MIXED FEELINGS AND VEXED PASSIONS

RESOURCES FOR BIBLICAL STUDY

Editors
Marvin A. Sweeney, Old Testament/Hebrew Bible
Tom Thatcher, New Testament

Number 90

MIXED FEELINGS AND VEXED PASSIONS

Exploring Emotions in Biblical Literature

Edited by

F. Scott Spencer

 **PRESS**

Atlanta

Copyright © 2017 by SBL Press

All rights reserved. No part of this work may be reproduced or transmitted in any form or by any means, electronic or mechanical, including photocopying and recording, or by means of any information storage or retrieval system, except as may be expressly permitted by the 1976 Copyright Act or in writing from the publisher. Requests for permission should be addressed in writing to the Rights and Permissions Office, SBL Press, 825 Houston Mill Road, Atlanta, GA 30329 USA.

Library of Congress Cataloging-in-Publication Data

Names: Spencer, F. Scott (Franklin Scott), editor.
Title: Mixed feelings and vexed passions : exploring emotions in biblical literature / edited by F. Scott Spencer.
Description: Atlanta : SBL Press, [2017] | Series: Resources for biblical study ; number 90 | Includes bibliographical references and index.
Identifiers: LCCN 2017032561 (print) | LCCN 2017033525 (ebook) | ISBN 9780884142560 (ebook) | ISBN 9781628371949 (pbk. : alk. paper) | ISBN 9780884142577 (hardcover : alk. paper)
Subjects: LCSH: Emotions—Biblical teaching. | Bible—Criticism, interpretation, etc.
Classification: LCC BS680.E4 (ebook) | LCC BS680.E4 M59 2017 (print) | DDC 220.8/1524—dc23
LC record available at https://lccn.loc.gov/2017032561

Printed on acid-free paper.

Contents

Preface vii
Abbreviations xi

Getting a Feel for the "Mixed" and "Vexed" Study of Emotions
in Biblical Literature
F. Scott Spencer 1

The Central Role of Emotions in Biblical Theology, Biblical Ethics,
and Popular Conceptions of the Bible
Matthew Richard Schlimm 43

A Prototype of Biblical Hate: Joseph's Brothers (Genesis 37)
Deena Grant 61

From Fear's Narcissism to Participatory Imagination:
Disrupting Disgust and Overcoming the Fear of Israel's
Ḥērem Laws
L. Juliana Claassens 77

Disgust in Body, Mind, and Language: The Case of Impurity in
the Hebrew Bible
Thomas Kazen 97

Understanding Grief and Reading the Bible
David A. Bosworth 117

Mourning over Sin/Affliction and the Problem of "Emotion" as
a Category in the Hebrew Bible
David A. Lambert 139

Emotion, Repentance, and the Question of the "Inner Life" of
Biblical Israelites: A Case Study in Hosea 6:1–3
Dennis Olson 161

The Pride of Babylon in Isaiah 47 Revisited in Light of the Theory
of Self-Conscious Emotions
Antony Dhas Prakasam 177

God and the "Happiness Formula": The Ethos and Ethics of
Happiness
Samuel E. Balentine 197

"Your Faith Has Made You Well" (Mark 5:34; 10:52): Emotional
Dynamics of Trustful Engagement with Jesus in Mark's Gospel
F. Scott Spencer 217

Not "Hardened Hearts" but "Petrified Hearts" (Mark 6:52):
The Challenge to Assimilate and Accommodate the
Vastness of Jesus in Mark 6:45–52
Ivar Vegge 243

Reflexivity and Emotion in Narratological Perspective: Reading
Joy in the Lukan Narrative
Michal Beth Dinkler 265

Why the Johannine Jesus Weeps at the Tomb of Lazarus
Stephen D. Moore 287

When Enough Is Never Enough: Philosophers, Poets, Peter, and
Paul on Insatiable Desire
David E. Fredrickson 311

The Missing Emotion: The Absence of Anger and the Promotion
of Nonretaliation in 1 Peter
Katherine M. Hockey 331

Afterword
David Konstan 355

List of Contributors 371
Ancient Sources Index 377

Preface

On a last minute whim at the 2011 Annual Meeting of the Society of Biblical Literature, I decided to pop into a session devoted to Matthew Schlimm's new book, *From Fratricide to Forgiveness: The Language and Ethics of Anger in Genesis* (Eisenbrauns, 2011). I was late, but I got there in time to hear some of Matt's response to the panel reviewers and to participate in the wider discussion with the audience. It was not a huge group, but we had a fruitful exchange of ideas.

I was drawn to the session not so much to learn more about Genesis (I work primarily in the New Testament), but to hear what Matt and other scholars were thinking about emotions (anger in this case) in the Bible. For a few years I had been nosing around in the burgeoning literature on emotions in a broad range of fields in the humanities and sciences. Emotions were clearly running hot across academia. My interest particularly caught fire in reading Martha Nussbaum's magisterial *Upheavals of Thought: The Intelligence of Emotions* (Cambridge University Press, 2001). Though Nussbaum is a philosopher, not a biblical scholar, her grounding in classical literature and thoughtful engagement with a breathtaking array of ethical, legal, and religious ideas (she holds appointments in the University of Chicago Law School and Divinity School as well as the Philosophy department) warmed my biblical heart and made me wonder how this surge of research and reflection on emotions might impact biblical studies.

So in that Society of Biblical Literature session six years ago, I posed to Matt some question to this effect, dropping Nussbaum's name in the process and off-handedly suggesting we might benefit from more of these sessions—even a working group devoted to investigating emotions in the Bible. I spoke as a fool, but Matt politely affirmed my Nussbaum reference and agreed that the time was ripe for further work in this whole emotion area. I briefly spoke to Matt after the session (we knew nothing of each other before), congratulated him on his book (I immediately went to the exhibit hall and bought it), and half-joked that I might be in touch about this "starting a new group" thing.

Of course, a lot of things are said at these heady Society of Biblical Literature meetings in the heat of the moment (yes, even biblical scholars are emotional beings). But in fact I did email Matt soon after the meeting, and we began to set the wheels in motion to propose a new Bible and Emotion unit to the Society of Biblical Literature Program Committee. In the Spring of 2012 we were approved as a three-year consultation (we have since been extended as an official group). As cochairs, Matt and I were joined by a wonderful team of Hebrew Bible/Old Testament and New Testament scholars on the initial Steering Committee: Bill Arnold, Jacq Lapsley, Ellen van Wolde, and David Fredrickson. Soon, for various reasons, Bill gave way to Deena Grant and Ellen to David Bosworth. It's been a joy and honor to work with all of these brilliant women and men. By salutary design, the work of the Society of Biblical Literature is a collaborative effort.

As it happened, our first Society of Biblical Literature meeting in November 2012 was in Chicago, and Nussbaum graciously consented to headline our inaugural panel on "Assessing the 'Utility' of the Work of Martha C. Nussbaum for the Study of the Bible and Emotion." We also had an open session of five papers on a variety of emotion topics across the biblical canon. We have continued this two-session (papers and panel) annual pattern and look forward to many more years of productive study. Response has been most encouraging, both in terms of attendance and in the number of proposals submitted.

The present volume of essays evidences the beginning and early gelling of this vibrant inquiry into emotions in biblical literature, including not only expanded versions of Society of Biblical Literature papers, but also several fresh contributions by an international team of scholars. All of these essays engage deeply with both ancient and modern contexts, including interdisciplinary soundings into emotions, both theoretical and evidentiary, to provide incisive case studies of "passions" ranging from joy, happiness, and trust to grief, hate, and disgust.

I am grateful for each contributor and what I have learned from them. Thanks, too, goes to the Society of Biblical Literature Resources in Biblical Study general editors, Marvin Sweeney and Tom Thatcher, who provided guidance and encouragement throughout the project. And a special shout out to Nicole Tilford, Production Manager at SBL Press, for her remarkable organizational skills and expert shepherding of this work to publication.

This volume represents a stimulating sample of first digs into the emotional terrain of the Bible, a "ground-breaking" of a new field of study, but by no means the finished product. Much work remains to be done, but we "feel" pretty good about these initial probes and where they might lead us.

Abbreviations

Primary Sources

1 Esd	1 Esdras
1 Glor.	Dio Chrysostom, *De gloria i* (*Or.* 66)
3 Kgdms	3 Kingdoms
4 Macc	4 Maccabees
4 Regn.	Dio Chrysostom, *De regno iv* (*Or.* 4)
Aen.	Virgil, *Aeneid*
Aff. dig.	Galen, *De propriorum animi cuiuslibet affectuum dignotione et cura*
Ag.	Aeschylus, *Agamemnon*
Ag. Ber.	Aggadat Bereshit
Agr.	Philo, *De agricultura*
Am.	Ovid, *Amores*
Amat.	Plutarch, *Amatorius*
Amic. mult.	Plutarch, *De amicorum multitudine*
Anab.	Arrian, *Anabasis*; Epictetus, *Anabasis*; Xenophon, *Anabasis*
Ant.	Josephus, *Jewish Antiquities*
Anth. Gr.	Anthologia Graeca
Argon.	Apollonius of Rhodes, *Argonautica*
Augustine	Augustine, *De Trinitate*
Buc.	Calpurnius Siculus, *Bucolicae*
Cat. Min.	Plutarch, *Cato Minor*
Chaer.	Chariton, *De Chaerea et Callirhoe*
Compunct. Dem.	John Chrysostom, *Ad Demetrium de compunctione*
Cons. ux.	Plutarch, *Consolatio ad uxorem*
Cor	Plutarch, *Marcius Coriolanus*
Crat.	Plato, *Cratylus*
Cyr.	Xenophon, *Cyropaedia*

ABBREVIATIONS

Daphn.	Longus, *Daphnis et Chloe*
De an.	Aristotle, *De anima*
Deipn.	Athenaeus, *Deipnosophistae*
Dial. mort.	Lucian, *Dialogi mortuorum*
Diatr.	Epictetus, *Diatribai*
Diss.	Musonius Rufus, *Dissertationum a Lucio Digestarum Reliquiae*
Dysk.	Menander, *Dyskolos*
Ecl.	Stobaeus, *Eclogae*
Ep.	Anacharis, *Epistulae*; Basil of Caesarea, *Epistulae*; Horace, *Epistulae*;. Philostratus, *Epistulae*; Seneca, *Epistulae morales*; Theodoros Kyzikos, *Epistulae*
Epitaph. Adon.	Bion, *Epitaphius Adonis*
Epitr.	Menander, *Epitrepontes*
Eth. nic.	Aristotle, *Ethica nicomachea*
Flor.	Stobaeus, *Florilegium*
Fr.	Charondas, *Fragmenta*; Perictione, *Fragmenta*; Pindar, *Fragmenta*; Sappho, *Fragmenta*; Timaeus, *Fragmenta*
Garr.	Plutarch, *De garrulitate*
Gen. Rab.	Genesis Rabbah
Gorg.	Plato, *Gorgias*
Hel.	Gorgias, *Helena*
Her.	Ovid, *Heroides*
Her. Leand.	Musaeus, *De Herone et Leandro*
Hist.	Herodotus, *Historiae*; Nymphis, *Historia*
Hymn. Dian.	Callimachus, *Hymnus in Dianam*
Id.	Theocritus, *Idylls*
Iph. aul.	Euripides, *Iphigenia aulidensis*
Iph. taur.	Euripides, *Iphigenia taurica*
Ir.	Philodemus, *De ira*
Ira	Seneca, *De ira*
Jdt	Judith
Jul.	Suetonius, *Divus Julius*
Leg.	Philo, *Legum allegoriae*; Plato, *Leges*
Legat.	Philo, *Legatio ad Gaium*
Leuc. Clit.	Achilles Tatius, *Leucippe et Clitophon*
Lib. phil. sect.	Arius Didymus, *Liber de philosophorum sectis*
Marc.	Tertullian, *Contra Marcellum*

Meg.	Megillah
Mem.	Xenophon, *Memorabilia*
Metaph.	Aristotle, *Metaphysics*
Mis.	Julian, *Misopogon*
Morb. sacr.	Hippocrates, *De morbo sacro*
Mut.	Philo, *De mutatione nominum*
Noct. Att.	Aulus Gellius, *Noctes Atticae*
Onom.	Pollux, *Onomasticon*
Op.	Hesiod, *Opera et dies*
Orest.	Euripides, *Orestes*
Paen.	Ambrose, *De paenitentia*
[*Pass.*]	Andronicus, *De passionibus*
Pers.	Aeschylus, *Persae*
Phaed.	Plato, *Phaedrus*
Princ.	Epicurus, *Principal Doctrines*
[*Probl.*]	Aristotle, *Problemata*
Prov. Alex.	Plutarch, *De proverbiis Alexandrinorum*
Psych.	Prudentius, *Psychomachia*
Purg.	Dante, *Purgatorio*
Resp.	Plato, *Respublica*
Rhet.	Aristotle, *Rhetorica*
Sanh.	Sanhedrin
Sir	Sirach/Ecclesiasticus
Spec.	Philo, *De specialibus legibus*
Stoic. rep.	Plutarch, *De Stoicorum repugnantiis*
Sum. theol.	Aquinas, *Summa theologiae*
Suppl.	Euripides, *Supplices*
Symp.	Plato, *Symposium*; Xenophon, *Symposium*
Ta'an.	Ta'anit
Tanh.	Tanhuma
Theb.	Statius, *Thebaid*
Tranq. an.	Plutarch, *De tranquillitate animi*
Trin.	Augustine, *De Trinitate*
Var. Hist.	Aelian, *Varia historia*
Ven.	Dio Chrysostom, *Venator* (*Or.* 7)
Virt.	Dio Chrysostom, *De virtute* (*Or.* 8)
Virt. prof.	Plutarch, *Quomodo quis suos in virtute sentiat profectus*
Vit. Mos.	Gregory of Nyssa, *De vita Mosis*

Vit. Phil.	Diogenes Laertius, *Vitae philosophorum*
Wis	Wisdom of Solomon
Yebam.	Yebamot

Secondary Resources

AB	The Anchor Bible
ABD	Freedman, David Noel, ed. *Anchor Bible Dictionary.* 6 vols. New York: Doubleday, 1992.
ADEBull	*Association of Departments of English Bulletin*
AEL	Lichtheim, Miriam. *Ancient Egyptian Literature.* 3 vols. Berkeley: University of California Press, 1971–1980.
AHD	*Attachment and Human Development*
AIL	Ancient Israel and Its Literature
AIPh	Annuaire de l'Institut de Philologie et d'Histoire Orientales et Slaves
AnBib	Analecta Biblica
ANF	*Ante-Nicene Fathers*
AOTC	Abingdon Old Testament Commentaries
AOTS	Augsburg Old Testament Studies
AP	*American Psychologist*
ATLAMS	American Theological Library Association Monograph Series
AusJP	*Australasian Journal of Philosophy*
AUSTR	American University Studies, Series 7: Theology and Religion
BBS	*Behavioral and Brain Sciences*
BC	*Brain and Cognition*
BCT	*The Bible and Critical Theory*
BDAG	Danker, Frederick W., Walter Bauer, William F. Arndt, and F. Wilbur Gingrich. *Greek-English Lexicon of the New Testament and Other Early Christian Literature.* 3rd ed. Chicago: University of Chicago Press, 2000. (Danker-Bauer-Arndt-Gingrich)
BDB	Brown, Francis, S. R. Driver, and Charles A. Briggs. *A Hebrew and English Lexicon of the Old Testament.* Oxford: Clarendon, 1907.

BECNT	Baker Exegetical Commentary on the New Testament
BETL	Bibliotheca Ephemeridum theologicarum Lovaniensium
Bib	*Biblica*
BibInt	*Biblical Interpretation*
BibInt	Biblical Interpretation Series
BibOr	Biblica et Orientalia
BICSSup	Bulletin of the Institute of Classical Studies Supplement
BJDP	*The British Journal of Developmental Psychology*
BJSUCSD	Biblical and Judaic Studies from the University of California, San Diego
BLPH	La Palabra (Hispanoamérica)
BMC	Bryn Mawr Commentaries
BMW	Bible in the Modern World
BRP	*Brill Research Perspectives in Biblical Interpretation*
Buc.	Calpurnius Siculus, *Bucolics*
BZ	*Biblische Zeitschrift*
BZAW	Beihefte zur Zeitschrift für die alttestamentliche Wissenschaft
CAS	Clarendon Aristotle Series
CBNT	*Commentaire biblique, Nouveau Testament*
CBQ	*Catholic Biblical Quarterly*
CBQMS	Catholic Biblical Quarterly Monograph Series
CC	Continental Commentaries
CC	*Cultural Critique*
CE	*Cognition and Emotion*
CEB	Common English Bible
CEI	Conferenza Episcopale Italiana
CHE	*Chronicle of Higher Education*
CI	*Critical Inquiry*
CIF	Classical Inter/Faces
CM	*Clinical Medicine*
CogL	*Cognitive Linguistics*
CON	*Current Opinion in Neurobiology*
ConBNT	Coniectanea Neotestamentica or Coniectanea Biblica: New Testament Series

COS	Hallo, William W., and K. Lawson Younger Jr., eds. *The Context of Scripture*. 4 vols. Leiden: Brill, 1997–2016.
CQS	Companion to the Qumran Scrolls
CR	*The Classical Review*
CSCP	Cornell Studies in Classical Philology
Di	*Dialogue*
DS	*Death Studies*
EBib	*Etudes Bibliques*
EBib	Etudes Bibliques
ECL	Early Christianity and Its Literature
EER	Early European Research
EH	Emotions in History
EHB	*Evolution and Human Behavior*
EJSP	*European Journal of Social Psychology*
EJud	Neusner, Jacob, Alan J. Avery-Peck, and William Scott Green, eds. *The Encyclopedia of Judaism*. 2nd ed. 5 vols. Leiden: Brill, 2005.
EKKNT	Evangelisch-katholischer Kommentar zum Neuen Testament
EmotRev	*Emotion Review*
Enc	*Encounter*
EncJud	Skolnik, Fred, and Michael Berenbaum, eds. Encyclopedia Judaica. 2nd ed. 22 vols. Detroit: Macmillan Reference USA, 2007.
ER	Jones, Lindsay, ed. *Encyclopedia of Religion*. 2nd ed. 15 vols. Detroit: Macmillan Reference USA, 2005
ERE	Hastings, James, ed. *Encyclopedia of Religion and Ethics*. 13 vols. New York: Scribner's Sons, 1908–1927. Repr., 7 vols. 1951.
ETMP	*Ethical Theory and Moral Practice*
FB	Forschung zur Bibel
FCB	Feminist Companion to the Bible
FOTL	Forms of the Old Testament Literature
GNB	Gute Nachricht Bibel
GPBS	Global Perspectives on Biblical Scholarship
GPIR	*Group Processes and Intergroup Relations*
HALOT	Koehler, Ludwig, Walter Baumgartner, and Johann J. Stamm. *The Hebrew and Aramaic Lexicon of the*

	Old Testament. Translated and edited under the supervision of Mervyn E. J. Richardson. 4 vols. Leiden: Brill, 1994–1999.
HBM	Hebrew Bible Monographs
HBT	*Horizons in Biblical Theology*
HCS	*Health, Culture and Society*
HDR	Harvard Dissertations in Religion
HNT	Handbuch zum Neuen Testament
HRR	*Human Rights Review*
HThKAT	Herders Theologischer Kommentar zum Alten Testament
HThKNT	Herders Theologischer Kommentar zum Neuen Testament
HTR	*Harvard Theological Review*
IBC	Interpretation: A Bible Commentary for Teaching and Preaching
ICC	International Critical Commentary
ICS	*Illinois Classical Studies*
IDB	Buttrick, George A., ed. *The Interpreter's Dictionary of the Bible*. 4 vols. New York: Abingdon, 1962.
Int	*Interpretation*
JAAR	*Journal of the American Academy of Religion*
JAJ	*Journal of Ancient Judaism*
JANER	*Journal of Ancient Near Eastern Religions*
JAOS	*Journal of the American Oriental Society*
JAPs	*Journal of Abnormal Psychology*
JBE	*Journal of Business Ethics*
JBL	*Journal of Biblical Literature*
JCPP	*Journal of Child Psychology and Psychiatry*
JEP	*Journal of Experimental Psychology*
JFSR	*Journal of Feminist Studies in Religion*
JHebS	*Journal of Hebrew Scriptures*
JLRS	*Journal of Law, Religion and State*
JLT	*Journal of Literature and Theology*
JNES	*Journal of Near Eastern Studies*
JNSL	*Journal of Northwest Semitic Languages*
JPS	Jewish Publication Society
JPs	*The Journal of Philosophy*
JPSBC	Jewish Publication Society Bible Commentary

JPSP	*Journal of Personality and Social Psychology*
JR	*Journal of Religion*
JSNT	*Journal for the Study of the New Testament*
JSNTSup	Journal for the Study of the New Testament Supplement Series
JSOT	*Journal for the Study of the Old Testament*
JSOTSup	Journal for the Study of the Old Testament Supplement Series
JTI	*Journal of Theological Interpretation*
JTPP	*Journal of Theoretical and Philosophical Psychology*
Kinema	*Kinema: A Journal for Film and Audiovisual Media*
KJV	King James Version
LBLA	La Biblia de las Américas
LCL	Loeb Classical Library
LHBOTS	The Library of the Hebrew Bible/Old Testament Studies
LNTS	Library of New Testament Studies
LSG	Louis Segond Bible
LSJ	Liddell, Henry George, Robert Scott, and Henry Stuart Jones. *A Greek English Lexicon*. 9th ed. with revised supplement. Oxford: Clarendon, 1996.
LXX	Septuagint
MBE	*Mind, Brain, and Education*
MoTh	*Modern Theology*
NA^{28}	*Novum Testamentum Graece*, Nestle-Aland, 28th ed.
NAB	New American Bible
NAC	New American Commentary
NASB	New American Standard Bible
NBR	*Neuroscience and Biobehavioral Reviews*
NBS	Nouvelle Bible Second
NCBC	New Cambridge Bible Commentary
Neot	*Neotestamentica*
NETS	Pietersma, Albert, and Benjamin G. Wright, eds. *A New English Translation of the Septuagint*. New York: Oxford University Press, 2007.
Next Wave	Next Wave: New Directions in Women's Studies
NIGTC	New International Greek Testament Commentary
NIV	New International Version

NJPS	*Tanakh: The Holy Scriptures: The New JPS Translation according to the Traditional Hebrew Text*
NLH	*New Literary History*
NovT	*Novum Testamentum*
NovTSup	Supplements to Novum Testamentum
NR	The Italian Nuova Riveduta
NRSV	New Revised Standard Version
NSIN	Norton Series on Interpersonal Neurobiology
NSyHL	The New Synthese Historical Library
NThT	*Nieuw Theologisch Tijdschrift*
NTS	*New Testament Studies*
NVI	Nueva Versión Internacional
OBO	Orbis Biblicus et Orientalis
OBT	Overtures to Biblical Theology
OLB	Orte und Landschaften der Bibel
OTL	Old Testament Library
OTM	Oxford Theological Monographs
OTS	Old Testament Studies
PBA	*Proceedings of the British Academy for the Promoting of Historical, Philosophical, and Philological Studies*
PCI	Post-contemporary Interventions
PDV	La Bible Parole de Vie
PG	Migne, Jacques-Paul, ed. Patrologia Graeca [= Patrologiae Cursus Completus: Series Graeca]. 162 vols. Paris, 1857–1886.
Phil	*Philosophy*
PMLA	*Proceedings of the Modern Language Association*
PRSt	*Perspectives in Religious Studies*
PsBull	*Psychological Bulletin*
PSPA	Publications of the Society for Psychological Anthropology
PsRev	*Psychological Review*
PTRSLB	*Philosophical Transactions of the Royal Society of London, Series B (Biological Sciences)*
RAC	Klauser, Theodor, et al. *Reallexikon für Antike und Christentum*. Stuttgart: Hiersemann, 1950–.
RBS	Resources for Biblical Study
REB	Revised English Bible
RMCS	Routledge Monographs in Classical Studies

RNBC	Readings: A New Biblical Commentary
RRCMS	Routledge Research in Cultural and Media Studies
SANT	Studien zum Alten und Neuen Testaments
SAOC	Studies in Ancient Oriental Civilization
SBLDS	Society of Biblical Literature Dissertation Series
SBLMS	Society of Biblical Literature Monograph Series
SBT	Studies in Biblical Theology
SC	Sources chrétiennes
SCE	Self-Conscious Emotions theory
ScEs	*Science et esprit*
SemeiaSt	Semeia Studies
SESI	Studies in Emotion and Social Interaction
SHE	*Studia Historiae Ecclesiasticae*
SLTHS	Siphrut: Literature and Theology of the Hebrew Scriptures
SNTS	Studiorum Novi Testamenti Societas
SPQ	*Social Psychology Quarterly*
SRSB	Studi e ricerche: Sezione biblica
SSI	*Social Science Information*
SSN	Studia Semitica Neerlandica
SSSA	Stockholm Studies in Social Anthropology
ST	*Studia Theologica*
StBibLit	Studies in Biblical Literature
STDJ	Studies of the Texts of the Desert of Judah
SubBi	Subsidia biblica
SVF	Arnim, Hans Friedrich August von. *Stoicorum Veterum Fragmenta*. 4 vols. Leipzig: Teubne, 1903–1924.
SymS	Symposium Series
TCS	*Trends in Cognitive Sciences*
TDOT	Botterweck, G. Johannes, and Helmer Ringgren, eds. *Theological Dictionary of the Old Testament*. Translated by John T. Willis et al. 8 vols. Grand Rapids: Eerdmans, 1974–2006.
THL	Theory and History of Literature
TIN	Theory and Interpretation of Narrative
TLA	Traducción en Lenguaje Actual
TLOT	Jenni, Ernst, ed., with assistance from Claus Westermann. *Theological Lexicon of the Old Testament*.

	Translated by Mark E. Biddle. 3 vols. Peabody, MA: Hendrickson, 1997.
TOB	Traduction Œcuménique de la Bible
TrGF	Snell, Bruno, Richard Kannich, and Stefan Radt, eds. *Tragicorum graecorum fragmenta*. 2 vols. Göttingen: Vandenhoeck & Ruprecht, 1971–2004.
TTC	Transdisciplinary Theological Colloquia
TynBul	*Tyndale Bulletin*
UBS	*The Greek New Testament*, United Bible Societies, 5th ed.
USQR	*Union Seminary Quarterly Review*
VT	*Vetus Testamentum*
VTSup	Supplements to Vetus Testamentum
Vulg.	Vulgate
WBC	Word Biblical Commentary
WCD	The Works of Charles Darwin
WMANT	Wissenschaftliche Monographien zum Alten und Neuen Testament
YCS	Yale Classical Studies
ZAW	Zeitschrift für die alttestamentliche Wissenschaft

Getting a Feel for the "Mixed" and "Vexed" Study of Emotions in Biblical Literature

F. Scott Spencer

"I am writing during a boom in the history of emotions; there is gold rush fever in the air." So says the historian Jan Plamper in his recent critical survey of emotion analysis in Western thought.[1] Plamper attributes a sharp spike in this emotional "fever" to the cataclysmic events of 9/11. From the smoldering ashes of the Twin Towers arose a fresh obsession with human "experience," not least *emotional* experience on both pathological (what drove these maniacal terrorists?) and parochial (East-West/ Muslim-Christian fundamentalist) levels. We were accustomed, of course, to xenophobic hate, religious zeal, and nationalist grief—but not to this shocking degree and not in the bright LED glow of a new millennium. Had Enlightenment *logos* not long ago won the day over Neanderthal *pathos*? Had the Scientific Revolution not become so digitized as to leave all sentiment in the dust? So why this resurgent tsunami of hate, fear, zeal, and grief—exploding with ferocious volume, velocity, and visibility through hyperlinked media—mixing bytes and guts, as it were?[2]

To be more precise, 9/11 turbocharged a fire for understanding emotions that had been burning at the close of the twentieth century across a wide range of disciplines. Plamper focuses on anthropology and biology, especially neuroscience with its glitzy new brain-imaging technology lighting up areas of emotional processing intertwined with perceptual-cognitive circuits.[3] But in fact almost every other field in the humanities and sciences has caught "emotion fever" as well, including, classics, literature,

---

1. Jan Plamper, *The History of Emotions: An Introduction*, trans. Keith Tribe, EH (Oxford: Oxford University Press, 2015), 297.
2. Ibid., 60–67, 297–98 (Plamper uses the tsunami image on p. 60).
3. In Plamper's survey, anthropology serves as the exemplar of a *social construc-*

linguistics, philosophy, psychology, sociology, political science, economics, and education.[4]

What about biblical studies? As a notoriously conservative field with a tendency to hole up in tight pockets of interest within its own discipline and even more isolated from other areas of inquiry, academic biblical studies remained largely immune from the scholarly emotion contagion—until the last several years. Following a few pioneering publications on emotions in the Bible,[5] the Bible and Emotion Consultation of the Society of Biblical Literature was established in 2012 (it became a continuing group in 2015) with the following rationale: "This consultation focuses on understanding the spectrum of emotions displayed throughout the Bible in their literary and cultural contexts, informed by the burgeoning cross-disciplinary study of emotion." This group has yielded stimulating papers and panel discussions at the annual meetings. This collection of essays reflects some of these contributions, as well as new offerings, by a range of specialists probing the significance of emotion(s) in both testaments. Independently of this endeavor, Françoise Mirguet and Dominika Kurek-Chomycz introduce the 2016 thematic issue of *Biblical Interpretation* devoted to "Emotions in Ancient Jewish Literature" as confirming evidence that "emotions are in full bloom in biblical scholarship."[6] I am

---

tivist approach to emotion study (ibid., 75–146); conversely the life sciences take a more *universalist* tack (147–250).

4. See the starter bibliography at the end of this essay.

5. Pre-2010, e.g., see Ellen J. van Wolde, "Sentiments as Culturally Constructed Emotions: Love and Anger in the Hebrew Bible," *BibInt* 16 (2008): 1–24; Jacqueline E. Lapsley, "Feeling Our Way: Love for God in Deuteronomy," *CBQ* 65 (2003): 350–69; Paul A. Kruger, "On Emotions and the Expression of Emotions in the Old Testament: A Few Introductory Remarks," *BZ* 48 (2004): 216–18; Gary A. Anderson, *A Time to Mourn, A Time to Dance: The Expression of Grief and Joy in Israelite Religion* (University Park, PA: Pennsylvania State University Press, 1991); Matthew A. Elliott, *Faithful Feelings: Rethinking Emotion in the New Testament* (Grand Rapids: Kregel, 2006); Stephen Voorwinde, *Jesus' Emotions in the Fourth Gospel: Human or Divine?*, LNTS 284 (London: T&T Clark, 2005); Thomas H. Olbricht and Jerry L. Sumney, eds., *Paul and Pathos*, SymS 16 (Atlanta: Society of Biblical Literature, 2001).

6. Françoise Mirguet and Dominika Kurek-Chomycz, "Introduction: Emotions in Ancient Jewish Literature," *BibInt* 24 (2016): 435. This thematic issue results from a comparable research group on Emotions and the Biblical World in the European Association of Biblical Studies (EABS), which convenes jointly at times with the Society of Biblical Literature International Meeting.

not sure how full the bloom is yet, but emotions are certainly beginning to blossom in our field with promise of bearing much fruit.

Nothing like a consensus strategy has emerged, which is appropriate for a developing subfield in conversation with such rich cross-disciplinary resources. The following emotion-focused essays stand alone and speak for themselves. But some common concerns affect the shape and scope of this ongoing research project.[7]

- *Terminological-taxonomic* concerns. What is an *emotion*, and how is it distinguished (or not) from associated terms like *feeling, passion, affect,* and *sentiment*? What ancient Hebrew or Greek terms (if any) reflect the experience of emotion? How much conceptual and emotional load do lexemes like "fear" (יראה, φόβος) carry in any given context?
- *Textual-generic* concerns. What distinctive challenges does our target text of *biblical literature* pose for emotion analysis? Although it features "feeling" divine and human figures in poignant situations, it is hardly a psychology or psychotherapeutic manual, even in its ethical and pastoral materials, or a psychological novel in its narrative sections. How do the various biblical genres disclose and delineate emotional experience?
- *Cross-cultural* concerns. The familiar nature-nurture, universalist-constructivist debate obviously pertains, since emotions have to do with human beings' natures expressed and experienced in cultural contexts. Many Americans became *afraid*, even *terrified*, of further terrorist attacks after 9/11. To what extent does this fear translate to the Gibeonites' and King Adoni-zedek's fear of the conquering Israelite army over three millennia earlier (Josh 9:24; 10:2), when world trade centers, skyscrapers, and passenger jets were inconceivable? Are people wired, biologically and/or culturally, to feel the same kinds of fear in the same ways across human history?
- *Cross-disciplinary* concerns. The never-ending flood of monographs and articles in multiple languages makes it virtually impossible to remain fully current in one's primary area of specialization,

---

7. The concluding section of Dennis Olson's essay and Michal Beth Dinkler's section on "Four Points of Departure" in this volume introduce similar questions and provide helpful responses.

even one as comparatively narrow, say, as the Megilloth or Synoptic Gospels. How then can a poor biblical scholar hope to become adequately informed about another humanities discipline, to say nothing about a daunting technical field like neuroscience? Are we not condemning ourselves from the start as hopeless dabblers and dilettantes? Maybe, but with due humility, is it not worth the struggle to avoid obscurantism and academic sectarianism in our increasingly interconnected information age?

I now try to flesh out these questions and provide some tentative guardrails guiding study of the Bible and emotion in general and this volume's essays in particular.

1. Terms and Taxonomies

The mash-up of *mixed feelings*, *vexed passions*, and *emotions* in the title of this volume may appear to assume a lazy synonymy among the three nouns. Why not throw in *sentiments*, *affections*, and other associated terms while we are at it? But the adjectives *mixed* and *vexed* provide important qualifiers, not only of particular "felt" and "passionate" experiences (e.g., mixed grief and anger over loss;[8] vexed fear or depression), but also of the broader classifications. In current colloquial English, *feelings*, *passions*, and *emotions* occupy a common semantic field (my *passion* for country music presumes an *emotional* engagement with it that makes me *feel* good when I sing along). Moreover, all of these terms typically collocate *over against* cognitive concepts of *intellect*, *reason*, and *rationality* ("I can't talk with you when you're being so emotional and unreasonable!").[9] Even so, the meaning of emotion language, as all language, is heavily dependent on

---

8. On mixed emotions, see Paul Ekman, *Emotions Revealed: Recognizing Faces and Feelings to Improve Emotional Life*, 2nd ed. (New York: Holt, 2007), 69–71, 105, 185–86, 211–12; Robert C. Solomon, *True to Our Feelings: What Our Emotions Are Really Telling Us* (Oxford: Oxford University Press, 2001), 170–79; Amelia Rorty, "A Plea for Ambivalence," in *The Oxford Handbook of Philosophy of Emotion*, ed. Peter Goldie (Oxford: Oxford University Press, 2010), 425–44.

9. The flip side of this antithesis, favoring emotion over against reason, might say: "Don't overthink your decision: just go with your gut!" Or in the words of the country love song: "This ain't no thinkin' thing … it goes a little deeper than that. It's a physical, chemical, emotional devotion, passion that we can't hold back" (Tim Nichols and Mark D. Sanders, "No Thinkin' Thing," recorded by Trace Adkins, 1997).

context, including the interpretive context of the experiencing self. Most American English speakers today, for example, more readily attach sexual elements to *passion* than to *feeling* or *emotion*.

1.1. Emotion Categories

These simple observations about the variable mixing of emotion language in contemporary English merely scratch the surface of the complex history of usage in English (sketched below in part 3) and—to ratchet up the vexatious tension even more—in ancient biblical languages of Hebrew and Greek. For starters no biblical Hebrew term precisely corresponds with the English *emotion*. The word usually rendered "desire" (תשוקה) in its (mere) three occurrences (Gen 3:16; 4:7; Song 7:10) may come close, but with obsessive tinges of "longing" and "craving."[10] Of course, this linguistic lacuna by no means indicates that the ancient Israelites were an unfeeling people or Vulcan-like embodiment of "pure reason." They had plenty of "heart" (לב) with which to "love God," no doubt including intense feelings of "love," though scarcely reduced to sappy romantic sentiments. Biblical "heartfelt" love and other "heart" responses involve as much or more decision (will), cognition (thought), and action (obedience) as emotion (see Deut 6:5–8).[11] In any case, the apparent lack of a conceptual *category* of emotion in the Hebrew Bible cautions us, as David A. Lambert argues in the present volume, against automatically infusing modern emotions into ancient religious practices, such as importing later (requisite) feelings of penitential sorrow into biblical fasting rituals.[12]

---

10. BDB, s.v. תשוקה; William L. Holladay, ed., *A Concise Hebrew and Aramaic Lexicon of the Old Testament* (Grand Rapids: Eerdmans, 1971), 396.

11. Note these statements from Jon D. Levenson, *The Love of God: Divine Gift, Human Gratitude, and Mutual Faithfulness in Judaism* (Princeton: Princeton University Press, 2016), typical of his rich and balanced treatment of love in the Bible: "The love of God in the Hebrew Bible, then, is a matter of both action and affect, with each influencing the other. Efforts to separate action and affect, and conceptions of the self that disjoin the two, can lead only to a drastic misunderstanding" (xiv); "Biblical psychology associates the heart at least as much with thought as with emotion" (69).

12. See Françoise Mirguet, "What Is an 'Emotion' in the Hebrew Bible? An Experience That Exceeds Most Contemporary Concepts," *BibInt* 24 (2016): 442–65; Phillip A. Lasater, "'The Emotions' in Biblical Anthropology? A Genealogy and Case Study with ירא," *HTR* (forthcoming).

If ancient Israelite sages were less philosophically preoccupied with emotion as a category of thought and experience, their Greek counterparts were not so constrained. In the second book of his *Rhetoric*, Aristotle devotes considerable attention to πάθος as a key factor in the art of persuasion: speakers must move (motivate) audiences (sym)pathetically, passionately, and emotionally. He defines the category and manifestations of πάθη (pl. of πάθος) as follows:

> The emotions [πάθη] are those things through which, by undergoing change, people come to differ in their judgments and which are accompanied by pain and pleasure, for example, anger, pity, fear, and other such things and their opposites. There is need to divide the discussion of each into three headings. I mean, for example, in speaking of anger, what is their *state of mind* when people are angry and against *whom* are they usually angry and for what sort of *reasons*. (*Rhet.* 2.1.8–9 [1378a])[13]

Aristotle assumes a broad, integrative view of πάθη such as anger and fear in human life, associated with positive (pleasurable) and negative (painful) experience within a triadic network of (1) *cognitive* ("state of mind"), (2) *social* (involved with "whom"), and (3) *motivational* ("what sort of reasons") *judgments* (κρίσεις). We might also add a presumed *somatic* or *embodied* "station" of all emotional experience, as διάκειμαι does not strictly denote "state of *mind*," but rather a broader condition: "to be in a certain state of *mind, body, or circumstances*, to be disposed or affected in a certain manner."[14] Elsewhere, Aristotle explicitly refers to "bodily emotions" (σωματικά ἐστι τὰ πάθη [*Eth. nic.* 10.3.8–9 (1173b)]) and links specific emotional experiences to somatic stimuli (e.g., anger to a hot feeling of boiling blood in the chest [*De an.*1.1.10–30 (403a)]). In any case, Aristotle's emphasis on the adjudicative, deliberative dimension of emotions (as "judgments") resists reducing them to irrational disturbances, though they can prove quite disturbing and unreasonable when applied to the wrong things for the wrong reasons in certain wrong times and situations.[15]

---

13. Aristotle, *On Rhetoric: A Theory of Civic Discourse*, trans. George A. Kennedy, 2nd ed. (New York: Oxford University Press, 2007), 113, emphasis original.

14. LSJ, s.v. "διάκειμαι."

15. See Aristotle, *Eth. nic.* 3.7.4 (1115b): "Error arises either from fearing what one ought not to fear, or from fearing in the wrong manner, or at the wrong time, or the

Classics scholars like George A. Kennedy (translator of *Rhetoric*) and David Konstan are happy to render Aristotle's πάθη as "emotions," even as they appreciate the approximate, provisional nature of all cross-linguistic work. Konstan, in particular, warns against a perfect correspondence of ancient Greek and modern English terms for the emotions while still allowing for sufficient correlation to have a reasonable cross-cultural conversation.[16] He is also careful to note that Aristotle's association of πάθη with pain and pleasure does not amount to absolute identification; rather, Aristotle dubs these hedonic elements as "sensations" ("sense perceptions" [αἰσθήσεις]) that may or may not accompany any particular emotion.[17]

Of the sixty-seven occurrences of πάθος in Greek biblical literature (LXX and New Testament), the lion's share (sixty-two) appears in 4 Maccabees, starting with the first verse: "Since I am about to discuss an eminently philosophical subject [φιλοσοφώτατον λόγον]—whether pious reason [εὐσεβὴς λογισμός] is absolute master of the passions [παθῶν]—I would duly advise you to attend diligently to the philosophy here set forth" (4 Macc 1:1 NETS).[18] Though the NRSV and CEB consistently render πάθη as "emotions" in 4 Maccabees, NETS opts for "passions." In any case, this Hellenistic-Jewish philosophical tract pits reason and passion against each other in mortal combat, arguing that superior reason/logic (λογισμός), if judiciously ("piously") exercised, can in fact master the inferior passions/emotions (πάθη), as exemplified in the serene commitment to rational devotion to Israel's God and Torah maintained by Eleazar (and his mother and seven brothers) in the face of excruciating torture exacted by the Hellenistic tyrant Antiochus IV. This stoical martyr is imaged as both a

---

like; and similarly with regard to occasions for confidence" (Aristotle, *Nichomachean Ethics*, trans. H. Rackham, LCL 73 [Cambridge: Harvard University Press, 1926]).

16. See the helpful introductory chapter, "*Pathos* and Passion," in David Konstan, *The Emotions of the Ancient Greeks: Studies in Aristotle and Classical Literature* (Toronto: University of Toronto Press, 2006), 3–40; see my quotation of Konstan below in section 3.2.2. "Cultural Twists" and Konstan's further reflections in his afterword to the present volume.

17. Konstan, *Emotions of the Ancient Greeks*, 21, 33–34; Aristotle, *Eth. nic.* 10.4 (1174a–1175b); *Aristotle's Nicomachean Ethics*, trans. Robert C. Bartlett and Susan D. Collins (Chicago: University of Chicago Press, 2011), 216–19; more generally, see William W. Fortenbaugh, *Aristotle on Emotion*, 2nd ed. (London: Duckworth, 2002); Elizabeth S. Belfiore, *Tragic Pleasures: Aristotle on Plot and Emotion* (Princeton: Princeton University Press, 1992).

18. All subsequent translations of 4 Maccabees are from NETS.

model "philosopher of divine life" (7:7) and "a most skillful pilot" guided by "reason ... [that] steered the ship of piety on the sea of the passions, and though buffeted by the stormings of the tyrant and ... mighty waves of the tortures ... in setting his mind firm like a jutting cliff, our father Eleazar broke the madly raging waves of the passions" (7:1–5).

In this violent prosecutorial situation, the passions engulfing Eleazar equate to the terrible *pains* he feels inflicted by the instruments of torture. Like Aristotle, the writer of 4 Maccabees associates the "two most comprehensive types" of passions with "pleasure and pain, and each of these pertains by nature both to the body [σῶμα] and to the soul [ψυχήν]" (1:20). Notice both somatic and "psychic," physical and mental, effects of passionate experience, whether pleasurable or painful. Further, these two passion categories interlink in a causal chain with related passions: "Before pleasure comes desire, and after pleasure, delight. Before pain comes fear, and after pain, sorrow" (1:22).

Desire (ἐπιθυμία) → PLEASURE (ἡδονή) → Delight/Joy (χαρά)
Fear (φόβος) → PAIN (πόνος) → Sorrow (λύπη)

In this scheme, pleasure is just as morally suspect as pain, constituting a "malevolent disposition, which of all the passions, assumes the most varied forms" threatening body (e.g., gluttony) and soul (e.g., greed) (1:25–27). Here 4 Maccabees drifts away from moderate Aristotelian thought to more rigid Stoic aims to control, if not eradicate, all passions by sober reason.

Proverbs 25:20—one of the two LXX references to πάθος outside 4 Maccabees—also stresses the painful aspect of passion: "As vinegar is harmful to a wound, so a calamity [πάθος] that befalls the body [ἐν σώματι] pains [λυπεῖ] the heart" (Prov 25:20 NETS). This Greek version considerably modifies its Hebrew *Vorlage*, which has no counterpart to πάθος. Rendered in NETS as "calamity," πάθος in this proverb denotes a bitter, vinegar-like *event* that exacerbates a bodily injury and the painful feelings that attend it deep within one's heart.[19]

---

19. The other LXX reference also stresses the grievous element of πάθος, identifying it with the specific sad experience of mourning associated with painful bodily affliction: "My skin has blackened greatly, and my bones, from heat. Yes, my lyre has been turned into *mourning* [πάθος], and my melody into weeping for me" (Job 30:30–31 NETS).

All three New Testament uses of πάθος continue to accentuate its negative moral-physical valence—entailing unreasonable, unrighteous, and unrewarding indulgence of bodily pleasures and avoidance of pains—albeit in a more *sexualized* manner than in 4 Maccabees, entangled in vice lists with lustful desires: Rom 1:26 ("degrading passions" [πάθη ἀτιμάς]; cf. 1:29–31); Col 3:5 ("fornication, impurity, passion [πάθος], evil desire"); and 1 Thess 4:5 ("passion of lust" [πάθει ἐπιθυμίας]). Of course, the passion of Christ in English ecclesiastical usage has no (conscious) connection with sexual experience, certainly not in any immoral sense. Rather, it associates exclusively with the verb πάσχω/παθεῖν (a cognate of πάθος), meaning "to suffer" and applied specifically to the model suffering of Christ in trial and death, similar to that of the Maccabean martyrs, though with unique messianic significance (see, e.g., Luke 17:25; 24:26, 46; 1 Pet 2:21, 23; 4:1).[20] This passion again involves *painful* experience, but paradoxically modulated to a major redemptive key in Christ's case from the perspective of the New Testament writers.

The seeming absence of a clear-cut emotion category in the Hebrew Bible and the highly restricted and chiefly negative use of passion language in the LXX and New Testament might appear to put a damper on our entire project. Categorical language, while hardly definitive of a complex culture, says something about the way it organizes significant personal and social experiences, perhaps even how it conceives of the self. The anthropologist Catherine A. Lutz, for example, discovered in her field study of the Ifaluk language and people "two major terms used to talk about aspects of the self, *nunuwan* and *tip-*," both "potentially emotion laden."[21] Though closely related concepts, they have distinct nuances: *nunuwan* representing a swirl of thoughts and emotions, especially those "extensively involved with local ideas about morality and maturity"; *tip-* having "stronger connotations of desire and movement toward and away from

---

20. 4 Maccabees also uses repeatedly uses the verb πάσχω/παθεῖν to denote the painful suffering the martyrs endured: 4:25; 9:8; 10:10; 14:9; cf. 2 Macc 6:30; 7:18, 32 (in 9:28 the verb also characterizes the horrible demise of the tyrant Antiochus who had tortured the martyrs: "having endured the most intense suffering [παθών], such as he had inflicted on others, came to the end of his life by a most pitiable fate").

21. Catherine A. Lutz, *Unnatural Emotions: Everyday Sentiments on a Micronesian Atoll and Their Challenge to Western Theory* (Chicago: University of Chicago Press, 1988), 91.

its object."[22] Both of these broader notions may be associated with more particular emotion words, such as *song*—"justifiable anger"—and *fago*—"a central part of their view of human relationships," combining aspects of "compassion, love, and sadness" within a "nurturing" social ethic for coping with a "fragile" existence.[23] Correlating sociolinguistics with ethnopsychology suggests to Lutz that the Ifaluk language reflects a culture in which emotions play a positive, integral role in shaping self and society.[24]

But granting that categorical language marks a certain salience of experience and self-conception in a given culture does not crown such language as all-determinative of identity. It is a reductive fallacy to dub the Israelites of the Hebrew Bible as a nonemotional—or still less, antiemotional—people because they lack a proper emotion folder in their linguistic database[25] or to dub the Hellenistic-Jewish writers of the LXX and New Testament as a glum, even masochistic bunch because a prime emotion (πάθος) category focuses on pain and suffering. The most we *might* venture, with all due tentativeness, is that *perhaps* emotions as we conceive them were not *as important, formative, or positive* in the biblical world as they are for Micronesian Ifaluk islanders or for the modern English-speaking world (in different ways). But "less important" is a fuzzy notion, impossible to measure; at any rate, it need by no means mean "*non*important" or "*non*existent." In fact, a number of emotion theorists argue that emotions, by whatever name and tone, are characteristically *important* and value laden in the sense that, as "concern-based construals," they signal what matters most to an individual or group, what people most care about, are "passionate" about.[26]

---

22. Ibid., 93.
23. Ibid., 119–21.
24. See summary of Lutz's work in Plamper, *History of Emotions*, 106–9.
25. On this broader cultural point Lambert would agree (see his essay below); see also Mirguet's argument that "the absence [in the Hebrew Bible] of a 'meta-description' for both our noun 'emotion' and our verb 'to feel,'" though suggesting a different conceptualization of what we would call emotional experience, scarcely eradicates such experience in the Bible ("What Is an 'Emotion'?," 463). In fact, Mirguet's approach is expansive, rather than reductive: "Biblical Hebrew words that are usually translated by emotional terms, such as love or fear, *exceed our emotional realm*, as they also include actions, ritual gestures, and physical sensations" integral to *social-communal* relations (463, emphasis added).
26. Robert C. Roberts, *Emotions: An Essay in Aid of Moral Psychology* (Cambridge: Cambridge University Press, 2003), 143, 320; Roberts, *Spiritual Emotions: A*

1.2. Emotion Catalogs

However limited overarching emotion *categories* might be in biblical Hebrew and Greek, a thicker *catalog* of particular emotion-related terms may be easily indexed in both testaments featuring words reasonably translated as "anger," "fear," "joy," and such. Of course, the problem remains of correlating and/or distinguishing the *connotations* of these emotion terms in source and target languages (did/would Jesus get "angry" at the same things in the same ways I do?). I will say more about the vexed issue of basic emotions in part 3. But for now, I consider a more fundamental lexical point, namely, that *no single term (or set of terms) in any language adequately captures the dense texture of emotional experience.* Designating an "angry God" or a "grieving Jesus" does not get us very far, no more so than simply declaring out of the blue, "I am mad" or "I am sad." Mad/sad at what or whom, why, for how long, how much? Appraising the heinous state of *sinners* in the hands of an *angry God*, as in Jonathan Edwards's famous sermon (discussed in Matthew Richard Schlimm's essay in the present volume) or the grievous state of the *weeping Jesus at Lazarus's tomb* (see Stephen D. Moore's essay below, which provocatively associates Jesus's "grief" with *disgust*), provides necessary *contextual grounding* for lexical meaning: "anger" or "sadness" rooted in, shaped in, coming to life in *this* sociolinguistic environment (Edwards's sermon in eighteenth-century America, John's Gospel in first-century Asia Minor) (see more below on genre).

The research psychologist Jerome Kagan has levied especially clear and strong indictments against lexical calcification in emotion study that fails to appreciate the complex "emotional profiles," "semantic networks," and "cascade" of processes—including originating triggers, valences (pleasant/

Psychology of Christian Virtues (Grand Rapids: Eerdmans, 2007), 11–14, 25; see also Martha C. Nussbaum, *Upheavals of Thought: The Intelligence of Emotions* (Cambridge: Cambridge University Press, 2001), 30–31: "The object of emotion is seen as *important for* some role it plays in the person's own life … that is, concerned with the person's flourishing" (emphasis original); Nico H. Frijda, "The Laws of Emotions," *American Psychologist* 43 (1988): 351: "Emotions arise in response to events that are important to the individual's goals, motives, or concerns"; Lei Liu et al., "The Value of Emotion: How Does Episodic Prospection Modulate Delay Discounting," *PLoS ONE* 8 (2013), doi:10.1371/journal.pone.0081717: "Positive or negative emotion influences the content of thought in which emotion serves as information about the value of whatever comes to mind."

painful), intensity/salience, and social and temperamental factors—that attend any felt-emotion experiences.[27]

> All conclusions about emotional states based only on verbal descriptions have distinctive meanings that usually do not apply to inferences that are based on biological or behavioral data. Most English terms for emotions do not name natural kinds but, rather, families of states whose members assume a different form in varied contexts or to different incentives. Americans use the word *fear* to name worry over possible harm to the body, loss of property, social rejection, task failure, unfamiliar situations, and being alone.... Feelings are dynamic, often fleeting, experiences that semantic concepts freeze-frame into static categories.[28]

Though primarily assessing social-scientific and biological-neurological models of emotion analysis, Kagan's sage conclusion proves just as apt for literary study: "The study of emotion is not mature enough to allow confidence in a great many premises."[29] And confidence in barebones, diagnostic emotion lexicography is especially ill-placed, however attractively "free of cumbersome detail" it might be.[30] Accordingly, Kagan ends his book (and summary article) with a clarion call: "Let us agree to a moratorium on the use of single words, such as *fear, anger, joy,* and *sad,* and write about emotional process with full sentences rather than ambiguous, naked concepts that burden readers with the task of deciding who, whom, why, and especially what."[31]

---

27. Jerome Kagan, "Once More into the Breach," *EmotRev* 2 (2010): 91–99; "cascade" (91); "semantic network" (94); "emotional profiles" (95). Also developing a cascade model of neural processing in forming emotion "predictions" and "concepts," see Lisa Feldman Barrett, *How Emotions Are Made: The Secret Life of the Brain* (Boston: Houghton Mifflin Harcourt, 2017), 119–22, 311–20 (appendix D); Barrett, "The Theory of Constructed Emotion: An Active Inference Account of Interoception and Categorization," *Social Cognitive and Affective Neuroscience* 12 (2017): 8–9, 11–12, 14.
28. Kagan, "Once More into the Breach," 94, emphasis original. See also Kagan, *What Is Emotion? History, Measures, and Meanings* (New Haven: Yale University Press, 2007), 119; Kagan, *On Being Human: Why Mind Matters* (New Haven: Yale University Press, 2017), 225–44.
29. Kagan, *What Is Emotion?*, 214.
30. Ibid., 216.
31. Ibid., 216, emphasis original; and Kagan, "Once More into the Breach," 98; Kagan, *On Being Human*, 244.

All contributors in the current volume write about various emotions in biblical literature—including all four emotions that Kagan lists in the previous citation—in not only full sentences, but also fleshed-out paragraphs integrated into substantive essays. Though offering no definitive profile of any emotion—a fool's errand in any case—these essays add several rigorous case studies to the dossier. Beyond abstract word or category studies of emotion(s), these investigations are rooted in the corpora of the Jewish and Christian Bibles bound together by historical and canonical processes, but internally distinguished by different books and genres. Our project thus confronts special literary challenges: How does the Bible's multifaceted literary context affect the study of emotions within it? How does its literary form(s) present emotional function(s)?

2. Texts and Types

The 1980s produced a burst of interest in the "Bible as Literature."[32] This focus on formalistic, generic, stylistic, thematic, even "novelistic" elements of the Bible (correlated with studies of secular literature) reacted against both the longstanding hegemony of atomistic historical-critical approaches to biblical scholarship and the parochial use of the Bible as a theological sourcebook. Bible courses could now be safely offered in nonsectarian college literature departments. On a fundamental level, however, acknowledging the Bible as literature is hardly some startling innovation. Though biblical interpretation might reflect historical, theological, or some other aims and interests, it must deal, in the nature of the documentary case, with biblical *literature*, with this body of historical, theological (or whatever) *literature*. Without delving into theoretical or ideological debates about what counts as literature or art, for the purposes of this discussion I take the Bible's *literary* classification as a patent, commonsense observation: this "book" is an anthology of various genres, such as narrative and poetry, typically regarded as "literary" rather than merely "textual." But even types of material not normally touted for artistic merit

---

32. See, e.g., Northrop Frye, *The Great Code: The Bible as Literature* (New York: Houghton Mifflin Harcourt, 1981); Leland Ryken, *How to Read the Bible as Literature ... and Get More Out of It* (Grand Rapids: Zondervan, 1984); John B. Gabel and Charles B. Wheeler, *The Bible as Literature: An Introduction* (New York: Oxford University Press, 1986); and Robert Alter and Frank Kermode, *The Literary Guide to the Bible* (Cambridge: Belknap, 1990).

tilt toward the literary side in the Bible. The so-called historical accounts, however factually accurate or not, are presented in stylized narrative form and in no case constitute a bare chronicle of events (including the books tagged "Chronicles" in English Bibles); genealogical and legal materials are embedded in narrative books (e.g., Genesis, Exodus, Matthew, Luke) as part of their stories, again nothing like a transcript of court minutes or congressional records; and the letters of Paul, for all their koine flavor, though not epistolary novels on the order of Chion of Heraclea[33] or *The Color Purple*, are scarcely business transactions or family "text messages" like the mundane papyri Deissmann published.[34] Paul's missives are chock full of rhetorical flourishes, literary references (especially from the Jewish scriptures), sophisticated arguments, and narrative backgrounds and substructures.[35] Genres routinely mix in literary productions.

Granting, then, the Bible as literature(s), it is no great leap to presume a vital concern with emotions in its pages. As the philosopher and classics scholar Martha C. Nussbaum succinctly states: "Literature is in league with the emotions"—in terms not only of emotional responses made by readers to moving passages and engaging characters, but also of emotional girders "built into the very structure" of literary works.[36] Keith Oatley and coauthors of a major psychology textbook on the emotions concur: "From the earliest times to the present, it is extraordinary that at the focus of poetic, fictional, and folk-historical narratives have been the emotions." As examples from antiquity, they cite Homer's *Iliad*, commencing with "Of rage sing, goddess," and the Hebrew Torah, especially the Genesis "family history in which the protagonists ... oscillate between fear and hopeful

---

33. See Patricia A. Rosenmeyer, *Ancient Epistolary Fictions: The Letter in Greek Literature* (Cambridge: Cambridge University Press, 2001).

34. Adolf Deissmann, *Light from the Ancient East: The New Testament Illustrated by Recently Discovered Texts of the Graeco-Roman World*, trans. Lionel R. M. Strachan (London: Hodder & Stoughton, 1927).

35. See, e.g., Bruce W. Longenecker, ed., *Narrative Dynamics in Paul* (Louisville: Westminster John Knox, 2002); Richard B. Hays, *The Faith of Jesus Christ: The Narrative Substructure of Galatians 3:1–4:11*, 2nd ed. (Grand Rapids: Eerdmans, 2002).

36. Martha C. Nussbaum, *Poetic Justice: The Literary Imagination and Public Life* (Boston: Beacon, 1995), 53 (part of a stimulating essay, "Rational Emotions," 53–78); see also Patrick Colm Hogan, *What Literature Teaches Us about Emotion*, SESI (Cambridge: Cambridge University Press, 2011); and the article by Dinkler in the present volume.

dependence on their god Yahweh."[37] Along with epic poetry, Greek tragedies featured tangled webs of emotional experience, much to the delight and education of popular audiences, but not always valued by professional thinkers then or since. Tensions between the different emotional tenors of philosophy and literature run long and deep in the history of thought.

Plato was no great fan of poets and playwrights, effectively banning them from public policy forums: "We must ask Homer and the other poets to excuse us if we delete all passages of this kind," like the account of Achilles's histrionic grieving over the death of Patroclus. "It is not that they are bad poetry or are not popular; indeed the better they are as poetry the more unsuitable they are for the ears of children or men who are to be free and fear slavery more than death" (*Resp.* 387b).[38] In this view, poetry's powerful emotional appeal, like that of the Sirens' song, entraps hearers/readers into its mind-numbing, self-sapping swell, leading to shipwreck and ruin.[39] But such a monodimensional, antirational perspective of the passions hardly does justice to literature's complex portrayals of emotional experience. As Nussbaum describes her personal epiphany: "I was finding in the Greek tragic poets a … deep sense of the problem of conflicting obligations, and a recognition of the ethical significance of the passions, that I found more rarely, if at all, in the thought of the admitted philosophers, whether ancient or modern."[40] Far from simply reversing Plato's bias, however, Nussbaum argues for a mutually informing and

---

37. Keith Oatley, Dacher Keltner, and Jennifer M. Jenkins, *Understanding Emotions*, 2nd ed. (Malden, MA: Blackwell, 2006), 400–1. Oatley also happens to be an accomplished novelist as well as research psychologist. See also two other works exclusively by Oatley dealing with emotion and literature: *Such Stuff as Dreams: The Psychology of Fiction* (Malden, MA: Wiley-Blackwell, 2011), 107–32; *The Passionate Muse: Exploring Emotion in Stories* (Oxford: Oxford University Press, 2012). In this section, I borrow some material from F. Scott Spencer, "A Woman's Touch: Manual and Emotional Dynamics of Female Characters in Luke's Gospel," in *Characters and Characterization in Luke-Acts*, ed. Frank Dicken and Julia Snyder, LNTS 548 (London: Bloomsbury T&T Clark, 2016), 75–79.

38. Quotation from Allan Bloom, trans., *The Republic of Plato*, 2nd ed. (New York: Basic Books, 1991), 64; see Martha C. Nussbaum, *Love's Knowledge: Essays on Philosophy and Literature* (New York: Oxford University Press, 1990), 17–18.

39. Nussbaum notes that the Stoics used Odysseus's lashing himself to the ship's mast to prevent surrendering to the Sirens' allures as an image of "critical detachment" from the passionate perturbations of literature (*Poetic Justice*, 57–58).

40. Nussbaum, *Love's Knowledge*, 14.

challenging engagement between philosophy and literature in navigating the dense thicket of entangled emotions (passions), thoughts (ideas), and actions (ethics).[41]

Though some portions of the Bible have a marked philosophical cast—wisdom literature (esp. Ecclesiastes and Wisdom of Solomon), 4 Maccabees (see above), Paul's Areopagus speech in Acts 17, parts of Paul's letters, Hebrews to some degree—and many more speak to key philosophical issues (e.g., the problem of evil, the nature of justice),[42] *generically*, the Bible would never be mistaken for a set of philosophical treatises. Moreover, its interest in emotions as part of its fundamental literary character easily elides into its more philosophical substrata. The biblical writer perhaps most conversant with Greek philosophy and sometimes called a philosopher in his own right, Saul/Paul of Tarsus,[43] is hardly a dispassionate, ivory-tower scholastic or Christian Socrates. Even a cursory reading of Paul's letters reveals a more populist than professional thinker who, along with spinning out rigorous conceptual (theological) arguments, often wears his emotions on his sleeves and even lets them get the best of him at times, with Galatians providing the most salient example.[44]

The essays in this volume examine texts within all the major genres of the Bible—narrative (including gospel *bioi*), legal, poetic (including prophetic), sapiential, epistolary—except for apocalyptic.[45] How might these

---

41. Nussbaum develops this point throughout *Love's Knowledge*; *Poetic Justice*; *Upheavals of Thought*; and *Not for Profit: Why Democracy Needs the Humanities* (Princeton: Princeton University Press, 2010).

42. For a sterling analysis of the vexed problem of evil and justice (theodicy) across the Hebrew Bible in light of the Holocaust, see Marvin A. Sweeney, *Reading the Hebrew Bible after the Shoah: Engaging Holocaust Theology* (Minneapolis: Fortress, 2008). For a stimulating discussion of philosophical reasoning *through* various literary genres in the Hebrew Bible, see Yoram Hazony, *The Philosophy of Hebrew Scripture* (Cambridge: Cambridge University, 2012).

43. See, e.g., Ward Benton and Hent de Vries, eds., *Paul and the Philosophers* (New York: Fordham University Press, 2013); Abraham J. Malherbe, *Paul and the Popular Philosophers* (Minneapolis: Fortress, 1989); Malherbe, *Paul and the Thessalonians: The Philosophical Tradition of Pastoral Care* (Philadelphia: Fortress, 1987).

44. Maia Kotrosits, *Rethinking Early Christian Identity: Affect, Violence, and Belonging* (Minneapolis: Fortress, 2015), 9, 206–11, discussing the "emotional intensity" of Brigitte Kahl's study of Galatians: *Galatians Re-imagined: Reading with the Eyes of the Vanquished*, Paul in Critical Contexts (Minneapolis: Fortress, 2010).

45. For recent investigations of affective dimensions of Revelation, see Stephen D. Moore, "Retching on Rome: Vomitous Loathing and Visceral Disgust in Affect Theory

literary types affect the interpretation of passions/emotions within them? The literary critic Philip Fisher writes: "In literature, the passions are not present merely as ... certain kinds of moments alongside other important moments like choosing, perceiving, remembering, talking, or acting. Key passions determine genres or literary kinds; large and ordered systems of aesthetic practices that generate the form of the whole."[46] This emphasis on "the form of the whole" again cautions us against atomistic analyses of emotion words, incidents, or experiences decoupled from wider literary (and social-cultural) contexts. Fisher cites *elegy* and *tragedy* as sample genres thoroughly formed and informed by passions of *grief and mourning*, in the former case, and *fear and pity*, in the latter (following Aristotle's *Poetics*). In the Bible, the book of Lamentations fits the elegiac mold, however many times it actually uses the word *grief* and related terms. Though shot through with "tragic" experiences, no biblical book or section in either testament fully fits the *tragedy* mold since an indomitable *comic* vision and cosmic hope for restoration prevails from Genesis to Revelation.[47]

A recent article by Petra von Gemünden provocatively, though not altogether persuasively, delineates the distinctive emotional orientations of narrative and paraenetic types of biblical and related literature. Her focal texts derive from the Testaments of the Twelve Patriarchs and New Testament gospels and letters. Comparing presentations of emotions in the subgenres of *narratio* (the patriarchs' recounting personal past negative emotions) and *paraenesis* (the patriarchs' warning descendants concerning emotional traps) *within* the macrogenre of testamentary/farewell literature, von Gemünden detects the *narrative* tendency to focus on multiple past emotions with bodily effects, in contrast with the *paraenetic* target of one emotion to be unequivocally resisted in future conduct.[48] The

---

and the Apocalypse of John," *BibInt* 22 (2014): 503–28; Kotrosits, *Rethinking Early Christian Identity*, 9, 211–16.

46. Philip Fisher, *The Vehement Passions* (Princeton: Princeton University Press, 2002), 8.

47. See J. William Whedbee, *The Bible and the Comic Vision* (Minneapolis: Fortress, 2002); Dan O. Via, *Kerygma and Comedy in the New Testament: A Structuralist Approach to Hermeneutic* (Philadelphia: Fortress, 1975); Kevin J. Madigan and Jon D. Levenson, *Resurrection: The Power of God for Christians and Jews* (New Haven: Yale University Press, 2008).

48. Petra von Gemünden, "Emotions and Literary Genres in the Testaments of the Twelve Patriarchs and the New Testament: A Contribution to Form History and Historical Psychology," *BibInt* 24 (2016): 514–35.

patriarch Simeon, for example, recalls his former swirl of jealousy, envy, anger, and sadness in his despicable dealings with younger brother Joseph, effecting the calcification of Simeon's *liver* and incapacitation of his *hand*. When he turns to exhortation, however, Simeon concentrates in a strict "either/or logic" on the singular "spirit of envy" that must be shunned "at all costs."[49] In New Testament narratives, "envy" (φθόνος) appears only in Matt 27:18 // Mark 15:10, describing Pilate's motivation for granting the chief priests and attendant mob's demand for Jesus's crucifixion. In the paraenetic material, however, von Gemünden focuses on the blanket prohibition of φθόνος in epistolary vice lists (Rom 1:29; Gal 5:21; 1 Tim 6:4; Tit 3:3; 1 Pet 2:1), continuing the unambiguous denunciation of corrosive emotions in the Testaments of the Twelve Patriarchs didactic sections, though collocated in the New Testament with other emotion-related vices rather than singled out.[50]

Though von Gemünden properly attends to generic literary contexts in studying emotions, she overplays her hand in the examples she cites. The admixture of narrative and paraenetic materials *within* individual testaments (and the corpus overall) weakens distinctions between them from the start. Subgenres are not separate, sealed compartments but rather mutually informing and interlacing units—like the narrative and legal sections in Exodus or narrative and sermonic discourses in Matthew—whose contents and perspectives, including those regarding emotions, inform and interpenetrate each other. More critically, the structure of von Gemünden's analysis of emotions in New Testament literature around three select terms (φθόνος, ὀργή, and ἐπιθυμία) hews too close for comfort to the lexical fallacy discussed above. Concerning φθόνος in particular, von Gemünden ignores the one Pauline case not in vice lists—"Some proclaim Christ from envy [φθόνον] and rivalry, but others from goodwill" (Phil 1:15 NRSV); this proves to be a glaring omission, not only because it misses the key context of missionary preaching, but also because it forecloses suggestive affinities between the envy of Paul's rivals and his own impassioned "longing" (πόθος) for Christ and for the Philippians, as David Fredrickson has so deftly teased out (ἐπιποθέω [Phil 1:8; 2:26]).[51]

---

49. Ibid., 519–21.
50. Ibid., 527–29.
51. David E. Fredrickson, *Eros and the Christ: Longing and Envy in Paul's Christology*, Paul in Critical Contexts (Minneapolis: Fortress, 2013), 107–22.

Both rooted in ἔρως, φθόνος and πόθος "bore a likeness to one another" as fierce passions of "lovesickness and longing" commonly expressed in images of bodily draining, including a desiccated "hollow eye" associated with exhaustive outpouring of tears.[52] This story of Paul's (and Christ's) envy-like, "erotic" loving and longing for God's people is not only signaled by various emotion terms and explicit statements but also seeps into the discursive gaps[53] and saturates the entire correspondence: Philippians is a passionate love letter. Significantly, what especially opens Fredrickson's eyes to this rich emotion-laden reading of Pauline and other New Testament letters (see his treatment of "insatiable desire" in the present volume) is his adroit, *multigeneric* conversation concerning the passions among philosophical, epistolary, and especially poetic literatures not usually convened around the same seminar table.

3. Twists and Turns

Having sketched above some historical "turns" in passion/emotion terminology from Hebrew biblical literature to Aristotle's Greek *Rhetoric* to the LXX and New Testament and some analytical "twists" in investigating emotion concepts and experiences (mixed feelings) within various literary forms (mixed genres), I now extend the horizons of the "turns" and delve deeper into the thicket of "twists" affecting studies of the Bible and emotion.

3.1. From *Émotion* to Emotion

3.1.1. The Emotive Turn

Here I return to the vexed English term *emotion*, which according to the historian of psychology and medicine Thomas Dixon represents a "keyword

---

52. Ibid., 109.
53. Reflecting on gaps in emotional expression, Fisher stresses a responsive tendency toward "a blank spot where the reader or spectator *volunteers* passion, stepping in to supply the missing fear, grief, shame, or anger" (*Vehement Passions*, 144, emphasis original). See further on "filling in [emotion] gaps" Peter Goldie, *The Mess Inside: Narrative, Emotion, and the Mind* (Oxford: Oxford University Press, 2012), 19–20. In her essay in the present volume, Katherine M. Hockey offers a fascinating assessment of the *absence* of (explicit) anger in 1 Peter's responses to a hostile social environment.

in crisis,"[54] echoed in research psychologist Carroll E. Izzard's assessment that emotion, as currently deployed in both everyday and scientific discourse, "cannot be defined as a unitary concept."[55] In what we might call the "emotive turn," the word came into English, according to Dixon, in the early seventeenth century as a transliteration of the French *émotion* (e.g., in the English version of Montaigne's essays), denoting various types of physical agitation in nature, the human body, and society ("public emotion").[56] Into the eighteenth century, the term developed into a general descriptor of "the bodily stirrings accompanying mental feelings"[57] designated variously as "passions," "desires," "affections," and "sentiments," clustering around a moral dualism of good versus evil "feeling" states, following the lead of Augustine, Aquinas, and other Christian thinkers. Not only was human experience beset by corrosive "passions" and "desires" (lusts) to be vigilantly nipped in the bud by rational argument, as the Stoics stressed, but it was also blessed by virtuous "sentiments" and "affections" (loves) to be nurtured and acted upon, in more Aristotelian fashion.[58] Though these moral mental dispositions accompanied emotive external excitations, they themselves were not yet regarded as constitutive of emotions.

But the emotive turn inward "from the bodily to the mental domain" had begun, receiving further impetus from influential Scottish scholars: first, David Hume and Adam Smith, in their sporadic and unsystematic use of emotion sometimes as a generic label "for any kind of mental feeling or agitation" and other times as a synonym for either "passion" or "affection";[59] and second, the early nineteenth-century philosopher-physicians Thomas Brown and Charles Bell, who solidified emotion as a major conceptual category, though still vaguely defined. After admitting the term's slippery meaning, Brown ventured a proposal: "Perhaps, if any

---

54. Thomas Dixon, "'Emotion': The History of a Keyword in Crisis," *EmotRev* 4 (2012): 338–44; summarizing and updating his fuller argument in *From Passions to Emotions: The Creation of a Secular Psychological Category* (Cambridge: Cambridge University Press, 2003).
55. Carroll E. Izzard, "The Many Meanings/Aspects of Emotion: Definitions, Functions, Activation, and Regulation," *EmotRev* 2 (2010): 363; see also 363–70.
56. Dixon, "Emotion," 340. In this section on the emotive turn (as I call it), I depend heavily on Dixon's work; see also Lasater, "'The Emotions' in Biblical Anthropology?"
57. Dixon, "Emotion," 340.
58. Ibid. 339; and Dixon, "Revolting Passions," in *Faith, Rationality, and the Passions*, ed. Sarah Coakley (Malden, MA: Wiley-Blackwell, 2012), 181–95.
59. Dixon, "Emotion," 340.

definition of [emotions] be possible, they may be defined to be vivid feelings, arising immediately from the consideration of objects, perceived, or remembered, or imagined, or from other prior emotions."[60] These "vivid feelings," however, in Brown's view, though "perceived" in the mind, were *not* regarded as deliberative cognitive assessments or moral judgments. Common to the psychology of his day, he maintained "a stark separation between intellectual thoughts and emotional feelings."[61] Bell sharpened and modified the picture, turning back toward the body with a causal theory of emotion as a "movement of the mind," both primed by bodily stimuli (from heart, lungs, and "organs of breathing and speech") and producing outward bodily effects (e.g., on the face).[62] Though situating emotional feelings in a body-mind loop, the "mental" part remained secondary to and subsumed by the "physical" signs and sensations.

This somatic-framed emotive theory persisted through the nineteenth and into the twentieth century, given classic formulation by the American philosopher-psychologist William James in his essay, "What Is an Emotion?":

> Our natural way of thinking about these standard emotions is that the mental perception of some fact excites the mental affection called the emotion, and that this latter state of mind gives rise to the bodily expression. My thesis on the contrary is that *the bodily changes follow directly the* PERCEPTION *of the exciting fact, and that our feeling of the same changes as they occur* IS *the emotion.*[63]

Again, though allowing for "mental/perceptual" aspects of emotional experience, this trajectory from French (Michel de Montaigne) to Scottish philosophy to American pragmatism (William James) tilts heavily toward biological/physiological accounts of psychic phenomena (with more than a little boost from Charles Darwin)[64] and away from intellectual moral evaluations of "passions," whether wholly malevolent (4 Maccabees; New

---

60. Cited in ibid., 340 (Brown pens this definition in 1820).
61. Ibid., 341.
62. Ibid.
63. William James, "What Is an Emotion?," in *What Is an Emotion? Classic and Contemporary Readings*, ed. Robert C. Solomon, 2nd ed. (Oxford: Oxford University Press, 2003), 66–76, quotation from 67, emphasis original.
64. Charles Darwin, *The Expression of the Emotions in Man and Animals*, ed. Paul Ekman, 4th ed. (London: Murray, 1872; repr., Oxford: Oxford University Press, 2009).

Testament vice lists) or of mixed value (bad "passions" versus good "affections"). Emotions may move through the mind, but they do not spend much time or energy there.

3.1.2. The Cognitive Turn

Deeper into the twentieth century, however, the mind began to matter more in a marked "cognitive turn" in psychology, sparked in part by new neuroscience technologies of brain imaging. Certain areas of the brain could now be demonstrated as receptors and transmitters of emotional "signals" triggered by situations demanding some decision, action, or other response and wired to memory data areas storing past responses. A leading researcher in this field, Antonio Damasio, distills this "somatic-marker hypothesis," as he calls it: "In brief, the signal *marks* options and outcomes with a positive or negative [emotional] signal that narrows the decision-making space and increases the probability that the action will conform to past experience."[65] In other words, "the emotional signal … covertly or overtly … focuses attention on certain aspects of the problem and thus enhances the quality of reasoning over it."[66] Emotion and reason thus partner together in rational decision making. This emotion theory remains bodily (somatic)-oriented, though, compared with earlier theories more concentrated on the *brain* as the central processing organ and more integrated with intellectual (cognitive) dimensions of that processing.[67]

The cognitive turn in neuroscience coordinates with *appraisal* theories of emotion in psychology, represented by Richard Lazarus, Keith Oatley, Philip Johnson-Laird, and Agnes Moors.[68] In Lazarus's terms, for

---

65. Antonio Damasio, *Looking for Spinoza: Joy, Sorrow, and the Feeling Brain* (Orlando: Harcourt, 2003), 148, emphasis original; see also Damasio, *The Feeling of What Happens: Body and Emotion in the Making of Consciousness* (Orlando: Harcourt, 1999), 40–42; Damasio, *Descartes' Error: Emotion, Reason, and the Human Mind* (New York: Penguin, 1994), 205–22; Damasio, "The Somatic Marker Hypothesis and the Possible Functions of the Prefrontal Cortex," *PTRSLB* 31 (1996): 1413–20.

66. Damasio, *Looking for Spinoza*, 147.

67. Essays by Dennis Olson and Ivar Vegge in the present volume engage with neuroscience studies of emotion.

68. Richard S. Lazarus, *Emotion and Adaptation* (Oxford: Oxford University Press, 1991); for a more popular treatment, see Richard S. Lazarus and Bernice N. Lazarus, *Passion and Reason: Making Sense of Our Emotions* (New York: Oxford Uni-

example, "*appraisal* [distinct from 'knowledge'] consists of a continuing evaluation of the significance of what is happening for one's personal well-being. Without personal significance, knowledge is cold, or nonemotional. When knowledge touches on one's personal well-being, however, it is hot, or emotional."[69] Breaking down further this evaluative emotional process, Lazarus posits three stages, appraising (1) *goal relevance* (emotions monitor success, failure, or indifference to achieving life goals), (2) *goal congruence* (positive/encouraging emotions)/*incongruence* (negative/discouraging emotions), and (3) *type of ego involvement* (assessing boosts and threats to self-flourishing).[70] Though mental judgments play a key role in emotional appraisal, they fit into a more complex, dynamic "cognitive-motivational-relational" process involving thoughts, attitudes, aspirations, and "action readiness."[71]

Philosophers of emotion like Nussbaum and Robert C. Solomon, among others, have embraced the cognitive-appraisal turn.[72] For Nussbaum in particular, this marks a much-needed turn *back* to Hellenistic moral philosophy, which took seriously the interplay, for good and ill, between emotion and reason in living a whole, satisfying, *eudaimonistic*

---

versity Press, 1994); Keith Oatley and Philip N. Johnson-Laird, "Towards a Cognitive Theory of Emotions," *CE* 1 (1987): 29–50; Oatley and Johnson-Laird, "Cognitive Approaches to Emotions," *TCS* 18 (2014): 134–40; Oatley, Keltner, and Jenkins, *Understanding Emotions*, 166–80; Agnes Moors, "Flavors of Appraisal Theories of Emotion," *EmotRev* 6 (2014): 303–7; Moors et al., "Appraisal Theories of Emotion: State of the Art and Future Development," *EmotRev* 5 (2013): 119–24; Moors, "Integration of Two Skeptical Emotion Theories: Dimensional Appraisal Theory and Russell's Psychological Construction Theory," *Psychological Inquiry* 28 (2017): 1–19.

69. Lazarus, *Emotion and Adaptation*, 144, emphasis original.

70. Ibid., 149–50.

71. Lazarus, *Emotion and Adaptation*, 115. On emotions as "action tendencies" prompting "some change in action readiness," see Frijda, "Laws of Emotion," 351; Frijda, *The Emotions* (Cambridge: Cambridge University Press, 1986), 69–93, 231–41; Frijda, *The Laws of Emotion* (New York: Routledge, 2013), 3–46.

72. For Martha C. Nussbaum, see *Upheavals of Thought*; "Rational Judgments" in Nussbaum, *Poetic Justice*, 53–78; "Emotions as Judgments of Value and Importance," in *Thinking about Feeling: Contemporary Philosophers on Emotions*, ed. Robert C. Solomon (Oxford: Oxford University Press, 2004), 183–99. For Robert C. Solomon, see *The Passions: Emotions and the Meaning of Life*, 2nd ed. (Indianapolis: Hackett, 1993); *True to Our Feelings*; "Emotions, Thoughts, and Feelings: Emotions as Engagements with the World," in Solomon, *Thinking about Feeling*, 76–88.

life.[73] Even in their hyperrational stance, the Stoics took emotions seriously as signs of the human condition and spurs to careful examination of what constitutes the "good life." In Nussbaum's "neo-Stoic" view, as she calls it, emotions *are* "judgments of value" (not simply preludes to such judgments) "suffused with intelligence and discernment," "part and parcel of the system of ethical reasoning."[74] They "involve judgments about important things, judgments in which, appraising an external object as salient for own well-being, we acknowledge our own neediness and incompleteness before parts of the world that we do not fully control."[75] Though thoroughly rational, emotions are typically not generative of calm and cool reason; rather they stir the ethical-deliberative pot as "upheavals of thought."[76]

While Damasio, Lazarus, Nussbaum, and the other cognitive emotion theorists cited above are all wide-ranging thinkers with broad visions of human experience in the world, their predominantly cognitive emphasis runs the risk of stuffing the emotions too tightly inside a personalized, internalized, and intellectualized box (or brain pod).[77] With this turn into the mind, particularly the self-conscious mind, and parking there, does the body—including the brain, but so much more—get shortchanged in all this emotional experience and disengaged from other bodies socially, politically, and environmentally? Has the body-mind loop lost its kinetic tension, like a floppy drive belt in a car?

---

73. See the essay by Samuel Balentine in the present volume for a wide-ranging assessment of *eudaimonism* in connection with ancient and modern perspectives on happiness.

74. Nussbaum, *Upheavals of Thought*, 1.

75. Ibid., 19.

76. Nussbaum's title *Upheavals of Thought* derives from Marcel Proust's description of love as "real geological upheavals of thought" in *Remembrance of Things Past*.

77. See the critique of Damasio and Nussbaum in Daniel M. Gross, *The Secret History of Emotion: From Aristotle's Rhetoric to Modern Brain Science* (Chicago: University of Chicago Press, 2006), 28–39, 74–78. Gross argues against what he judges as a biological-scientific reductionism in cognitive theories of emotion that fail to appreciate core *social-rhetorical* factors: "Subjective experiences such as emotion have an essential social component and are best treated with *social analysis* of the sort developed in the rhetorical tradition" (33–34, emphasis original). Although I think Gross unduly reduces Damasio's and Nussbaum's more sophisticated, expansive arguments, his point about the social (relational) environment of emotions is well taken (see below).

3.1.3. The Affective Turn

At this point the "affective turn" in cultural studies turns *back* to the body (again!), ratcheting up its "intensity"[78] and capacity to affect behavior at precognitive/subconscious levels of response.[79] Moore provides an outstanding introduction to affect theory in this volume, accessible and applicable to biblical scholars, which is not as easy to see as with cognitive-based models of emotion, partly because of affect theory's more abstruse theorizing, but also because cognitive approaches fit more congenially with biblical interpreters' traditional interests in theological and moral reasoning. I need not reprise Moore's careful tracking of two primary strains of affect discourse (Silvan Tompkins and Guattari Deleuze). I simply focus on the body-mind configuration of the affective turn and its import for studying emotion in the Bible. In this discourse, affect is related but not equated to emotion, though hard definitions of either term are hard to find. Introducing their *Affect Theory Reader*, Melissa Gregg and Gregory Seigworth describe affect in terms of "in-between-ness," which tellingly resists clear-cut definition:

> Affect arises in the midst of *in-between-ness*: in the capacities to act and be acted upon.... That is, affect is found in those intensities that pass body to body (human, nonhuman, part-body, and otherwise), in those resonances that circulate about, between, and sometimes stick to bodies

---

78. "Intensity" is a major concept of the leading affect theorist Brian Massumi; the term is used some fifty-eight times in his *Parables of the Virtual: Movement, Affect* (Durham, NC: Duke University Press, 2007). With reference to Massumi (and Félix Guatarri), Lone Bertelsen and Andrew Murphie stress the bountiful, boundless nature of this intensity—"the multiplicity of intensities"; "an excess of affective intensity." See Bertelsen and Murphie, "An Ethics of Everyday Intensities and Powers: Félix Guatarri on Affect and the Refrain," in *The Affect Theory Reader*, ed. Melissa Gregg and Gregory J. Seigworth (Durham, NC: Duke University Press, 2010), 153, see more broadly 138–57.

79. On this turn, see Patricia Ticineto Clough, ed., with Jean Halley, *The Affective Turn: Theorizing the Social* (Durham, NC: Duke University Press, 2007); Simon Thompson and Paul Hoggett, eds., *Politics and the Emotions: The Affective Turn in Contemporary Political Studies* (New York: Bloomsbury Academic, 2012); Louise J. Lawrence, "Emotions in Protest in Mark 11–13: Responding to an Affective Turn in Social-Scientific Discourse," in *Matthew and Mark Across Perspectives: Essays in Honour of Stephen C. Barton and William R. Telford*, ed. Kristian A. Bendoraitis and Nijay K. Gupta (London: Bloomsbury T&T Clark, 2016), 83–107.

and worlds, *and* in the very passages or variations between these intensities and resonances themselves. Affect, at its most anthropomorphic, is the name we give to those forces—visceral forces beneath, alongside, or generally *other than* conscious knowing, vital forces insisting beyond emotion—that can serve to drive us toward movement, toward thought and extension, that can likewise suspend us (as if in neutral) across a barely registering accretion of force-relations.[80]

This fluid, dynamic, "vital," and volatile kaleidoscope of affect moves us not only "beyond emotion" but beyond "conscious knowing" (cognition) and, to say the least, beyond highlighted brain circuits on an fMRI readout.

But going beyond need not mean leaving behind, and if affect theory is anything, it is expansive rather than reductive: "It makes easy compartmentalisms give way to thresholds and tensions, blends and blurs." It may drive us *toward* thought and emotion as well as away/beyond. Crisply put, "Affect and cognition are never fully separable—if for no other reason than that thought is itself a body, embodied."[81]

Hebrew Bible scholar Amy Cottrill employs affect theory to good effect in her stimulating analysis of Ehud and Jael's forceful, bodily "handlings" ("armed" assaults) of Israel's enemies in Judg 3–5 interlaced with emotional fears, anxieties, and insecurities on both sides. Drawing on the work of Sara Ahmed and Teresa Brennan, among others, Cottrill explains the critical corporeal-cognitive nexus of affect theory informing her reading of biblical narrative: "Bodily affect—the visceral response of the body to its environment, which happens mostly on an unconscious level—evokes thought.... We may think *through* our feelings and bodily

---

80. Gregory J. Seigworth and Melissa Gregg, "An Inventory of Shimmers," in Gregg and Seigworth, *Affect Theory Reader*, 1, emphasis original.

81. Seigworth and Gregg, "Inventory of Shimmers," 2–3. Given this acknowledged junction of bodily affect and cognition, Ruth Leys ("The Turn to Affect: A Critique," *CI* 37 [2011]: 443) overstates her critique of affect theory (and neuroscience a la Damasio): "What the new affect theorists and the neuroscientists share is a commitment to the idea that there is a gap between the subject's affects and its cognition or appraisal of the affective situation or object, such that cognition come 'too late' for reasons, beliefs, intention, and meanings to play the role in action and behavior usually accorded to them." "Later," perhaps (by milliseconds at times), but not necessarily "*too* late" for substantive cognitive engagement.

reactions, finding thoughts that match the physical registers of our corporeal experiences."[82]

New Testament and early Christian literature specialist Maia Kotrosits utilizes affect theory to interpret canonical (Acts, Paul, Revelation) and extracanonical (Secret Revelation of John, Gospel of Truth) writings enmeshed in vulnerable diaspora environments fraught with traumatic tension. Her goal is to "make sense" of these materials, but in a much richer sense than usual, in which "thinking and feeling are hopelessly interwoven experiences.... My choice of the word 'sense' ... implies *both cognition and emotion*."[83] Further, she regards affect theory not as a rigid method of analysis but "as a set of cross-disciplinary reflections on the bodily, social, and linguistic entanglements of that which is often more colloquially understood as 'emotion.' ... To say we 'make sense' ... is to accord an intuitive, bodily, non- or beyond-conscious force to knowing."[84] Kotrosits thus values core "impressionistic" facets of cognitive reasoning as more than mere adornments for hard logical proofs or philosophical tenets; but this perspective does not reinforce the reason/emotion dichotomy from the other side (now privileging emotion) as much as it engages the entire cognitive-affective process.

These various emotive, cognitive, and affective turns in the modern era all, in their own ways, provide as much challenge as clarification to biblical studies. At root they remind us that emotion, however delineated, matters a lot in human experience and can never be excised from sense or meaning making, which biblical scholars call "hermeneutics" partly to make our efforts at "exegesis" (another favored term) appear more scientific. The Enlightenment project of rational historical criticism(s) has been very productive in biblical scholarship and will continue apace. But it is high time to face up, as Kotrosits puts it, to the "acutely depersonalizing" and highly "dispassionate language of historical inquiry," amounting to a

---

82. Amy C. Cottrill, "A Reading of Ehud and Jael through the Lens of Affect Theory," *BibInt* 22 (2014): 435–36, emphasis original, drawing here especially on Teresa Brennan, *The Transmission of Affect* (Ithaca, NY: Cornell University Press, 2004), 7.

83. Kotrosits, *Rethinking Early Christian Identity*, 3, emphasis added.

84. Ibid., 4. See also Barrett, *How Emotions Are Made*, 126: "*Emotions are meaning.* They explain your interoceptive changes and corresponding affective feelings, in relation to the situation. They are a prescription for action. The brain systems that implement concepts, such as the interoceptive network and the control network, are the biology of meaning-making" (emphasis original).

kind of repressive "disavowing [of the] affective motive and force" pulsing in the biblical texts under investigation and in the scholars who examine them, to say nothing of the Bible's pervasive social-cultural effects—and affects!—"injuriously burned into folks' skin."[85]

Those biblical scholars of a more theological bent working in seminaries or divinity schools can also fall prey to hyperscholastic, dispassionate analyses. Theologies of the Torah, Deuteronomic History, Prophets, Luke-Acts, or Paul have too often reduced to a system of logical ideas (soteriology, eschatology, Christology, and so on) void of any pathology—that is, the study of *pathos*. Perhaps the most notable exception to this rule is Abraham Joshua Heschel's monumental two-volume *The Prophets*, shot through with a "theology of pathos" in interpreting both divine and human character(s).[86] The present volume may be viewed as both a tacit tribute to and an extension of Heschel's work.

3.2. Tapestry and Threads

It should be obvious by now that the turns in emotion theory we have sketched involve as much circuitous twisting around and back to each other as straight, linear movement. The twisting image may be usefully extended to evaluating emotions themselves as well as the language and methods used to analyze them in terms of *intertwining networks*. Hence the textile picture of tapestry and threads, which could also be imaged as arachnid "web and strands," cybernetic "web and links," or the quantitative "Problem of Parts and Plenty."[87] Discrete parts collocate into patterns, both unified and diversified. But while due attention must be paid to loose threads, rough patches, and bumpy knots and pills—which give the tapestry its distinctive character and can threaten its integrity (if pulling the dangling thread unravels the whole)—making sense of words, texts,

---

85. Kotrosits, *Rethinking Early Christian Identity*, 6–9; in the "disavowing" phrase, Kotrosits cites Eve Sedjwick, *Touching Feeling: Affect, Pedagogy, Performativity* (Durham, NC: Duke University Press, 2003), 126.

86. Abraham Joshua Heschel, *The Prophets: Two Volumes in One* (Peabody, MA: Hendrickson, 1962; repr., 2009); see esp. chs. "The Theology of Pathos," "The Philosophy of Pathos," and "Anthropopathy," 2:1–58.

87. See Jesse J. Prinz, *Gut Reactions: A Perceptual Theory of Emotion* (Oxford: Oxford University Press, 2004), 18–19, 241–45; discussed in Goldie, *Mess Inside*, 60–61.

emotions, and most anything entails *making* (shaping/forming) some connections between—and "in-between"—parts and parcels. Otherwise, we have *non-sense*. If the devil is in the details, is God in the designs (both intelligent and passionate)?

Trying to pull together the threads of this introductory survey of emotion study in relation to biblical literature, I propose three functional twists without tightening the strands into straitjackets.

3.2.1. Linguistic Twists

The vexed question of political correctness (PC) seems to haunt almost all communication these days, dangling speakers and writers between the Scylla of having to define every word with clockwork precision and the Charybdis of "speaking from the heart" whatever happens to bubble up there without thought of possible offences or other consequences. Of course, words *really matter* to most biblical scholars—for good reason, I must say. Readers of the following essays will find a good bit of semantic analysis involving Hebrew and Greek terms and their English counterparts. But most contributors (Lambert excepted), myself included, do not sweat too much over fine lines between the categorical terms *emotions*, *passions*, and *feelings*. In other words, we blithely mix them without being overly vexed. This casual twisting on a broad level of emotion descriptors may not be such a problem *if* we tighten things up at the level of particular emotion expressions, experiences, and episodes in particular contexts—with appropriate awareness of the historical trajectories of emotion-related discourse discussed above. Whether I designate "faith" or "trust" as an emotion, passion, or feeling in my essay below may not matter so much *if* I carefully unpack (as I try to do) the emotional valences (or lack thereof) of πίστις/*fides* in Greco-Roman thought and Mark's Gospel in conjunction with other feelings and attitudes coursing between and around Jesus and other Markan characters (thus avoiding the one-term lexical fallacy decried by Kagan). But, of course, that may just be special pleading on my part.

Still, even Thomas Dixon, after summarizing his meticulous plotting of the historical linguistic-conceptual shift from passions to emotions, admits:

> If the science of emotion is supposed to provide an explanation of a widely experienced kind of mental state, and in terms that can be communicated to the general public, then it might be better to stick

with the complexity, fuzziness, and overinclusivity of "emotion" than to retreat still further from the world of everyday concerns into new scientific jargons.[88]

To be sure, he does not leave matters there. He cannot resist commending some "subcategories," like Paul Griffiths's "more primitive 'affect programs' and the 'higher cognitive emotions.'"[89] But this stricter scheme does not nullify Dixon's more relaxed preceding proposal. Accessible communication with the general public about everyday concerns is not a bad thing and, as it happens, increasingly motivates the mission of the Society of Biblical Literature.[90]

3.2.2. Cultural Twists

The following essays investigate an array of emotions in biblical literature: anger, fear, sadness (grief), disgust, joy, happiness, surprise (awe/wonder), pride, shame, insatiable desire, compassion, and faith/trust. A number of researchers have regarded the first six or seven in this list as basic emotions common to most human cultures across time and coded in near-universal facial expressions: for example, downturned lower lip, scrunched up upper lip and nose, and narrowed eyes signal *disgust* pretty much everywhere, regardless of what someone may be disgusted *about* (though such facial movements, individually or together, may also express non-disgust-oriented feelings and judgments in distinct contexts).[91] But this *about-ness* is

---

88. Dixon, "Emotion," 343.
89. Ibid., 343. See Paul Griffiths, *What Emotions Really Are: The Problem of Psychological Categories* (Chicago: University of Chicago Press, 1997), 77–136.
90. See the Society of Biblical Literature's Bible Odyssey project at www.bibleodyssey.org. Matt Schlimm's essay in the present volume has an insightful section on popular culture in relation to the study of the Bible and emotion.
91. See Darwin, *Expression of the Emotions*, 146–359; Paul Ekman, "Afterword: Universality of Emotional Expression? A Personal History of the Dispute," in Darwin, *Expression of the Emotions*, 363–93; Ekman, *Emotions Revealed*; Paul Ekman and Daniel Cordaro, "What Is Meant by Calling Emotions Basic," *EmotRev* 3 (2011): 364–70. Barrett has recently leveled a broadside critique against the spate of studies that undergird the hypothesis of universal facial expressions of emotions. In her thoroughgoing constructivist model accentuating *context-specific variations* in interpreting facial-muscular configurations and emotion concepts among different cultures, Barrett resists identifying innate, cartographic "emotion fingerprints"—whether on the face or in the brain (*How Emotions Are Made*, 4–15, 42–55). Though appreciating

what matters most about *understanding* emotions—not least for our purposes since the Bible has limited facial descriptions and no pictures—and emotional *meaning* remains heavily shaped by social-cultural forces. Even within an otherwise homogeneous society, absolute universalism breaks down. As a lifelong tenderfoot city boy, I tend to be considerably more disgusted at the sights, smells, and even thoughts of horse or (literal) bull shit than a rancher from my native state of Texas of the same age, race, gender, marital status, economic class, and church denomination. Nevertheless, with similar language facility, we can still reasonably communicate with one another about disgusting things and easily find something that evokes a disgusting face from both of us (eating a maggot sandwich, maybe).

Dealing with biblical languages and cultures far removed from south Texas (or Micronesia or Papua New Guinea)[92] undoubtedly places a heavier burden on resisting anachronistic and ethnocentric transfers of emotional interpretation. Translation on any level—words, concepts, practices, experiences, cultures—is never pristine and often traitorous (*traduttore traditore*). But it makes the world go around and keeps us talking to one another with *some* mutual understanding. Efforts at universal communication, whether related to basic emotional expressions or more scientific linguistic schemes like Natural Semantic Metalanguage (NSM) may not be as widespread as claimed, but at least provide sound encouragement for cross-cultural understanding. An avid proponent of NSM and sometimes analyst of biblical literature, Anna Wierzbicka, argues that we can properly grasp the tenor of Jesus's passion experience in Gethsemane, according to Mark 14:34 ("And he said to them, 'My soul/psyche [ψυχή] is deeply sad/distressed [περίλυπος], even to death"), with the following NSM code:

And he said to them something like this:
    "something very bad is happening to me now
    I feel something very bad because of this

---

her emphasis on careful contextual analysis of emotions, I am not persuaded that she has dethroned the prevailing paradigm of remarkably widespread consistency (I will grant that "universality" is a chimera) among facial registers of certain emotions. Of course, Paul Ekman is not persuaded either; see the brief post by Paul Ekman and Dacher Keltner, "Darwin's Claims of Universals in Facial Expression Not Challenged," *The Blog*, 10 June 2014, https://tinyurl.com/SBL0396b. I anticipate a more substantive defense soon.

92. Sites of Lutz's and Ekman's research, respectively.

> I can't not feel like this
> I can't not think like this now: 'I can die because of this.' "[93]

Good enough, though beyond rendering ψυχή as "I" without all the Christian accretions of "soul" or Freudian notions of "psyche," I am not sure how much this paraphrase aids our understanding of Jesus's angst at this hour ("feeling very bad" seems a rather bland description of Jesus' intense experience). But I think it is on the right track in granting that we moderns, with due openness and diligent study, can still have a reasonable cross-cultural exchange with our ancient brothers and sisters about emotions, that we can truly, though not fully, sympathize—feel with—them. As Konstan avers, "The *pathē* thus appear to correspond broadly to the kinds of sentiments that we typically or at least sometimes classify as emotions. Often, however, the context will demand some variation."[94] A nice, balanced working hypothesis, it seems to me.

3.2.3. Methodological Twists

In this survey, I have alluded to various developments in philosophy, psychology, classical studies, anthropology, literature, linguistics, affect theory, neuroscience, and cognitive research, as these relate to our Bible and Emotion project. So I have freely engaged in methodological twisting already, perhaps on the brink of madness (is there really method in it?) and tying myself in knots. But I think we have little choice, unless we resort to the silly ostrich strategy, but to join the fray, to jump into the spaghetti junction of highways interlacing the burgeoning metropolis of emotion research in the humanities and sciences. (Yes, I am mixing/twisting metaphors now.) We need to drive as smartly and alertly as we can, and taking our time in the slow lane is highly advised in these new territories. But there is too much exciting and potentially illuminating material out there to ignore. Even so, the last thing we should do is abandon our critical faculties, honed in long practice of more traditional biblical criticisms. Considerable debate swirls *within* other fields of emotion study, to say nothing of problems of transferring insights from other humanities disciplines and results from biological and social sciences research to biblical

---

93. Anna Wierzbicka, "Language and Metalanguage: Key Issues in Emotion Research," *EmotRev* 1 (2009): 6; see also 3–14.

94. Konstan, *Emotions of the Ancient Greeks*, 4.

studies. David A. Bosworth's essay on grief in the present volume provides useful guidance for avoiding pitfalls and maximizing profits of contemporary psychological research. In a similar vein, Samuel Balentine critically exposes the limits of positive psychology for understanding happiness and emotional well-being in biblical theology. Other essays work out the illuminating potential of various cross-disciplinary approaches in the course of investigating particular emotions in the Bible.

No single essay, of course, can take account of all the possible twists and turns of emotion analysis. It may be useful, however, in this introduction to map out a range of emotion characteristics to bear in mind in an eclectic and dialectic framework at this still formative and fluid stage of research. In an earlier article, I charted four broad intersecting aspects of emotions—cognitive, motivational, relational, and value laden—with corrective checks on common misperceptions.[95] I now add two additional features that I failed to highlight sufficiently in that prior study: (1) a *somatic* dimension, acknowledged, as we have seen, in different ways from Aristotle to James to such distinct projects as neuroscience technology and affect theory (body *matters* in emotion as in all human experience); and (2) a *narrative* dimension.

Though I hinted at this latter facet of emotion above (part 2: Texts and Types), a narrative concept of emotions, focusing on their episodic more than static or momentary character, extends beyond a literary genre to encompass common human experience. The British philosopher Peter Goldie, a leading proponent of this view, argues: "An emotion … is a relatively complex state, involving past and present episodes of thoughts, feelings, and bodily changes, dynamically related in a narrative of part of a person's life, together with dispositions to experience further emotional episodes, and to act out of the emotion and to express that emotion."[96] Though the narrative *process* (a key concept for Goldie) of emotions seeks to provide some coherence and causal explanation for the vicissitudes of life and thus "tidy up the mess inside," the process

---

95. F. Scott Spencer, "Why Did the 'Leper' Get under Jesus' Skin? Emotion Theory and Angry Reaction in Mark 1:40–45," *HBT* 36 (2014): 112–18. For a fuller discussion of misconceptions in emotion study, see the eight myths exposed by Solomon, *True to Our Feelings*, 127–200; see also Richard J. Davidson, "Seven Sins in the Study of Emotion: Correctives from Affective Neuroscience," *BC* 52 (2003): 129–32.

96. Peter Goldie, *The Emotions: A Philosophical Exploration* (Oxford: Oxford University Press, 2000), 144.

itself and often the final product are rarely neat and tidy.[97] But this side of complete breakdown, the emotional sense-making story we tell ourselves keeps the mess at bay.

Here is my larger chart, then, with full recognition that the lines and boxes of a table immediately oversimplify the twists and turns of emotion theory and practice. But perhaps a survey map gets us heading in the right direction.

Common Characteristic	Comparative Elements	Corrective Emphases
Somatic	Physical, biological, embodied, sensual, neurological, affective, felt	*Not simply* psychological, self-conscious, intellectual, conceptual, attitudinal
Narrative	Structural, processual, contextual, coherent (though not necessarily tidy), causal at times, cross-temporal scope (past to future)	*Not simply* incidental, haphazard, a state or event, momentary
Cognitive	Mental, rational, connected with appraisals, evaluative judgments and construals	*Not simply* impulsive, instinctual, mindless, unreasonable, external, (merely) impulsive, instinctual, physically reactive
Motivational	Volitional, behavioral, intentional, conative, purposive, connected with "action tendencies" or "action readiness"	*Not simply* passive, arbitrary, disruptive, unsettling
Relational	Social, rhetorical, political, communicative	*Not simply* personalized, internalized, private, self-contained, individualistic
Value laden	Axiological, moral, meaningful, vital, concern based, attachment oriented	*Not simply* trivial, petty, disengaged, insignificant, unserious, hysterical, low level, vapid

While I am in table-making mode, I end with a modified table of contents or a "setting the table," if you will, for the rich fare of essays to follow. Again, this chart does scant justice to the complex and creative twists of

---

97. Ibid., 59.

these pieces both separately and as part of this overall volume, but it offers a useful at-a-glance place to start.

Author	Emotions	Texts/Genres	Approaches/Resources
Matthew Richard Schlimm	Love (compassion), anger, joy, surprise, sadness, fear, jealousy	Exod 34:6–7; 1 John 4:8, 16; an array of other Hebrew Bible and New Testament texts appropriate for this survey essay	cultural psychology (Schweder); popular theology and culture, the new atheism (Dawkins)
Deena Grant	Hate, anger	Gen 37; 45 (Joseph story); 2 Sam 13:22–32; 1 Kgs 22:8–27	cognitive psychology; cognitive linguistics; prototype emotion-script models
L. Juliana Claassens	Disgust, fear	Num 21:2–3; Deut 7:1–5 (ḥerem ban); Josh 2; 6 (Rahab story)	modern philosophy (Nussbaum); cultural politics and affect theory (Ahmed); South African history and culture; postcolonial theory; film criticism
Thomas Kazen	Disgust	Ezra 9:11; Isa 30:22; 64:6; Ezek 36; various other texts in Law, Prophets, and Writings	conceptual metaphor theory; cognitive science; psychology
David A. Bosworth	Grief	Lam 1–2; 2 Sam 12:15–23; an array of other Hebrew Bible texts dealing with mourning and weeping	attachment theory; grief studies; psychology research; ancient Near Eastern materials

David A. Lambert	Remorse, regret, contrition, distress, mourning associated with repentance and fasting, shame	Lev 16:1–31; 23:26–32; 1 Sam 1–2 (Hannah story); 2 Sam 12:16–23; 13:12–19; Pss 69:11–12; 109:24–26; Isa 58:2–9; Joel 1:8–14; Jonah 3:5–10	linguistic studies; ritual studies
Dennis Olson	Remorse, regret, contrition, distress associated with repentance, God's emotional responses to insincere repentance (sorrow vs. spite), loyal love	Hos 6:1–6; 14:1–7 (*shuv* texts); Judg 10:10–16; Priestly, Deuteronomic, and prophetic material	affective neuroscience; cognitive science; narrative studies; social psychology
Antony Dhas Prakasam	Pride	Isa 47	self-conscious emotions (SCE) theory
Samuel E. Balentine	Happiness	Tablet of Cebes (Prodicus); Tablet of Cebes woodcut (Hans Holbein)	positive psychology; happiness studies; ancient Greek philosophy, medicine, and tragedy
F. Scott Spencer	Faith/trust (primarily), fear, doubt, shame, pity, grief, goodwill, compassion, gratitude	Mark 5:24–34; 10:46–52	ancient Jewish, Greek, and Roman literature; modern theology, philosophy, psychology, and cognitive science
Ivar Vegge	Vastness, awe, wonder, fear, trauma	Mark 6:45–52 (primarily); Mark 3:5; 4:35–41; Gen 45 (Joseph); Exod 15:11–16; Job 17:6–7; 1 Sam 25 (Abigail)	psychology; neurology; trauma studies; ancient Greek literature

Michal Beth Dinkler	Joy	Luke 4:16–30; 8:1–15; Acts 8:26–40; 13:27, 40–41; Mark 16:1–8; an array of other New Testament texts dealing with joy	literary theory and narrative studies, ancient and modern; narrative reflexivity; linguistic studies; affect theory; ancient Greek and Roman literature; classics studies
Stephen D. Moore	Disgust	John 11:35–38; an array of other Johannine texts; *Psycho* shower scene	affect theory; literary and cultural studies
David E. Fredrickson	Insatiable desire, love (*erōs*), longing, grief, mourning, sadness	1 Cor 13:12; 1 Pet 3:6–7	ancient Greek amatory poetry, philosophy, and literature; postmodern philosophy (Caputo; Derrida)
Katherine M. Hockey	Anger (absence thereof)	1 Peter	Greco-Roman philosophical and rhetorical literature

Starter Bibliography on Emotions in Various Disciplines

(See further the select bibliographies at the end of each essay in this volume)

Affect Theory

Ahmed, Sarah. *The Cultural Politics of Emotion*. 2nd ed. New York: Routledge, 2014.
Clough, Patricia Ticineto, ed., with Jean Halley. *The Affective Turn: Theorizing the Social*. Durham, NC: Duke University Press, 2007.
Gregg, Melissa, and Gregory J. Seigworth, eds. *The Affect Theory Reader*. Durham, NC: Duke University Press, 2010.

Anthropology

Darwin, Charles. *The Expression of the Emotions in Man and Animals.* Edited by Paul Ekman. 4th ed. London: Murray, 1872. Repr., Oxford: Oxford University Press, 2009.

Hinton, Alexander Laban. *Biocultural Approaches to the Emotions.* PSPA. Cambridge: Cambridge University Press, 1999.

Lutz, Catherine A. *Unnatural Emotions: Everyday Sentiments on a Micronesian Atoll and Their Challenge to Western Theory.* Chicago: University of Chicago Press, 1988.

Business/Economics

Graham, Carol. *The Pursuit of Happiness: An Economy of Well-Being.* Washington, DC: Brookings Institution, 2011.

Mitchell, Vale Hawkins. *The Cost of Emotions in the Workplace: Bottom Line Value of Emotional Continuity Management.* Edited by Kristen Noakes-Fry. Brookfield, CT: Rothstein Associates, 2013.

Solomon, Robert C., and Fernando Flores. *Building Trust in Business, Politics, Relationships, and Life.* Oxford: Oxford University Press, 2001.

Classics

Fitzgerald, John T., ed. *Passions and Moral Progress in Greco-Roman Thought.* Routledge RMCS. London: Routledge, 2008.

Graver, Margaret. *Stoicism and Emotion.* Chicago: University of Chicago Press, 2007.

Konstan, David. *The Emotions of the Ancient Greeks: Studies in Aristotle and Classical Literature.* Toronto: Toronto University Press, 2006.

Education

Boler, Megan. *Feeling Power: Emotions and Education.* New York: Routledge, 1999.

Immordino-Yang, Mary Helen. *Emotions, Learning, and the Brain: Exploring the Educational Implications of Affective Neuroscience.* New York: Norton, 2016.

Immordino-Yang, Mary Helen, and Antonio Damasio. "We Feel, Therefore We Learn: The Relevance of Affective and Social Neuroscience to Education." *MBE* 1 (2007): 3–10.

History

Matt, Susan J., and Peter N. Stearns, eds. *Doing Emotions History*. Urbana: University of Illinois Press, 2013.
Plamper, Jan. *The History of Emotions: An Introduction*. Translated by Keith Tribe. EH. Oxford: Oxford University Press, 2015.
Reddy, William M. *The Navigation of Feeling: A Framework for the History of Emotions*. Cambridge: Cambridge University Press, 2001.

Linguistics

Kövecses, Zóltan. *Emotion Concepts*. New York: Springer, 1990.
Lakoff, George, and Mark Johnson. *Philosophy in the Flesh: The Embodied Mind and Its Challenge to Western Thought*. New York: Basic Books, 1999.
Wierzbicka, Anna. *Emotions across Language and Cultures: Diversity and Universals*. Cambridge: Cambridge University Press, 1999.

Literature

Fisher, Philip. *The Vehement Emotions*. Princeton: Princeton University Press, 2002.
Hogan, Patrick Colm. *What Literature Teaches Us about Emotion*. SESI. Cambridge: Cambridge University Press, 2011.
Nussbaum, Martha C. "Rational Emotions." Page 53–78 in Nussbaum, *Poetic Justice: The Literary Imagination and Public Life*. Boston: Beacon, 1995.
Oatley, Keith. *The Passionate Muse: Exploring Emotion in Stories*. Oxford: Oxford University Press, 2012.

Neuroscience

Barrett, Lisa Feldman. *How Emotions Are Made: The Secret Life of the Brain*. Boston: Houghton Mifflin Harcourt, 2017.

Damasio, Antonio. *Descartes' Error: Emotion, Reason, and the Human Mind.* New York: Penguin, 1994.
Frazzetto, Giovanni. *Joy, Guilt, Anger, Love: What Neuroscience Can—and Can't—Tell Us about How We Feel.* New York: Penguin, 2013.
LeDoux, Joseph. *The Emotional Brain: The Mysterious Underpinnings of Emotional Life.* New York: Simon & Schuster, 1996.
Panksepp, Jaak, and Lucy Biven. *Archaeology of the Mind: Neuroevolutionary Origins of Human Emotions.* New York: Norton, 2012.

Philosophy

Goldie, Peter, ed. *The Oxford Handbook of Philosophy of Emotion.* Oxford: Oxford University Press, 2010.
Nussbaum, Martha C. *Upheavals of Thought: The Intelligence of Emotions.* Cambridge: Cambridge University Press, 2001.
Price, Carolyn. *Emotions.* Key Concepts in Philosophy. Cambridge: Polity, 2015.
Solomon, Robert C. *The Passions: Emotions and the Meaning of Life.* 2nd ed. Indianapolis: Hackett, 1993.
——, ed. *What Is an Emotion? Classic and Contemporary Readings.* 2nd ed. Oxford: Oxford University Press, 2003.

Politics

Clarke, Simon, Paul Hoggett, and Simon Thompson, eds. *Emotions, Politics, and Society.* New York: Palgrave Macmillan, 2006.
Nussbaum, Martha C. *Political Emotions: Why Love Matters for Justice.* Cambridge: Harvard University Press, 2013.
Westen, Drew. *The Political Brain: The Role of Emotion in Deciding the Fate of the Nation.* New York: PublicAffairs, 2007.

Psychology

Barrett, Lisa Feldman, Michael Lewis, and Jeannette M. Haviland-Jones, eds. *Handbook of Emotions.* 4th ed. New York: Guilford, 2016.
Kagan, Jerome. *What Is Emotion? History, Measures, and Meanings.* New Haven: Yale University Press, 2007.
Keltner, Dacher, Keith Oatley, and Jennifer M. Jenkins. *Understanding Emotions.* 2nd ed. Malden: Blackwell, 2006.

Lazarus, Richard S. *Emotion and Adaptation*. Oxford: Oxford University Press, 1991.

Sociology

Barbalet, Jack, ed. *Emotions and Sociology*. Oxford: Blackwell, 2002.
Goodwin, Jeff, James M. Jasper, and Francesca Polletta, eds. *Passionate Politics: Emotions and Social Movements*. Chicago: University of Chicago Press, 2001.
Harris, Scott R. *An Invitation to the Sociology of Emotions*. New York: Routledge, 2015.
Stets, Jan E., and Jonathan H. Turner, eds. *Handbook of the Sociology of Emotions*. New York: Springer, 2006.
Turner, Jonathan H., and Jan E. Stets. *Sociology of Emotions*. Cambridge: Cambridge University Press, 2005.

The Central Role of Emotions in Biblical Theology, Biblical Ethics, and Popular Conceptions of the Bible*

Matthew Richard Schlimm

Across the humanities and even in fields of empirical science, emotions have become an incredibly fruitful area of study. Philosophers, linguists, neurobiologists, anthropologists, and psychologists have discovered that emotions are fascinating and integral elements of human existence that merit careful attention.[1] Martha C. Nussbaum, one of the leading public intellectuals of our day, has published multiple books on the topic.[2]

Instead of explaining why philosophy, neuroscience, or another field suggests that emotions merit careful scholarly attention, this essay focuses on why biblical scholars must understand emotion in order to achieve key advances in (1) biblical theology, (2) biblical ethics, and (3) popular conceptions of the Bible. Because I am a specialist in the Hebrew Bible, I will focus the bulk of my attention on that corpus, though I will also make some observations about the Christian New Testament.

---

* A version of this essay was initially presented at the Bible and Emotion Consultation at the Annual Meeting of the Society of Biblical Literature, Chicago, November 17, 2012. The author would like to thank Annette B. Huizenga and Christina L. Ennen for their feedback on earlier drafts of this essay.

1. See the literature cited in Robert C. Fuller, "Spirituality in the Flesh: The Role of Discrete Emotions in Religious Life," *JAAR* 75 (2007): 25–51.

2. Martha C. Nussbaum, *Upheavals of Thought: The Intelligence of Emotions* (Cambridge: Cambridge University Press, 2001); Nussbaum, *Anger and Forgiveness: Resentment, Generosity, Justice* (New York: Oxford University Press, 2016); Nussbaum, *Political Emotions: Why Love Matters for Justice* (Cambridge: Harvard University Press, 2013); Nussbaum, *Hiding from Humanity: Disgust, Shame, and the Law* (Princeton: Princeton University Press, 2004).

1. Biblical Theology

The first reason why emotions merit our attention is that the Bible consistently portrays God in emotional terms. When one reads the Bible's descriptions of God, one simply cannot get very far without wading into emotional language. Repeatedly, both the Hebrew Bible and the New Testament have a propensity to describe the divine life with emotions, often emphasizing love and anger.

1.1. Exodus 34:6-7

In fact, at the Bible's most significant moments, the text portrays God with emotions like love and anger. A key example is Exod 34:6-7.[3] These verses describe, as Jewish tradition puts it, the Thirteen Attributes of God. Countless biblical scholars have recognized this text as central to the field of biblical theology, including George Ernest Wright, Brevard Childs, Dale Patrick, Terence Fretheim, Walter Brueggemann, John Goldingay, James Crenshaw, and Walter Moberly.[4] Dennis Olson describes it as "one of the

---

3. Another important example would be the more than fifty times that the biblical text says, "[God's] loyal love is forever" (*ləʿôlām ḥasdô*), about half of which appear in Ps 136.

4. G. Ernest Wright writes, "The nearest the Bible comes to an abstract presentation of the nature of God by means of his 'attributes' is an old liturgical confession embedded in Exod. 34.6-7 and quoted in part in many other passages.... The emphasis in the confession is upon the gracious, loyal and forgiving nature of God, an emphasis which lies at the centre of the Biblical *kerygma*. Yet this Divine grace is a two-edged sword which appears in the human scene as a power working both for salvation and for judgment that salvation may be accomplished" (*God Who Acts: Biblical Theology as Recital*, SBT 8 [London: SCM, 1952], 85-86). Brevard S. Childs writes, "The frequent use through the rest of the Old Testament of the formula in v. 6 by which the nature of God is portrayed (Num. 14.18; Neh. 9.17; Ps. 86.15, etc.) is an eloquent testimony of the centrality of this understanding of God's person" (*The Book of Exodus: A Critical, Theological Commentary*, OTL [Louisville: Westminster, 1974], 612). In a chapter entitled, "The Identity of God," Childs also speaks of Exod 34:5-6 as "the decisive passage" by which God reveals his name (*Biblical Theology of the Old and New Testaments: Theological Reflection on the Christian Bible* [Minneapolis: Fortress, 1992], 354). Dale Patrick, describing Exod 34:6, writes, "The biblical tradition has established a 'center' of the divine personality which conditions and circumscribes all depictions" (*The Rendering of God in the Old Testament*, OBT 10 [Philadelphia: Fortress, 1981], 39). Terence E. Fretheim writes, "The confessional statement in [Exod 34:6-7] ... cuts

most important and definitive definitions of the character of God in the entire Bible."[5] Olson and others see this text as pivotal to the entire Hebrew Bible in part because it reverberates throughout these Scriptures. Depending on how one counts, as many as two dozen texts display some type of intertextual relationship with these two verses from Exodus.[6] Diverse genres and traditions join together in echoing Exod 34:6-7.[7]

Strikingly, these verses speak of God *not* in terms of saving acts in history, *not* in terms of creative activity, *not* in terms of stoic attributes,

---

across the Old Testament as a statement of basic Israelite convictions regarding its God. It thus constitutes a kind of 'canon' of the kind of God Israel's God is, in the light of which God's ongoing involvement in its history is to be interpreted" (*Exodus*, IBC [Louisville: John Knox, 1991], 302). Elsewhere, Fretheim calls these verses "Israel's central confession" (*God and World in the Old Testament: A Relational Theology of Creation* [Nashville: Abingdon, 2005], 333 n. 6). Walter Brueggemann observes, "Scholars believe this is an exceedingly important, stylized, quite self-conscious characterization of Yahweh, a formulation so studied that it may be reckoned to be something of a classic, normative statement to which Israel regularly returned, meriting the label 'credo'" (*Theology of the Old Testament: Testimony, Dispute, Advocacy* [Minneapolis: Fortress, 1997], 215-16). John Goldingay calls these verses "Yhwh's ... self-definition" and "Yhwh's classic self-definition" (*Israel's Gospel*, vol. 1 of *Old Testament Theology* [Downers Grove, IL: InterVarsity Press, 2003], 338, 828). James L. Crenshaw writes, "In the Bible the classic text that expresses the tension between justice and mercy within God is Exod 34:6-7, which has the deity proclaim the various divine attributes to Moses.... The struggle to balance these qualities of justice and mercy in describing God's interaction with a covenanted people permeates much of the Bible—indeed, exposing a conflict within the soul of Israel" (*Defending God: Biblical Responses to the Problem of Evil* [Oxford: Oxford University Press, 2005], 3-4). Walter Moberly talks about Exod 34:6 as "the fullest statement about the divine nature in the whole Bible." He continues, calling these words "foundational within Israel's scriptures" (*Old Testament Theology: Reading the Hebrew Bible as Christian Scripture* [Grand Rapids: Baker Academic, 2013], 192).

5. Dennis T. Olson, "Exodus," in *The CEB Study Bible with Apocrypha* (Nashville: Common English Bible, 2011), 81-153 (esp. 143-44).

6. The following texts have been mentioned as intertextually related to Exod 34:6-7 (whether through quotation, echo, paraphrase, or allusion): Num 14:18; Deut 4:31; 5:9-10; 7:9-10; 2 Chr 30:9; Neh 1:5; 9:17, 31; Pss 77:9-10[8-9]; 78:38; 86:5, 15; 103:8, 17; 111:4; 112:4; 116:5; 145:8; Jer 32:18-19; Lam 3:32; Dan 9:4; Joel 2:13; Jonah 4:2; Nah 1:2-3; 4 Ezra 7:132-140; see also Exod 20:5-6; Fretheim, *Exodus*, 302; Crenshaw, *Defending God*, 8, 93, 95, 197 n. 2, 227 n. 42; Victor P. Hamilton, *Exodus: An Exegetical Commentary* (Grand Rapids: Baker Academic, 2011), 576; Phyllis Trible, *God and the Rhetoric of Sexuality*, OBT 2 (Philadelphia: Fortress, 1978), 1-5.

7. Fretheim, *Exodus*, 302.

but in terms of emotional relationality. The text occurs when Moses is on Mount Sinai after the golden calf debacle, and the human insists on seeing the divine. As the Lord passes before Moses, who hides in the cleft of a rock, readers gain their clearest picture of God's identity. Readers expect to learn what God looks like physically, but there is no account of God's hair, clothing, or stature. Instead, it is as though readers see God's heart.[8] The text permits various translations. Here is my attempt: "The Lord: the Lord is a compassionate and warm-hearted God; slow to anger and filled with reliable, loyal love; a keeper of loyal love to thousands; a forgiver of iniquity, crime, and sin—but hardly acquitting everything; a visitor of parents' punishment upon children and grandchildren, to third and fourth generations" (Exod 34:6–7, my trans.). It is clear that emotional terms abound as God's love and anger reside in uneasy tension with one another.

On the side of love, God is described as "compassionate" (*raḥûm*), a word that many scholars associate with tender, motherly affection.[9] God also appears as "warm hearted" (*ḥannûn*). Though the Hebrew word can mean "gracious," it also has strong emotional dimensions. To find "grace" (*ḥēn*) in the eyes of someone means that the person has a warm disposition without any anger or sadness.[10] God is also portrayed as "slow to anger" (*'erek 'appayim*), a concept that is foundational to the Hebrew Bible's thinking about God.[11] The text then describes God as filled with

---

8. Here I invoke language of the heart not because biblical authors necessarily saw the heart as the center of emotion but because the English-speaking world tends to see the heart this way.

9. Trible, *God and the Rhetoric of Sexuality*, 34–56; T. C. Vriezen, *An Outline of Old Testament Theology* (Oxford: Blackwell, 1958), 163–64; J. Gerald Janzen, *Exodus*, WBC (Louisville: Westminster John Knox, 1997), 252. Although these scholars may be guilty of what James Barr calls the "etymological fallacy," the word clearly conveys an emotional intensity related to compassion and mercy (*Semantics of Biblical Language* [London: Oxford University Press, 1961], 100–60).

10. See Janzen, *Exodus*, 254; David Noel Freedman and Jack R. Lundbom, "*ḥānan*," in *TDOT* 5:22–36 (esp. 5:24). The affective dimensions of this word are visible in the common idiom, "If I find *ḥēn* in your eyes," which means essentially, "If you are warmly disposed toward me" or "If I bring any gladness to you" (e.g., Gen 33:8, 10). The term *ḥēn* is clearly set in opposition to anger and grief toward a person. Thus Gen 6:6–8 differentiates Noah, who receives *ḥēn* in divine eyes, from the rest of humanity, which grieves (*'ṣb*) God.

11. It is possible to read all of 1–2 Kings as a lengthy description of how God is slow to anger. The displacement, death, and loss of 587 BCE do not follow on the heels of one king doing evil. Only after many generations of unrepentant sin is God's pun-

"reliable, loyal love" (*ḥesed weʾĕmet*), which is preserved for thousands.[12] This loving characterization of God is rounded out by presenting the deity as one who lifts the burden of iniquity, crime, and sin.[13]

The remainder of this description makes clear, however, that divine love exists in tension with divine anger. The prior emphasis on God's slowness to anger speaks to divine patience. Yet, embedded in this language is the notion that God can indeed become angry if continually provoked. As the text concludes, God will not simply acquit everything, but rather visit punishments on children, grandchildren, and great-grandchildren. Crenshaw astutely observes the following:

> This daring attempt to penetrate to the very heart of God's nature rather than resting content with descriptive accounts of his actions pushes aside the veil of darkness and discloses the split within the deity's being. Justice or mercy? That is the eternal question. Judging from the sheer number of related attributes, the confessional formulation seems to be weighted on the side of mercy. But the last word, far from compassionate, acts as a mighty corrective on the side of justice.[14]

Exodus 34:6–7 emphasizes divine love while at the same time preventing readers from forgetting the ominous potential of God's anger.

In short, this text provides one of the central portraits of God in the entire Hebrew Bible, "Yhwh's classic self-definition," as Goldingay puts it, describing God in an array of explicitly emotional or emotion-related

---

ishment set in motion. For more on the importance of this expression, see Matthew Richard Schlimm, *This Strange and Sacred Scripture: Wrestling with the Old Testament and Its Oddities* (Grand Rapids: Baker Academic, 2015), 189–91.

12. Following the lead of Nelson Glueck, who recognized that *ḥesed weʾĕmet* functions as a hendiadys, I translate these two Hebrew words together, first using "reliable" to capture the sense of truthfulness and faithfulness conveyed by *ʾĕmet* and then "loyal love" to capture the sense of loyalty conveyed by *ḥesed*. See Glueck, *Hesed in the Hebrew Bible*, trans. Alfred Gottschalk (Cincinnati: Hebrew Union College, 1967), 102. Moreover, although *ʾmt* does not initially seem to be a particularly emotional word, over 25 percent of the verses containing *ʾmt* also contain *ḥsd*, suggesting some shared emotional overtones.

13. On the visualization of sin as a burden, see Gary A. Anderson, *Sin: A History* (New Haven: Yale University Press, 2009), 15–26.

14. Crenshaw, *Defending God*, 93.

terms.[15] Such terms dominate verse 6, and the next verse explains the wobbly balance between loyal love and anger.

1.2. 1 John 4:8, 16

Emotion dominates not only the above description of the divine life in the Hebrew Bible, but also descriptions of God in the New Testament. In the Johannine corpus, readers receive something akin to definitions of who God is. They find God equated with the *logos* (John 1:1), with being true (*alēthēs* [3:33]), with spirit (*pneuma* [4:24]), and with light (*phōs* [1 John 1:5]). They also repeatedly find God equated with love (*agapē* [1 John 4:8, 16]).[16] So even centuries after Exod 34:6–7 became something of a creedal statement in Israel, New Testament texts evoke the realm of emotion when describing God's core being.[17]

1.3. Diversity of Emotions Ascribed to the Biblical God

In addition to using emotional language at particularly important moments when God's character is revealed, the Bible also displays a remarkable variety in the types of emotion used to describe God. When looking at the major emotions, it is clear that the Bible describes God with nearly all of them. In a well-respected study, Phillip Shaver and colleagues argue that there are six basic types of human emotion: (1) love, (2) joy, (3) surprise, (4) anger, (5) sadness, and (6) fear.[18] The Hebrew Bible and New Testament describe God with all of these emotional categories, except perhaps fear.

---

15. Goldingay, *Israel's Gospel*, 828.

16. Given the anarthrous nature of the Greek predicate nominative, the epistle conveys that a core quality of God is love, not that God is only love or that love is God; see Daniel B. Wallace, *Greek Grammar beyond the Basics: An Exegetical Syntax of the New Testament* (Grand Rapids: Zondervan, 1996), 264; Raymond E. Brown, *The Epistles of John*, AB 30 (Garden City, NY: Doubleday, 1982), 194–95, 515.

17. On the dating of Exod 34:6–7, Carol L. Meyers observes that these verses may have served as a creedal statement even before the exile and at the latest were incorporated into Jewish liturgy during the rabbinic period. See Carol L. Meyers, *Exodus*, NCBC (Cambridge: Cambridge University Press, 2005), 264. On the importance of 1 John 4:8, see D. Moody Smith, *First, Second, and Third John*, IBC (Louisville: John Knox, 1991), 109: "Obviously 1 John 4:7–12 is a classic text dealing with a central Christian teaching and concern."

18. Phillip Shaver et al., "Emotion Knowledge: Further Exploration of a Prototype

THE CENTRAL ROLE OF EMOTIONS IN BIBLICAL THEOLOGY   49

The emotion of love has already been discussed, so let us turn to the second basic emotion: joy. Biblical writers repeatedly ascribe this emotion to God. In Jer 32:41, for example, God says, "I will rejoice [śûś] in doing good to them." Jesus similarly speaks of a deity who rejoices ([syn]chairō), celebrates (euphrainō), and expresses joy (chara) over finding a lost sheep, coin, and child (Luke 15:5–7, 9–10, 32).

Strikingly, biblical authors even imply that their God experiences surprise and amazement, the third basic category of emotion named by Shaver and associates. Divine surprise does not receive the attention that God's love or anger does, but in Jer 3:7 readers do find God saying, "I thought that after she had done all this she would return to me, but she didn't" (CEB).[19] Or, in Jesus's parable of the tenants, the landowner (a God figure in the story) says, "They will respect my son." But then the servants kill the son (Matt 21:37–39 // Mark 12:6–8 // Luke 20:13–15). At the very least, the text implies a tinge of divine surprise.

A fourth basic emotion is anger. I touched on this emotion earlier when discussing Exod 34:6–7, but it is worth noting that biblical examples of divine anger abound. From the continually provoked deity of Numbers to the raging God of the Prophets to the New Testament deity sending people to fire where there will be "weeping and gnashing of teeth," a wrathful God constitutes one of the Bible's overarching theological images. In fact, Bruce Edward Baloian says that over 70 percent of the Hebrew Bible's 714 references to anger apply to *divine* anger.[20] Isaiah 13:9 is typical: "See,

---

Approach," *JPSP* 52 (1987): 1061–86, esp. 1067. It is debatable whether God experiences particular minor types of emotions, such as those akin to sexual arousal and disgust. With regard to the first, Jeremiah does accuse God: "You seduced me, and I was seduced" (Jer 20:7). With regard to the second, one could easily argue that God is disgusted by certain practices. In Ezek 23:18, God says, "When she carried on her whorings so openly and flaunted her nakedness, I turned in disgust [wattēqaʿ napšî] from her, as I had turned from her sister" (Ezek 23:18 NRSV; cf. NJPS, NASB, NIV). See also places where God uses tôʿēbâ, which can be translated "disgusting thing" (e.g., Lev 18:26).

19. See also: "And I thought you would call me, My Father, and would not turn from following me. Instead, as a faithless wife leaves her husband, so you have been faithless to me, O house of Israel, says the Lord" (Jer 3:19–20 NRSV). For more examples, see Terence E. Fretheim, *The Suffering of God: An Old Testament Perspective*, OBT 14 (Philadelphia: Fortress, 1984), 45–59.

20. Bruce Edward Baloian asserts that 518 of 714 (= 72.5 percent) occurrences of anger in the Hebrew Bible refer to divine anger (*Anger in the Old Testament*, AUSTR

the day of the Lord is coming—a cruel day, with wrath and fierce anger—to make the land desolate and destroy the sinners within it" (NIV). Or, in Rom 2:6–8, one reads, "God will repay everyone based on their works.... There will be wrath and anger for those who obey wickedness instead of the truth" (CEB).

A fifth basic emotion is sadness. Scholars like Abraham Heschel, Terence Fretheim, and Walter Brueggemann have called attention to long-neglected texts, allowing interpreters to see in fresh ways how the God of the Hebrew Bible suffers because of, with, and for human beings.[21] Already in Gen 6:6 we read, "The LORD regretted making human beings on the earth, and he was heartbroken" (CEB). In the New Testament, the Gospel of John, even with its high Christology, does not flinch at saying that Jesus wept (11:35). Meanwhile, Ephesians talks about grieving God's holy s/Spirit (4:30).[22]

A sixth and final emotion category is fear. Here, readers are hard pressed to find crystal-clear examples of the biblical God being afraid. In many ways, this emotional omission makes sense: the biblical God is second to no one, and therefore has no one to fear; indeed, God is characteristically the object of fear.

Despite the omission of fear, most basic emotions are ascribed to God. Furthermore, as we have seen, emotions characterize the divine life precisely at moments when the Bible speaks its most crucial definitions of

---

99 [New York: Lang, 1992], 189). I disagree with some of the specifics of Baloian's calculations. For example, he sees *rgz* as referring to human anger only two times, whereas I believe it refers to human anger more frequently. Nevertheless, his numbers provide useful ballpark estimates.

21. Key works where these authors explore divine sadness include Abraham Joshua Heschel, *The Prophets: Two Volumes in One* (Peabody, MA: Hendrickson, 1962; repr., 2009); Fretheim, *Suffering of God*; Brueggemann, *Theology of the Old Testament*, esp. 267–313. I compare and contrast these three authors' interpretive approaches to texts depicting divine emotion in Matthew Richard Schlimm, "Different Perspectives on Divine Pathos: An Examination of Hermeneutics in Biblical Theology," *CBQ* 69 (2007): 673–94.

22. Markus Barth writes: "Though an explicit reference to 'grieving' the Father is not found in 4:30, this text comes near an affirmation of patripassionism.... The God proclaimed in Ephesians is not an unmoved mover" (*Ephesians*, AB 34A [Garden City, NY: Doubleday, 1974], 548). On the same page, Barth avers that this text is likely related to Isa 63:10, which speaks of grieving God's spirit.

who God is. Such facts not only speak to the centrality of emotions to biblical theology, but also raise important questions.

One major issue concerns the possible function of divine emotion as a rhetorical device designed to help humans wrap their minds around abstract concepts. Are the Bible's anthropopathic depictions of God akin to hyperboles: figures of speech that should not be taken too literally? To phrase the same question differently, do emotional depictions of God pertain strictly to God's office and actions rather than to God's personality and being?[23] Or, to be more specific, is an emotion such as God's sadness simply a rhetorical way of saying that God does not approve of sin?[24]

Another important and related question for biblical theologians: how is divine emotion similar to and different from human emotion? Clearly, human affections provide a proximate reference point in these texts, but how is God's emotional life different from humanity's? For example, is God ever incapacitated by strong emotion? To understand the highly emotional God of the Bible, interpreters need to give serious thought to such questions.[25]

2. Biblical Ethics

Emotions play an essential role not only in biblical theology, but also in biblical ethics. To illustrate, the comments below focus on anger, fear, and love.

2.1. Anger

Since antiquity, great philosophers have recognized that right living is both impaired and fostered by the emotions we experience. Anger, in

---

23. See Schlimm, "Different Perspectives on Divine Pathos," 687–90.
24. For example, interpreting Hos 11:8, E. B. Pusey does not say that God's heart is actually burdened, but rather that God "deigneth," that is, condescends or accommodates to a human level, speaking "as if" divine suffering were taking place (*The Minor Prophets with a Commentary Explanatory and Practical and Introductions to the Several Books* [London: Walter Smith, 1883], 73).
25. Some works have begun to examine such questions, e.g., Deena E. Grant, *Divine Anger in the Hebrew Bible*, CBQMS 52 (Washington, DC: Catholic Biblical Association of America, 2014), 1; Matthew Richard Schlimm, review of *Divine Anger in the Hebrew Bible*, by Deena E. Grant, *JHebS* 15 (2015), doi:10.5508/jhs.2015.v15.r8; Schlimm, "Different Perspectives on Divine Pathos," esp. 690–94.

particular, has received the most attention, for obvious reasons.[26] As a response to a perceived wrongdoing, anger is activated by one's sense of ethics and morality—what is right and wrong. However, this volatile emotion also prompts people to take vengeance or seek justice, even when they lack all the facts, thus leading people to commit morally questionable behaviors while angry. So a full account of the moral life needs to make sense of emotions like anger.

On this basic link between emotions and ethics, the biblical writers agree with ancient philosophers. The book of Proverbs, for example, echoes the Instruction of Amenemope in focusing repeatedly on human anger.[27] Or, as I have argued in my own publications, human anger constitutes an important motif in the book of Genesis.[28] Every patriarch and many of the matriarchs have significant encounters with this emotion, ranging from Cain's blood-seeking anger at the beginning of Genesis to Joseph and his brothers' abatement of anger through forgiveness at the end of the book. Genesis offers readers moral instruction about how to handle this perplexing emotion by multiple narrative examples.

Anger is hardly a foreign topic for New Testament authors. Jesus focuses on it during the Sermon on the Mount (Matt 5:22), among other occasions (Luke 15:28; John 7:23). Moreover, New Testament letters repeatedly admonish recipients to hold their anger in check, which is hardly surprising given how conflict threatened to divide the first churches (2 Cor 12:20; Gal 5:20; Eph 4:26, 31; Col 3:8).

An interesting avenue for moving forward is comparing and contrasting biblical teachings on anger. Points of tension, if not contradiction, exist on the surface of things. For example, Eph 4:26 seems diametrically opposed to 4:31. The former verse tells believers that they can be angry as long as they refrain from sinning, while the latter urges avoiding anger altogether. Before concluding that these ideas contradict one another, however, it is worth noting that only four verses separate these statements, suggesting that it is conceptually possible to hold both ideas

---

26. David E. Aune, review of *Restraining Rage: The Ideology of Anger Control in Classical Antiquity*, by William Harris, *JR* 83 (2003): 678–80, esp. 678.

27. See Prov 22–23 (e.g., 22:24); Instruction of Amenemope (*COS* 1:115–22; see esp. chs. 2–4, 9–10, 12). See also the Instruction of Ptahhotep (*AEL* 1:61–80), esp. §§2–4, §25 (*AEL* 1:63–64, 70).

28. See esp. Matthew Richard Schlimm, *From Fratricide to Forgiveness: The Language and Ethics of Anger in Genesis*, SLTHS 7 (Winona Lake, IN: Eisenbrauns, 2011).

THE CENTRAL ROLE OF EMOTIONS IN BIBLICAL THEOLOGY   53

together. Perhaps one verse presents a realistic perspective while the other reflects an idealistic vision. Perhaps verse 31 has harsher forms of anger in view, since it groups anger alongside other vices like bitterness, wrath, and slander. Or, perhaps with an emotion like anger, no one-size-fits-all analytical principle holds true in every circumstance. The emotional life may be better guided by proverbs and narratives than universal precepts.[29] All this is to say that biblical ethics can move forward by appreciatively and generously approaching Scripture's diverse teachings about emotion.

2.2. Fear

To name another avenue for inquiry: what should interpreters make of the Bible's love-hate relationship with fear? On numerous occasions, fear is upheld as a positive emotion. Biblical authors, of course, name fear as the beginning of wisdom (Ps 111:10; Prov 1:7; 9:10). Sometimes "the fear of the Lord" is even employed as an idiom for Yahwism (e.g., Ps 34:12[11]). This positive association with fear extends to the New Testament. Different texts associate the fear of the Lord with praising God (Luke 7:16), comfort from the Holy Spirit (Acts 9:31), and working out one's salvation (Phil 2:12).

But then, in a variety of texts, people are specifically commanded *not* to be afraid. Such commands form a standard part of biblical theophanies that make clear that people should *not* fear God (Gen 15:1; 21:17; 26:24; Judg 6:23; Acts 18:9; Rev 1:17; cf. Matt 28:5, 10). Elsewhere, 1 Pet 3:6, 14 form intertextual bridges with Prov 3:25 and Isa 8:12, encouraging people not to fear. Isaiah also urges people not to fear while Jerusalem is under the shadow of the Assyrians (2 Kgs 19:6 // Isa 37:6), much as Jesus later urges people not to worry while Jerusalem is under the shadow of the Romans (Matt 6:25–34).

So what should interpreters make of the Bible's love–hate relationship with fear?[30] Many Western interpreters easily understand texts where fear is cast in negative terms because their culture tends to view fear as a source of weakness and shame. It is not so easy, however, to see why some biblical texts speak of fear in virtuous terms. An important task of biblical ethics is to explain texts that describe fear so positively. We may be aided

---

29. Schlimm, *From Fratricide to Forgiveness*, 91–132.
30. See F. Scott Spencer, "To Fear and Not to Fear the Creator God: A Theological and Therapeutic Interpretation of Luke 12:1–34," *JTI* 8 (2014): 229–49.

in this project by various anthropological studies of South Pacific cultures, where terms for fear have positive moral connotations. In these contexts, the emotion is something to be prized, even celebrated.[31] By recognizing that cultures often have differing ideas about emotions, and by looking for anthropological analogues to biblical texts, interpreters can unlock the meaning of perplexing emotional phrases such as "the fear of the Lord."

2.3. Love

Another important avenue for research in biblical ethics pertains to the emotion of love. Both the Hebrew Bible and New Testament place highest priority on loving God and neighbor.[32] What feelings should accompany the act of loving others? How are these feelings shaped? Is it perhaps, as Deuteronomy suggests, only through a community engaged in continually remembering God's loving acts that people develop within themselves the appropriate sort of disposition that facilitates loving feelings towards God and neighbor?[33] How do writers of New Testament epistles understand the Holy Spirit, particularly regarding the pneumatological shaping of inner dispositions that lead toward loving attitudes?[34]

As these questions begin to illustrate, biblical ethics involves much more than human behavior. Following the lead of the texts, biblical ethicists need to inquire about the emotions that drive human behavior, whether that be anger, fear, love, or something else. We will never arrive at a crystal-clear picture of what biblical texts expect of humans

---

31. Catherine A. Lutz, *Unnatural Emotions: Everyday Sentiments on a Micronesian Atoll and Their Challenge to Western Theory* (Chicago: University of Chicago Press, 1988), 18–85; Robert I. Levy, *Tahitians: Mind and Experience in the Society Islands* (Chicago: University of Chicago Press, 1973), 307–8.

32. The importance of loving God and neighbor is of course explicitly named by Jesus in Matt 22:35–40. In the Hebrew Bible the importance of these commandments is highlighted by their textual location. The command to love God with all of one's being follows on the heels of the Shema (Deut 6:5), while the command to love one's neighbor appears in the central chapter of Leviticus (Lev 19:18); see Jacob Milgrom, *Leviticus: A Book of Ritual and Ethics*, CC (Minneapolis: Fortress, 2004), 7.

33. See Deut 5:15; 7:17–18; 8:2, 18; 9:7; 15:15; 16:3, 12; 24:9, 18, 22; 32:7; see also Walter Brueggemann, *Deuteronomy*, AOTC (Nashville: Abingdon, 2001), 25.

34. See Richard B. Hays, *Moral Vision of the New Testament: A Contemporary Introduction to New Testament Ethics* (San Francisco: HarperSanFrancisco, 1996), 43–45, esp. 45.

unless we also study the essential roles that emotions play in shaping what humans do.

3. Popular Conceptions of the Bible

I turn, finally, to popular conceptions of the Bible. Here again, emotions loom large. The most famous sermon in American history is arguably Jonathan Edwards's "Sinners in the Hands of an Angry God." Here is an excerpt:

> How awful are those Words, Isai. 63. 3. which are the Words of the great God, *I will tread them in mine Anger, and will trample them in my Fury; and their Blood shall be sprinkled upon my Garments....* [God] will know that you can't bear the Weight of Omnipotence treading upon you, yet he won't regard that, but he will crush you under his Feet without Mercy; he'll crush out your Blood, and make it fly, and it shall be sprinkled on his Garments.... He will not only hate you, but he will have you in the utmost Contempt; no Place shall be thought fit for you, but under his Feet, to be trodden down as the Mire of the Streets.[35]

Edwards seizes upon the Bible's wrathful depictions of God, burning them into his audience's consciousness.

If images of a wrathful God were popular in Edwards's time, they are no longer. In fact, one reason the Bible has come under fire is because of its emotional portrayals of the divine. Among Christians of various types, it is quite common to hear the expression, "the New Testament God is just so much more loving than the angry Old Testament God."[36] Such an idea smacks of ancient Marcionite heresy and persisting anti-Semitic prejudice.[37] It certainly fails to ring true, given that ideas of eternal damnation are more at home in the New Testament than the Old Testament (e.g., Matt 18:8; 25:41).

Among church leaders willing to offer overt criticism of the Bible, John Shelby Spong finds fault precisely with the emotions that the Bible ascribes

---

35. Michael Warner, ed., *American Sermons* (New York: Library of America, 1999), 359, emphasis original.
36. See Richard Dawkins, *The God Delusion* (New York: Houghton Mifflin Harcourt, 2008), 283.
37. Doctoral candidate David M. Stark of Duke University made this comment to me in a personal conversation. His work focuses on Christian preaching from the Hebrew Bible.

to God. He laments, "The Bible, again and again, portrays a wrathful God's intention to punish the chosen people."[38] Or, to turn to popular atheistic ideas, Richard Dawkins writes, "The God of the Old Testament is arguably the most unpleasant character in all fiction." He gives many reasons why this God is this way, but the first one he names is an emotional reason: The Old Testament God is "jealous and proud of it." Dawkins speaks of God's jealousy as "maniacal," in addition to referring to God's "characteristic fury."[39]

Much of this sentiment can be traced back at least to the time of Marcion. Although Marcion's writings have not survived, the following quotation from Tertullian suggests that Marcion's supreme deity was immune to certain emotions and incapable of anger: "[Marcion and others] refuse to ascribe to [God] such emotions of mind as they censure in their Creator.... [Marcion's God] is susceptible of no feeling of rivalry, or anger, or damage, or injury" (Tertullian, *Marc.* 1.26 [*ANF* 3:291]). Carolyn J. Sharp teaches a class at Yale Divinity School entitled "Exorcising Marcion's Ghost."[40] As it suggests, the church has had difficulty shaking Marcion's basic impulse to reject the Old Testament deity.

Today, if people do not outright reject portrayals of an angry God, they often find themselves fearing that their deity is some sort of cosmic cop. As T. S. Matthews describes in his memoir *Under the Influence*: "I still think of God ... as a watchful, vengeful, enormous, omniscient policeman, instantly aware of the slightest tinge of irreverence in my innermost thought, always ready to pounce (though with ominous patience he might hold his hand for a time) if I curse, if I mention him in anger, fun or mere habit, if I (O hell-fire and horror!) blaspheme his holy name."[41] As countless religious leaders can testify, Matthews is hardly alone. Many religious folk remain haunted by the idea that an angry God is out to get them.[42]

---

38. John Shelby Spong, *The Sins of Scripture* (New York: Harper Collins, 2005), 169–170, 260.

39. Dawkins, *God Delusion*, 51, 279, 278, respectively.

40. Carolyn J. Sharp, "Curriculum Vitae," 11, https://tinyurl.com/SBL0396a.

41. T. S. Matthews, *Under the Influence: Recollections of Robert Graves, Laura Riding, and Friends* (London: Cassell, 1977), 343; Fretheim introduced me to this quotation (*Suffering of God*, 1).

42. See Phil Zuckerman, *Faith No More: Why People Reject Religion* (Oxford: Oxford University Press, 2012), 162.

THE CENTRAL ROLE OF EMOTIONS IN BIBLICAL THEOLOGY   57

Given the profound effect that emotions play in popular opinions of the Bible, it is incumbent upon us as interpreters to shed as much light on emotions as possible. One area that cries out for additional research regards the extent to which modern ideas of emotions actually match up with biblical conceptions. As I have argued in *From Fratricide to Forgiveness*, interpreters should not automatically assume that biblical writers conceived of emotions the same way people do today. In fact, I wonder if a great deal of what is wrong with American religion is that people have taken modern ideas of love and anger and then simplistically imposed these ideas onto biblical characterizations of divine and human emotion. Such an imposition is immensely problematic because different cultures can have differing views about:

- what types of feelings people experience;
- which situations elicit which emotions; and
- how emotions can and should be expressed.[43]

An important task for interpreters is explaining how biblical emotions differ from present perceptions of them.

For example, consider the emotion of jealousy—which, as I have mentioned, Dawkins upholds as a primary reason for rejecting the biblical God. Jealousy is loaded with negative connotations nowadays. Although in our consumer culture, people are supposed to feel a healthy amount of greed, the passion for acquiring things is not supposed to get out of hand. When it does, words such as *jealousy* and *envy* are often invoked. In such contexts, these emotions entail an irrational desire to see harm or loss come to someone more fortunate.[44]

The Hebrew Bible, however, thinks about jealousy differently.[45] Here jealousy stems from the perception that someone has something that they

---

43. See Richard A. Shweder, *Thinking through Cultures: Expeditions in Cultural Psychology* (Cambridge: Harvard University Press, 1991), 242–52.
44. See the useful discussion of English, Hebrew, and Greek terminology in John H. Elliott, "God—Zealous or Jealous but Never Envious: The Theological Consequences of Linguistic and Social Distinctions," in *The Social Sciences and Biblical Translation*, ed. Dietmar Neufeld (Atlanta: Society of Biblical Literature, 2008), 79–96.
45. As I have pointed out in *From Fratricide to Forgiveness* (65–67), in the Hebrew Bible jealousy is a subset of anger. Like other types of anger, jealousy is an emotion that arises in response to a perceived wrongdoing.

should not legitimately possess.[46] It signified an ordinary reaction to a world where people did not always get what they deserved. In this environment, God naturally feels jealousy when the worship, adoration, and sacrifices that God alone *should* receive go to other gods instead.[47]

For biblical authors, then, jealousy was less about desire gone overboard and more about cases where someone (e.g., other gods) received what they should not have (e.g., the allegiance due to God alone). If interpreters ignore the logic of the biblical text, however, and presuppose that modern negative perceptions of jealousy are at work wherever God is called "jealous," then we naturally end up with a highly negative view of the biblical God. In that case, we cannot help but agree with Dawkins that belief in this deity is delusional.

On the other hand, if we take the biblical text on its own terms, suspending our preconceptions about what an emotion like jealousy is all about, then an image of God emerges that actually makes sense. Then, interpreters can shed proper light on why a text describing God as jealous would (1) be written, (2) be preserved, and (3) attain canonical status.

4. Conclusion

Biblical emotion matters deeply to the world we inhabit. The nature of the biblical God, what biblical texts portray as driving human behavior, and what the general populace thinks about the Bible are matters of highest significance. By investing time and energy into the dynamics of biblical emotions, interpreters can achieve key advances in the fields of biblical theology and biblical ethics. We may even have an impact on how the broader public thinks about the Bible, God, and their faith.

Select Bibliography

Elliott, John H. "God—Zealous or Jealous but Never Envious: The Theological Consequences of Linguistic and Social Distinctions." Pages 79–96 in *The Social Sciences and Biblical Translation*. Edited by Dietmar Neufeld. Atlanta: Society of Biblical Literature, 2008.

---

46. See Matthew Richard Schlimm, "Jealousy or Furnace Remelting? A Response to Nissim Amzalag," *JBL* (forthcoming).

47. See the conclusions in Elliott, "God—Zealous or Jealous," 94–96, which also deal with New Testament materials.

Fretheim, Terence E. *The Suffering of God: An Old Testament Perspective.* OBT 14. Philadelphia: Fortress, 1984.

Fuller, Robert C. "Spirituality in the Flesh: The Role of Discrete Emotions in Religious Life." *JAAR* 75 (2007): 25–51.

Glueck, Nelson. *Hesed in the Hebrew Bible.* Translated by Alfred Gottschalk. Cincinnati: Hebrew Union College Press, 1967.

Grant, Deena E. *Divine Anger in the Hebrew Bible.* CBQMS 52. Washington, DC: Catholic Biblical Association of America, 2014.

Heschel, Abraham J. *The Prophets: Two Volumes in One.* Peabody, MA: Prince, 1999.

Nussbaum, Martha C. *Upheavals of Thought: The Intelligence of Emotions.* Cambridge: Cambridge University Press, 2001.

Schlimm, Matthew Richard. "Different Perspectives on Divine Pathos: An Examination of Hermeneutics in Biblical Theology." *CBQ* 69 (2007): 673–94.

———. *From Fratricide to Forgiveness: The Language and Ethics of Anger in Genesis.* SLTHS 7. Winona Lake, IN: Eisenbrauns, 2011.

Spencer, F. Scott. "To Fear and Not to Fear the Creator God: A Theological and Therapeutic Interpretation of Luke 12:1–34." *JTI* 8 (2014): 229–49.

A Prototype of Biblical Hate: Joseph's Brothers (Genesis 37)

Deena Grant

Classical definitions of hate display a wide variety of contradictory perspectives. According to Aristotle, hate is a painless feeling that arises even without a preceding offense and precipitates attack (Aristotle, *Rhet.* 2.4.31 [1382a]).[1] In stark contrast, Baruch Spinoza argues that hate *is* pain that *does* have an external cause, while René Descartes contends that hate brings about aversion, not attack.[2] In David Hume's view, hate cannot even be defined because feelings are "irreducible" and possess "the introspective immediacy of sensory impressions."[3]

Some of these differences can be attributed to opposing perspectives about whether feelings or thoughts are more essential to hate's definition.[4] Today, though, most scholars recognize that emotions, hate among them, comprise *both* feelings and thoughts as well as actions.[5] The cognitive

---

1. Cited from Aristotle, *Rhetoric*, trans. W. Rhys Roberts (Oxford: Clarendon, 1924), available online at https://tinyurl.com/SBL0396c.

2. Robert J. Sternberg and Karin Sternberg, *The Nature of Hate* (Cambridge: Cambridge University Press, 2008), 16, citing Edwin Curley, *The Collected Works of Spinoza*, 2 vols. (Princeton: Princeton University Press, 1985), esp. 1:408–617. See René Descartes, *On the Passions of the Soul*, trans. S. Voss (Indianapolis: Hackett, 1991), esp. 62. Cited by Edward B. Royzman, Clark McCauley, and Paul Rozin, "From Plato to Putnam: Four Ways to Think about Hate," in *The Psychology of Hate*, ed. Robert J. Sternberg (Washington, DC: American Psychological Association, 2005), 4.

3. Royzman, McCauley, and Rozin, "From Plato to Putnam," 4. See David Hume, *A Treatise of Human Nature* (Oxford: Clarendon, 1980), esp. 67.

4. Spinoza and Hume appear to emphasize negative feelings while Aristotle emphasizes negative judgments; see Royzman, McCauley, and Rozin, "From Plato to Putnam," 4.

5. See Ervin Staub, "The Origins and Evolution of Hate, with Notes on Preven-

approach to psychology, which developed initially out of observations made in the course of therapy, focuses on delineating just *how* the content of individuals' thoughts influences their feelings and behaviors.[6]

1. The Cognitive Approach to Modern and Biblical Hate

In his book *Prisoners of Hate*, Aaron Beck, a pioneering figure in the field of cognitive therapy, applies the cognitive approach to the emotion of hate. Beck argues that hate is preceded by a belief "(realistic or not) that one is persistently wronged, damaged, coerced or corrupted."[7] The appraisal of wrongdoing can include both conscious judgments as well as subconscious automatic thoughts, any of which may contain a number of cognitive distortions.[8] Justified or not, these thoughts lead to unpleasant feelings, such as jealousy, and to an intense and persistent form of anger, which Beck describes as hatred.[9] In sum, "Assigning responsibility to another for unjustly 'causing' an unpleasant feeling is a prelude to feeling angry. The persistence of a sense of threat and the fixed image of a malicious person leads to at least a temporary feeling of hate."[10] Ultimately, these thoughts

---

tion," in Sternberg, *Psychology of Hate*, 51–66; Rob B. Briner and Tina Kiefer, "Psychological Research into the Experience of Emotion at Work: Definitely Older but Are We Any Wiser," in *The Effect of Affect in Organizational Settings*, vol. 1 of *Research on Emotion in Organization*, ed. Charmine E. J. Härtel, Neal M. Ashkanasy, Wilfred J. Zerbe (Oxford: Elsevier, 2005), 282. Nonetheless, scholars do maintain differing emphases even today. For example, Willard Gaylin describes emotions as "the irrational underpinnings of human behavior and the darker side of the human spirit," and he defines hate, in particular, as "an intense and irrational emotion that is a passion" (*Hatred: The Psychological Descent into Violence* [New York: PublicAffairs, 2003], 28). By contrast, Aaron T. Beck emphasizes the cognitive aspects of hate, arguing that hate stems from an appraisal of wrongdoing (*Prisoners of Hate: The Cognitive Basis of Anger, Hostility, and Violence* [New York: Perennial, 1999], 43–44).

6. Aaron Beck and James Pretzer, "A Cognitive Perspective on Hate and Violence," in Sternberg, *Psychology of Hate*, 68.

7. Beck and Pretzer, "Cognitive Perspective on Hate and Violence," 68–69.

8. Cognitive distortions include, for example, overgeneralization, dichotomous thinking, and catastrophizing. See Beck and Pretzer, "Cognitive Perspective on Hate and Violence," 69–70; Beck, *Prisoners of Hate*, 71–86.

9. Beck is among many scholars who draw connections between anger and hate. For a discussion of these scholars' views, see Royzman, McCauley, and Rozin, "From Plato to Putnam," 334.

10. Beck, *Prisoners of Hate*, 44.

and feelings precipitate retaliation, revenge seeking, rebelling, or destroying the source of the corruption.[11]

Conclusions derived from the cognitive approach to hate, such as employed by Beck, can contribute to our understanding of biblical hate because the Bible's portrait of hate in many ways resembles Beck's description of modern hate. Biblical hate, as expressed by the root שנא (śnʾ), arises often in response to a perceived wrongdoing and leads to injury.[12] For instance, when Amnon rapes Tamar and then refuses to marry her, Absalom hates Amnon and then kills him. Second Samuel 13:22–32 reads:

> But Absalom spoke to Amnon neither good nor bad; for Absalom hated Amnon [כי-שנא אבשלום את-אמנון] because he had raped his sister Tamar. Then Absalom commanded his servants, "Watch when Amnon's heart is merry with wine, and when I say to you, 'Strike Amnon,' then kill him. Do not be afraid; have I not myself commanded you? Be courageous and valiant." So the servants of Absalom did to Amnon as Absalom had commanded.... And Jonadab, the son of Shimeah, David's brother, responded, "Do not let my lord suppose they have put to death all the young men, the king's sons, for Amnon alone is dead; because by the intent of Absalom this has been determined since the day that he violated his sister Tamar." (NRSV)[13]

Similarly in 1 Kgs 22:8–27, King Ahab is offended by the prophet Micaiah's prophecies, hates him, and consequently sends him to prison:

> And the king of Israel said to Jehoshaphat, "There is yet one man by whom we may inquire of the Lord, but I hate him [ואני שנאתיו], because he does not prophesy good concerning me, but evil. He is Micaiah son of Imlah." But Jehoshaphat said, "Let not the king say so."... Then the king of Israel said, "Take Micaiah and return him to Amon the governor of the city and to Joash the king's son; and say, "Thus says the king, 'Put this man in prison, and feed him sparingly with bread and water until I return safely.'" (NASB)

---

11. According to Beck, only "hot and reactive violence" derives from hate. He also perceives "cold and calculated violence" as another form of *violence* that does not derive from hate (*Prisoners of Hate*, 16–17, 31, 44–45).

12. E. Lipiński, "אנש," *TDOT* 14:164.

13. The violence that characterizes Absalom's hate stands in stark contrast to the benign nature of David's anger at Amnon (2 Sam 13:21–22).

Resemblances between Beck's description of modern hate and these biblical examples of hate are not surprising since some aspects of human emotional experience are universal.[14] However, the Bible's depiction of hate is distinct in a number of ways. First, in contrast to modern hate, which can occur in a number of social frameworks, biblical hate primarily characterizes those in positions to act out against their objects of hate (e.g., elder brothers, husbands) and not those impotent to act against their offenders. For example, Joseph's elder brothers hate him (Gen 37:4, 5, 8), Jacob hates his wife Leah (29:31, 33), and the Psalmist is hated by an overwhelming number of powerful enemies (Pss 18:18; 25:19; 38:19).[15] This narrow framework of social empowerment suggests that biblical hate is perceived as actionable, even if the hater chooses not to act on it.[16]

A second way in which the Bible's portrait of hate diverges from Beck's description of modern hate is in distinguishing the provoker from the object of hate. In contrast to Beck's view of modern hate as arising in response to a party's perceived characteristic flaw or behavior (warranted or not),[17] biblical hate frequently targets parties who have *not* perpetrated a crime. For example, Amnon hates Dinah after he rapes her (2 Sam 13:14b–15a), the Philistines hate Isaac because his wells are successful and he is mighty (Gen 26:27), Jacob hates Leah after her father tricks him into marrying her (29:31), and the Psalmist's haters hate him without cause (Ps 35:19).[18] In none of these cases are the hated parties culpable or do they

---

14. Carroll Izzard argues that feelings such as interest, joy, surprise, distress, anger, fear, shame, disgust, contempt and guilt are universally perceived as distinct emotions, recognizable in the way they are expressed (*The Face of Emotion* [New York: Appleton-Century-Crofts, 1971]). More recently, Paul Ekman uses cross-cultural studies of facial expressions to argue for the universality of emotions such as happiness, anger, disgust and sadness (*Emotions Revealed: Recognizing Faces and Feelings to Improve Communication and Emotional Life* [New York: Holt, 2003], esp. 1–51).

15. Deut 21:15–16 admonishes an individual against offering the rights of firstborn to the son of a beloved wife instead of to the firstborn son of a hated wife. The passage offers no explanation as to why the individual might hate his wife, which suggests there may be no justified reason.

16. This same social structure is also evident in biblical depictions of anger. For more, see Deena Grant, *Divine Anger in the Hebrew Bible*, CBQMS 52 (Washington, DC: Catholic Biblical Association of America, 2014).

17. Beck, *Prisoners of Hate*, 44.

18. In fact, the Psalmist often refers to his "haters" but neglects to explain why they hate him; see Pss 9:14; 18:17, 41; 21:8; 25:19; 35:19.

display untoward behavior or even a flaw in character. This suggests that revenge/retaliation, which is integral to Beck's definition of hate, may not be as potent a motivator of biblical hate as we might assume.

Third, in contrast to Beck's understanding of hate as "persistent,"[19] a number of cases in the Bible portray haters reconciling with their objects of hate. Moreover, just as the hated parties do nothing to deserve the hate they receive in the first place, they also do nothing to bring about the reconciliation granted them later on. For example, after hating Isaac and kicking him out of their land, the Philistines choose to reunite in a covenant with him (Gen 26:28–29). Similarly, after kicking Jephthah out of the community in their hate, the people of Gilead request that he return to become their chief and to protect them against their enemies (Judg 11:7–10).

Thus we see that aspects of the biblical portrait of hate do not wholly accord with a modern notion of hate derived from cognitive psychology. This divergence is to be expected since the experience of emotion is, to some degree, influenced by culture.[20] As the cross-cultural linguist Anna Wierzbicka explains, "Emotions are not merely individual sensations or biophysical responses to external stimuli but are mediated by cognitive processes embedded in a particular culture."[21] Her point is supported by a number of cross-cultural ethnographic studies that show stark differences in the conceptions and experiences of emotions across diverse communities.[22] Similarly, we should not expect biblical conceptions about and depictions of hate to fully match our own presumptions about and experiences of the emotion.

---

19. As well as Aristotle's description of hate as incurable by time in *Rhet.* 2.4.31 (1382a).

20. The study of assumptions, ideas, and attitudes about emotions held by members of different sociocultural groups entails various ethnotheories of emotion; see Jane C. Wellenkamp, "Ethnotheories of Emotion," in *Everyday Conceptions of Emotion: An Introduction to the Psychology, Anthropology and Linguistics of Emotion*, ed. James A. Russell et al., NATO Science Series D 81 (Dordrecht: Kluwer Academic, 1995), 167–80, esp. 171.

21. Anna Wierzbicka, *Semantics, Culture and Cognition: Universal Human Concepts in Culture Specific Configurations* (Oxford: Oxford University Press, 1992), 125.

22. For examples see James A. Russell, "Culture and Categorization of Emotion," *PsBull* 110 (1991): 426–50; Wellenkamp, "Ethnotheories of Emotion," 169–79; Anna Wierzbicka, *Emotions across Language and Cultures: Diversity and Universals* (Cambridge: Cambridge University Press, 1999); Wierzbicka, *Semantics, Culture and Cognition*.

But if our own emotional experiences do not fully explain the nature of biblical hate, how might we discern the presumptions and motivations that *do* underlie this biblical emotion?[23]

2. A Prototype Emotion Script Model of Biblical Hate

The prototype emotion script model, deriving from the field of cognitive linguistics, offers insight into the presumptions and motivations that govern biblical hate. A prototypical emotion script refers to "the patterns or chains of events that prototypically constitute the content of an emotion as expressed in language."[24] According to this model, repeated experiences with similar events lead individuals to form a conceptually generic representation of an emotion. These traits are then ordered in a causal sequence, "similar to how actions are ordered in a playwright's script."[25] In order to understand the concepts that make up a particular emotion, we must learn the emotion's "characteristic behavioral patterns, including its particular series of expected actions."[26] In other words, we must learn its prototypical script.

Importantly, since emotion scripts are formed through repeated experiences with similar events, they are culturally dependent.[27] Therefore, scholars can discern cross-cultural differences in emotion concepts by contrasting various cultures' distinctive prototypical emotion scripts.[28]

The general concept of a prototypical emotion script stands in contrast to classical definitions of conceptual categories, in particular, Aristotle's

---

23. Ultimately, some aspects of emotion appear to be more universal, such as physiological changes related to emotions, while other aspects of emotions appear to be more socially constructed and societally specific, such as behavioral consequences of emotions. For more discussion, see Phillip Shaver et al., "Emotion Knowledge: Further Exploration of a Prototype Approach," *JPSP* 52 (1987): 1061–86, esp. 1061–63.

24. Ellen van Wolde, *Reframing Biblical Studies: When Language and Text Meet Culture, Cognition, and Context* (Winona Lake, IN: Eisenbrauns, 2009), 63.

25. Russell, "Culture and Categorization of Emotion," 442; for more on applying prototype theory to the cross-cultural study of emotion, see Beverly Fehr and James A. Russell, "Concept of Emotion Viewed from a Prototype Perspective," *JEP* 113 (1984): 464–86; Shaver et al., "Emotion Knowledge," 1063, also 1072–81.

26. Van Wolde, *Reframing Biblical Studies*, 63.

27. See n. 23 above.

28. Van Wolde, *Reframing Biblical Studies*, 26.

idea of necessary or sufficient features.[29] Contrary to the classical approach of defining an emotion by means of an essential trait (e.g., sadness is defined by the presence of weeping), the prototype emotion script model asserts that no single trait or set of traits necessarily defines an emotion.[30] Instead, a number of traits, ordered in a particular sequence, represent the *expected* progression of the emotion. The more closely a series of traits resembles a particular emotion script, the more likely it will be perceived as constituting that emotion.[31]

To offer an example, Zoltán Kövecses applies the prototype emotion script model to anger, as expressed in American English. By analyzing the typical metaphors and metonymies of anger in American English, Kövecses discerns five stages of an anger script: (1) an offending event, (2) anger, (3) an attempt at control, (4) a loss of control, and (5) an act of retribution. According to Kövecses, none of these stages are, in themselves, necessary or sufficient to constitute anger. Rather, individual speakers of American English evaluate the degree to which a set of perceived traits resembles or diverges from this prototypical script. The more closely a series resembles this anger script, the more likely an individual will perceive it as constituting anger.[32]

Returning to the Bible, Ellen van Wolde applies the prototype approach to the cross-cultural study of biblical anger. By singling out the expressions most often used to designate anger, the location of anger in the body, the grammatical subject of anger and the question of whether anger expresses a feeling or something else, van Wolde identifies four stages of a biblical anger script: (1) a report of an offense or offending event, (2) anger rising to the head, (3) a willingness or eagerness to correct, and (4) an act of retribution. With these stages, van Wolde demonstrates that the Bible's prototypical anger script diverges from the modern American English anger script discerned by Kövecses in its social framework, per-

---

29. For a discussion of the classical approach to categorization and of the many objections raised against it (most prominently by Ludwig Wittgenstein), see John R. Taylor, *Linguistic Categorization*, 3rd ed., Oxford Textbooks in Linguistics (Oxford: Oxford University Press, 2009), 35–39.

30. Put otherwise, no single trait or set of traits is necessary or sufficient for membership in an emotion category.

31. Taylor, *Linguistic Categorization*, 44 and 69.

32. Zoltán Kövecses, *Metaphors of Anger, Pride and Love: A Lexical Approach to the Structure of Concepts* (Amsterdam: Benjamins, 1987), 28–32.

ceived physiological expression, expectation of correction, and absence of control.[33]

A similar approach can be applied to the study of biblical hate. As prototype theory predicts, biblical hate tends to be associated with a variety of typical, but not necessary, features. A study of these features—in particular, the typical social framework, antecedents, cognitive appraisals, ways of feelings, and action tendencies associated with hate—uncovers a number of prototypical hate scripts that resemble the portrait of modern hate laid out by Beck but also diverge in ways that reflect some dissimilar underlying concepts.

A particularly salient hate script that pervades narrative-prose texts throughout the Bible involves an interpersonal relationship in which a more powerful party wants to avoid and/or injure a less powerful party. Its causal sequence of traits runs as follows: (1) an individual or group is offended by a more powerful perpetrator, (2) the offended party ("subject") appraises a loss, (3) the subject directs negative feelings such as envy or anger at a third party ("object") who has benefitted at his expense, (4) the subject estranges the object, perhaps to avoid being reminded of the offense, and (5) after some time, the subject's drive to separate gives way to a drive to profit from or despite the offense. Profit is realized either by injuring, exploiting, or reconciling with the object of hate.

The following chart delineates the hate script:

Trait	Script	Texts
Social framework	More powerful subject toward vulnerable object	Gen 26:27; 29:31, 33; 37:4, 5, 8 Judg 11:7; 15:2 2 Sam 13:15, 22 1 Kgs 22:8 2 Chr 18:7
Antecedent	Offense committed by a third party	Gen 26:27; 29:31, 33; 37:4, 5, 8 Judg 11:7; 15:2

---

33. Van Wolde, *Reframing Biblical Studies*, 62–72. Van Wolde builds on the work of Paul Kruger, who more generally addresses the cognitive representation of anger in the Bible ("A Cognitive Interpretation of the Emotion of Anger in the Hebrew Bible," *JNSL* 26 [2000]: 181–93).

Appraisal	Loss has been/will be incurred	Gen 26:27; 29:31, 33; 37:4, 5, 8 Judg 11:7; 15:2 2 Sam 13:15
Feelings	Negative feelings: envy or anger	Gen 26:27 [envy in 26:14]; 37:4, 5, 8 [envy in 37:11] Judg 15:2 [anger in 14:19]
Action tendency	Estrangement	Gen 26:27; 29:31, 33; 37:4, 5, 8 Judg 11:7; 15:2 2 Sam 13:15, 22 1 Kgs 22:8 2 Chr 18:7
Later action tendency	Profiting from/despite the loss via exploitation, injury, or rapprochement	Gen 26:27; 37:4, 5, 8 Judg 11:7; 15:2 2 Sam 13:15, 22 1 Kgs 22:8 2 Chr 18:7

As this chart illustrates and as the prototype approach to the study of emotion anticipates, not all instances of biblical hate possess the same traits in exactly the same order and, conversely, no single trait is present in all instances of biblical hate. Nonetheless, many hate scenarios possess many of these traits, and in this order. Thus it appears that the relationship between the biblical designation of a set of traits as involving "hate" (שׂנא) and resemblance to this biblical hate script is fluid.

3. A Case Study: Joseph and his Brothers (Genesis 37)

The prototypical hate script outlined above offers a heuristic through which to understand better the thoughts, feelings, and behaviors of Joseph's brothers in Gen 37. This expression of the prototypical script runs as follows:

- ▶ Social framework: A group of older brothers hate Joseph
- ▶ Antecedent: Jacob bestows a garment on Joseph
- ▶ Appraisal: Joseph threatens his brothers' status
- ▶ Feelings: Joseph's brothers are envious
- ▶ Action tendency: Joseph's brothers estrange themselves from him
- ▶ Later action tendency: Joseph's brothers assault and profit from him

Genesis 37 introduces Joseph as hated by his elder brothers. Outnumbered and the youngest of the brood, he possesses the least clout. Emphasizing this latter point, the narrative describes him as a mere "lad" relegated to attending the maidservants' sons.[34] The passage presents three episodes as contributing to the overall negative fraternal relations: Joseph's bad report about the brothers, Jacob's preferential treatment of Joseph, and Joseph's dreams. However, the narrative distinguishes only the second episode as the initial source of the brothers' hate: "Now Israel loved Joseph more than any other of his children, because he was the son of his old age; and he had made him a long robe with sleeves. But when his brothers saw that their father loved him more than all his brothers, they hated him, and could not speak peaceably to him" (37:3–4 NRSV).[35]

Claus Westermann argues that the brothers' hate is incited not by Jacob's emotional predilection for Joseph but by the consequence of his preference in the form of a distinctive garment. The "richly ornamented robe" is both an affront and a loss, for it signifies a change in Joseph's social standing.[36] Whereas this mere "lad" who attends to the maidservants' sons

---

34. "Lad" (נער) could mean young male anywhere between the ages of infancy to young adulthood. It may also refer to the subservient role of "servant." The latter meaning would underscore Joseph's particularly humble role as subservient to the sons of the concubines. See Victor H. Matthews, "The Anthropology of Clothing within the Joseph Narrative," *JSOT* 65(1995): 688.

35. The passage adds that, upon hearing the dreams, the brothers come to hate him even more (ויוספו עוד שנא אתו [Gen 37:5, 8]). Nonetheless, the inception of hate lies with the garment. Moreover, the many contradictions, repetitions and disruptions throughout the chapter indicate that the passage comprises a number of sources. In this light, scholars tend to view Joseph's tale telling and dreams as only secondarily associated with the brothers' hate. Klaus Westermann, among others, points out that Joseph's report does not concern all the brothers but only the four sons of Jacob's secondary wives. Therefore, his behavior would not explain why *all* the brothers hate him. See Claus Westermann, *Genesis 37–50: A Commentary*, CC (Minneapolis: Fortress, 2002), 34. For a discussion of the multiple sources of Gen 37, see Westermann, *Genesis 37–50*, 34–38; Baruch J. Schwartz, "Joseph's Descent into Egypt: The Composition of Genesis 37 from Its Sources" [Hebrew], *Beit Mikrah* 55 (2010): 1–30. The association of hate with Joseph's bad report and with his dreams in the chapter's final form may reflect an attempt to shift the burden of blame for the subsequent events off Jacob's shoulders and onto Joseph's. In any event, the fact that the narrator does not reveal the content of the bad report underscores the passage's lack of interest in specifically connecting Joseph's behavior to the brothers' hate.

36. The precise meaning of כתנת פסים remains uncertain and has been translated

should serve his elder brothers, Jacob elevates Joseph above his brothers by means of a conspicuous inheritance.[37]

Westermann suggests that the portrait of the brothers hating Joseph instead of Jacob—the perpetrator—reflects the narrator's "profound understanding of the human condition.... [He] touches on an experience that he can presuppose in his hearers: the hatred of the one slighted is often directed not toward the one who favors unjustly, but toward the one favored."[38] More pointedly, the scenario reflects the narrator's understanding of hate as actionable; unable to act against Jacob, their patriarchal authority, the men direct hate at their vulnerable younger brother whose status has been elevated at the expense of theirs.

The brothers respond to Joseph's dreams of hierarchical superiority with jealousy (37:11). Their jealousy arises not from any new information offered in Joseph's dreams but from the confirmation that Jacob's gift portends a future reality in which Joseph possesses authority over his elder brothers. As George Coats elaborates, "Joseph's preferred position with his father, symbolized by the coat of authority, suggests his power. The power position is highlighted in the dreams of the next element."[39]

The brothers' hate is immediately followed by an estrangement: "But when his brothers saw that their father loved him more than all his brothers, they hated him, and could not speak peaceably to him [דברו לשלם]" (37:4). The term שלם is a greeting of welcome and farewell that also involves an inquiry into one's well-being and health. Westermann interprets its absence as a "rupture in the fellowship" between the brothers and Joseph.[40] The relational rift is realized, in the next scene, through a physical separation: the brothers shepherd together in the field while

---

in various ways. The traditional translation as "coat of many colors" follows the LXX and Vulg. understandings (as reflected in NIV, NJPS). The alternative interpretation is "a long robe with sleeves" (NRSV, REB) or "long tunic" (NAB). For more, see Matthews, "Anthropology of Clothing," 31–32.

37. Joseph is "set above" them, according to Robert E. Longacre, *Joseph: A Story of Divine Providence; A Text Theoretical and Textlinguistic Analysis of Genesis 37 and 39–48*, 2nd ed. (Winona Lake, IN: Eisenbrauns, 2003), 34. The bestowal and removal of attire is a well-known theme in cultural studies and signifies a change in social standing; see Matthews, "Anthropology of Clothing," 29.

38. Westermann, *Genesis 37–50*, 37.

39. George W. Coats, *Genesis with an Introduction to Narrative Literature*, FOTL 1 (Grand Rapids: Eerdmans, 1983), 268.

40. Westermann, *Genesis 37–50*, 37.

Joseph remains at home, alone with their father. Joseph's proximity to his father underscores his favored status, which is the very trigger of the brothers' hate.

Jacob then sends Joseph to seek out his brothers' שלם (well-being), a request that ironically augurs the violence to come. As the hate script anticipates and as the passage has already made clear, the brothers no longer wish Joseph שלם in return. On the contrary, they are fixated on the threat that he poses and that his dreams foretell. Consequently, when they confront Joseph in the field, they address him not as "brother" but as "the dreamer" (הנה בעל החלמות הלזה בא [37:19]), and they plot to kill him. In fact, the brothers persistently refuse to acknowledge Joseph as their brother, referring to him as "your son" (בנך) even when they relay his death to their father (37:32).

Joseph's estrangement facilitates the violence with which the brothers attempt to sideline him and regain their status. The passage preserves two versions of the brothers' assault on Joseph. In the first variant, Joseph's brothers conspire to murder him, but Reuben convinces them to throw him into a pit instead, presumably to die anyway.[41] Then, unbeknown to them all, Midianites retrieve Joseph from the pit and sell him to Ishmaelites (37:18–22, 29–30). In the second variant, the brothers strip off Joseph's coat and cast him into a waterless pit to die. Afterwards, while the brothers are eating, they decide to sell him to Ishmaelites who happen to be walking by (37:23–28).

Despite differences between the versions, a common salient trait emerges. In both accounts, the brothers are motivated by a desire to recoup loss and attain profit. In the first variant, the brothers act against Joseph *specifically* so that his dreams will not come to fruition: "Come now, let us kill him and throw him into one of the pits; then we shall say that a wild animal has devoured him, and we shall see what will become of his dreams" (37:20 NRSV). The brothers do not argue with Reuben when he suggests that they throw Joseph into a pit instead of murdering him because they are primarily invested in regaining their position within the family—less so in the nature or extent of any injury they might inflict on Joseph in pursuing this goal. Accordingly, though the brothers do not kill

---

41. The narrator tells us that Reuben intends to rescue him later on (Gen 37:22).

Joseph, they do strip him of his tunic, the garment that represents their own diminishment.[42]

In the second variant, the brothers are similarly quick to listen to Judah's suggestion that they profit off Joseph rather than bear the guilt of fratricide: "Then Judah said to his brothers, 'What profit is it if we kill our brother and conceal his blood? Come, let us sell him to the Ishmaelites, and not lay our hands on him, for he is our brother, our own flesh.' And his brothers agreed" (37:26–27 NRSV). As in the first variant, the brothers are less interested in what becomes of Joseph than in profiting from his departure. Kenneth A. Mathews explains, "Murder and its cover-up will not pay as handsomely as a slave's price."[43] Ironically, this very sale "actualizes the dreams that the brothers meant to subvert."[44]

Chapters ahead and years later, the brothers turn to Joseph for food in his capacity as an Egyptian official (Gen 45). The brothers are no longer empowered to act against Joseph, and notably, their hate appears to vanish. This transformation becomes immediately evident following Joseph's offers to provide for the brothers and their families. The brothers respond to Joseph's offer by engaging in the very same act they had previously refused; when they had hated him, they could not even speak to him (ולא יכלו דברו לשלם [37:4]), but in this new context of subservience to a "Lord of Egypt," they begin to speak. Genesis 45:4–15 reads:

> Then Joseph said to his brothers, "Come closer to me." And they came closer. He said, "I am your brother Joseph, whom you sold into Egypt.... Hurry and go up to my father, and say to him, 'Thus says your son Joseph, God has made me lord of all Egypt; come down to me, do not delay. You

---

42. By stripping him of the garment, the brothers reverse the investiture ceremony in which his father clothed Joseph in a special robe. The stripping of this garment and the later seizure of one of his garments by Potiphar's wife represents his "descending status from favored son to slave, and from slave overseer to prisoner," according to Kenneth A. Mathews, *Genesis 11:27–50:26: An Exegetical and Theological Exposition of Holy Scripture*, NAC 1B (Nashville: Broadman & Holman, 2005), 689. A precedent for systematic disrobing as a reflection of diminishing authority is evident in the removal of Inana's garments as she makes her way down the underworld. As each garment is removed, her power and life force is drained until she becomes a mere corpse; see Matthews, "Anthropology of Clothing," 31.

43. Mathews, *Genesis 11:27–50:26*, 699.

44. Ibid., 685. Thus we see that the brothers' hate—fomented in response to Joseph's ascension—ironically foreshadows their future subservience to him.

shall settle in the land of Goshen, and you shall be near me, you and your children and your children's children, as well as your flocks, your herds, and all that you have. I will provide for you there—since there are five more years of famine to come—so that you and your household, and all that you have, will not come to poverty....'" Then he fell upon his brother Benjamin's neck and wept, while Benjamin wept upon his neck. And he kissed all his brothers and wept upon them; *and after that his brothers talked with him* [ואחרי כן דברו אחיו אתו]. (NRSV)

It is with this act of reconciliation that the prototypical hate script concludes.

4. Conclusion

Modern cognitive psychology is a useful tool with which to study biblical hate, but it is only partially instructive. Since cognition is embedded in culture, we cannot assume that modern conceptions and experiences of this emotion wholly underlie its biblical depiction. Instead, biblical hate (and, in fact, biblical emotions more broadly) must be explored on its own terms. The prototype emotion script approach, derived from the field of cognitive linguistics, offers a means to do this.

A study of the sequence of traits that characterizes biblical hate reveals a number of discernible hate scripts. A particularly salient script portrays an individual (or group) who is affronted by a more powerful party and appraises a loss. In response, the hater directs negative feelings (anger, jealousy) and harmful actions (estrangement, injury) against a third party who has benefited from his loss, and against whom the subject is empowered to act. Later on, however, the hater's motivations shift as he attempts to profit off his object of hate, whether through injury, exploitation, or reconciliation. This prototypical hate script offers a conceptually generic, culturally dependent, and rationally organized representation of biblical hate that allows us to understand further, for example, why Joseph's brothers feel what they feel and do what they do.

Select Bibliography

Beck, Aaron T. *Prisoners of Hate: The Cognitive Basis of Anger, Hostility, and Violence*. New York: Perennial, 1999.

Kövecses, Zoltán. *Metaphors of Anger, Pride and Love: A Lexical Approach to the Structure of Concepts.* Amsterdam: Benjamins, 1987.
Russell, James A. "Concept of Emotion Viewed from a Prototype Perspective." *JEP* 113(1984): 464–86.
———. "Culture and Categorization of Emotion." *PsBull* 110 (1991): 426–50.
Shaver, Phillip, Judith Schwartz, Donald Kirson, and Cary O'Connor. "Emotion Knowledge: Further Exploration of a Prototype Approach." *JPSP* 52 (1987): 1061–86.
Sternberg, Robert J., ed. *The Psychology of Hate.* Washington, DC: American Psychological Association, 2005.
Sternberg, Robert J., and Karin Sternberg. *The Nature of Hate.* Cambridge: Cambridge University Press, 2008.
Taylor, John R. *Linguistic Categorization.* 3rd ed. Oxford Textbooks in Linguistics. Oxford: Oxford University Press, 2009.
Van Wolde, Ellen. *Reframing Biblical Studies: When Language and Text Meet Culture, Cognition, and Context.* Winona Lake, IN: Eisenbrauns, 2009.
Wierzbicka, Anna. *Emotions across Language and Cultures: Diversity and Universals.* Cambridge: Cambridge University Press, 1999.
———. *Semantics, Culture and Cognition: Universal Human Concepts in Culture Specific Configurations.* Oxford: Oxford University Press, 1992.

From Fear's Narcissism to Participatory Imagination: Disrupting Disgust and Overcoming the Fear of Israel's Ḥērem Laws

L. Juliana Claassens

Many laws, both ancient and contemporary, are rooted in a primal emotion of fear that is deeply narcissistic in nature and primarily concerned with the survival of the self. So argues Martha C. Nussbaum in *The New Religious Intolerance: Overcoming the Politics of Fear in an Anxious Age*.[1] Nussbaum cites the example of a national referendum in Switzerland that passed a bill in November 2009 with 70 percent of the vote to add the following law to the Constitution: "The building of minarets is prohibited." Nussbaum employs this example and the rhetoric used in the buildup to the referendum to show something of the underlying fears associated with laws such as these. For instance, in an internet video game called Minaret Attack, minarets were shown rising up all over the picturesque Swiss countryside, looking like missiles spread across the landscape. The game ended with a message running across the screen: "Game Over! Switzerland is covered in minarets. Vote to ban them on November 29."[2] Another argument pertained to the rights of women with leading feminists supporting the ban. Nussbaum cites one female voter: "If we give them a minaret, they'll have us all wearing burqas.... Before you know it, we'll have sharia law and women being stoned to death in our streets."[3]

Such fear mongering in the public realm is not a new problem. In an article that was deeply formative for my own thinking about the "self"

---

1. Martha C. Nussbaum, *The New Religious Intolerance: Overcoming the Politics of Fear in an Anxious Age* (Cambridge: Belknap, 2012), 55–56.
2. Ibid., 45.
3. Ibid.

and the "other," "The Dangers of Deuteronomy: A Page from the Reception History of the Book," Ferdinand Deist showed how biblical laws had an unfortunate history of reception in South Africa when the Afrikaner readers were inspired by Deuteronomic regulations to create boundaries that culminated in apartheid laws and practices intended to keep people of different races separate.[4] Deist shows how a shared sense of anxiety was responsible for erecting boundaries between "us" (the people of God) and "them" (the heathen nations) in the sixth and seventh centuries BCE (the proposed sociohistorical context of Deuteronomy) and was racialized in the case of South Africa.[5]

Of the laws in Deuteronomy, probably most disconcerting in its association with violence is the infamous *ḥērem* ban in Deut 7:1–5, in which God commands Israel to destroy utterly the Hittites, Girgashites, Amorites, Canaanites, Perizzites, Hivites, and Jebusites upon entering the promised land. The Israelites are further commanded to "make no covenant with them and show them no mercy" (7:2). Moreover, in 7:5 the Israelites are ordered to "break down their altars, smash their pillars, hew down their sacred poles, and burn their idols with fire." Whether this violence occurred in the way this text commands is a much debated question.[6] Yet its intention to divide ethnic and religious groups is clear, and

---

4. Ferdinand E. Deist, "The Dangers of Deuteronomy: A Page from the Reception History of the Book," in *Studies in Deuteronomy: In Honour of C.J. Labuschagne on the Occasion of His Sixty-Fifth Birthday*, ed. Florentino García Martínez, VTSup 53 (Leiden: Brill, 1994), 13–29.

5. Deist, "Dangers of Deuteronomy," 20–21. In addition to this shared sense of anxiety, Deist also identifies a shared sense of promise according to which the Afrikaners, like the Israelites in Deuteronomy, viewed themselves as God's chosen people who should keep themselves pure/holy and hence separate themselves from the people of the land.

6. Jonathan Klawans argues that many writers on religion and violence such as Hector Avalos, Regina Swartz, and Joseph Hoffman assume that Israel engaged in a historical genocide of the Canaanites during the time of Joshua. However, Klawans states, "Never mind that the book of Joshua is full of miraculous fantasy; the walls we are told came tumbling down as Israel marched around the city." Moreover, he points to archaeological evidence that all but negates the historical accuracy of much of Joshua. See Klawans, "Introduction: Religion, Violence, and the Bible," in *Religion and Violence: The Biblical Heritage*, ed. David A. Bernat and Jonathan Klawans (Sheffield: Sheffield Phoenix, 2007), 8. See also the nuanced line of argumentation in John J. Collins, "The Zeal of Phinehas: The Bible and the Legitimation of Violence," *JBL* 122 (2003): 10–12.

the numerous scholars who struggle with these laws attest to their dangerous potential to sanction violence in the name of God against ethnic and religious others.

Even though the law prohibiting the building of minarets in Switzerland has not yet led to violence, nor could one demonstrate a direct link between the ḥērem laws in Deuteronomy and their South African readers during the apartheid years,[7] Nussbaum rightly shows the potential for violence associated with religious intolerance. She cites the example of the Norwegian Anders Behring Breivik, who on 23 August 2011 shot and killed seventy-seven students and injured more than three hundred others on Utøya island. It later became evident that Breivik's actions traced back to anti-Islamic rhetoric that Nussbaum describes as the "world of paranoid blogging about a Muslim takeover."[8] Even the way the media reported the attacks in Norway is revealing, quickly linking the attack to Islamic terrorism. For instance, the headline of the *Sun* in Britain read: "Al Qaeda massacre: Norway's 9/11."[9]

This essay pursues two aims. First, drawing on the work of Sara Ahmed and Martha C. Nussbaum, I explore the link between powerful emotions such as fear and disgust to help us better understand religious laws that draw sharp boundaries based on race, religion, gender, and sexual orientation, among other differences. Second, engaging with Nussbaum and the Deuteronomic ḥērem laws, I investigate what it might take for a society to transcend narcissistic notions of fear that foment laws preoccupied with preservation of the self.

1. Fear's Narcissism and the Stickiness of Disgust

Nussbaum highlights some important aspects regarding the mechanics of fear. She argues in the first place that fear typically emerges from some real problem, such as people's anxiety about economic and political insecurities.[10] Such angst characterized the Afrikaner community during the heyday of apartheid. Deist outlines a situation of great socioeconomic

---

7. Though note the application of Deist's argument in Rannfrid I. Thelle, "The Biblical Conquest Account and Its Modern Hermeneutical Challenges," *ST* 61 (2007): 74–75.
8. Nussbaum, *New Religious Intolerance*, 50.
9. Ibid., 49.
10. Ibid., 23.

vulnerability in the aftermath of the Anglo-Boer War (1899–1902), two World Wars, the Great Depression, and a series of droughts and epidemics triggering large-scale urbanization. Moreover, Afrikaners, threatened by black migrants competing for unskilled employment in the city, "insisted that the principle of 'no equalization' (*geen gelykstelling*) between black and white people had to be applied."[11] It is no surprise, as Deist has demonstrated, that Deuteronomy's "circling-the-wagons" approach, which viewed the world, according to Louis Stulman, as "fragile and fraught with danger" with "chaotic social forces ... threat[ening] to undermine its social and cosmic order," resonated with the Afrikaners during the 1930s and 1940s.[12]

Moreover, as Nussbaum points out, though people "react to *perceived* danger, ... that is not always the same thing as *real* danger."[13] Sometimes people are quite wrong about what really threatens their well-being, perhaps by having the wrong information or overestimating a real danger.[14] Nonetheless, "a sudden tear in the fabric of [one's sense of] invulnerability" may be responsible for people seeking to regain control, often by devising laws to protect the self.[15] As Nussbaum writes, "People don't feel fear if they think that they control everything important and cannot be harmed."[16]

Second, Nussbaum notes that fear is often projected onto some other unpopular target.[17] In this regard, she exposes the intricate link between fear and disgust, "fear's first cousin."[18] Various groups across history, including Jews, Muslims, women, gays and lesbians, African Americans, and also black, colored, and Indian individuals in South Africa have been

---

11. Deist, "Dangers of Deuteronomy," 14–15. See also Robert Vosloo, "From a Farm Road to a Public Highway: The Dutch Reformed Church and Its Changing Views Regarding the City and Urbanisation in the First Half of the Twentieth Century (1916–1947)," *SHE* 39 (2013): 19–32.

12. Louis Stulman, "Encroachment in Deuteronomy: An Analysis of the Social World of the D Code," *JBL* 109 (1990): 626; Susan Niditch, *War in the Hebrew Bible: A Study of the Ethics of Violence* (Oxford: Oxford University Press, 1995), 75; Deist, "Dangers of Deuteronomy," 20–21.

13. Nussbaum, *New Religious Intolerance*, 27, emphasis added.
14. Ibid., 33.
15. Ibid., 34.
16. Ibid., 30.
17. Ibid., 23.
18. Ibid., 36.

subjected to "projective disgust," that is, associations with offensive food, dirt, feces, blood, and vomit that all evoke a strong reflex of recoiling or distancing oneself from the contaminant "other."

Ahmed demonstrates how expressions of disgust typically correlate stereotypical perceptions of "sticky" substances to bodies, marking sharp boundaries between "us" and "them."[19] For example, the term *Paki* in Ahmed's London context has become an insult through repeated association with "immigrant, outsider, dirty." However, she argues that "such words do not have to be used once the sign becomes sticky. To use a sticky sign is to evoke other words, which have become intrinsic to the sign through past forms of association."[20] Moreover, in the most extreme manifestation of disgust, certain bodies may become fixed as objects of hate and violent hate crimes.[21]

This link between disgust, fear, and violence elucidates the *ḥērem* laws in the Hebrew Bible. Rannfrid I. Thelle notes that the rationale for annihilating the inhabitants of the land focuses on the contaminating potential of their despicable religious practices.[22] It is thus the fear of becoming like the Canaanites—linked to Israel's forfeiture of their land in the Deuteronomistic Historian's worldview—that catalyzes divinely sanctioned violence against "them." For instance, Deut 20:16–18 reinforces the divine commandment to destroy utterly "the towns of these peoples that the LORD your God is giving you as an inheritance; you must not let anything that breathes remain alive … so that they may not teach you to do all the abhorrent [or one could say 'disgusting'] things that they do for their gods, and you thus sin against the LORD your God" (NRSV).

Ahmed notes that the speech act "That is disgusting!" serves as a form of vomiting, a form of abjection typifying the expulsion of the contaminant or threat.[23] Actually, Lev 18:25 draws an even stronger link between the other nations and disgust, stating that the land became polluted due to the

---

19. Sara Ahmed, *The Cultural Politics of Emotion* (Edinburgh: Edinburgh University Press, 2004), 64, 92.

20. Ibid., 92.

21. Ibid., 57, 60.

22. Thelle, "Biblical Conquest Account," 64.

23. Ahmed, *Cultural Politics of Emotion*, 94. Nussbaum rightly suggests that the language of "vomit" communicates that "the disgusting remains 'other' and it is always possible to imagine removing it from the world the way one flushes away feces or disposes of spoiled food" (*Upheavals of Thought: The Intelligence of Emotions* [Cambridge: Cambridge University Press, 2001], 222).

"fleshy practices of the Canaanites."[24] As a result, the land will vomit out its inhabitants. As Erin Runions puts it: "Forbidden sexuality is expelled from the land like bad-tasting food from the body."[25] This "vomiting" is no passive action, however. In this regard, Ziony Zevit writes that "Deuteronomy provided a practical clarification of how the land would disgorge the iniquitous Canaanites and purge itself. It mandated genocide."[26]

Third, Nussbaum shows how often "fear is nourished by the idea of a disguised enemy." Whether it is the wolf pretending to be Grandmother, ready to pounce on the unsuspecting Red Riding Hood, or the deranged Glenn Close in *Fatal Attraction* seducing Michael Douglas, "fear thrives on the idea of hiddenness, of danger lurking beneath the façade of normalcy."[27] There is a long history of viewing the Other in terms of a concealed threat. Nussbaum cites an example of conspiracy fiction, *Protocols of the Elders of Zion*, first published in Russia (1902), exposing a Jewish conspiracy to achieve world domination. As Nussbaum describes the novel's premise of hidden danger under the auspice of normalcy, "Jews are all around you,

---

24. Ziony Zevit, "The Search for Violence in Israelite Culture and in the Bible," in Bernat and Klawans, *Religion and Violence*, 27. Erin Runions employs an antigay cartoon by Jack Chick in "The Gay Blade" that illustrates this link between disgust, sexuality, and violence in terms of the Canaanites. In this cartoon, one sees how the Canaanite "other" is associated with filth and ensuing disgust when a group of archaeologists uncover Canaanite religious practices. Runions writes: "Given the overall message of the tract, the reader is left to surmise that these religious practices include nonheteronormative sex. Not only does the image suggest a visceral (and therefore, presumably natural) response to nonheteronormativity, but it also implies violence is the appropriate response to objects of disgust." See Runions, "From Disgust to Humor: Rahab's Queer Affect," in *Bible Trouble: Queer Reading at the Boundaries of Biblical Scholarship*, ed. Theresa J. Hornsby and Ken Stone, SemeiaSt 67 (Atlanta: Society of Biblical Literature Press), 50.

25. Runions, "From Disgust to Humor," 50. Runions notes that in the text anxiety and disgust are not only associated with "Canaanite same-sex desires but also with other kinds of nonheteronormative, nonmonogamous practices. Many scholars have associated so-called Canaanite fertility rites with the biblical phrase 'whoring after other gods' and so with literal prostitution" (51).

26. Zevit, "Search for Violence," 27. Niditch similarly argues that the ḥērem laws served as a means of "gaining God's favor through expurgation of the abomination" of those practices that the Deuteronomistic tradition considered to be "idolatrous, contaminating, and degenerate" (*War in the Hebrew Bible*, 56–57).

27. Nussbaum, *New Religious Intolerance*, 23–24.

masquerading as nice normal people. But a day will come when they will leap out of hiding and kill you."[28]

A similar propensity for fear politics in our global context should be obvious. Nussbaum concludes that it is too easy for individuals or a society "to fall into the fairy tale trap of imagining that what's feared is easily identified as a single group, already unpopular, whose differences in religion and dress had already marked them out for suspicion."[29] With regard to the minaret law in Switzerland, Nussbaum states, "Immigrants, rather than being seen as full people, were seen from the narrow perspective of the ego, as missiles attacking the homeland."[30] The same argument could be made with regard to the struggles facing many other European countries, the United States, and South Africa concerning the influx of immigrants, leading one to ask the following critical questions: Is it possible for individuals and communities to overcome this narcissistic fear preoccupied with safeguarding the self? Can one unlearn disgust? Nussbaum seems to answer in the affirmative.

In the following section, I explore three conditions that Nussbaum introduces as necessary for communities to overcome fear's narcissism. By way of illustration, I focus the discussion on the ḥērem law rooted in the dangerous combination of fear and disgust, exploring how the biblical tradition and its interpreters counter/undo this law's nefarious effects.

2. Transcending Fear, Disrupting Disgust

Nussbaum argues that in order for a community to transcend fear and to disrupt disgust, it must embrace the following three principles: (1) political (and I would add religious) principles that express equal respect and dignity for all people, (2) rigorous critical thinking that criticizes inconsistencies leading to human rights violations, and (3) an empathetic or participatory imagination regarding how the world looks from a different cultural or religious point of view.[31]

---

28. Ibid., 38, see also 22–23.
29. Ibid., 25.
30. Ibid., 56.
31. Ibid., 2–3.

2.1. Valuing All Human Life

First and foremost, Nussbaum argues that necessary to overcome religious (and I would add racial) intolerance is the bedrock principle "that all human beings are equal bearers of human dignity." Even though "people may be unequal in wealth, class, talent, strength, achievement, or moral character," they are "equal as bearers of inalienable basic human dignity that cannot be lost or forfeited."[32] In terms of the Hebrew Bible, Carol Fontaine applies this basic tenet that human rights "belong to every human simply by virtue of being born human" to theological biblical interpretation.[33]

> By the very fact of existence, all (created) life-forms have the inherent worth of simply *being embodied here*. Some may claim that "what exists" is here because God created it so, and blessed the creation. Others may reject that account, choosing instead the complexities of evolution and science as explanation, but that does not obviate the ethical implications of the existence of being. From either perspective, religious or secular, the evidentiary function of simply being, as a part of known creation, conveys a dignity proper to whatever form of existence we may be speaking of, and creates a duty in the one who perceives it.[34]

Such a principle of human dignity or equality encourages readers who are troubled by the violence in the Old Testament to employ interpretive strategies that, as proposed in the subtitle of Eric A. Siebert's book, "overcome the Old Testament's troubling legacy."[35] For instance, Seibert utilizes a "consistent ethics of life" concerned with valuing *all* people to critique "all readings that condone the use of violence and lethal force against

---

32. Ibid., 61. Nussbaum continues to modify this initial definition of human dignity in light of its overemphasis on humans' abilities to reason, which potentially denies equal respect to mentally disabled persons. Accordingly, Nussbaum extends her initial definition of being human to include capacities to perceive, to move, to feel emotions, to love, and to care (64). See also Nussbaum, *Frontiers of Justice: Disability, Nationality, Species Membership* (Cambridge: Belknap, 2006); Nussbaum, *Creating Capabilities: The Human Development Approach* (Cambridge: Belknap, 2011).

33. Carole R. Fontaine, *With Eyes of Flesh: The Bible, Gender and Human Rights*, BMW 10 (Sheffield: Sheffield Phoenix, 2008), 8, emphasis original.

34. Ibid., 28, emphasis original.

35. Eric A. Seibert, *The Violence of Scripture: Overcoming the Old Testament's Troubling Legacy* (Minneapolis: Fortress, 2012).

others, even when such force is ostensibly exercised in the name of justice. Valuing *all* human life precludes the possibility of using violence and lethal force against *any* human life."[36]

2.2. The Need for Critical Thinking

Nussbaum laments the popular tendency to make decisions in an uncritical way with little self-reflection. Hence people's actions are often marred by what she describes as "limited experience, by tradition and peer pressure, by fear..., by self-interest and self-protective bias." In this regard, Nussbaum highlights the importance of "the examined life" in showing the inconsistencies in people's reasoning that may contribute to human rights violations.[37]

Actually, the numerous biblical interpreters, both ancient and modern, who have grappled with overtly violent texts such as the ḥērem laws and their subsequent manifestations bear witness to a rigorous process of critical thinking rooted in principles of equality, justice, and human dignity. For instance, Susan Niditch looks to the ancient Near Eastern background of the ḥērem texts to propose another interpretation beyond the one introduced earlier. She cites Num 21:2–3, in which Israel makes a vow promising to devote the cities and their inhabitants to destruction if God gave the people into their hands. Regarding other texts from Deuteronomy and Joshua, Niditch argues that the ban represents a sacrifice to God, implying a worldview in which the deity appreciates human sacrifice.[38] "Paradoxically," she contends, "the ban as sacrifice may be viewed as admitting more respect for the value of human life than other war ideologies that allow for the arbitrary killing of soldiers and civilians." Accordingly, "the enemy is not the unclean 'other,' but a mirror of the self, that which God desires for himself."[39] John Collins dryly responds to Niditch's suggestion that the enemy was deemed worthy of sacrificial offering: "One hopes that the Canaanites appreciated the honor."[40] Collins

---

36. Ibid., 69. Two additional criteria inform his ethical critique: "The Rule of Love: Reading for the Love of God and Others" and "A Commitment to Justice: Setting Things Right" (67–69).
37. Nussbaum, *New Religious Intolerance*, 99.
38. Niditch, *War in the Hebrew Bible*, 33–35.
39. Ibid., 50.
40. Collins, "Zeal of Phinehas," 6.

adds that in this understanding of the ban as sacrifice welcomed by God puts "the practice into context in the ancient world, but increases rather than lessens its problematic nature from an ethical point of view."[41]

This debate demonstrates the significance of dissenting voices within the interpretive tradition. Niditch cites two cases from rabbinic interpreters exemplifying the refusal to accept either ḥērem as sacrifice or ḥērem as justice as the definitive norm. First, Midrash Tanhuma imagines God saying:

> *I did not command* Jephthah to sacrifice his daughter, *I did not speak* to the king of Moab (saying) that he should sacrifice his son, *neither came it into My mind* to tell Abraham to slay his son.... Our Rabbis say: Why in connection with the king of Moab is the verb *speak* employed? Because the Holy One, blessed be He said: Did I ever hold a conversation with him, etc? Why, I never spoke as much as a word to him—and of all things, that he is to sacrifice his son? (Tanh. 50)[42]

Moreover, Niditch cites the rabbinic tradition in b. Meg. 10b (also b. Sanh. 39b) in which God admonishes the angels' jubilation after the the Red Sea crossing: "The work of my hands has drowned in the sea and shall you chant songs?" According to the rabbis, God does not "rejoice in the downfall of the wicked." In other words, the Egyptians are also God's children, the work of the Creator God.[43]

2.3. Looking at the World through the Eyes of Another

These voices dissenting against an uncritical acceptance of biblical policies that advocate violently killing "the Other" exemplify ongoing attempts to challenge harmful texts and their interpretations. Nussbaum's third point, promoting an empathetic or participatory engagement with different religious and cultural traditions, offers further guidance in countering the politics of fear that is often rooted in disgust. In what she calls "cultivat[ing] the inner eyes," Nussbaum stresses the importance of a "curious, questioning, and receptive demeanor that says, in effect, 'Here

---

41. Ibid., 7.
42. Text from Niditch, *War in the Hebrew Bible*, 45 (citing Shalom Spiegel, *The Last Trial*, trans. Judah Goldin [New York: Pantheon, 1967], 79–80). See also Ag. Ber. 31; b. Ta'an. 41; Gen. Rab. 55.5.
43. Text from Niditch, *War in the Hebrew Bible*, 150.

is another human being. I wonder what he (or she) is seeing and feeling right now."[44]

Considering that the basic criterion for human dignity is being born, the "other" must be valued simply for being there. As Fontaine writes: "The Other does not need to disappear, to be done away with, or contained; the Other needs only to be acknowledged, truly and properly seen, through the fleshy eyes of another embodied entity."[45]

An intriguing biblical example of such participatory imagination, with potential to disrupt processes of disgust and undermine the *ḥērem* tradition, is Rahab, the Canaanite prostitute (Josh 2; 6). Runions sees Rahab's story as a case of breaking through stereotypes that circulate and stick to an individual and group, or in Ahmed's terms, enabling disgusting entities to "lose their stickiness."[46] As Runions argues: "It seems to be that signs are never quite so static as they might appear. With some pushing and pulling, objects and affect can perhaps be unstuck and reconfigured."[47]

Considerable irony underlies Rahab's story. Her "prostitute" designation (Josh 2:1) carries throughout the story up to 6:25, which reports her salvation by Joshua and incorporation into the Israelite community.[48] At first glance Rahab's "prostitute" label affirms the perception that all Canaanites engage in lewd sexual practices. However, the Joshua text deconstructs these initial impressions, registering no moral judgment regarding Rahab's profession.[49] Rather, Rahab, the only named character other than Joshua, is cast in a positive light. The subject of several active verbs, Rahab emerges as the classic trickster who cleverly (and humorously) tricks the king in order to save herself and her family.[50]

---

44. Nussbaum, *New Religious Intolerance*, 140–43.
45. Fontaine, *With Eyes of Flesh*, 29.
46. Runions, "From Disgust to Humor," 66.
47. Ibid., 54.
48. Runions notes tongue in cheek that this "story could be called sex-trade positive," conceivably serving as an etiological tale explaining the existence of the sex trade in Israel (ibid., 66).
49. Ibid., 58. Throughout Josh 2 and 6, Rahab is only identified as prostitute, never as wife or mother, thus subverting the traditional heteronormative paradigm.
50. Ibid., 65. Connecting the city-destruction stories involving Lot and Rahab, L. Daniel Hawk argues that both Lot and the Israelite spies are portrayed as passive and impotent figures. By contrast, however, Rahab actively "negotiates her own salvation by saving others, and thereby effectively rescues her family" ("Strange Houseguests: Rahab, Lot and the Dynamics of Deliverance," in *Reading Between Texts: Intertextual-*

This comedic portrayal of Rahab's outwitting the king and his men moves affect in another direction, away from the disgust sticking to all those filthy Canaanites. As Runions says: "No longer disgusting and repulsive, but instead brilliant, assertive and funny, the racialized, non-heteronormative woman has the upper hand, which she demonstrates by turning military proceedings into futile silliness."[51] Melissa Jackson also highlights the story's comedic elements that subvert not only the Canaanites' authority but also the Israelites', thereby undermining "any Israelite self-depiction as a superior people invulnerable to foolishness."[52] Moreover, Jackson notes that the theologically orthodox tenor of Rahab's speech serves as a way of disrupting disgust, certifying that not all Canaanites are "evil, idol-worshipping foreigners who must destroyed before they pervert God's chosen people." On the contrary, "Rahab's profession of Israel's Yahweh is so outstanding that the spies plagiarize it for their own report to Joshua."[53]

Rahab's very presence in Israel's story deconstructs the totalizing notion of the *ḥērem* as utter destruction, as does the overall picture in Judges of Israel's gradual infiltration into the land and continual skir-

---

ity and the Hebrew Bible, ed. Danna Nolan Fewell [Louisville: Westminster John Knox, 1992], 96). Danna Nolan Fewell and David M. Gunn quip that foreigners' ability to quote Deuteronomy better than the Israelites raises vital questions concerning who is chosen and who is not (*Gender, Power, and Promise: The Subject of the Bible's First Story* [Nashville: Abingdon, 1993], 120).

51. Runions, "From Disgust to Humor," 69. Runions further concludes that trickster Rahab's story "shifts affective energies so that what we might become is not conscribed by signifiers of scripture sticky with the regurgitations of disgust" (70).

52. Melissa A. Jackson, *Comedy and Feminist Interpretation of the Hebrew Bible: A Subversive Collaboration*, OTM (Oxford: Oxford University Press, 2012), 93.

53. Jackson, *Comedy and Feminist Interpretation*, 93. Jackson describes this "truly 'orthodox' theologian" as voicing the best of Deuteronomistic theology. For example, the phrase "God in heaven above and on earth below" (Josh 2:11b) appears only two other times in the Hebrew Bible: voiced by Moses in the wilderness (Deut 4:39) and by Solomon at the temple's dedication (1 Kgs 8:23). See also Judith McKinlay's argument that the reason Rahab sounds like an Israelite is that "she is an Israelite construct and constructed as a pawn of the text which makes her into the all-important Other, and so a significant part of the justification for the dispossession of her people's land." In a context in which the Israelites were probably not a distinct ethnical group, "Rahab was created 'Other' in order to provide the 'Us' of Israel with an identity" (*Reframing Her: Biblical Women in Postcolonial Focus* [Sheffield: Sheffield Phoenix, 2004], 47).

mishes between various Israelite tribes and other peoples.[54] In the story of Rahab, disgust at this Canaanite prostitute dissipates, resulting in the salvation of all who belong to her when the Israelite spies offer "our lives for yours" (Josh 2:14).[55] Since Achan the Israelite will soon be killed together with his whole family for violating the *ḥērem* (7:25), Rahab's survival is all the more remarkable.[56]

Indeed, in this compelling narrative incorporated into Israel's story of itself, Rahab the Canaanite prostitute has become a person with a father, mother, brothers, and sisters whose lives must be delivered from death (2:13). In this regard, Seibert reminds us that "humanizing Canaanites is critical" in any attempt to "undermin[e] efforts to justify genocide."[57] Drawing on the work of Daniel Hawk, Seibert proposes that "later editors may have revised some of these stories to recast the Canaanites in a more favourable light, making it more difficult to dehumanize and demonize them."[58]

The rabbis supply further details that humanize this Canaanite "other," depicting her as one of the world's four most beautiful women (together with Sarah, Abigail, and Esther), whose mere name caused men to experience sexual pleasure (ejaculate) (b. Meg. 15a). In contrast

---

54. Runions, "From Disgust to Humor," 67. Mark G. Brett speculates that Rahab's story "may have been constructed precisely in order to oppose the [*ḥērem*] law in Deuteronomy" (*Decolonizing God: The Bible in the Tides of Empire* [Sheffield: Sheffield Phoenix, 2008], 86).

55. McKinlay ironically remarks that "if Rahab has been reading Deuteronomy, the spies obviously have not, or they would have remembered that Deut 7:2 and 20:16–18 categorically forbid any such arrangements. In Holy War there were to be no survivors at all" (*Reframing Her*, 41). Note also Runion's suggestion that there was "an entertaining earlier indigenous tale that undercuts the story's impulse to subjugation and genocide." Hence she proposes that "the preredactional layer comically works against the later conquest narrative and the identity construct it supports" ("From Disgust to Humor," 46).

56. Jackson, *Comedy and Feminist Interpretation*, 89. Jackson further argues that boundaries are blurred in the book of Joshua: "Rahab, who ought to be an outsider, assists the spies, professes faith in Yahweh, and becomes an insider." In contrast, "Achan, an insider, violates God's command and thus is moved outside" (92).

57. Seibert, *Violence of Scripture*, 101. Further: "We must learn to see Canaanites as real people—moms and dads, aunts and uncles, brothers and sisters, nephews and nieces, grandmas and grandpas … [with] hopes and dreams, strengths and weaknesses, virtues and vices, just like we do" (101).

58. Jackson, *Comedy and Feminist Interpretation*, 99.

to Flavius Josephus, who tried to recast Rahab as an innkeeper offering food and lodging and food to travelers (*Ant.* 5.1–7), the rabbis remained interested in Rahab's occupation as prostitute. So they elaborated on her sexual exploits, proposing that she started her career at age ten and that eventually every leader and king in the realm paid her a visit![59] The rabbis touted the profound piousness of Rahab—"this golden-hearted worthy-of-inclusion Canaanite"[60] prostitute who found her way to Israel's God and even married Joshua, the leader of Israel. Moreover, late Jewish literature presents her as a prophetess, and she appears in three New Testament texts: Matt 1:5 includes her in Jesus's genealogy; Heb 11:31 celebrates her as a model of faith; and Jas 2:23–25 commends her as a paragon of good works along with Abraham.[61] This rich reception history testifies that the initial disgust associated the Canaanite prostitute Rahab had been disrupted or overturned.

The Rahab narrative in Joshua and its reception history nicely illustrate the use of participatory imagination, which Nussbaum advocates as vital to disrupting disgust and overcoming narcissistic notions of fear. Much of Nussbaum's supporting evidence comes from classical Greco-Roman tragedies and comedies that so vividly reveal common human vulnerabilities.[62] Of course, quality literature is seldom simplistic or one dimensional. Good stories, stories that succeed in keeping our attention, quite often are complex and multifaceted in nature. So Rahab's story admits to different readings, such as those by postcolonial (feminist) interpreters. Judith McKinlay, for example, argues that the Deuteronomistic Historian co-opts this Canaanite prostitute by filling her with the orthodox words of Yahwist theology.[63] Musa Dube describes Rahab as the ultimate colonizer's

---

59. Admiel Kosman, "Rahab: Prostituierte und Prophetin," in *Jewish Lifeworlds and Jewish Thought: Festschrift Presented to Karl E. Grözinger on the Occasion of His Seventieth Birthday*, ed. Nathanael Riemer (Wiesbaden: Harrassowitz, 2012), 178. This interpretation of Rahab also explains why the spies visited her: to get information from this Mata Hari-type figure.

60. Jackson, *Comedy and Feminist Interpretation*, 95.

61. Kosman, "Rahab," 179.

62. For instance, Nussbaum argues that bodily elements associated with excrement, sex, food, and drink featured in comedies function as signs of human vulnerability "common to all, as just a part of being alive, connected to life's joy." See Martha C. Nussbaum, *Political Emotions: Why Love Matters for Justice* (Cambridge: Belknap, 2013), 272.

63. McKinlay, *Reframing Her*, 44–45, 54. She proposes that Israel had taken "what

fantasy, a figure constructed to herald "the colonizer's superiority, pledge absolute loyalty, and surrender all [her] rights voluntarily."[64] Lori Rowlett sees the assimilated Rahab as the "good native" celebrated for turning her back on her own people and collaborating with the enemy.[65] Read from the "enemy's" side, Rahab's story emerges as a "text of terror" not only for all Canaanites, but also for contemporary immigrants coerced to assimilate or be expulsed.[66]

McKinlay warns that instead of inviting her "to question any of these assumptions, the text's strategy has been to lead [the reader], almost unawares, to accept its values and interests as the story itself is accepted."[67] As she passionately writes in "Rahab Reviewed":

> As I read the narrative afresh, I am struck by how the story itself functions as a *mise en abyme* for the conquest tradition as a whole: her door is open to the spies, so with Israel already inside … all is programmed for Israel's victory and Jericho's failure. By opening up her city to Israel, Rabah has laid open the country: cities and towns will be destroyed; Canaanites will be killed and driven out in greater numbers, even if there is some resistance. Blood soaked imperialism in action. How can this be positive?[68]

---

once was a folk tale and reshaped it as a tool of its own political ideology" (44); see also Jackson, *Comedy and Feminist Interpretation*, 96–97.

64. Musa W. Dube, *Postcolonial Feminist Interpretation of the Bible* (St. Louis, MO: Chalice, 2000), 78.

65. Lori Rowlett, "Disney's Pocahontas and Joshua's Rahab in Postcolonial Perspective," in *Culture, Entertainment and the Bible*, ed. George Aichele, JSOTSup 309 (Sheffield: Sheffield Academic, 2000), 66.

66. McKinlay argues that Rahab has become a "'foreigner' in her own land"; further: "assimilation means loss for Rahab, loss of culture, loss of identity as Canaanite, with a forced forgetting of her origins, of the stories and myths that have made her who she is. See Judith McKinlay, "Rahab Reviewed," in *Troubling Women and Land: Reading Biblical Texts in Aoteara New Zealand*, BMW 59 (Sheffield: Sheffield Phoenix, 2014), 118.

67. McKinlay, *Reframing Her*, 47. She further warns of a twofold danger. One is that "other dominant cultures, such as [her own New Zealand context] will find it all too easy to identify with the dominant voice, which justifies the taking of land, on the assumption that Canaanites are inherently wicked. But an even more disturbing danger is that such a voice may also lead those who have lost their land to Christian invaders and settlers to read against their own history and identity," something that she describes as "bleeding without knowing one has been cut" (49).

68. McKinlay, "Rahab Reviewed," 114.

I propose, however, that engaging in participatory imagination with Ruth's story has compelled McKinlay, who is keenly aware of her colonizer position in Aotearoa (New Zealand), to uncover the many different complex layers embedded in this intriguing narrative. In another case, McKinlay affirms her need to hear the story of Ruth and Naomi in more than one key: on the one hand, celebrating Ruth and Naomi as "strong women, as part of the scriptural blessings"; on the other hand, critiquing the assimilation underlying the notion of the "model immigrant" turning her back on Moab and gladly disappearing into the dominant culture.[69] Could one not say the same thing about Rahab? Does this complex figure who transcends all attempts at containment, even by the editor, not challenge readers to engage her from more than one point of view? To be sure, McKinlay concludes her article by outlining various divergent interpretations of Rahab,[70] agreeing with Tikva Frymer-Kensky that the reader, both individually and communally, ultimately determines meaning. Nevertheless, McKinlay herself chooses to read Rahab's tale in a single key ending on this final note: "But be careful—this is no innocent text."[71] It seems that Rahab has also become an object of disgust for her postcolonial interpreters, effectively blocking alternative meanings.

Nussbaum's first two principles for countering the politics of fear—(1) critical, self-aware thinking and (2) the equality and dignity of all persons—come back into play. To read a complex biblical story like Rahab's from different vantage points helps the reader to comprehend that humans are even more complex than the portraits constructed in multifaceted literature.[72] Participatory imagination, in conjunction with vital skills of

---

69. McKinlay, *Reframing Her*, 55. See also Laura Donaldson, "The Sign of Orpah: Reading Ruth through Native Eyes," in *Ruth and Esther*, ed. Athalya Brenner, FCB 2/3 (Sheffield: Sheffield Academic, 1999), 130–44.

70. McKinlay asks: "Is the strange woman rehabilitated, albeit the continuing mote in Israel's eye? Is she Frymer-Kensky's 'quintessential downtrodden from whom Israel comes' and is thus 'a new Israel?'... Is she Dube's 'a literary phantom of imperialism's 'cultural bomb'? Or is she Runions's postcolonial trickster, the 'indeterminate figure' who 'starts up laughing with others and at ourselves'?" ("Rahab Reviewed, 118–19).

71. McKinlay, "Rahab Reviewed," 119. McKinlay also notes that the fact that many Maori still feel like foreigners in their own land confirms for her that the "Rahab narrative is no 'once upon a time' tale, which is why I continue to turn it this way and that" (118).

72. Laurel Dykstra seeks to read Israel's story from the "other side" point of view

critical thinking and attributions of dignity to all people, may help individuals and groups to appreciate the histories, motivations, joys, and sorrows of the "other"; to allow one to be truly drawn into the life story of "another." In this way, as Nussbaum avers, "the muscles of the imagination [are exercised], making people capable of inhabiting for a time, the world of a different person, and seeing the meaning of events in that world from the outsider's viewpoint."[73]

3. Conclusion

Overcoming a politics of fear is not easy. One need only consider the flood of anti-immigration sentiments on the internet to get a sense of the uphill battle to disrupt and transcend narcissistic notions of fear. As recent cases in point, witness (1) the Dutch Geert Wilders, who proclaims, "Send them all back and close our borders!," referring to recent migrants to Europe after a treacherous, even deadly, journey across the Mediterranean;[74] (2) "Anti-Muslim Attacks after Charlie Hebdo Highlight France's Long History of Islamophobia," headlining a recent article in the Huffington Post;[75] and (3) the oft-heard "The *kwerekwere* (foreigners) are stealing our jobs" accompanying xenophobic violence in South Africa.[76]

Within such a context, the principles proposed by Nussbaum and expounded in this essay are vital to help build a society in which values of love and compassion triumph over powerful emotions of fear, disgust,

---

of Rahab the prostitute who typifies "agents of resistance and solidarity in the life project called survival" (*Set Them Free: The Other Side of Exodus* [Maryknoll, NY: Orbis Books, 2002], 41).

73. Nussbaum, *Upheavals of Thought*, 431.

74. Geert Wilders, *Geert Wilders Weblog*, 30 May 2015, https://tinyurl.com/SBL0396d.

75. Alissa Schneller and Jan Diehm, "Anti-Muslim Attacks after Charlie Hebdo Highlight France's Long History of Islamophobia," *Huffington Post*, 9 January 2015, https://tinyurl.com/SBL0396e. The authors cite a 2013 survey indicating that 74 percent of French respondents believe Islam is incompatible with French society. Moreover, Islamophobic attacks in France have sharply been on the rise since 2005.

76. Kate Wilkinson, "South Africa's Xenophobic Attacks: Are Migrants Really Stealing Jobs?," *The Guardian*, 20 April 2015, https://tinyurl.com/SBL0396f. As she introduces her article: "Shops are torched. Streets are barricaded. Tyres [sic] are set alight. People are stabbed, shot and burned to death. Mobs hound Somalis, Mozambicans, Zimbabweans, Pakistanis and Bangladeshis from their homes and businesses."

and hatred.[77] Such efforts demand transformative encounters with both "real" embodied persons and "re-presented" characters in narratives and other literary media, whereby we may "learn to appreciate the diversity of circumstances in which human beings struggle for flourishing."[78]

In an interesting article engaging with three Swiss-German films about migration and border-crossing, Gisela Hoecherl-Alden argues that *Die Schweizermacher* (*The Swissmakers*, 1978), directed by Rolf Lyssy;[79] *Reise der Hoffnung* (*Journey of Hope*, 1990), by Xavier Koller; and *Pastry, Pain and Politics* (1998), by Stina Werenfels, offer candid and critical views at the way Switzerland has dealt with cultural and religious diversity. Moreover, these films offer a glimpse into the life stories of a number of immigrants who seek to make a life in Switzerland, and as a result they "try to revise mainstream stereotypes about the ethnic groups in question."[80]

For instance, *Journey of Hope* offers a painful portrayal of a Turkish family who travels through Istanbul to Italy and then by foot over the Swiss border, culminating in an arduous climb over the snow-covered Swiss Alps. The film poignantly depicts the difficult immigrant condition: "a painful, disquieting experience," according to Hoecherl-Alden, "where changing places results in harsh confrontations and ... leads from one marginal or

---

77. Nussbaum, *Upheavals of Thought*, 401.
78. Ibid., 432. Nussbaum further argues that it is difficult for individuals to think in the abstract about such a sensitive matter (388). But "when we move the outer circles closer to the self, as an education in proper compassion urges, our inclination to favour projects of revenge toward these distant people, should we even have such projects, will be likely to diminish. Through this channelling of concern we will become concerned for others as for members of our own families, and see any damage befalling them as a damage to ourselves as well" (395).
79. Gisela Hoecherl-Alden, "On the Road to Multiculturalism: Challenging Concepts of Neutrality and Tolerance in Swiss-German Cinema," *Kinema* 25 (2006), https://tinyurl.com/SBL0396g. In *The Swissmakers*, two immigration officials must decide which immigrants may be naturalized as Swiss citizens. The film begins with a training session where the chief immigration authority informs the "trainees that an assimilated foreigner is someone who is no longer noticeable. Eliciting adjectives, that describe a true citizen of Switzerland, the trainees provide him with 'dependable,' 'neutral,' 'serious,' 'righteous,' 'hard-working,' and 'militant,' after which they begin their quest for those worthy of Swiss citizenship." Hoecherl-Alden notes that these Swiss stereotypes feature throughout the film, related to the director's "question as to what being Swiss or becoming Swiss really means, and whether unconditional assimilation at the price of cultural identity should be the stated goal of immigration policies."
80. Hoecherl-Alden, "On the Road."

peripheral place to another." This is hauntingly illustrated when the family arrives at the first Swiss village that looks just like the picturesque postcard that lured the father to come to this land of plenty. However, the director "recasts [this postcard] as a powerful image of exclusion: as the exhausted, freezing immigrants stand in the snow, mountains behind them, they look through the glass at the lush greenery surrounding an indoor swimming pool from which the owner yells the word 'closed' ('*geschlossen!*')."[81]

When the father is detained for illegally entering Switzerland, he heartbreakingly asks: "How could [I] have known that this place is so cold?" Hoecherl-Alden notes that "he is clearly referring to the cold-heartedness of the Swiss authorities, which Koller also underscores visually through the brilliantly white sterility of the prison." Yet, echoing the title of the film, the family's motive for taking on the treacherous, costly journey is evident in the father's answering the immigration official's query "Who and what brought you here?" with one word: "Hope."

Films like *Journey of Hope* indeed underscore Nussbaum's point that a participatory imagination implies "not just learning some facts about classes, races, nationalities, sexual orientations other than her own but being drawn into their lives through the imagination, becoming a participant in those struggles."[82]

Select Bibliography

Ahmed, Sara. *The Cultural Politics of Emotion*. Edinburgh: Edinburgh University Press, 2004.
Bernat, David A., and Jonathan Klawans, eds. *Religion and Violence: The Biblical Heritage*. Sheffield: Sheffield Phoenix, 2007.
Butler, Judith. *Frames of War: When is Life Grievable?* London: Verso, 2009.
———. *Notes Toward a Performative Theory of Assembly*. Cambridge: Harvard University Press, 2015.
———. *Precarious Life: The Powers of Mourning and Violence*. London: Verso, 2004.
Nussbaum, Martha C. *The New Religious Intolerance: Overcoming the Politics of Fear in an Anxious Age*. Cambridge: Belknap, 2012.

---

81. Ibid.
82. Nussbaum, *Upheavals of Thought*, 432.

———. *Political Emotions: Why Love Matters for Justice.* Cambridge: Harvard University Press, 2013.
———. *Upheavals of Thought: The Intelligence of Emotions.* Cambridge: Cambridge University Press, 2001.
Runions, Erin. "From Disgust to Humor: Rahab's Queer Affect." Pages 45–74 in *Bible Trouble: Queer Reading at the Boundaries of Biblical Scholarship.* Edited by Theresa J. Hornsby and Ken Stone. SemeiaSt 67. Atlanta: Society of Biblical Literature, 2011.
Seibert, Eric A. *The Violence of Scripture: Overcoming the Old Testament's Troubling Legacy.* Minneapolis: Fortress, 2012.

Disgust in Body, Mind, and Language: The Case of Impurity in the Hebrew Bible

Thomas Kazen

The present article explores the multileveled function of disgust in biblical purity discourse as an embodied emotion, a conceptual framework, and a rhetorical strategy. The methodological approach is broadly evolutionary (biopsychological) and cognitive conceptual, including insights from neuroscience and linguistics (metaphor and blending theories). The texts referred to and analyzed represent a variety of genres (legal, narrative, prophetic) and are selected to illustrate different aspects and functions of disgust, ranging from ritual indexing and taboos to moral indignation and general value judgments to ostracism and ethnocentrism. The aim is to demonstrate how biological underpinnings and cultural constructions of disgust interact and thereby provide resources for a better understanding of impurity and disgust reflected in biblical texts. The argument builds on my previous studies on impurity and disgust and incorporates some of their analyses and conclusions.[1]

---

1. Thomas Kazen, "Dirt and Disgust: Body and Morality in Biblical Purity Laws," in *Perspectives on Purity and Purification in the Bible*, ed. Baruch J. Schwartz et al., LHBOTS 474 (London: T&T Clark, 2008), 43–64; Kazen, *Emotions in Biblical Law: A Cognitive Science Approach*, HBM 36 (Sheffield: Sheffield Phoenix, 2011), 9–94; Kazen, "The Role of Disgust in Priestly Purity Law: Insights from Conceptual Metaphor and Blending Theories," *JLRS* 3 (2014): 62–92; Kazen, "Levels of Explanation for Ideas of Impurity: Why Structuralist and Symbolic Models Often Fail While Evolutionary and Cognitive Models Succeed," *JAJ* 8 (forthcoming). For more detailed and overarching discussions of impurity, see also Kazen, *Jesus and Purity Halakhah: Was Jesus Indifferent to Impurity?*, ConBNT 38 (Stockholm: Almqvist & Wiksell, 2002; corrected repr. ed., Winona Lake, IN: Eisenbrauns, 2010); Kazen, *Issues of Impurity in Early Judaism*, ConBNT 45 (Winona Lake, IN: Eisenbrauns, 2010); Kazen, *Scripture, Interpretation,*

1. Evolved Survival Strategy and Cultural Construction

From an evolutionary perspective, emotional disgust has evolved as a survival strategy in order to protect living creatures from poison and pathogens in air, water, and potential food as well as from contact with contaminated matter and individuals.[2] The extent to which various species of animals display signs of disgust is a much-discussed issue,[3] but for our purposes we can stay content with results from research on human beings.

Core disgust is usually understood as a primary emotion, a direct bodily response to repulsive stimuli. From this innate, ultimate base, a set of secondary emotions has evolved that are also important for survival—but within a social framework, as they have evolved in parallel with culture.[4] Hence certain levels of disgust have predominantly cultural or proximate bases, although the biological and cultural underpinnings are not fully separable, as the final "wiring" of the human brain occurs through interaction with social and cultural experiences during periods of plasticity in childhood and adolescence.[5]

The psychological research of Paul Rozin and his colleagues is now well known. Rozin identifies nine empirically demonstrated triggers for

---

or *Authority? Motives and Arguments in Jesus' Halakic Conflicts*, WUNT 320 (Tübingen: Mohr Siebeck, 2013), 113–94.

2. See Paul Rozin, Jonathan Haidt, and Clark McCauley, "Disgust," in *Handbook of Emotions*, ed. Michael Lewis and Jeanette M. Haviland-Jones, 2nd ed. (New York: Guildford, 2000), 639–40. For the argument that disease avoidance is a main function of disgust, see Carlos David Navarrete and Daniel M. T. Fessler, "Disease Avoidance and Ethnocentrism: The Effects of Disease Vulnerability and Disgust Sensitivity on Intergroup Attitudes," *EHB* 27 (2006): 270–82; Valerie Curtis, *Don't Look, Don't Touch, Don't Eat: The Science Behind Revulsion* (Chicago: University of Chicago Press, 2013), 1–40.

3. See Charles Darwin, *The Expression of the Emotions in Man and Animals*, WCD 23 (London: Murray, 1872; repr., New York: New York University Press, 1989); Curtis, *Don't Look*, 3–40.

4. Antonio R. Damasio, *Descartes' Error: Emotion, Reason, and the Human Brain* (New York: Putnam, 1994), 129–39; Heather Looy, "Embodied and Embedded Morality: Divinity, Identity, and Disgust," *Zygon* 39 (2004): 219–35; Rozin, Haidt, and McCauley, "Disgust," 647–48. See also Kazen, *Emotions in Biblical Law*, 9–19.

5. Jonathan Haidt, "The Emotional Dog and Its Rational Tail: A Social Intuitionist Approach to Moral Judgment," *PsRev* 108 (2001): 814–34; see also Stephanie D. Preston and Frans B. M. de Waal, "Empathy: Its Ultimate and Proximate Bases," *BBS* 25 (2002): 1–72.

disgust: food, body products, animals, sexual behaviors, contact with death or corpses, violations of the exterior envelope of the body (including gore and deformity), poor hygiene, interpersonal contamination (contact with unsavory human beings), and certain moral offenses.[6] It is interesting to note the degree to which all of these triggers combine biologically evolved (ultimate) underpinnings with culturally construed (proximate) responses. Emotional disgust as we know it is always a mixture of innate and acquired capacities that have coevolved with culture, a combination of biological and psychological reactions blended and shaped within social contexts.

This complex emotional matrix is important to keep in mind as we take a closer look at a number of texts that explicitly or implicitly associate disgust with impurity. Although certain things that are labeled impure may be near universally experienced as disgusting, others do not commend themselves as particularly repulsive unless so learned through socialization in a particular context. Since culture pervades all human life, some measure of cultural construction is always present in disgust reactions, but the degree of visceral immediacy sometimes becomes quite acute. As we will see, such "gut reactions" may be transferred to and invested in new fields through culture, particularly through language and cognition.

2. Conceptualization and Experience

Although many understand disgust as primarily triggered by taste and centered on the mouth (in line with the etymology of the term), others have instead emphasized the role of smell and touch.[7] A number of studies, from Charles Darwin's *The Expression of the Emotions in Man and Animals* and onwards, have pointed out the ambiguous character of disgust as based on something "actually perceived or vividly imagined."[8] As a

---

6. Rozin, Haidt, and McCauley, "Disgust," 637.
7. See some of the classical studies of disgust. For an emphasis on taste and the mouth, see Darwin, *Expression of the Emotions*, 195; Andras Angyal, "Disgust and Related Aversions," *JAPs* 36 (1941): 395, 402, 411. For inclusion of smell and touch, see Aurel Kolnai, *On Disgust*, ed. Barry Smith and Carolyn Korsmeyer (Chicago: Open Court, 2004); William Ian Miller, *The Anatomy of Disgust* (Cambridge: Harvard University Press, 1997), 6, 12, 60–79.
8. Darwin, *Expression of the Emotions*, 195.

secondary emotion, disgust can be triggered by sight, memory, or thought, without direct engagement of other senses.[9]

The fact that disgust can be associated with a number of senses and can be not only imagined but actually felt without any physical catalyst is important to notice. An emotion is no less an emotion—and resides just as much in the body—when caused by nonphysical stimuli.[10] Disgust can erupt from remembering or conceptualizing various objectionable items, situations, people, or behaviors that normally evoke disgust in one's social and cultural context. This capacity makes disgust useful also for rhetorical purposes, since merely associating something with another typically disgusting item is quite efficient—a kind of "disgust by association." Disgust thus becomes a ready way of expressing and transmitting values.

Morality, as increasingly acknowledged in recent thought, is not a matter of human rationality fighting against animalistic and selfish natural propensities but a complex interaction of emotion and cognition, in which most of our "moral" behaviors derive from evolutionary adaptations and develop further through cultural and contextual coevolution. According to John Teehan, morality results from "our emotions, our cognitive processes, and the complex relationship between the two."[11] Hence we can talk of "moral emotions," with disgust usually counting among them. In Jonathan Haidt's view, moral emotions *are linked to the interests or welfare either of society as a whole or at least of persons other than the judge or agent.*[12] These include emotions that motivate prosocial action, but also other-condemning emotions, such as contempt, anger, and disgust. The latter put constraints on people in social contexts by responding to injustice and protecting human integrity.

That disgust plays a prominent role in this game is clear from the way it often signifies moral dislike. As many have pointed out, however, the involvement of disgust in moral evaluation does not mean that moral rules

---

9. Miller, *The Anatomy of Disgust*, 60–88; Jonathan Haidt, "The Moral Emotions," in *Handbook of Affective Sciences*, ed. Richard J. Davidson, Klaus R. Scherer, and H. Hill Goldsmith (Oxford: Oxford University Press, 2003), 852–70, esp. 857; Curtis, *Don't Look*, 1–40.

10. This applies to all sense perceptions. The brain processes them in basically the same way, regardless of where the input comes from. See, for example, Damasio, *Descartes' Error*, 83–164, esp. 129–39.

11. John Teehan, "Kantian Ethics: After Darwin," *Zygon* 38 (2003): 58.

12. Haidt, "Moral Emotions," 853, emphasis original.

should be based on universally felt disgust.¹³ Socially conditioned emotions can hardly be trusted for moral guidance, since they are precisely that—socially conditioned. To use disgust as a normative yardstick is risky, not to say dangerous.¹⁴ Such caveats notwithstanding, disgust remains a rhetorically powerful tool, a bodily emotional reaction that can be evoked not only by exposure to physical experiences, but also by mere conceptualization. In the following, we will examine some expressions of disgust in biblical texts to see how they resonate with bodily experiences, mental conceptualizations, and rhetorical use of language.

3. Disgust and Impurity in the Law, Prophets, and Writings

The concept of impurity is especially suited as a topos for exploring disgust emotions, since it frequently uses disgust terminology, and even when not explicitly employing expressions of revulsion, the context usually implies aversive feelings. Although priestly legal discourse on impurity and purification is often phrased in fairly "neutral" language,¹⁵ the underlying visceral aspects of impurity are not far below the surface.

The food laws patently associate impurity and disgust. Deuteronomy 14:3 introduces its list of clean and unclean animals with the injunction not to eat anything abominable (tôʿēbâ). The complex text of Lev 11 brands all three categories of "swarmers" (šereṣ)—water, winged, and ground swarmers—as detestable (šeqeṣ), just like birds of prey.¹⁶

The subsequent "ritual" purity laws concerning impure conditions (skin diseases, molds, genital discharges) and their purification through ablutions, shaving, scraping, and certain apotropaic practices (Lev 12–15) do not explicitly employ disgust language. This does not mean, however, that these conditions were not regarded as repulsive; it only shows that

---

13. John Kekes, "Disgust and Moral Taboos," *Phil* 67 (1992): 438, 441.
14. See Martha C. Nussbaum, *Hiding from Humanity: Disgust, Shame, and the Law* (Princeton: Princeton University Press, 2004), 13–15, 72–171.
15. As in the discharge laws of Lev 15. See David P. Wright, "The Spectrum of Priestly Impurity," in *Priesthood and Cult in Ancient Israel*, ed. Gary A. Anderson and Saul M. Olyan, JSOTSup 125 (Sheffield: Sheffield Academic, 1991), 150–81.
16. For a discussion of "swarmers" in Lev 11 and the relationship between Lev 11 and Deut 14, see Kazen, *Emotions in Biblical Law*, 72–80; Kazen, "Purity and Persia," in *Current Issues in Priestly and Related Literature: The Legacy of Jacob Milgrom and Beyond*, ed. Roy E. Gane and Ada Taggar-Cohen, RBS 82 (Atlanta: SBL Press, 2015), 445–47, 457–59.

the technical instructions for removing the impurity did not require emotional motivation. The culturally conditioned attitude to such conditions is evident from other texts. Though no disgust terminology is used, Aaron's description of the "leprous" Miriam (Num 12:10–13) clearly appeals to the disgust felt at the sight of particular types of skin disease (ṣāraʿat). The contempt with which people with skin diseases and discharges are mentioned in 2 Sam 3:29 also strongly suggests an underlying emotional attitude of disgust toward their physical conditions.

The clearest example of emotional disgust associated with genital bleeding may be found in Ezekiel's use of menstrual imagery (niddâ) for defiling behavior (36:17), which in the larger context (36:31) is characterized as abominations (tôʿēbôt) and associated with loathing (qûṭ). Similarly, the impurity of menstruants (ṭəmēʾat hanniddâ) in Ezek 22:10 is juxtaposed with abomination (tôʿēbâ) and pollution (ṭimmēʾ) in 22:11. In certain contexts, as in Lev 20:21 (and probably also in 2 Chr 29:5), the term niddâ takes on a broader meaning, denoting something indecent and objectionable or aversive in general. In Ezra 9:11, the land to which the exiles return is described as a niddâ land, defiled by the niddâ of the people of the land and by their abominations (tôʿēbôt); here niddâ is juxtaposed to, and more or less synonymous with, the disgust term tôʿēbâ. Isaiah's reference to idols and ephods being thrown out like a bleeding woman (kəmô dāwâ [30:22]) also breathes disgust, although no such terminology explicitly appears.[17]

When impurity language characterizes disapproved behavior, such as various sexual acts, worship of other gods, or bloodshed, a common term is tôʿēbâ. The term is especially prominent in the Holiness Code, Deuteronomy, Proverbs, and Ezekiel, at times seemingly *without* its affective character, simply meaning "disapproved."[18] However, in contexts of impurity, it tends to retain its aversive character. For example, the sexual behaviors denounced in Lev 18 are summarized (18:24–30) as abominations (tôʿēbôt) and characterized as defiling both the people and the land, to the point that the land will vomit (qîʾ) the people out. The argument recurs in 20:22–24, this time with even more overt disgust terminology—God is said to loathe (qûṭ) people with such behavior—and juxtaposed to

---

17. See Elizabeth Goldstein, *Impurity and Gender in the Hebrew Bible* (Lanham, MD; Rowman & Littlefield, 2015), but with slightly different interpretations.

18. Kazen, *Emotions in Biblical Law*, 86–87; Paul Humbert, "Le substantif toʿēbā et le verbe tʿb dans l'Ancien Testament," ZAW 72 (1960): 217–37.

an injunction not to become detestable (*šāqaṣ*) by eating unclean animals (20:25–26).[19]

All of this serves to emphasize that emotional disgust frequently associates with impurity language, whether the issue is prohibited foods, various conditions involving genital discharges or skin ailments (pathological or not, but technically understood as unclean and possible to purify), or disapproved behaviors.[20] The point is not to claim that every use of impurity language must involve emotional disgust, but to show that disgust attends very different "types" of impurity. There has been a tendency to classify impurity into various categories, which are then easily multiplied. A basic differentiation between "ritual" and "moral" impurity has long been suggested—a differentiation frequently referred to in the form it has received through the work of Jonathan Klawans.[21] Others have suggested different categories, and some have added genealogical impurity, sin impurity, sexual pollution, gentile impurity, and the like.[22] In our human urge for categorization, we run the risk of an essentialism of sorts. We are probably seduced into endless categorization because of the one area in which purity discourse is very precisely employed and technically treated: the priestly ritual "system." This is the only purity discourse in the Bible to which a set of purification rites are attached.

So how do we understand other purity discourses? To some, the simplest solution categorizes ritual impurity as "literal" and other uses of

---

19. See Kazen, *Emotions in Biblical Law*, 87–88.

20. For the sake of space, I have not included corpse impurity or molds on houses or clothing in this brief summary.

21. Jonathan Klawans, *Impurity and Sin in Ancient Judaism* (Oxford: Oxford University Press, 2000).

22. For genealogical impurity, see, e.g., Christine E. Hayes, *Gentile Impurities and Jewish Identities: Intermarriage and Conversion from the Bible to the Talmud* (Oxford: Oxford University Press, 2002). For sin impurity, see, e.g., Mila Ginsburskaya, "The Idea of Sin-Impurity: The Dead Sea Scrolls in The Light Of Leviticus," *TynBul* 60 (2009): 309–12. For sexual pollution, see, e.g., Eve Levavi Feinstein, *Sexual Pollution in the Hebrew Bible* (Oxford: Oxford University Press, 2014). For gentile impurity, see, e.g., Hayes, *Gentile Impurities*, including her discussion of the views of Emil Schürer, Gedaliah Alon, and Adolf Büchler; Klawans, *Impurity and Sin*; Hannah K. Harrington, "Keeping Outsiders Out: Impurity at Qumran," in *Defining Identities: We, You, and the Other in the Dead Sea Scrolls*, ed. Florentino García Martínez, Peter W. Flint, and Eibert J. C. Tigchelaar, STDJ 70 (Leiden; Boston: Brill, 2008), 187–203; Mira Balberg, *Purity, Body, and Self in Early Rabbinic Literature* (Berkeley: University of California Press, 2014).

purity language as "metaphorical." To others, this distinction has proved unsatisfactory, since some usages of purity language appear difficult to classify. Deficient theories of metaphor have confused the issue further, resulting in discussions of whether "moral" or "genealogical" impurity should be taken literally or metaphorically.[23]

My view is that taxonomies of purity issues—which could theoretically be multiplied even further—are largely futile and misguided. Although we might want to continue using some of these labels for the sake of convenience, they need to be seriously questioned. I want to suggest that by carefully exploring the relationship between emotional disgust and impurity in terms of human cognition and language, we will find more satisfying explanations for the ways in which purity discourse develops and mutates in biblical texts.

4. Disgust in Body: Literal Impurity

We must, of course, beware the etymological fallacy, by which *present-day meaning* is falsely deduced from lexical history; nevertheless, terminology may reveal something about the *conceptualization* of experiences and the *evolution* of word *usage* in various contexts. Purity terminology suggests a concrete, literal understanding at the roots. The underlying meaning for Hebrew ṭāmēʾ/ṭûmʾâ is probably "dirt." The Syriac cognate verb can mean to be "soiled" or "sticky," and the corresponding Egyptian Arabic root means "silt." Later Arabic ṭamā means "be choked with mud," and ṭammay is "mud of the Nile."[24] Paschen suggests *feuchter Schmutz* ("moist dirt") as the original meaning of ṭāmēʾ.[25] Hebrew ṭāhôr/ṭohŏrâ, like its Ugaritic cognate, can mean "shining" or "radiance." This can be compared to Akkadian terms for purity (*ellu*, *ebbu*, and *namru*), which refer to being clean, clear, or bright, in contrast to being dim, tainted, or sullied.[26]

---

23. See my discussions of this problem elsewhere in Kazen, "Dirt and Disgust"; Kazen, "Role of Disgust"; Kazen, "Levels of Explanation."

24. Gunnel André, "טָמֵא," *TDOT* 5:330. See also Eve Feinstein, "Sexual Pollution in the Hebrew Bible" (PhD diss., Harvard University, 2010), 51.

25. Wilfried Paschen, *Rein und Unrein: Untersuchung zur biblischen Wortgeschichte*, SANT 24 (Munich: Kösel, 1970), 27.

26. See Karel van der Toorn, *Sin and Sanction in Israel and Mesopotamia: A Comparative Study*, SSN 22 (Assen: Van Gorcum, 1985), 27–37; van der Toorn, "Sin, Pollution, and Purity: Mesopotamia," in *Religions of the Ancient World: A Guide*, ed. Sarah Iles Johnston (Cambridge: Belknap, 2004), 499–501; Yitzhaq Feder, "The Semantics of

When this linguistic data is taken seriously, we see that much of the literal-metaphorical debate is misguided. "Ritual" impurity is taken to be literal by default due to its concrete effects, and to some, even certain "moral" issues are presumed to be more literal than metaphorical because of their "real" consequences.[27] Yet metaphor is not an ontological but a *linguistic* category. How one conceptualizes the effects of various "types" of impurity has little to do with whether or not the language is used figuratively. From a linguistic point of view, much of what is generally called "ritual" impurity reflects a metaphorical use of purity language. The contagion that ritual impurity incurs via contact has no physical substance, even in the case of contact with corpses. Skin disease impurity does manifest material signs, but the scales and rashes involved are not precisely "dirt"; rather, they represent a secondary use of impurity language.[28] Only genital fluids, with their capacity to become smeary and smelly, might earn their place as "literal" impurities, except that in the priestly legislation it is no longer the substance per se that defiles but the impure state of the discharger, regardless of the amount of fluid. Excrement constitutes the prototypical literal impurity, but although it figures as unclean in certain biblical contexts, it is conspicuously excluded from the priestly system.[29]

Thus impurity and disgust have a complex, equivocal relationship. Not everything disgusting is called impure and not everything called impure is disgusting from a biopsychological point of view. While some "disgusting" impurities lack emotional and ultimate evolutionary underpinnings, associations between disgust and impurity in biblical texts are ultimately based on experiences of visceral, bodily, emotional disgust towards literal impurities of dirt, contaminated matter, and other physical entities understood as harmful to ingest, breathe, or contact. The feeling of disgust antipathetic to "dirt" is, however, easily transposed to other experiences,

---

Purity in the Ancient Near East: Lexical Meaning as a Projection of Embodied Experience," *JANER* 14 (2014): 87–113.

27. Especially so by Klawans, *Impurity and Sin*.
28. See also Kazen, "Levels of Explanation."
29. See Deut 23:12–14; 2 Kgs 10:27; Ezek 4:12–15; Zech 3. For a discussion of the biblical evidence, see Tracy Lemos, "Where There Is Dirt Is There System? Revisiting Biblical Purity Constructions," *JSOT* 37 (2013): 285–87. For discussions of the impurity of excrement in Qumran (including comparisons with biblical and rabbinic evidence), see Hannah K. Harrington, *The Purity Texts*, CQS 5 (London: T&T Clark, 2004), 19, 64–65, 106–8; Jodi Magness, *Stone and Dung, Oil and Spit: Jewish Daily Life in the Time of Jesus* (Grand Rapids: Eerdmans, 2011), 130–44.

and with it often follows their conceptualization as "impure." This is a process that takes place in the *body*, through the *mind*, and by figurative use of *language*.

5. Disgust in Mind: Impurity as Conceptual Metaphor

What are the conceptual mechanisms that made it possible for purity issues to develop into such an overarching and influential paradigm, especially in Second Temple Judaism? How do we explain the transfer of dirt properties and disgust feelings from the literal level to other domains? I suggest that conceptual metaphor and blending theories can help us understand this process.[30] I employ these theories here in an eclectic and simplified manner. Conceptual metaphor theory in Mark Johnson and George Lakoff's popularized version contends that metaphors carry notions from one cognitive or conceptual domain to another, providing the latter with new impetus, different understanding, and change of meaning. Metaphors are cross-domain mappings from a source to a target domain that relate to the way we conceptualize and influence actions and behaviors (see fig. 1).[31]

Source Domain	Target Domain
X X X X X	X X X X X

Applied to purity discourse, such cross-domain mapping suggests that "impurity" carries notions from its source domain (dirt) to various target domains, thus influencing the ways we think about those target domains and relate to them. The most conspicuous of those notions is disgust, and hence avoidance, but others may also follow, such as washing away the

---

30. See further Kazen, "Role of Disgust."
31. This diagram is the author's own, based on the research and diagram of George Lakoff and Mark Johnson, *Metaphors We Live By* (Chicago: University of Chicago Press, 1980); Lakoff and Johnson, "Conceptual Metaphor in Everyday Language," *JPs* 77 (1980): 453–86; Lakoff and Johnson, *Philosophy in the Flesh: The Embodied Mind and Its Challenge to Western Thought* (New York: Basic Books, 1999).

(now metaphorical) "dirt." This process clearly plays out when the concept of disgusting "impurity" is mapped onto target domains of unsavory human beings, objectionable behavior, and repulsive creatures (dietary taboos). By mapping the notion of dirt onto detestable people, their state is classified as *ṭāmēʾ* (dirty) and contact with them or their fluids or scaly residues becomes a kind of defilement that can be purified by water. By mapping dirt onto objectionable behavior, certain acts are understood as impure and disgusting, in need of being "removed," whether by atonement, the *kārēt* penalty, expulsion from the land, or blood revenge.[32] By mapping dirt onto certain animal species, they are tainted with disgust and classified as unfit to eat.

This model partly explains what happens when we "think with" (or "experience with") literal dirt in other domains. But why does disgust get involved in certain domains and not in others? Why do certain dirt-related conceptualizations, such as washing, scraping, or other types of removal, emerge here but not there? Blending theory offers a somewhat different way of construing mental (and experiential) processes. It explains some of the more sophisticated mechanisms involving secondary uses of purity language in new domains, and it proves particularly helpful in cases where conceptions of impurity are expanded or used in unusual or unexpected circumstances. Blending theory focuses on conceptual spaces or frames within which images or mental representations function as a network. Rather than conceptualizing figurative expressions as one-way mapping processes, blending suggests that input spaces, which already have certain common elements (generic space), provide a blended space with other elements that are not common and do not necessarily or entirely fit together. The resulting blend is not really inherent in any of the input spaces, nor indicated by the generic space (common elements) that makes blending possible in the first place. The outcome of the process is thus in a sense "unanticipated," which is precisely why it results in new conceptual frameworks, new meanings, and new behaviors (see fig. 2).[33]

---

32. This example (mapping dirt onto objectionable behavior) partly corresponds to the "moral impurities" of the Holiness Code (Lev 17–26). Note also the provisions for unintended manslaughter (cities of refuge) and the magical/apotropaic rite of breaking a heifer's neck to "effect removal" for the people and free them from blood-guilt in case the murderer could not be found and removed by blood revenge or refuge (Num 35:9–34; Deut 19:1–13; 21:1–9). See Kazen, *Emotions in Biblical Law*, 135–37.

33. This diagram is the author's own, based on the research and diagram of Gilles

Conceptual Blending

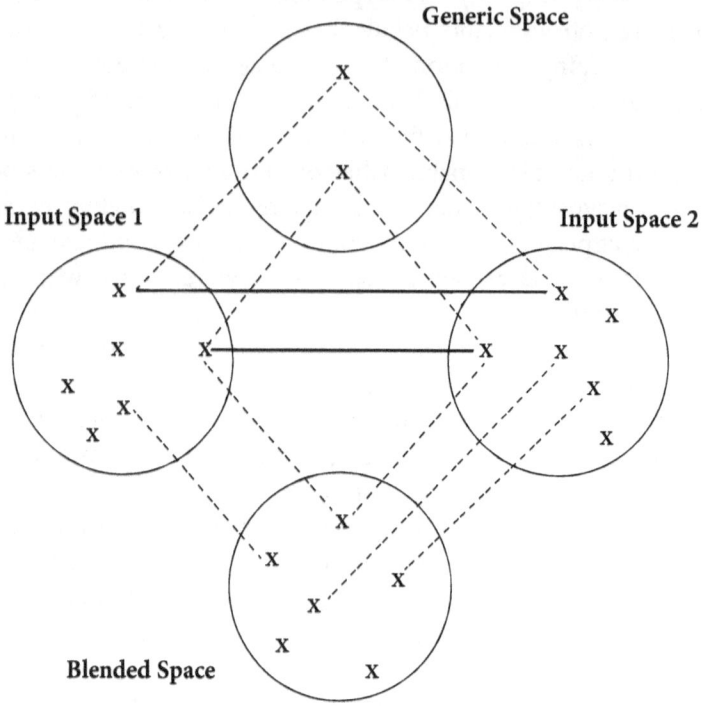

Blending theory can be effectively applied to the three domains just discussed. Contact with dirt and contact with unsavory people can be understood as two input spaces that share avoidance and aversion (disgust) but little else. These shared items, however, make possible the evolution of a blended space that conceives of such people as "impure" and their impurity as contagious ("sticky"), requiring removal by water. In a further step (see Ps 51), a blend between contact contamination, disapproved ("sinful") behavior, and dirty laundry (again sharing avoidance and aversion) envisages certain sexual behaviors as impure stains on one's inner being, necessitating "cleansing" by water and hyssop. The first blend results in "ritual" impurity being purified by literal water; in the second blend, however, the water and hyssop function as symbolic

---

Fauconnier and Mark Turner, *The Way We Think: Conceptual Blending and the Mind's Hidden Complexities* (New York: Basic Books, 2002), 17–57; Seanna Coulson and Todd Oakley, "Blending Basics," *CogL* 11 (2000): 75–96.

elements for removing evil rather than as literal components of a purification ritual. But this makes little difference to the fact that the *impurity* imagined in both cases represents a metaphorical mapping on physical dirt. This point becomes even clearer concerning the impurity of the pig (see Lev 11), which may be explained as a blending of traditional avoidances of certain meats and aversions to slimy and rotting vermin.[34] The resulting blended space becomes imbued with notions of impurity and disgust, even though pork seems no more intrinsically disgusting or dirty than any other animal flesh.[35]

While in the first two cases (unsavory people and disapproved behavior) disgust seems to belong to the generic space, which makes blending possible and sometimes even likely, it operates differently in the third example. What is shared here is avoidance: neither "swarmers" nor pigs are eaten (for whatever reasons), but the visceral disgust felt for small, creepy animals (vermin, slimy water creatures, and the like) is imported into the category of non-cud-chewing and non-cleft-footed quadrupeds. This creative blend constitutes a rhetorical move as much as a conceptual one, resulting in a kind of "disgust by association." This point leads into the next section focusing more fully on the role of language and social construction in developing conceptions of impurity and purity discourse.

6. Disgust in Language: Impurity as Rhetoric

As the grounds for viewing the pig (or camel or hare) as both impure and disgusting are scarcely obvious, the same problem applies to several other phenomena. Why, for example, are new mothers severely restricted and regarded as impure for a long time according to priestly law? Although never explicitly labeled disgusting, does their impurity evoke notions of aversion by virtue of being associated with—mapped onto the domain of—genital dischargers in general? On what grounds do the authors of the Holiness Code, Isaiah, Ezekiel, and Ezra-Nehemiah associate foreign practices and worship of other gods, implicitly or explicitly, with

---

34. Figures illustrating these and other examples of blends are found in Kazen, "Role of Disgust."

35. Although the dirty character and scavenger status of the pig is sometimes referenced, anyone who owned a he-goat will have a hard time finding reasons why one should evoke disgust but not the other.

emotional disgust?[36] There is little ultimate, biopsychological basis for visceral aversive reactions to culturally proximate religious practices and worship. How is Ezra-Nehemiah able to muster such aversive feelings against other ethnic groups (or perhaps against people of the same ethnic group as well), separated by circumstances and differing fates and experiences (see, e.g., Ezra 9-10; Neh 13)?

The conceptual processes by which such mutations take place can be profitably described and understood with the help of blending theory. The genital bleeding of a woman with pathological (long-term) discharge impurity (*zābâ*) and a new mother are similar enough to constitute grounds (generic space) for blending. Whether the ensuing blend at some point actually resulted in viewing a parturient with disgust is not, however, certain. The possibility would, in any case, lie close at hand.

Aversion to certain practices and worship rites can be interpreted as part of a general tendency to shun that which is different and "foreign." A large body of literature discusses the evolutionary basis and adaptive function of ethnocentrism and xenophobia.[37] From this starting point, a long step extends to the cultural construction of "the other" and the rhetorical creation of an ethnic and national identity, as evidenced in texts like the Holiness Code, Ezra-Nehemiah, and many prophetic writings. Although the differences between the groups are relatively minor, mechanisms of group dynamics and social-identity formation make it easy to exploit them.

My argument is that feelings of disgust, associated with experiences of impurity ("dirt"), are sufficiently grounded in human bodies and minds for human language to exploit rhetorically. Such rhetorical effects (and

---

36. E.g., Lev 12; 18; 20; 26; Isa 30; Ezek 22; 36; Ezra 9. See further the discussion in part 3 above.

37. E.g., Navarrete and Fessler, "Disease Avoidance and Ethnocentrism"; Curtis, *Don't Look*; Jason Faulkner et al., "Evolved Disease-Avoidance Mechanisms and Contemporary Xenophobic Attitudes," *GPIR* 7 (2004): 333-53; Chad Joseph McEvoy, "A Consideration of Human Xenophobia and Ethnocentrism from a Sociobiological Perspective," *HRR* 3.3 (2002): 39-49; Daniel G. Freedman, "The Infant's Fear of Strangers and the Flight Response," *JCPP* 2 (1961): 242-48; Robin I. M. Dunbar, "Sociobiological Explanations and the Evolution of Ethnocentrism," in *The Sociobiology of Ethnocentrism: Evolutionary Dimensions of Xenophobia, Discrimination, Racism, and Nationalism*, ed. Vernon Reynolds, Vincent Falger, and Ian Vine (London: Croom Helm, 1987), 48-59; Harold D. Fishbein, *Peer Prejudice and Discrimination: The Origins of Prejudice*, 2nd ed. (Mahwah, NJ: Erlbaum, 2002).

DISGUST IN BODY, MIND, AND LANGUAGE 111

affects) happen when purity discourse breaks away from its physical-literal anchoring and invades domains or blends with spaces where it has little foothold, often including disgust as a secondary emotion. To some degree, purity and disgust rhetoric always reflects general conceptual developments, so that texts express what people feel and think.[38] But these evolutionary and cultural conditions provide a ready playground, or a resonating sounding board, for exploitative and rhetorical innovations, whether fortuitous or studied, to associate emotional disgust with actions, items, or peoples through the use of impurity language.

A few examples indicated in the list of questions above may suffice to illustrate this point. Let us first look at two fairly late Isaianic texts.[39] In Isa 64:5 (Isa 64:6 in English), the anonymous prophet confesses: "Everyone of us has become like impurity [*ṭāmēʾ*], and like a menstrual cloth [*beged ʿiddîm*] all our righteous acts."[40] Although the rendering "menstrual cloth" is partly conjectural, it is a likely option.[41] The sentence is an obvious parallelism in which impurity or a thing classified as *ṭāmēʾ* is synonymous

---

38. I.e., texts express what at least *some* people feel and think. Texts are, of course, biased: most texts reflect a patriarchal bias, some have priestly bias, and all texts have been more or less processed by scribal elites. Still, socially and culturally conditioned expressions ultimately rest on general conceptual developments.

39. The lament in Isa 63:7–64:11 is usually understood to be either exilic or early postexilic; see P. A. Smith, *Rhetoric and Redaction in Trito-Isaiah: The Structure, Growth and Authorship of Isaiah 56–66*, VTSup 62 (Leiden: Brill, 1995), 44–47. For a postexilic dating, see Paul D. Hanson, *The Dawn of Apocalyptic: The Historical and Sociological Roots of Jewish Apocalyptic Eschatology*, rev. ed. (Philadelphia: Fortress, 1979), 79–100. For a date during the second half of the sixth century BCE, see Lena-Sophia Tiemeyer, "The Lament in Isaiah 63:7–64:11," in *The Book of Isaiah: Enduring Questions Answered Anew; Essays Honoring Joseph Blenkinsopp and His Contribution to the Study of Isaiah*, ed. Richart J. Bautch and J. Todd Hibbard (Grand Rapids: Eerdmans, 2014), 52–70; John Goldingay, *A Critical and Exegetical Commentary on Isaiah 56–66*, ICC (London: Bloomsbury, 2014), 382. H. G. M. Williamson remarks that Isa 30:19–26 "is nowadays widely agreed to be post-exilic" in "Idols in Isaiah in the Light of Isaiah 10:10–11," in *New Perspectives on Old Testament Prophecy and History: Essays in Honour of Hans M. Barstad*, ed. Rannfrid I. Thelle, Terje Stordalen, and Mervyn E. J. Richardson (Leiden: Brill, 2015), 24; see also Hans Wildberger, *Isaiah 28–39*, trans. Thomas H. Trapp, CC 3 (Minneapolis: Fortress, 2002), 170–72.

40. All translations are my own. See also Joseph Lam, *Patterns of Sin in the Hebrew Bible: Metaphor, Culture, and the Making of a Religious Concept* (Oxford: Oxford University Press, 2016), 194.

41. Translations like "stained clothes" are common, but imprecise. Although the exact meaning of *ʿēd* is unclear, it is used in rabbinic texts for the test rag with which

with a menstrual cloth. Human beings and their (purportedly righteous) actions are likened to dirt, impurity, and genital blood. These expressions, based on emotional revulsion against dirt and genital discharges, tell us something about cultural and contextual conceptions of menstrual blood. The blend of dirt and discharge is common enough, and the setting is not particularly legal or ritual. The rhetorical dynamics depend on an inseparable mixture of evolutionary (ultimate, emotional, visceral) conditions and culturally constructed conceptions. The resulting blend, however, evokes and invokes disgust reactions against behaviors of quite a different character. The rhetoric enlists visceral and emotional elements in the service of a value-laden and programmatic agenda: to blame the present disasters on the actions of the people.

Another late Isaianic example is found in Isa 30:22: "You will defile [*wǝtimmēʾtem*] the plating of your silver idols [or: your silver-plated idols] and the gold covering of your ephods [or: your gold-covered images]. You will throw them out like a bleeding [woman] [*dāwâ*]. 'Get out!' you will say to it/him." Certain translation issues complicate the interpretation of this passage. Concerning the referent in the last suffix (*lô*), it cannot refer to the *dāwâ* as such, but rather to that which is thrown out and for which the *dāwâ* serves as a simile. For the sentence to be grammatically correct, this can refer either to the first masculine noun in the phrase, plating (*ṣippû*), or possibly to the silver (*kesep*) and gold (*zāhāb*), respectively, that cover the idols. In any case, the ultimate reference must be to the *idols*, comparing the defilement (in the sense of desecration) of silver and gold images to a menstruating woman. But again, to what precisely does this comparison refer? One suggestion envisions the people disposing their idols in the same manner as a woman disposes her menstrual *cloth*.[42] However, I consider this an overinterpretation, especially as the cloth is not in the text, but must be supplied.[43] More probably, the passage likens the disparaging, expulsive treatment of former idols (throwing them out) with the disparaging treatment of a menstruating woman expected by the text's male recipients: "Get out of here!" Once more we sense a combination of ultimate-emotional and proximate-cultural reactions against dirty,

---

Jewish women checked for signs of menstruation. See further Lam, *Patterns of Sin*, 194-95.

42. Lam, *Patterns of Sin*, 197-98.

43. Also, rags were likely to have been washed and reused, even as cloth diapers are in modern times.

sticky, or smelly substances in general, and genital discharge in particular, rhetorically exploited for religious propaganda against unacceptable types of worship.

Ezekiel 36 affords a similar rhetorical use of impurity language. Here Israel is accused of having defiled (*wayṭamməʾû*) the land by their ways and deeds, like the impurity of menstruation (*kəṭumʾat hanniddâ*). The defiling ways and deeds are identified as bloodshed and idol worship (Ezek 36:17-18). For this reason, God scattered Israel among the nations, but since they profaned his name there, he will now gather them from these countries in order to defend his honor (name). The logic of this argument may be faltering, but the argument continues: "I will sprinkle pure waters on you and you will be pure from all your impurities [*ṭumʾôtêkem*] and from all your idols I will purify you" (36:25). Further: "I will rescue you from all your impurities [*ṭumʾôtêkem*]" (36:29). When this salvation happens, the Israelites will remember their former evil deeds and loathe (*nəqōṭōtem*) themselves because of their sins and abominations (*tôʿăbôtêkem*) (36:31).

Here we observe the full register of disgust and impurity language at work. The imagery is partly inconsistent, but the author's ultimate purpose is evocative and rhetorical, not declarative and logical. Feelings of disgust, based on various causes ranging from evolutionary adaptive avoidances of dirt and pathogens to patriarchal aversions to female blood, blend with notions of murder and misguided divine worship. The rhetoric produces an implicit value statement of unequaled strength: the people need cleansing from their disgusting state. The fact that the defiled land recedes into the background does not seem to trouble the author and probably did not trouble the recipients either. The intended effect is that they feel disgust for themselves because of their (or their ancestors') past behavior, which makes purification necessary. As the purity metaphors evoke: God will sprinkle them with pure water to purify them from the idols (36:25). These rhetorical effects depend on the previous blend of idol worship with impurity and disgust and thus should not be taken literally, just as the next verse's language about replacing the heart of stone with a heart of flesh is obviously figurative (36:26).

Our last example comes from Ezra 9:11. An overly literal interpretation reads: "The land you are coming to possess is a *niddâ* land by the *niddâ* of the people of the land by their abominations [*tôʿēbôt*] by which they have filled it from mouth to mouth by their impurities [*ṭumʾātām*]." It is a moot point to what extent *niddâ* retains its visceral character and reference to genital bleeding.[44] It is not used as a simile but rather seems to designate impurity in a strong sense. In any case, it complements and reinforces two very general terms for impurity (*ṭumʾâ*) and disgust (*tôʿēbâ*). The Ezra author exploits *niddâ* in order to evoke strong emotional disgust towards groups of people designated by "the people of the land," from which the audience must separate themselves, and towards their practices, stereotyped as "abominations" and "impurities." Again, rhetorical use builds on underlying metaphorical and literal levels. Disgust is evoked by language, through the mind, in the body.

7. Conclusion

In this essay I have tried to demonstrate the multileveled character of disgust, ranging from visceral emotional *body* reactions towards physical substances, animals, and human beings that evoke aversive feelings because of their characteristics, through various types of metaphorical conceptualizations in the *mind*, to conscious rhetorical *language* strategies for influencing moral values, behaviors, and actions against disapproved individuals or groups. This essay has focused on the case study of the concept of purity/impurity in biblical literature, which interacts and intersects with emotional disgust at all levels, albeit in various ways and degrees.

We have found that the rhetorical effects and uses of the disgust-impurity paradigm rest on a diversified metaphorical framework, which can be profitably interpreted with the help of conceptual metaphor and blending theories. We have also found that at all levels rhetorical and/or metaphorical expressions of disgust in relation to various types of impurity build on and presuppose visceral core disgust reactions as their emotional underpinnings. Although disgust and impurity language may occasionally become fairly conventionalized, it always presupposes aversive feelings as an underlying and innate capacity. Biblical textual expressions of disgust rest on and receive their power from an inseparable blend of ultimate and proximate emotional triggers: reactions due to evolutionary adaptation and to contextual cultural construction.

---

44. For various views on the use of *niddâ* in this text and others, such as Zech 13:1 and those discussed above, see, e.g., Hyam Maccoby, *Ritual and Morality: The Ritual Purity System and Its Place in Judaism* (Cambridge: Cambridge University Press, 1999); Goldstein, *Impurity and Gender*; Tarja Philip, *Menstruation and Childbirth in the Bible: Fertility and Impurity*, StBibLit 88 (New York: Lang, 2006), 19–42.

Select Bibliography

Curtis, Valerie. *Don't Look, Don't Touch, Don't Eat: The Science behind Revulsion*. Chicago: University of Chicago Press, 2013.
Damasio, Antonio R. *Descartes' Error: Emotion, Reason, and the Human Brain*. New York: Putnam, 1994.
Darwin, Charles. *The Expression of the Emotions in Man and Animals*. WCD 23. London: Murray, 1872. Repr., New York: New York University Press, 1989.
Fauconnier, Gilles, and Mark Turner. *The Way We Think: Conceptual Blending and the Mind's Hidden Complexities*. New York: Basic Books, 2002.
Kazen, Thomas. *Emotions in Biblical Law: A Cognitive Science Approach*. HBM 36. Sheffield: Sheffield Phoenix, 2011.
———. "The Role of Disgust in Priestly Purity Law: Insights from Conceptual Metaphor and Blending Theories." *JLRS* 3 (2014): 62–92.
Klawans, Jonathan. *Impurity and Sin in Ancient Judaism*. Oxford: Oxford University Press, 2000.
Lakoff, George, and Mark Johnson. *Metaphors We Live By*. Chicago: University of Chicago Press, 1980.
Lam, Joseph. *Patterns of Sin in the Hebrew Bible: Metaphor, Culture, and the Making of a Religious Concept*. Oxford: Oxford University Press, 2016.
Lemos, Tracy. "Where There Is Dirt Is There System? Revisiting Biblical Purity Constructions." *JSOT* 37 (2013): 265–94.
Miller, William Ian. *The Anatomy of Disgust*. Cambridge: Harvard University Press, 1997.
Navarrete, Carlos David, and Daniel M. T. Fessler. "Disease Avoidance and Ethnocentrism: The Effects of Disease Vulnerability and Disgust Sensitivity on Intergroup Attitudes." *EHB* 27 (2006): 270–82.
Nussbaum, Martha C. *Hiding from Humanity: Disgust, Shame, and the Law*. Princeton: Princeton University Press, 2004.
Rozin, Paul, Jonathan Haidt, and Clark McCauley. "Disgust." Pages 637–53 in *Handbook of Emotions*. Edited by Michael Lewis and Jeanette M. Haviland-Jones. 2nd ed. New York: Guilford, 2000.

Understanding Grief and Reading the Bible

David A. Bosworth

I first began to research scientific studies on grief when I wanted to understand David's strange behavior surrounding the sickness and death of Bathsheba's firstborn (2 Sam 12). I quickly learned that in order to understand grief one has to understand attachment theory (see below). I also discovered that much of what passes for "common wisdom" about grief in the United States is wrong.

Although Elizabeth Kübler-Ross's five stages have become an extraordinarily popular model of grief, this model has not held up well under empirical research. She developed these stages in her personal experience of how dying people faced their own deaths, not through research on how bereaved people coped with the loss of others.[1] Mourners and those around them consequently harbor expectations about the grief process that do not mimic reality well and can lead the bereaved and those around them to wonder whether there is something wrong with them when their experience does not fit expectations. Similarly, the idea that emotions flow like fluids and, if stopped, build up pressure that explodes in mental illness does not reflect reality. For example, catharsis (the idea that one must express emotional memories to alleviate emotional weight) is not real. Well-intentioned but misinformed supporters of the bereaved may seek to force them to confront their hidden sadness and grieve "appropriately"

---

1. Elizabeth Kübler-Ross, *On Death and Dying* (New York: Macmillan, 1969). She did think that the stages applied equally to the dying and the bereaved, although evidence has not borne this out. See Ruth David Konigsberg, *The Truth about Grief: The Myth of the Five Stages and the New Science of Loss* (New York: Simon & Schuster, 2011); George A. Bonanno, *The Other Side of Sadness: What the New Science of Bereavement Tells Us about Life after Loss* (New York: Basic Books, 2009).

while in fact creating social pressures that cause bereaved people to feel rejected and isolated.[2]

Grief looks different in different people, and people cope with grief in many ways. Some coping strategies prove better than others: locating supportive people is preferable to abusing drugs and alcohol. Although individual behavior varies considerably, researchers have observed four grief trajectories: resilience, recovery, prolonged grief, and delayed grief.[3]

- ▶ Resilience involves little or no loss of function in work, relationships, and practical tasks of living.
- ▶ Recovery involves some loss of function for a period of time followed by a gradual recovery.
- ▶ Prolonged grief involves extended loss of function and lack of recovery.
- ▶ Delayed grief involves little or no loss of function initially, but symptoms of grief arise later (and then follow a prolonged or recovery trajectory).

The first two trajectories are common; the other two relatively rare. Contrary to expectations about catharsis, people who manifest few grief symptoms soon after loss are unlikely to develop symptoms later. Rather, resilience is more common than previously believed. People experiencing a resilient grief trajectory may be harassed for their apparent lack of sadness and accused of being cold and callous, caring little for the deceased, or avoiding their feelings of sadness and risking further complications because of their "unresolved feelings." Those experiencing prolonged grief may be stigmatized as weak and told to "get over it" because their sorrow makes others uncomfortable. These four trajectories do not neatly

---

2. Bonanno, *Other Side of Sadness*, esp. 45–65. Although avoidant coping strategies can be effective, they may collapse under the weight of significant stress. Thus there is some truth to this myth, but pressuring the avoidant to face personal pain may not be kind or therapeutic, and some people cope with loss rather well without obvious signs of grief or long-term difficulties.

3. George A. Bonanno, "Loss, Trauma, and Human Resilience: Have We Underestimated the Human Capacity to Thrive after Extremely Adverse Events?," *AP* 59 (2004): 20–28; George A. Bonanno, Kathrin Boerner, and Camille B. Wortman, "Trajectories of Grieving," in *Handbook of Bereavement Research and Practice: Advances in Theory and Intervention*, ed. Margaret Stroebe et al. (Washington, DC: American Psychological Association, 2008), 287–307; Bonanno, *Other Side of Sadness*, 59–60.

correspond to types of people. A person may experience resilience following one loss and prolonged grief or recovery following another. Many variables affect an individual's experience of grief, including the nature and quality of the relationship with the deceased, the manner of death, and cultural beliefs about death.

Already this summary of scientific studies of grief supplies a useful framework for analyzing biblical material by stripping away misconceptions. Consider the curious behavior of David around the sickness and death of Bathsheba's firstborn that sparked my own entry into grief and bereavement studies.[4] Modern scholars have often read David as a cold, heartless man because he immediately resumes his normal life after hearing of the baby's death. His seeming unconcern is all the more striking because of his weeklong petition to God to save the infant's life. His own servants ask David "What have you done?" with a decidedly judgmental overtone (Gen 4:10; 12:18; 20:9; 26:10; Judg 15:11; 1 Sam 13:11) reflecting the negative evaluation shared by many modern readers. While one *may* read David as cold hearted, the recognition of resilience opens up another possibility: David may experience a resilient grief trajectory that does not reflect monstrous callousness or unconcern for his baby. Consequently, this story may not be the best resource for comforting bereaved parents who do not experience a resilient trajectory following the death of their child. A mother and father may resemble Bathsheba's recovery trajectory or, like Bathsheba and David, may react differently their child's loss. In short, David need not be judged so harshly by scholars or presented as a normative model to bereaved parents. The description of David's behavior seems to be used in the Bible to characterize David, not to tell other parents how to mourn.[5]

---

4. David A. Bosworth, "Faith and Resilience: King David's Reaction to the Death of Bathsheba's Firstborn," *CBQ* 73 (2010): 691–707; "'David Comforted Bathsheba' (2 Sam 12:24): Gender and Parental Bereavement," in *Seitenblicke: Literarische und historische Studien zu Nebenfiguren im zweiten Samuelbuch*, ed. Walter Dietrich, OBO 249 (Göttingen: Vandenhoeck & Ruprecht, 2011), 238–55.

5. David is upheld as a model of grief and acceptance in various sources, most significantly Harold Kushner, *Why Bad Things Happen to Good People* (New York: Schocken, 1981), and Harriett Sarnof Schiff, *The Bereaved Parent* (New York: Penguin, 1977).

1. Weird Science

Biblical scholars sometimes object that studies on modern people cannot be applied to ancient people. This same objection may be raised any time a modern person reads an ancient text no matter what methods are used, but humanities scholars especially react to scientifically-grounded approaches with this criticism. The sciences hold considerable social power in many quarters, and scientific authority may go unquestioned or its methods and findings go uncritically accepted. Although such "scientism" should be rejected, science cannot be ignored. The philosopher Martha C. Nussbaum understands that she cannot provide a credible account of emotions without engaging relevant scientific research.[6] In the same way, biblical interpreters interested in emotions in the Bible cannot ignore the extensive and growing scientific research on emotions. But a scientifically literate account should seek to grasp both the insights and limitations of emotion research.

One limitation drew considerable attention following the publication of "The Weirdest People in the World?" by a team of psychologists.[7] The article appeared with multiple peer evaluations and the authors' response. The authors argue that the field of psychology suffers from a major selection bias: published studies rely too heavily on US college students because they are a convenient population for psychology professors to test. They demonstrate that these students score differently on multiple psychological measures compared to most other populations and therefore do not constitute a representative sample of human beings. They derive a rhetorically effective description of this population as WEIRD: Western, Educated, Industrialized, Rich, and Democratic. Although this acronym may not fully characterize the peculiar qualities of this population, it makes the point.[8] Accordingly, the writers of this article call for more cross-cultural

---

6. Martha C. Nussbaum, *Upheavals of Thought: The Intelligence of Emotions* (Cambridge: Cambridge University Press, 2001).

7. Joseph Heinrich, Steven J. Heine, and Ara Norenzayan, "The Weirdest People in the World?," *BBS* 33 (2010): 61–135.

8. The weirdness of this population might be better captured with other descriptors. For example, Western cultures generally are "individualist," meaning that Westerners tend to think of themselves as autonomous agents with their own goals. By contrast, almost all other cultures studied are "collectivist," meaning they tend to think of themselves as embedded in social networks and relationships. Consequently, I often mistakenly think that the "I" in WEIRD stands for "individualist."

research involving non-WEIRD populations to mitigate this selection bias. This concern about the limited applicability of modern psychological study raises questions about using psychology to interpret ancient texts.

The article describing this weirdness depends on a robust, decades-long tradition of cross-cultural research.[9] The importance of cross-cultural study is not a recent realization, and some universities (including my own) intentionally incorporate cross-cultural work in their training of research and clinical psychologists. This important research tradition remains underdeveloped because it is often logistically difficult and expensive, and granting agencies and other stakeholders desire efficiency. The field of evolutionary psychology has heightened the motivation for researchers to engage in cross-cultural research because it seeks to disentangle evolved behaviors within the web of cultural diversity. In sum, someone seeking to apply modern psychological research to ancient texts needs to be aware of the selection bias in the relevant research and seek cross-cultural evidence to discern whether a given insight is limited to a specific culture or has wider applicability. For example, while people weep over the death of a loved one across all cultures, mourning rituals vary considerably.[10] The cultural selection bias in many psychological studies does not render psychological research useless for biblical interpretation.

There are forms of selection bias other than WEIRD. For example, much psychological research on grief focused on clinical populations or people who sought professional help for coping with bereavement. The resilient grief trajectory was underappreciated until prospective longitudinal studies revealed more about it. Instead of asking bereaved people about their fallible recollections of their grief process (retrospective study), a prospective study follows a group over time (longitudinal) to see how they respond to bereavement when/if it occurs. By this method, researchers learned that many bereaved people do not seek therapy, and resilience

---

9. For example, four volumes of Harry C. Triandis, ed., *Handbook of Cross-Cultural Psychology*, 6 vols. (Boston: Allyn & Bacon, 1980–1981) summarized extensive research conducted over preceding decades. A second edition was published in 1997. More recently, see Jaan Valsiner, ed., *The Oxford Handbook of Psychology and Culture* (Oxford: Oxford University Press, 2012); Joan Y. Chiao et al., eds., *The Oxford Handbook of Cultural Neuroscience* (Oxford: Oxford University Press, 2016).

10. Tom Lutz, *Crying: The Natural and Cultural History of Tears* (New York: Norton, 1999), 195.

is more common than previously believed.¹¹ This insight has held up in cross-cultural research, and biblical texts seem to reflect trajectories of resilience (David), recovery (Judah in Gen 38:12), and prolonged grief (Jacob in Gen 37:35).

Psychologists and other social scientists have many opportunities to make serious methodological errors in their research, and selection bias is just one example. These sciences are presently in the grip of a "replicability crisis" grappling with the widespread practice of poor research methods.¹² These poor methods have been driven in part by publication bias, or the preference of journal editors and reviewers to publish positive results (a statistically significant correlation between two variables) over negative results (lack of correlation), even though both advance knowledge. Furthermore, journal editors do not like to publish replications of previous findings. These problems do not render scientific findings useless, but they do require caution on the part of those using scientific work for biblical interpretation. It is helpful to recall that a single study is just a single study, and almost no study is as important as science journalists make it out to be. Published metastudies can be extremely helpful because they are critical evaluations of a large number of studies. Sometimes the few high-quality studies reviewed offer results that differ from a much larger number of lower-quality studies.¹³ Several recent works provide helpful guidance about how to read scientific articles and evaluate their methodology.¹⁴ As for popular science writing accessible to lay audiences, it is advisable to consult works written by active researchers in the field

---

11. George A. Bonanno, "Resilience to Loss and Chronic Grief," *JPSP* 83 (2002): 1150–64; Bonanno, *Other Side of Sadness*, 64–94.

12. Brian A. Nosek et al., "Estimating the Reproducibility of Psychological Science," *Science* 349 (2015): 4716. Christopher D. Green focused on the issue of replication and poor research design without noting the WEIRD selection bias ("The Flaw at the Heart of Psychological Research," *CHE*, 26 June 2016, https://tinyurl.com/SBL0396h). Cross-cultural studies are worthless if poorly designed.

13. See Richard P. Sloan, *Blind Faith: The Unholy Alliance of Religion and Medicine* (New York: St. Martin's Griffin, 2008), which describes how a few good studies undercut the connection between religiosity and health claimed by more poorly designed projects.

14. For a detailed yet accessible discussion of research methods, see R. Parker Bausell, *The Design and Conduct of Meaningful Experiments Involving Human Participants: Twenty-Five Scientific Principles* (Oxford: Oxford University Press, 2015). Bausell, *Snake Oil Science: The Truth about Complementary and Alternative Medicine*

(though some science journalists do excellent work) who cite extensive notes and bibliography and steer away from sensational claims.

All biblical interpretation necessarily employs a psychology or theory of mind. There is nothing to be gained by forming psychological theories in ignorance and then applying them to the texts. For example, too many scholars have drawn on Sigmund Freud's psychoanalytic writings to elucidate texts, while demonstrating ignorance of post-Freudian developments, including serious discrediting of Freud's legacy.[15] More often, scholars assume a psychology that they have not made explicit even to themselves. This "naïve" approach is almost always preferable to relying on Freud, but it is possible to do better. If we want to read the Bible at all, then we inevitably bring a psychology with us. We do well to examine our assumptions, and one way to do that is to read (critically) literature from disciplines that have credible insight into the human mind.

2. Attachment Theory

Attachment theory is one of the great achievements of modern psychology, and I have invested considerable time and energy into learning about it and applying it to ancient texts.[16] I have three primary reasons for this investment. First, attachment theory describes the relationships that infants and children forge with their caretakers and therefore involves the reciprocal bonds that caregivers form with children. Since becoming a parent, research on the parent-child relationship has resonated with me as both a son and a father. Second, attachment theory arises in almost every context involving emotion and relationship because the first relationships children experience shape their emotional and relational lives within and beyond romantic partnerships (I am also a husband, friend, colleague,

---

(Oxford: Oxford University Press, 2007) is even more accessible, but limited to medical research methods and alternative treatments.

15. Freud's legacy has been intensely debated. For an overview, see Morton Hunt, *The Story of Psychology*, rev. ed. (New York: Anchor, 2007), 225–32.

16. Attachment theory underlies my project on weeping. See David A. Bosworth, *Infant Weeping in Akkadian, Hebrew, and Greek Literature* (Winona Lake, IN: Eisenbrauns, 2016); Bosworth, "The Tears of God in the Book of Jeremiah," *Bib* 94 (2013): 25–46; Bosworth, "Weeping in the Psalms," *VT* 62 (2013): 36–46; Bosworth, "Weeping in Recognition Scenes in Genesis and The Odyssey," *CBQ* 77 (2015): 219–39. Attachment theory has also shaped my understanding of prayer: Bosworth, "Ancient Prayers and the Psychology of Religion: Deities as Parental Figures," *JBL* 134 (2015): 681–700.

etc.). For these two reasons, this field has enormous intrinsic interest and wide application. Third, attachment theory is well grounded in decades of research across many cultures.[17] It is integrated into evolutionary theory, offering insights that span species as well as cultures, and its underlying neurology is becoming increasingly clear.[18] Therefore, I have a high degree of confidence that attachment theory is not going to collapse in a replication crisis or turn out to be a "weird" Western phenomenon.[19]

Attachment theory originated with research on children whose mental health issues appeared to be related to early experiences of loss, separation, or family dysfunction.[20] These investigations combined with insights from other fields led to the realization that babies engage in "attachment behaviors" like crying, grasping, and following (when they can crawl) that, after about six months of age, are preferentially directed to known

---

17. Mary D. Ainsworth's pioneering work began in Uganda, where the foundations were laid for subsequent studies on Western populations (a reversal of the usual direction of influence). See Ainsworth, *Infancy in Uganda: Infant Care and the Growth of Love* (Baltimore: Johns Hopkins University Press, 1967); Ainsworth et al., *Patterns of Attachment: A Psychological Study of the Strange Situation* (Hillsdale, NJ: Erlbaum, 1978). See also Klaus E. Grossmann, Karin Grossmann, and Anika Keppler, "Universal and Cultural-Specific Aspects of Human Behavior: The Case of Attachment," in *Culture and Human Development: The Importance of Cross-Cultural Research for the Social Sciences*, ed. Wolfgang Friedlmeier, Pradeep Chakkarath, and Beate Schwarz (New York: Psychology Press, 2005), 75–97; Judi Mesman, Marinus H. van Ijzendoorn, and Abraham Sagi-Schwartz, "Cross-Cultural Patterns of Attachment: Universal and Contextual Dimensions," in *Handbook of Attachment: Theory, Research, and Clinical Applications*, ed. Jude Cassidy and Phillip R. Shaver, 3rd ed. (New York: Guilford, 2016), 852–77.

18. See several articles in Cassidy and Shaver, *Handbook of Attachment*. For example: Jeffry A. Simpson and Jay Belsky, "Attachment Theory within a Modern Evolutionary Framework," 91–116; Inge Bretherton and Kristine A. Munholland, "Internal Working Model Construct in Light of Contemporary Neuroimaging Research," 63–90; Amie A. Hane and Nathan A. Fox, "Studying the Biology of Human Attachment," 223–41; James A. Coan, "Toward a Neuroscience of Attachment," 224–71.

19. However, attachment theory is subject to misunderstanding and popularizing fads, such as some attachment-based therapies and "attachment parenting," inspired by attachment theory but sometimes drawing conclusions well beyond the evidence and provoking unnecessary and harmful anxiety in parents.

20. If you only read one book about attachment theory, read Robert Karen, *Becoming Attached: First Relationships and How They Shape Our Capacity to Love* (Oxford: Oxford University Press, 1998). He describes attachment theory in the course of narrating its origins and development in an engaging style.

caregivers and elicit care from these calming and protective "attachment figures" (usually parents). Even older children seek to maintain proximity to their attachment figures and turn to them as a "safe haven" when they experience distress (e.g., physical pain, hunger, appearance of a stranger). Children learn to regulate their emotional states with attachment figures and, once the attachment behavior has "switched off," they use the caregiver as a "secure base" from which to explore the world. A child that does not feel safe cannot engage in nonattachment behaviors that facilitate learning activities like exploring the environment and engaging in social relations. Persistent patterns of unalleviated distress in childhood may lead to serious problems later in life.

Children form "internal working models" based on their experiences with attachment figures. These models, developed from experience, represent the self and others and help the child predict how interactions will unfold and regulate their behavior accordingly. Ideally, they develop "secure attachments" to their caregivers and form a model of the self as loved and lovable and of others as generally reliable and trustworthy. However, if they experience substandard care or suffer the loss of attachment figures or separation from them, they may develop "insecure attachments" manifesting as "anxious" or "avoidant." Anxiously attached children intensify their attachment behaviors in desperate efforts to elicit the care they need from unresponsive or rejecting caregivers. Avoidantly attached children reduce their attachment behaviors in attempts to become self-sufficient and deny the importance of their attachment needs unmet by unresponsive or rejecting caregivers.[21] Although only about 30 percent of Western adults are insecurely attached, they constitute 75 percent of people seeking professional psychological services.[22] This statistic is one way of representing the ongoing influence of childhood attachment relationships over the life span. The internal working models of attachment relationships become ingrained as personality traits that influence future relationships. Indeed, it seems all relationships are subject to some influence from early bonds. The avoidantly attached child, for example, typically grows up to be

---

21. The category of "disorganized attachment" identifies children who manifest no organized system of attachment behaviors, but mix them randomly or engage in odd behaviors. These children have often suffered serious abuse.

22. Marian J. Bakermans-Kraneburg and Marinus H. van IJzendoorn, "The First Ten Thousand Adult Attachment Interviews: Distribution of Adult Attachment Representations in Clinical and Non-Clinical Groups," *AHD* 11 (2009): 223–63, esp. 230.

an adult who experiences discomfort with physical contact and intimacy, seeks emotional distance, and focuses on his or her own comfort to the neglect of others' feelings and interests. However, infancy is not destiny. As we age, early experiences become more remote and their influence wanes amid new and challenging experiences. Early relationships forever influence, but do not determine, our subsequent relationship patterns.

Another way to understand the impact of childhood attachment relationships on adult life lies in emotion regulation. As noted above, children learn to regulate their emotion in connection with their attachment figures. For example, caregivers calm babies with lullabies or arouse them with play. Emotion regulation does not only entail effortful control, as when people seek to hold back their tears, but also subconscious shaping of emotion. Researchers generally agree that the attachment system is, at its core, an emotion regulation system. Our relational life and emotional life are indistinguishable. Emotional regulation in children involves a social process engaging other people, but regulation models sometimes avoid acknowledging that adults similarly use interpersonal methods and strategies.[23] In the absence of relationship partners, adults and children can invoke their internal working models of them and engage in relational coregulation with these represented others, including God.[24] Since emotional regulation is really coregulation, attachment patterns shape emotional life.

3. Grief

Attachment theory explains that humans evolved to seek to be close to their attachment figures. The grief reactions that infants show in response to the loss of an attachment figure resemble the responses of adults to the loss of close relationship partners. Indeed, grief is more than bereavement; it encompasses a range of losses and trauma. Grief responses may occur in connection to any serious threat to a valued relationship (both the seriousness of the threat and the importance of the relationship are determined

---

23. Bernard Rimé, "Emotion Elicits the Social Sharing of Emotion: Theory and Empirical Review," *EmotRev* 1 (2009): 60–85. Rimé and others have developed a rich research tradition around the social sharing of emotions.

24. Shane Sharp, "How Does Prayer Help Manage Emotions?," *SPQ* 73 (2010): 417–37; Lee A. Kirkpatrick, *Attachment, Evolution, and the Psychology of Religion* (New York: Guilford, 2005).

in the culturally-embedded mind of the person who appraises them). For example, one may weep at the death of a spouse or at the spouse's threat of divorce. Furthermore, people may form close bonds with objects or goals that, if denied or threatened, may evoke grief reactions. Like others, I was previously skeptical of Saul Olyan's combination of mourning and petition, but now see that both are forms of grief.[25] One may grieve the loss of things one never had, but hoped, prayed, and worked to have. Thus, attachment theory helped me make sense of Olyan's findings.

Attachment theorists observed the reactions of infants and young children to separation from parents later found that these patterns also hold for adults. Grieving behaviors can be organized into "stages," although there is no fixed sequence. The behaviors described sometimes manifest in the biblical text.

Numbing. This initial reaction, although potentially present in children separated from an attachment figure, is more obvious in adults who have lost a loved one.[26] It refers to the shock and disbelief that many people experience upon first learning of a loved one's death. The detailed narrative setting up David's hearing about Absalom's death features David's expectation of good news (2 Sam 18:19–32), which then rudely gives way to horror over the shocking news of his son's demise (2 Sam 19:1; cf. Gen 44:30–31; 1 Sam 4:12–22; 1 Kgs 21:27).

Protest. Infants and small children strongly protest the absence of an attachment figure and vigorously seek to regain proximity.[27] This may involve screaming, crying, and frantic searching behavior. Recall seeing (or being) the small child separated from its parent in a grocery store. The child typically experiences overwhelming anxiety and panic in its sense of separation and isolation, often called "separation anxiety." In many psalms, the speaker seeks God, and the text reflects this desire for proximity. In these cases, the speaker reacts to the apparent loss of God (Pss 13:2–5; 22:2–3; 42:2–4) and may engage in seeking (77:6) and crying out (5:2–3; 18:7; 39:13; 120:1). As babies, Moses and Ishmael cry when abandoned

---

25. Saul Olyan, *Biblical Mourning: Ritual and Social Dimensions* (Oxford: Oxford University Press, 2004), esp. 19–27. See Simon B. Parker, review of *Biblical Mourning: Ritual and Social Dimensions*, by Saul M. Olyan, *JAOS* 125 (2005): 478–79; and Bosworth, "Faith and Resilience," 694 n. 10.

26. Phillip R. Shaver and R. Chris Fraley, "Attachment, Loss, and Grief: Bowlby's Views and Contemporary Views," in Cassidy and Shaver, *Handbook of Attachment*, 43.

27. Shaver and Fraley, "Attachment, Loss, and Grief," 41–42.

(Gen 21:17; Exod 2:6).[28] Saul, abandoned by God, escalates his attachment behavior (seeking) and finally resorts to illicit means (1 Sam 28:4–11). Job also frequently voices his desire to find God.

Despair. This response is characterized by sadness, depression, and hopelessness, manifest as mental and physiological disorganization.[29] Infants in despair stop crying and may quietly whimper, making no active effort to engage the environment. This deep mourning is sometimes mistaken for "self-soothing" and misinterpreted as a positive development. Adults may similarly sink into depression and dysregulation and, in prolonged grief trajectories, become stuck in ruminating on their pain and loss. Jacob provides a famous example of a bereaved father who refuses to be comforted (Gen 37:33–35; 44:27–31), and the figure of Rachel is likewise inconsolable (Jer 31:15). The speaker in Ps 77:2 refuses comfort, and Job famously gives voice to anger and despair that may be better understood through an attachment perspective rather than the much-discussed legal metaphor.

Detachment/Reorganization. In detachment, the infant defensively suppresses emotion in an effort to cope with separation or loss of the attachment figure. Since adults can verbally express their distress and cognitively cope with loss, and often do not want defensively to detach from their lost loves, this stage in adult grief is often called "reorganization" to indicate the mourner's revision of internal working models both to accommodate the loss and to perpetuate a relationship with the deceased.[30] For example, mourners commonly talk to their deceased loved ones. These continuing bonds find expression in multiple cultures that communicate with the dead through funerary offerings and other means.[31] David finds comfort in the prospect of seeing his dead son in Sheol (2 Sam 12:23).

The above responses do not neatly map into sequential stages of grief, but there is some evidence of development over time.[32] Bereaved people may oscillate among responses over both short and long time frames, as

---

28. Bosworth, *Infant Weeping*, 67–92.
29. Shaver and Fraley, "Attachment, Loss, and Grief," 42.
30. Shaver and Fraley, "Attachment, Loss, and Grief," 42–43, 55–57. Mourners vary between seeking defensive detachment from the deceased and preferring to readjust internal working models to maintain fellowship amid the post-loss reality.
31. Brian Schmidt, *Israel's Beneficent Dead: Ancestor Cult and Necromancy in Ancient Israelite Religion and Tradition* (Winona Lake, IN: Eisenbrauns, 1996).
32. Shaver and Fraley, "Attachment, Loss, and Grief," 46–47.

the grieving process prompts new working models and integrations of the new reality. One model understands this process as an alternation between a "loss orientation" that triggers a hyperactive attachment system (including yearning and ruminating) and a "restoration orientation" that defensively suppresses the attachment system to allow for distraction from grief and engagement in necessary tasks and new experiences and relationships.[33] Biblical scholars may recognize that this model correlates with Walter Brueggemann's categorization of Psalms as expressing "orientation," "disorientation," or "new orientation."[34] The latter two correspond with the loss and restoration orientations of this model of grief. The first corresponds to the state that precedes the experience of loss and subsequent grief.

4. Case Study: Lamentations 1–2

Grief is the dominant emotion in Lamentations and the personified figure of Zion significantly heightens the emotional power of the poetry. The text draws on the strong emotions of the parent-child bond and other emotionally intense relationships (e.g., romance) to induce powerful reactions in the audience. As we will see, the book represents social sharing of emotions within its text and induces sharing in its reception history. It thereby offers comfort to the bereaved and traumatized, reinforces communal bonds, and contributes to the construction of social memory. It accomplishes these ends through the emotional dynamics briefly described above. I have elsewhere discussed the emotion of personified Zion but without describing how attachment theory informed my work.[35] I will summarize aspects of my prior work, expand on it, and indicate the role of theoretical considerations in shaping interpretation.

The personification of Zion is one of the most striking and emotionally effective elements of Lam 1–2.[36] The human qualities that establish her per-

---

33. Margaret Stroebe and Henk Schut, "The Dual Process Model of Coping with Bereavement: Rational and Description," *DS* 23 (1999): 197–224.

34. Walter Brueggemann, *The Message of the Psalms: A Theological Commentary*, AOTS (Minneapolis: Augsburg, 1984).

35. David A. Bosworth, "Daughter Zion and Weeping in Lamentations 1–2," *JSOT* 38 (2013): 217–37.

36. Bosworth, "Daughter Zion," 119–23; Knut M. Heim, "The Personification of Jerusalem and the Drama of Her Bereavement in Lamentations," in *Zion, City of Our*

sonification focus specifically on her grief. Her human-like relationships with others (friends, lovers, and enemies in 1:2), her emotional expressiveness (speaking in 1:9b, 11b–22; groaning in 1:22), and body parts (cheeks in 1:2; heart in 1:20, 22) occur in connection with her suffering. Relational language clarifies Zion's connection to the community of people she represents: she is their mother. The voices of the narrator and Zion employ relational language: "her young women" (1:4), "her little ones" (1:5), "her leaders" (1:6), "her people" (1:7, 11), "my strong men" (1:15), "my young men" (1:15), "my children" (1:16), "my young women and my young men" (1:18), and "my priests and elders" (1:19). Her maternal relationship to the community comes through most clearly in her use of the relational term בני. Cognitive linguists distinguish independent nouns like "child" that refer to a concept (young person) and relational nouns like "son" that refer to a concept (young male) that necessarily involves one or more other people (mother and father).[37] Relational nouns in Lamentations include kinship terms and terms for friend, enemy, master, and the like. As noted above, these relational terms in Lamentations are often reinforced with possessive suffixes referring to Zion. The use of בני in 1:16 identifies Zion as the mother of these children and the multiple references to Israelites subsumed under this category. The stanza that employs בני also describes Zion's weeping and identifies the cause of her sorrow as the suffering of the Israelites ("On account of these things I weep" [1:16], namely, "her people" [1:11], "my warriors" [1:15]). Consequently, the suffering and deaths of all the various Israelites affect Zion in the same manner that the suffering and death of her children affect a mother. Although Lam 2 uses far more architectural language for Zion than Lam 1, the personification of Zion coheres with the image of her as mother of the community.[38]

The image of Zion as mother has implications for understanding the phrase "daughter (of) Zion" and similar בת-plus-GN (geographical name) constructions. This phrase reliably indicates personification and has attracted considerable scholarly attention. The historical origins of the expression are lost along with the origins of the personification it denotes.[39]

God, ed. Richard S. Hess and Gordon J. Wenham (Grand Rapids: Eerdmans, 1999), 129–69.

37. Ellen van Wolde, *Reframing Biblical Studies: When Language and Text Meet Culture, Cognition, and Context* (Winona Lake, IN: Eisenbrauns, 2009), esp. 110–14.

38. Bosworth, "Daughter Zion," 121–23.

39. See Julie Galambush, *Jerusalem in the Book of Ezekiel: The City as Yahweh's*

Discussion of בת ציון has tended in two opposite directions. One empties בת of its feminine-relational content and translates "dear Zion" or "fair Zion," or drops the supposedly weak meaning of בת altogether in favor of simply "Zion."[40] The other approach retains the feminine and kinship sense of בת and understands Zion as literally a daughter, typically of God.[41] The first interpretation identifies the phrase as an appositional genitive "daughter Zion," rather than "daughter of Zion," and assumes a diminutive nuance ("dear, fair"). Most scholars and translators have followed this analysis. The "dear, fair" interpretation of בת derives from contexts where בת plus GN (e.g., Isa 1:8; Lam 1:6; 2:1)[42] connotes "desired, vulnerable, endangered femininity."[43] However, this tender aspect of the בת-plus-GN construction derives precisely from the feminine and relational nature of בת, which should therefore not be emptied of its meaning "daughter." Israelite daughters were embedded within a family system in which they were both valued and devalued. Scholarship has sometimes focused so much on the devaluation of daughters that one scholar has felt the need to write a book demonstrating that daughters were also loved.[44] Stories like the sacrifice of Jephthah's daughter do not indicate that daughters were worthless, but in fact depend on the notion that they were cherished. The

---

Wife, SBLDS 130 (Atlanta: Society of Biblical Literature, 1992), 35; H. G. M. Williamson, *Isaiah 1–5*, ICC (London: T&T Clark, 2006), 69.

40. William F. Stinespring, "No Daughter of Zion: A Study of the Appositional Genitive in Hebrew Grammar," *Enc* 26 (1965): 133–41; followed by, for example, Adele Berlin, *Lamentations: A Commentary*, OTL (Louisville: Westminster John Knox, 2002), 10–12; Othmar Keel, *Geschichte Jerusalems und die Entstehung des Monotheismus*, 2 vols, OLB 4 (Göttingen: Vandenhoeck & Ruprecht, 2007), 1:632; R. B. Salters, *Lamentations*, ICC (London: T&T Clark, 2010), 51–53. For a critique of this position, see Michael H. Floyd, "Welcome Back, Daughter of Zion!," *CBQ* 70 (2008): 484–504.

41. J. Andrew Dearman, "Daughter Zion and Her Place in God's Household," *HBT* 31 (2009): 144–59. For a critique of this position, see Michael H. Floyd, "Daughter of Zion Goes Fishing in Heaven," in *Daughter Zion: Her Portrait, Her Response*, ed. Mark J. Boda, AIL 13 (Atlanta: Society of Biblical Literature, 2012), 177–220.

42. For a complete catalogue of examples, see Marc Wischnowsky, *Tochter Zion: Aufnahme und Überwindung der Stadtklage in den Prophetenschrift des Alten Testaments*, WMANT 89 (Neukirchen-Vluyn: Neukirchener Verlag, 2001), 15–18.

43. Keel: "begehrter, verletztlicher, bedrohter, Weiblichkeit" (*Geschichte Jerusalems*, 1:632). Similarly, Salters: "an element of vulnerability and concern" (*Lamentations*, 520).

44. Johanna Steibert, *Fathers and Daughters in the Hebrew Bible* (Oxford: Oxford University Press, 2013).

general preference for sons over daughters does not mean that daughters were despised, and the wider cultural bias can serve to make parents especially solicitous and concerned for their vulnerable daughters. The term "my daughter" also appears outside kinship relations to indicate parental care and love (Ruth 2:2, 8, 22; 3:1, 10–11, 16, 18; Ps 45:11; cf. "my son" in 1 Sam 26:21, 25; 2 Sam 19:1, 5; Prov 1:8, 10). Nathan illustrates a man's tender care for his lamb by saying that he treated it "like a daughter" rather than like a son. Evidently, father-daughter imagery best captured the vulnerability of the lamb and the man's love for it. Similarly, the בת-plus-GN construction draws on parental care for a daughter, and the emotional impact of the expression draws in significant measure on the parent-daughter relationship familiar to many in the audience. Consequently, the term should not be emptied of its feminine and relational meaning. That said, however, Zion is never identified as God's daughter or placed within an Israelite pantheon.[45]

The personification of Zion in Lam 1–2 identifies her as the mother of the people of Israel (living and dead) and induces empathy and concern for her suffering and grief through the term *daughter*. Although she is a mother, the term daughter also places her in solidarity with other children. Since all the people are also her children, the text also places her in solidarity with the adult members of the community. The mother is inextricably linked with all her children, whom she represents. Thus, Zion understands the pain of a broken relationship from multiple perspectives: she knows the separation anxiety of the child who has lost his or her attachment figure and the intense grief of the mother who has suffered the death of a child or witnessed her child's pain. The maternal figure may express a more intense pain than a paternal figure would. Fathers and mothers both suffer grievously over the death of a child, but maternal grief is generally perceived as more severe and bereaved mothers are powerfully emotional figures (2 Sam 21:10–14; Isa 49:17–23; 54:1–3; Jer 31:15).[46]

---

45. Contra Dearman, "Daughter Zion." Keel rightly cautions that Zion is not a literal daughter (*Geschichte Jerusalems*, 2:791; see also 2:630–32, 879–900) but overreacts by reducing בת to a term of endearment (1:632).

46. Amy Kalmanovsky, "Women of God: Maternal Grief and Religious Response in 1 Kings 17 and 2 Kings 4," *JSOT* 36 (2011): 55–74; Archie Chi Chung Lee, "Mother Bewailing: Reading Lamentations," in *Her Masters Tools? Feminist and Postcolonial Engagements of Historical-Critical Discourse*, ed. Caroline Vander Stichele and Todd Penner, GPBS 9 (Atlanta: Society of Biblical Literature, 2005), 195–210. David G.

Parental bereavement is influenced by culture and circumstances, but even those who expect to suffer the death of children due to high infant mortality in their society still grieve their losses.[47] The personification of Zion represents the suffering of the Israelite people through the lens of child death and maternal grief. Other relational experiences, such as spousal bereavement (1:1), loss of social status (1:1, 11), and social isolation (1:1, 2, 9, 17), fit this overarching image of an attachment relationship and parental bond. Empathy for any person's suffering can be magnified by seeing/feeling their pain through the eyes of someone who loves them. Catholic tradition has drawn on this insight by presenting the suffering and death of Jesus from the perspective of his mother, thereby placing any Christian in the intensely emotional context of a mother watching her son's torturous death.[48] Indeed, the personified Zion has influenced Catholic thought about Mary and the "mother" church.[49]

The complex relationships involved in the personification facilitate the social sharing and consequent coregulation of emotions. The primary

---

Wing et al. summarize research on subjects in the United States, United Kingdom, and Australia in "Understanding Gender Differences in Bereavement Following the Death of an Infant: Implications for Treatment," *Psychotherapy* 38 (2001): 60–73. See further Monica McGoldrick, "Gender and Mourning," in *Living beyond Loss: Death in the Family*, ed. Froma Walsh and Monica McGoldrick, 2nd ed. (New York: Norton, 2004), 99–118; Bosworth, "David Comforted Bathsheba."

47. Some argue that high infant mortality rates inhibit parents from forming attachments to their newborns, commonly citing Nancy Scheper-Hughes, *Death without Weeping: The Violence of Everyday Life in Brazil* (Berkeley: University of California Press, 1992), esp. 340–45. However, Jónína Einarsdóttir challenges Scheper-Hughes in her study of another society with high infant mortality, *"Tired of Weeping": Child Death and Mourning among Papel Mothers in Guinea-Bissau*, SSSA 46 (Stockholm: Elander Gotab, 2000). See also Melvin Konner, *Evolution of Childhood: Relationships, Emotion, Mind* (Cambridge: Belknap, 2010), 412–25; Bosworth, *Infant Weeping*, 6–10; Bosworth, "Faith and Resilience," 700–3.

48. Mary's perspective of her son's life is enshrined in the Catholic rosary, which includes reciting the Hail Mary repeatedly while meditating on episodes from the passion narratives known as the "sorrowful mysteries" (agony in the garden, scourging, crowing with thorns, carrying the cross, crucifixion).

49. Vatican II, *Lumen gentium*, 21 November 1964, 55; Paul VI, *Signum magnum*, apostolic exhortation, 13 May 1967, 3; John Paul II, *Redemptoris mater*, encyclical, 25 March 1987, 47. Although some have sought this typology in Luke, it appears to be a later development. See Raymond E. Brown et al., eds., *Mary in the New Testament: A Collaborative Assessment by Protestant and Roman Catholic* (New York: Paulist, 1978), 228–32; *Catechism of the Catholic Church* §559.

benefits of socially sharing emotional memories are eliciting empathy, motivating help, and solidifying memory of emotional experiences.[50] These benefits necessarily involve strengthening relationships. Two voices in Lam 1 share Zion's emotion with the text's human and divine audiences. We may call one voice the "narrator" and the other "Zion." R. B. Salters invokes the helpful analogy of the news reporter to describe the relationship between them. The narrator functions like a reporter describing an area devastated by disaster in emotionally evocative ways. Zion's voice, however, reflects eyewitness testimony of the victim with poignant first-person emotional impact. These combined voices share emotional experiences with a wider audience removed from the place of devastation in hopes of motivating them to aid those in distress.

After the narrator describes Zion's isolation and lack of a comforter, Zion invites the audience to adopt the comforter role: "Look, Yhwh, at my affliction, for the enemy exults" (1:9). She employs the imperative-plus-vocative-plus-כי clause common in prayers of petition (e.g., Pss 3:8; 5:2–3; 6:2–3; 43:1–2; 69:2; 88:2–4), which she reprises in 1:11 and 1:20. In all three cases, Zion's grief provides the motive for Yhwh's sympathetic attention. The narrator likewise addresses God (1:10). Zion also directly addresses passersby (1:12, 18) and places them in the position of "guilty bystanders" who should do more than watch. For her human audiences, Zion articulates her grief and isolation and seeks consolation (1:19, 21), and the narrator cooperates in this project (1:7–9). The support she seeks from God has a more specific stated purpose: she asks God to make her enemies suffer as they have made her suffer (1:22). Both the narrator and Zion admit Zion's guilt (1:5, 8, 12, 14, 18).[51] This admission may be understood as an attempt to make sense of the catastrophe and current pain and to express contrition that may elicit mercy from Yhwh. The focus of the poetry remains on Zion's suffering and grief, suggesting

---

50. Rimé, "Emotion Elicits the Social Sharing of Emotion"; Rimé et al., "The Social Sharing of Emotions in Interpersonal and Collective Situations: Common Psychosocial Consequences," in *Emotion Regulation and Well-Being*, ed. Ivan Nyklíček, Ad Vingerhoets, and Marcel Zeelenberg (New York: Springer, 2011), 147–63.

51. Another admission of guilt appears in Lam 1:20, but C. L. Seow persuasively argues that the original reading מרר מרתי ("how bitter am I") was mistakenly changed to מרר מריתי ("I have been very rebellious") ("A Textual Note on Lamentations 1:20," *CBQ* 47 [1985]: 416–19).

both that Zion's punishment is disproportionate to her sin and that Yhwh should relent.[52]

The narrator's voice develops between Lam 1 and 2, in the first chapter cooperating with Zion to articulate her grief and elicit comfort and in the second chapter identifying himself as part of the community via the second-person plural pronoun.[53] He also addresses Zion in the second person (2:13-17). The narrator does neither of these things in chapter 1, which has led some to read him as cold and unemotional.[54] However, Salter's reporter analogy may be helpful.[55] Reporters can engender significant empathy in their audiences without inserting themselves into the story. Indeed, they may be most effective when they maintain some sense of objectivity. By contrast, talk show hosts who insert themselves into the story can distract the audience from the supposed target of interest. While the narrator in chapter 1 adopts a rhetorical strategy of presenting Zion and her situation directly, the narrator in chapter 2 inserts himself into the story and almost totally displaces Zion's voice, which is heard only in 2:21-22. The narrator in chapter 2, however, need not be understood negatively, since he models the empathy called for in the previous chapter.

The voices of Zion and the narrator seek to elicit empathy and help from humans and Yhwh. Within Lamentations, alas, no help arrives. However, these pleas have had impacts, or a history of effects (*Wirkungsgeschichte*). Many scholars have indicated that Isa 40–55 depends on Lamentations. The opening words (Isa 40:1) answer Zion's repeatedly expressed need for a comforter (see 49:13; 51:3, 12, 19; 54:11). God restores Zion's children to her (49:14-21), ending her punishment and restoring her community (Isa

---

52. F. W. Dobbs-Alsopp, "Tragedy, Tradition, and Theology in the Book of Lamentations," *JSOT* 74 (1997): 36–37. Kim Lan Nguyen shows by comparison with Psalms that admissions of guilt are rare in biblical lament (*Chorus in the Dark: Voices in the Book of Lamentations* [Sheffield: Sheffield Phoenix, 2013]).

53. The gender of the narrator's voice is not clear, but most writers adopt the masculine pronoun for ease of contrast with the feminine Zion.

54. Kathleen M. O'Connor, *Lamentations and the Tears of the World* (Maryknoll, NY: Orbis Books, 2002), 17; Tod Linafelt, *Surviving Lamentations: Catastrophe, Lament, and Protest in the Afterlife of a Biblical Book* (Chicago: University of Chicago Press, 2000), 45–48.

55. For further argument that the narrator and Zion work together, see Robin Parry, "The Ethics of Lament: Lamentations 1 as a Case Study," in *Reading the Law: Studies in Honor of Gordon J. Wenham*, ed. J. Gordon McConville and Karl Möller, LHBOTS 461 (New York: T&T Clark, 2007), 138–55, esp. 149–51.

43). God humiliates Babylon (Isa 47) as Zion had asked (Lam 1:21–22). Furthermore, the text facilitates emotional sharing within the religious communities that regard it as Scripture. In the process, it both reinforces community and shapes memory of the events it describes and subsequent similar events in the histories of these communities. In Jewish tradition, Lamentations is recited on Tisha b'Av commemorating the destruction of the first temple along with other catastrophes in Jewish history.[56] In Catholic tradition, Lamentations forms the text of the Holy Week Tenebrae liturgy.[57] Within both communities, Lamentations provides a liturgical expression of emotion. This secondary sharing of emotion helps explain why these traumas continue to be commemorated long after the generation that experienced them has passed away. The experience becomes part of collective memory and identity.[58] Therefore, individuals interpret their grief and trauma through the lens of this communal memory, and communal rituals allow the congregation, individually and collectively, to express their grief and benefit from mutual understandings, empathy, social support, and reinforcement of relationships.

4. Conclusion

A scientifically-informed theory of grief can liberate us from common cultural misunderstandings about grief and help us gain a clearer idea of what grief is, why we experience it, and what it looks like behaviorally. Many observations of biblical interpreters achieve greater sense and clarity with the evidence and theory that psychology can provide. My reading in the field of psychology has persuaded me of the potential of this and related fields to help us read biblical texts with greater feeling and therefore greater understanding. The more I read, the more I am struck by how a field with a highly individualistic bias developed within an individualistic culture has

---

56. E. R. Stern, "Lamentations in Jewish Liturgy," in *Great is Thy Faithfulness? Reading Lamentations as Sacred Scripture*, ed. Robin A. Parry and Heath A. Thomas (Eugene, OR: Pickwick, 2011), 88–91.

57. A. Cameron-Mowat, "Lamentations in Christian Worship," in Parry and Thomas, *Great is Thy Faithfulness?*, 139–41.

58. Bernard Rimé and Véronique Christophe, "How Individual Emotional Episodes Feed Collective Memory," in *Collective Memory of Political Events: Social Psychological Perspectives*, ed. James Pannebaker, Dario Paez, and Bernard Rimé (Mahwah, NJ: Earlbaum, 1997), 131–46.

discovered community and relationship at the very core of the individual. That humans are social animals is a platitude, but we are social in ways and degrees that few people imagine. Our memories and emotions are profoundly relational, and we never become as autonomous as we like to believe. The pioneers of attachment theory encountered strong resistance from colleagues who simply refused to believe that humans could be such dependent creatures, that love could matter so much that the lack of it could be fatal. These results refuted cherished assumptions about rational humans acting as independent agents and challenged the very notion of human autonomy. Grief serves as a powerful and painful reminder of just how dependent we are on others, and the study of this pain leads us back to relationship and attachment theory.

Bibliographic Essay

The research on grief, attachment theory, and the overlap between them makes biblical studies seem like a tiny field. However, it is possible for nonexperts to gain an understanding of grief and attachment sufficient to use these insights to illuminate biblical texts. Several works orient readers to the literature. For an exceptionally good introduction to attachment theory that tells the engaging story of its origins and development, see Robert Karen, *Becoming Attached: First Relationships and How They Shape Our Capacity to Love* (Oxford: Oxford University Press, 1998). For comparably friendly introductions to research on grief, see George Bonanno, *The Other Side of Sadness: What the New Science of Bereavement Tells Us about Life after Loss* (New York: Basic Books, 2009) and Ruth David Konigsburg, *The Truth about Grief: The Myth of the Five Stages and the New Science of Loss* (New York: Simon & Schuster, 2011). In *Seeing through Tears: Crying and Attachment* (New York: Routledge, 2005), Judith Kay Nelson persuasively argues that weeping across the lifespan retains its connection to attachment. For a comprehensive summary of the science of crying, see Ad Vingerhoets, *Why Only Humans Weep: Unraveling the Mysteries of Tears* (Oxford: Oxford University Press, 2013).

John Bowlby, the father of attachment theory, resembles Charles Darwin, whom he admired. Like Darwin, Bowlby published excellent and accessible science writing and articulated a theory that has held up remarkably well over time. His attachment trilogy remains foundational: Bowlby, *Attachment and Loss*, 3 vols. (New York: Basic Books): vol. 1, *Attachment*, 2nd ed. (1982); vol. 2, *Separation: Anxiety and Anger* (1973); vol. 3, *Loss:*

Sadness and Depression (1980). Several of his lectures provide short introductions to his thinking: Bowlby, *A Secure Base: Clinical Applications of Attachment Theory* (New York: Routledge, 1988); Bowlby, *The Making and Breaking of Affectional Bonds* (New York: Routledge, 1989). Sarah Blaffer Hrdy is another scientist (anthropologist) who has published accessible works involving attachment theory and its significance in human evolution. See Hrdy, *Mothers Nature: Maternal Instincts and How They Shape the Human Species* (New York: Ballentine, 1999); Hrdy, *Mothers and Others: The Evolutionary Origins of Mutual Understanding* (Cambridge: Harvard University Press, 2009).

Although it is a big volume with small print, the many essays in Judy Cassidy and Phillip R. Shaver, eds., *Handbook of Attachment: Theory, Research, and Clinical Applications*, 3rd ed. (New York: Guilford, 2016) are surprisingly accessible to laypeople and collectively provide a magisterial overview of the many facets of attachment theory including its application to grief and the psychology of religion. A comparable volume on grief is Margaret Stroebe and Wolfgang Stroebe, eds., *Handbook of Bereavement Research and Practice* (Washington, DC: American Psychological Association, 2008).

For books specifically about attachment in adults, see Mario Mikulincer and Phillip R. Shaver, eds., *Attachment in Adulthood: Structure, Dynamics, and Change*, 2nd ed. (New York: Guilford, 2016); Omri Gillath, Gery C. Karantzas, and R. Chris Fraley, *Adult Attachment: A Concise Introduction to Theory and Research* (London: Academic Press, 2016). Bernard Rimé and colleagues have pioneered work on the social sharing of emotions that is becoming increasingly integrated into attachment theory and provides helpful models for understanding responses to grief and trauma. See Rimé, *Le partage social des émotions* (Paris: Presses universitaires de France, 2005); Rimé, "Emotion Elicits the Social Sharing of Emotion: Theory and Empirical Review," *EmotRev* 1 (2009): 60–85.

Mourning over Sin/Affliction and the Problem of "Emotion" as a Category in the Hebrew Bible

David A. Lambert

A variety of concerns—theological, ethical, textual, even therapeutic—bring us to a shared discussion of emotions as a category in the Hebrew Bible, as represented in the present volume. These studies have their own reasons and legitimacy as well as a strong undercurrent of representation in the faith communities that have treated this collection of ancient Israelite texts that we now often term "Hebrew Bible" as Scripture. My contribution comes from a rather different place and, to some extent, situates itself outside of these endeavors. Rather than seeing the Bible itself as a source of our values and thinking about "emotions," I turn to the Bible as a resource for engaging in what the theorist of canon Charles Altieri refers to as a "dialectical process of differing from ourselves."[1] Viewed in this light, biblical studies affords an opportunity to identify the contemporary, dominant frameworks in which we place the Bible and, at the same time, to discern alternatives that challenge some of our most basic thinking about the nature of the self and society. Surely how we think about being human has changed over time, and, if so, a study of the Bible in conjunction with its history of interpretation should offer us an opportunity to grapple with this change and give it sharper definition.[2]

---

1. Charles Altieri, *Canons and Consequences: Reflections on the Ethical Force of Imaginative Ideals* (Evanston, IL: Northwestern University Press, 1990), 24.

2. These methodological considerations and how they relate to the history of the field of biblical studies are laid out in further detail in the introduction to my recent monograph, David A. Lambert, *How Repentance Became Biblical: Judaism, Christianity, and the Interpretation of Scripture* (New York: Oxford, 2016), 1–10.

I say all of this to help make sense of the claim I will make that "emotion" does not exist as a category in the Hebrew Bible.³ I am not trying to delegitimize those theological and ethical endeavors that would seek to develop a theory of emotion in conversation with the Bible; indeed, the Bible gives us plenty of suggestive raw materials to work with. Nor am I trying to cast as primitive the world of ancient Israel. That is a common misperception of those dedicated to both contemporary notions of emotions and biblical priority, accordingly seeing any questioning of interiority in the Bible as belittling it as an externally oriented and cynical document or, in different terms, as shallow and insincere. Rather, I aim to highlight a meaningful difference between the ways in which ancient Israelites talked about themselves and the ways we do,⁴ and how, in that sense, a discourse around "emotion" can be seen as pertaining to later (though no less meaningful) periods of the Bible's history and interpretation—periods that tended to promote a more pronounced dichotomy between mind and body, reason and feeling. Such a statement constitutes neither a philosophical stance against "emotion" nor a critical view of ancient Israelites' inner worlds but rather an attempt to attain greater theoretical precision about the different sorts of available discourses around the self. We can acknowledge the shared biological unity of humanity and, therefore, the aptness of speaking of emotion, as long as we recognize it to be a social-scientific (or theological) category and not, necessarily, an aspect of the ancient Israelites' self-representation or particular cultural formations.

Of course, those conversant in the Hebrew Bible will readily recall terms that we translate today into English words like "love," "fear," and "hate," fitting into our category of emotion as presently constituted. William Moran and Gary Anderson have already demonstrated how current understandings of אהב and שמח, respectively, seem to privilege subjective feeling over behavioral or performative dimensions.⁵ I am currently work-

---

3. See also, most recently, Françoise Mirguet, "What is an 'Emotion' in the Hebrew Bible? An Experience That Exceeds Most Contemporary Concepts," *BibInt* 24 (2016): 442–65.

4. On changing notions of the self over the course of Western history and, in particular, an emerging interest in interiority, see Charles Taylor, *Sources of the Self: The Making of the Modern Identity* (Cambridge: Cambridge University Press, 1989), 111–207. For an application of this type of analysis to the Hebrew Bible, see Robert A. Di Vito, "Old Testament Anthropology and the Construction of Personal Identity," *CBQ* 61 (1999): 217–38.

5. See William Moran, "The Ancient Near Eastern Background of the Love of

ing on further clarifying translation problems for a range of biblical terms and have published a programmatic statement on the topic, "Refreshing Philology: James Barr, Supersessionism, and the State of Biblical Words."[6]

Addressing the theme of "Emotional Responses to Sin and Suffering,"[7] I focus on a specific example that I developed in my recent monograph, *How Repentance Became Biblical: Judaism, Christianity, and the Interpretation of Scripture*.[8] I argue that penitential readings of various passages in the Hebrew Bible are an important, but not necessarily inevitable, component of its interpretation. Repentance as an inchoate negative feeling in the face of wrongdoing and affliction may (or may not) be universal, but the development of an active discourse around "repentance" as the inner act of regret intended by the common Jewish and Christian terms *təšûbâ*, *metanoia*, and *paenitentia* is a hallmark of the late Second Temple period and beyond, not the earlier biblical material. Now, again, I must hasten to acknowledge many narratives, prayers, prophetic oracles, and biblical Hebrew terms that we commonly associate with repentance today. For example, the common phrase "(re)turning to YHWH" has often been claimed as the biblical equivalent of repentance. In fact, the biblical Hebrew root *šûb* comes to be used for the later rabbinic term for "repentance," *təšûbâ*. But in no way does it spell out that concept in full. In early prophetic literature, it consistently occurs in contexts of appeal. Even the later formulation in biblical Hebrew "turning away from sin" reveals important differences with the eventual late Second Temple usage of "repentance" language by, among other things, not locating the change as interior to the human being. The LXX, in fact, seems to recognize that *šûb* does not quite equate to *metanoeō* and, contrary to common assumption, never once uses

---

God in Deuteronomy," *CBQ* 25 (1963): 77–87; Gary A. Anderson, *A Time to Mourn, a Time to Dance: The Expression of Grief and Joy in Israelite Religion* (University Park, PA: Pennsylvania State University Press, 1991).

6. That article appeared as David A. Lambert, "Refreshing Philology: James Barr, Supersessionism, and the State of Biblical Words," *BibInt* 24 (2016): 332–56. There I engage further with the pertinent work of Michael Carasik and Ellen van Wolde, among others. See Carasik, *Theologies of the Mind in Biblical Israel*, StBibLit 85 (New York: Lang, 2006); van Wolde, *Reframing Biblical Studies: When Language and Text Meet Culture, Cognition, and Context* (Winona Lake, IN: Eisenbrauns, 2009).

7. This was the topic for the Bible and Emotion panel at the Society of Biblical Literature annual meeting, November 2016, where a version of this essay was presented.

8. David A. Lambert, *How Repentance Became Biblical: Judaism, Christianity, and the Interpretation of Scripture*, (Oxford: Oxford University Press, 2016).

the term as its translation, preferring, instead, variations of *-strephō*. In short, *šûb* does not appear to be depicted discursively as an "emotion" in the Hebrew Bible.[9]

I contend that we have been widely reading the Hebrew Bible with what I term a "penitential lens." My book shows how this lens operates and proposes alternatives in chapters focused on rites of fasting, appeal, and confession; the phrase "return to YHWH"; the institution of prophecy; and redemptive expectations. This essay constitutes a slightly modified, abbreviated version of the chapter "Fasting and the Artistry of Distress."[10] The standard view has been that fasting, especially in a context of sin, should be understood as penitential, that is, an external expression of inner contrition. I challenge that view by laying out an alternative vision of what fasting does without depending on the category of "emotion" as native to the biblical texts.[11] I demonstrate my proposed alternative through narrative texts featuring Hannah and David; several Psalms texts; passages in the books of Joel, Isaiah, and Jonah; and the priestly laws of the Day of Atonement.

1. The Study of Fasting in the Hebrew Bible

With respect to fasting in the Hebrew Bible, the central interpretive problem has been to explain how a single practice can figure in so many different contexts. Texts represent acts of fasting in times of mourning the dead, in response to drought, and in contexts of sin. Biblical scholarship has commonly addressed such diversity by utilizing an ethnography of fasting developed at the beginning of the last century. This ethnography sought to classify various reasons why people around the world fast. In the words of one influential account, fasting "may be an act of penitence or of propitiation; a preparatory rite before some act of sacramental eating or an initiation; a mourning ceremony; one of a series of purification rites; a means of inducing dreams and visions; a method of adding force to

---

9. For a full discussion of this phrase and its history, see Lambert, *How Repentance Became Biblical*, 71–89.

10. The material is reproduced by permission of Oxford University Press. For the full text, see Lambert, *How Repentance Became Biblical*, 13–31.

11. That said, in my book I myself resorted in a few places to a language of "emotions" to give rhetorical force to my present expression. If I were writing the chapter today, I suspect I would seek other ways to formulate my points.

magical rites."¹² Among biblical texts, evidence has been found for several of these types: mourning, petition, penitence, and visionary preparation.¹³

We should pause, perhaps, to ask: what view of the human subject is bound up in this particular kind of account, which posits, on one hand, the stable identity of a ritual performance, "fasting," throughout the world and, on the other hand, its diversity of types? This rendering is also marked by a strong emphasis on liminality, the sense in which rites serve to transition the human subject toward a more essential state. In view of the multiplicity of the act's possible meanings, it is the performer's intention that comes to define its nature. By objectifying fasting as a universal *practice*, such scholarly representations thus position the individual human as *actor*, endowed with agency and consciousness.¹⁴ While this classificatory scheme appears to limit the standard association of fasting with repentance, it ultimately establishes an overall platform quite conducive to the constructions of interiority, autonomy, and transformation bound up in the idea of repentance.¹⁵

On an interpretive level, this reading of the fasting rite eschews any substantive attempt to translate the communicative, material conditions of the behavior. It focuses instead on *intention*, on determining the

---

12. John A. MacCulloch, "Fasting," *ERE* 5:759. Later treatments (e.g., Rosemary Rader, "Fasting," *ER* 5:286–90) draw heavily on MacCulloch's article.

13. Hendrik A. Brongers, "Fasting in Israel in Biblical and Post-biblical Times," in *Instruction and Interpretation: Studies in Hebrew Language, Palestinian Archaeology and Biblical Exegesis; Papers Read at the Joint British-Dutch Old Testament Conference Held at Louvain, 1976, from 30 August to 2 September*, ed. Hendrik A. Brongers, OTS 20 (Leiden: Brill, 1977), 1–21; John Muddiman, "Fasting," *ABD* 2:773–74; Jacob Milgrom, "Fasting and Fast Days," *EncJud* 6:1190; Harvey Guthrie Jr., "Fast, Fasting," *IDB* 2:241–43; Thomas Podella, *Ṣôm-Fasten: Kollektive Trauer um den verborgenen Gott im Alten Testament* (Neukirchen-Vluyn: Neukirchener Verlag, 1989), 117–223; Saul Olyan, *Biblical Mourning: Ritual and Social Dimensions* (Oxford: Oxford University Press, 2004).

14. On ways to move beyond a focus on the intention of the individual actor in ritual performance, see William S. Sax, "Agency," in *Issues, Topics, Approaches, Concepts*, vol. 1 of *Theorizing Rituals*, ed. Jens Kreinath, Jan Snoek, and Michael Stausberg, Numen Book Series114 (Leiden: Brill, 2006), 473–81.

15. "The claim of many radical critics that hegemonic power necessarily suppresses difference in favor of unity is quite mistaken. To secure its unity—to make its own history—dominant power has worked best through differentiating and classifying practices" (Talal Asad, *Genealogies of Religion: Discipline and Reasons of Power in Christianity and Islam* [Baltimore: Johns Hopkins University Press, 1993], 17).

nature of the act by attending to the most privileged aspect of the context in which the rite unfolds and at which the actor is presumed to take aim. Accordingly, fasting tends to be interpreted as penitential whenever it appears in a context of sin. In such instances, it is commonly understood as "indicat[ing] repentance for transgressions committed."[16] Fasting is thereby rendered an external sign, an expression of an internal feeling whose generation and experience are the primary matters of importance.[17]

An alternative starting point for interpretation would be to step back from the analysis of fasting as a specialized rite and allow it to merge with the broader behavioral manifestations with which it frequently occurs in the Hebrew Bible—the weeping, donning of sackcloth, application of ashes, and other forms of self-affliction that accompany deprivation from nourishment. Various texts develop aspects of this behavioral complex, but elements of a unified meaning are broadly attested in ancient Israelite and other ancient Near Eastern literatures. This suggestion of commonality undercuts the autonomy usually attributed to both practitioners and authors in determining the meaning of fasting in favor of a broad cultural account of the practice.

2. Fasting as an Act of Mourning

The image of fasting and its concomitant rites that I would set forth is of a dramatic material response to disaster, a manifestation and communication

---

16. Olyan, *Biblical Mourning*, 75. Extended self-imposed affliction is also readily read as a sign of "penitent shame." Consider the comments of the noted anthropologist, Victor Turner on the Ndembu rituals of afflictions: "In the idiom of the rituals of affliction it is *as though* the Ndembu said: 'It is only when a person is reduced to misery by misfortune, and repents of the acts that caused him to be afflicted, that ritual expressing an underlying unity in diverse things may fittingly be enacted for him.' For the patient in rituals of affliction must sit, clad only in a waistcloth, in an attitude of penitent shame.... This is not to imply that Ndembu paganism is on an ethical or epistemological parity with the great world religions, but there is some satisfaction from a humanistic standpoint in finding similarities between men's modes of worship the world over" (*The Drums of Affliction: A Study of Religious Processes among the Ndembu of Zambia* [Oxford: Clarendon, 1968], 22, emphasis added). Here too we find a clear sense of the universality of ritual expression.

17. For a critique of the tendency in modern biblical scholarship to view "emotional experience" as "prior to any behavioral expression," see Gary A. Anderson, "Introduction: The Expression of Emotion in Cross-Cultural Perspective," in Anderson, *Time to Mourn*, 1–18.

of diminishment whereby the afflicted party comes to be defined by a perceived object of dread.[18] Such practices, conforming to patterns of mourning found throughout the ancient Near East,[19] do not respond to adversity by deflecting its claim over the sufferer, as Stoic exercises might aim to do, but rather by encoding that suffering upon the body. At times, this decision appears particularly odd to modern sensibilities. Tamar pleads with her brother Amnon not to rape her on account of the "shame" (*ḥerpâ*) she would bear. Yet after being raped and driven from Amnon's home, Tamar herself publicly reveals this *ḥerpâ* by placing dust upon her head, rending her garments, and screaming loudly (2 Sam 13:12–19). Loss is perceived along objective lines as an actual lessening of the person rather than merely as shame, a subjective account of how one feels in the view of others. Because status and possession, not to mention health, are seen as basic to the ontology of the self, not extraneous to it, the sufferer has no choice but to reflect his or her circumscribed status. Above all, fasting and its associated practices suggest a way around the supposedly inherent problem of pain's inarticulacy.[20] It uses the body as a canvas upon which to represent that suffering, to externalize a state that, in another cultural milieu, might remain private.

---

18. In this respect and others, the phenomenon fits into what the literary critic Philip Fisher sees as the workings of *passion*, as opposed to mere expressions of *emotion* (*The Vehement Passions* [Princeton: Princeton University Press, 2002]). The passions direct attention to "one monopolizing fact," focusing exclusively on an object of dread (57–58) and displaying what Fisher refers to as "thoroughness," by which all else, including the prudential self, is pushed out (44). It also bears similarities to the way in which the standard subject–object distinction breaks down in Julia Kristeva's notion of "abjection," whereby that which is rejected, the "abject," comes to define the subject (*Powers of Horror: An Essay on Abjection*, trans. Leon S. Roudiez [New York: Columbia University Press, 1982], esp. 1–8).

19. On mourning in general, see Anderson, *Time to Mourn*; David P. Wright, *Ritual in Narrative: The Dynamics of Feasting, Mourning, and Retaliation Rites in the Ugaritic Tale of Aqhat* (Winona Lake, IN: Eisenbrauns, 2001), 139–97; Olyan, *Biblical Mourning*.

20. Elaine Scarry, *The Body in Pain: The Making and Unmaking of the World* (New York: Oxford University Press, 1985), 3–11. See the critique of Scarry in Talal Asad, *Formations of the Secular: Christianity, Islam, Modernity* (Stanford, CA: Stanford University Press, 2003), 80–81. On pain as being subject to varied forms of cultural construction, see Mary-Jo DelVecchio Good et al., eds., *Pain as Human Experience: An Anthropological Perspective* (Berkeley: University of California Press, 1992), 1–28 and the literature cited there.

When suffering is of apparent divine authorship, mourning serves as a visible manifestation of the deity's power, part of the destruction left in its wake. Indeed, grief ultimately indicates the subjection of the human will to the superior power that has overwhelmed it, evidencing the inability to retrieve what has been lost. That is why weeping or tearing a garment is deemed the pious response to prophetic oracles of doom attached to Israel's god, YHWH.[21] Instead of indicating contrition, such performances show that the threatened divine punishment has registered with its victims. It marks the bodies of its victims and thereby goes part of the way toward a restitution of the deity's power, as measured by his ability to impose justice.[22]

The mourning dynamic functions whether a loss is already actualized or still only imagined. In fact, fasting and other rites of self-affliction tend to operate in situations where loss remains oblique, where it effects a diminishment of the self that is real but otherwise would not exist or yet be evident upon the body. Thus, the timing of the disaster matters little. That is why fasting can occur not only in mourning the dead but also in the vicinity of petition. That the loss is still only threatened, and therefore potentially reversible, does not change the meaning of the fast. For ancient Israelites, only one occasion for fasting seems salient: that of *loss*.

Once penitential assumptions are held at bay, the nature of the mechanism at work becomes clear. In many biblical texts, fasting appears closely related to prayer.[23] The visual manifestation of distress leads into and attends the verbal articulation of that distress. Seeing and heeding go together, and one may speak of the peculiar contribution of the visual toward eliciting divine pity.[24] Indeed, throughout the literary corpora of ancient Israel, the

---

21. In addition to the cases that appear below, see Isa 32:11–12 and Jer 6:26. Upon hearing the Torah read, the people weep in Neh 8:9 on account of the doom pronounced for those who have transgressed its stipulations. The refusal to mourn is particularly problematic (see Jer 36:24), as it calls into question the deity's power.

22. The practice of fasting in ancient Israel therefore fits well with premodern disciplinary procedures as described by Michel Foucault (*Discipline and Punish: The Birth of the Prison*, trans. Alan Sheridan [New York: Vintage Books, 1979]).

23. Patrick D. Miller takes an important step in recognizing the connection between fasting and prayer, though he associates these rites with "contrition and humility" (*They Cried to the Lord: The Form and Theology of Biblical Prayer* [Minneapolis: Fortress, 1994], 52–54).

24. Miller stresses the centrality of affliction in the biblical experience of prayer

prayers of the poor and afflicted are especially heard.²⁵ As the Covenant Code states, "You shall not afflict any widow or orphan. If you do afflict them and they cry out to me, I will heed their outcry" (Exod 22:21–22).²⁶ Potentially little difference emerges between persistent deprivation and induced affliction, between the poor/widows/orphans and those who, subject to some oblique distress, assume the persona of the afflicted, altering their ontological status through rites of self-diminishment.²⁷ Suffering only moves the deity when writ large upon the body itself, an impossible demand (without fasting) for those who occupy an otherwise respectable societal position.²⁸ This situation suits the anthropopathic qualities of the

---

(*They Cried to the Lord*, 55–134). See also James L. Kugel, "The Cry of the Victim," in Kugel, *The God of Old: Inside the Lost World of the Bible* (New York: Free Press, 2003), 109–36. Compare the position of Moshe Greenberg, who stresses the importance of the speaker's moral status and sincerity as major determinants of prayer's effectuality (*Biblical Prose Prayer: As a Window to the Popular Religion of Ancient Israel* [Berkeley: University of California Press, 1983], 48–51). For the particular contribution of vision, see Susan Sontag, *Regarding the Pain of Others* (New York: Farrar, Straus & Giroux, 2003), 3–17. Photographs of anonymous victims of war cause viewers to condemn *all* war. The justice of the victim's cause becomes irrelevant in the face of this immediate human response to suffering.

25. A connection of sorts may obtain between one biblical term for an afflicted person, ʿānî (see further below), and one term used to denote fasting. The phrase ʿinnâ nefesh/hitʿanneh, generally understood as constituting or at least including fasting (see Ezra 8:21; Ps 35:13; Isa 58:3, 5; Dan 10:12), was probably understood as "to afflict oneself," as suggested by the use of the reflexive form hitʿanneh in Ezra 8:21 and Dan 10:12. (The possible, original etymological sense of the phrase, "afflicting the throat," does not appear to be in play.) Some have viewed this term as inherently penitential, suggesting the translation, "to afflict one's soul" (see Muddiman, "Fasting," 773). We may loosely gloss the phrase as "to engage in certain acts of ritual affliction that render oneself afflicted"—that is, functionally equivalent to an ʿānî. Fasting is precisely one of those kinds of acts.

26. Indeed, it is the deity's responsibility *in his capacity as king* to protect the disempowered. See F. Charles Fensham, "Widow, Orphan, and the Poor in Ancient Near Eastern Legal and Wisdom Literature," *JNES* 21 (1962): 129–39. Translations of Hebrew Bible passages are a modified form of the New Jewish Publication Society translation (NJPS).

27. What Judith Butler writes concerning the relationship between the body and gender holds with regard to the body and grief as well (*Gender Trouble: Feminism and the Subversion of Identity* [New York: Routledge, 1990], 128–41). In fasting, the body does not express some inner essence, i.e., suffering. Rather, it performs that suffering and brings into effect the actor's identity as afflicted.

28. Victor Turner discusses the need for the privileged to engage in "status rever-

deity, his *pathos*, as frequently portrayed in the Bible.[29] Human impotence and dependence are physically demonstrated just prior to the sudden and total reversal that divine intervention brings. One may also speak of the power of mourning rites to elicit empathy as a sort of irritant to the deity. Like the lament literature with which it is frequently associated, physically manifesting distress protests that distress and challenges God to remove it from his sight.[30] Through its extreme, stark[31] expression, it creates an untenable situation that demands divine response. In that sense, fasting is not desired by the deity but is rather a human prerogative, an appropriate recourse in a time of need.

This general account, which we will now fill in and test through an examination of specific texts, leaves little room for repentance and, by extension, "emotion," at least in its conventional senses: distress is a response to disaster, not sin; fasting is an integrated material response to suffering, not an outward signifier of repentance; and fasting possesses no atoning power but rather marks a direct appeal to divine mercy. Actually, fasting, as generally represented in the Bible, may have been closer in aim to the modern-day hunger strike than to current religious rites.[32] The refusal to eat, like the lamenter's refusal to fall silent, is in many ways the last recourse of protest for one otherwise powerless to change the course of events.

---

sal," i.e., humiliation, at key religious junctures ("Humility and Hierarchy: The Liminality of Status Elevation and Reversal," in Turner, *The Ritual Process: Structure and Anti-structure* [Chicago: Aldine, 1969], 166–203).

29. See the introductory comments of Yochanan Muffs, *Love and Joy: Law, Language, and Religion in Ancient Israel* (New York: Jewish Theological Seminary of America, 1992), 4–5.

30. Walter Brueggemann emphasizes the protest element of the lament. See Brueggemann, "A Shape for Old Testament Theology, I: Structure Legitimation," *CBQ* 47 (1985): 28–46; Brueggemann, "A Shape for Old Testament Theology, II: Embrace of Pain," *CBQ* 47 (1985): 395–415.

31. Patrick D. Miller applies this term to the lament ("Trouble and Woe: Interpreting the Biblical Laments," *Int* 37 [1983]: 32–45, esp. 34).

32. For an account of one modern hunger strike that, like the biblical version, involved other bodily performances, see Begoña Aretxage, "Dirty Protest: Symbolic Overdetermination and Gender in Northern Ireland Ethnic Violence," *Ethos* 23 (1995): 123–48.

3. The Power of the Poor

One highly successful "hunger striker" was the biblical figure Hannah. Her narrative (1 Sam 1:1–28) furnishes our discussion with an in-depth example of the relationship between affliction, prayer, and the refusal to eat. Great anguish over her barrenness and the cumulative taunts of her rival wife leads Hannah to pray. Her state of affliction (ʿŏnî) is fundamental to her ultimate success, and she directly alludes to it in her votive prayer: "O Lord of Hosts, if you will look upon the affliction [ʿŏnî] of your maidservant and will remember me" (1:11). That Hannah is a woman is significant; it highlights her powerless, marginal position in light of her barrenness, and yet it paradoxically provides her with the nearly unstoppable power of the pathetic plea.[33] The deity notes her anguish and bestows upon her not just any child but the great leader Samuel.

The psalm of thanksgiving that Hannah is subsequently said to recite fittingly reprises the theme of the afflicted being exalted through the agency of God: "He raises the *poor* from the dust, lifts up the *needy* from the dunghill, setting them with nobles, granting them seats of honor" (2:8). Indeed, the book of Psalms consistently emphasizes the oppressed position of the petitioner who frequently refers to himself as an ʿānî (a term related to "affliction"), one who is poor or, perhaps better, afflicted: "Good and faithful as you are, save me. For I am afflicted [ʿānî] and needy" (Ps 109:22). A state of affliction is directly linked to prayer being heard: "Here was an afflicted man [ʿānî] who called, and the Lord listened, and delivered him from all his troubles" (Ps 34:7).[34] Hannah's plea can be regarded as an enactment of such verses.

Hannah also "wept and would not eat" (1 Sam 1:6). Her refusal to eat, not depicted here as a formal fast, represents a spontaneous reaction to affliction. But it also entails a rejection of her elevated status as preferred wife—a status represented precisely by the honored portion

---

33. For the connection between pain and power in the lament psalms, see Amy C. Cottrill, "The Articulate Body: The Language of Suffering in the Laments of the Individual," in *Lamentations in Ancient and Contemporary Cultural Contexts*, ed. Nancy C. Lee and Carleen Mandolfo, SymS 43 (Leiden: Brill, 2008), 103–22.

34. For a discussion of ʿānî as a technical term in these and other prayers, see Jonas Greenfield, "The Zakir Inscription and the Danklied," in *ʿAl Kanfei Yonah: Collected Studies of Jonas C. Greenfield on Semitic Philology*, ed. Shalom M. Paul, Michael E. Stone, and Avital Pinnick, 2 vols. (Boston: Brill, 2001), 1:178–80.

of the sacrifice she now foregoes—and embraces instead the persona of the ʿānî—her status as an isolated, barren, taunted woman. She thereby manifests an absence or loss, the significance of which might not be otherwise noted and is in fact contested by her husband. These stark choices compound the pathos of the narrative's central dramatic moment, Hannah's outpouring to YHWH (1:11). She eats as soon as her prayer concludes (1:18).

Like Hannah, David fasts on behalf of a child, the condemned fruit of his illicit union with Bathsheba (2 Sam 12:16-23). Unlike Hannah, however, David is portrayed as purposely refraining from food and as aware of the potential efficacy of such fasting. "I fasted and wept because I thought: 'Who knows? The Lord may have pity on me, and the child may live'" (12:22). This unusually clear programmatic statement of a religious phenomenon's function provides essential clarity to our current discussion. Against the common penitential reading of David's fast, a function of its appearance in a context of sin and its proximity to David's confession, which requires separate discussion, it manifestly functions as a form of entreaty.[35] Fasting and "lying on the ground" (12:16) enable the king to assume the lowered persona that is necessary to a successful appeal. The degree of intentionality behind David's act contributes to the narrative— it presents the king's religious behavior as innovative, in that he mourns before rather than after the death of his son—but it hardly changes the basic meaning of the act. Fasting again serves as a response to anguish that highlights the afflicted state of the supplicant and has the potential to move the deity to overturn the present crisis.

4. The Unseemliness of Affliction

When subjected to careful analysis, one apparently minor detail in the above account offers us further insight into the social dynamics of fasting: "The senior servants of his household tried to induce him to get up from the ground; but he refused, nor would he partake of food with them" (2 Sam

---

35. See, for instance, F. Stolz, "צום," *TLOT* 2:1066. In the preceding passage, David had already confessed his sin and had it commuted (12:13). The problem is that, as the fruit of an illicit union, the infant continues to constitute an affront to God and must be eradicated (12:14)—hence David's *subsequent* appeal. For further discussion, see Lambert, *How Repentance Became Biblical*, 51–67 (esp. 63–64, treating David's confession in particular).

12:17). In assuming the persona of an afflicted person, David has cut himself off from normal society, and his servants are disquieted. They attempt to persuade him to join them in their customary repast, to shed his mourner's garb and relinquish the extreme stance he has adopted. They withhold from him word of his son's death lest he extend this position in unimaginable new ways. Later on, they even question the king's behavior (12:18). Why do they exhibit so little understanding of David's comportment?

Returning to an odd moment in the Hannah narrative may provide some useful insight into David's situation. Elkanah, Hannah's husband, challenges her: "Hannah, why are you crying and why aren't you eating? Why are you so sad? Am I not more devoted to you than ten sons?" (1 Sam 1:8). He protests because Hannah, through her extreme manifestation of affliction, has effectively removed herself from participation in the feast and therefore from his society. By assuming the persona of the ʿānî, she has chosen to descend into a position of isolated distress that grants her potency before the merciful God. But to those remaining in the world of joyous festivities, like Elkanah, or of everyday affairs, like David's servants, there is an unseemliness in the affliction manifested by these individuals with their private difficulties. Indeed fasting and its accompanying rites produce results that are grotesque: dirty, bedraggled bodies—the abject.[36] The natural human impulse is either to withdraw from these wretches or to force them to clean themselves up.[37] To maintain its integrity, society has a stake in preventing individuals from slipping into the stark and horrid.

The unseemliness of affliction also figures in the Psalms. As in the narrative passages examined, fasting in the Psalms serves as a manifestation of affliction that flows naturally and quickly into petition: "My knees give way from fasting; my flesh is lean, has lost its fat. I am an object of scorn [ḥerpâ] for them; when they see me, they shake their head. Help me, O Lord, my God; save me in accord with your faithfulness" (Ps 109:24–26).[38] The psalmist uses the image of his fasting-induced emaciation to produce an evocative visual image of need; then he sets forth his verbal petition. Two of the three explicit references to fasting in the Psalms connect fasting to ḥerpâ, a word that we saw applied to Tamar as well. The term signifies the diminishment of the victim vis-à-vis others through misfortune and ritual enactment of loss. In these passages, those around the psalmist taunt

---

36. See Kristeva, *Powers of Horror*, 2–4.
37. See also Esther's response to Mordecai in Esth 4:4.
38. Ps 35:13, like the David narrative, also connects fasting to prayer for the sick.

him as a result of his fast. In addition to the passage just quoted, consider the following: "When I wept and fasted, I was reviled for it. I made sackcloth my garment; I became a byword among them" (Ps 69:11–12). Why should the psalmist be so reviled (*laḥărāpôt*) for fasting?[39] Extreme fasting and its concomitant rites have so altered the psalmist's appearance as to produce disgust in others at the sight of him.

In part, the portrayal of societal disgust sharpens the individual's fasting-induced affliction by adding an element of isolation. More fundamentally though, it provides a mirror through which to view the horror and starkness of the individual's assumed stance.[40] What is wretched to humanity, and hence subject to suppression, irritates the deity as well. However, he is in a position to remove the source of irritation rather than merely mask its effect. The portrayal of a negative societal response serves as a powerful tool in the hands of both narrator and psalmist to emphasize the depth of affliction experienced and to underscore the need for divine intervention. This tool helps point to the nature of fasting and its efficacy: a manifestation of affliction that has an immediate, concrete effect on those who perceive it.

Until now, we have only considered passages that explicitly mention fasting. However, throughout the Psalms and other lament literature, a strong emphasis is placed on the dissolution of the mourner's body.[41] Consider the following passage: "I am poured out like water; all my bones are disjointed; my heart is like wax, melting within me; my vigor dries up like a shard; my tongue cleaves to my palate; You commit me to the dust of earth" (Ps 22:15). Scholars believe that statements like these would have been uttered by the infirm seeking healing.[42] There is undoubtedly some

---

39. Reflecting a common spiritualizing tendency in reading the Psalms, Hermann Gunkel and Joachim Begrich suggest that the afflicted would have been reviled in ancient Israel because of presumed underlying sin (*Introduction to Psalms: The Genres of the Religious Lyric of Israel*, trans. James D. Nogalski [Macon, GA: Mercer University Press, 1998], 149). My proposed reading of these passages, however, suggests that the source of repulsion is material, not spiritual.

40. Indeed, the lament psalms are marked by a focus on what enemies say. See Claus Westermann, *Praise and Lament in the Psalms*, trans. Keith R. Crim and Richard N. Soulen (Atlanta: John Knox, 1981), 189–90.

41. Miller, *They Cried to the Lord*, 80. See further Amy C. Cottrill, *Language, Power, and Identity in the Lament Psalms of the Individual*, LHBOTS 493 (London: Bloomsbury T&T Clark, 2008), 29–57.

42. Gunkel and Begrich, *Introduction to Psalms*, 135.

truth to this view. However, in the poetics of lament, there is a fine line between the undesired dissolution wrought by illness and the purposeful dissolution of body wrought by fasting. Affliction is very much a *stance*, a state adopted and articulated by the supplicant. When distress did not directly impinge upon the body, fasting and its concomitant rites could be used to induce such a state.

5. "Great and Small Alike" (Jonah 3:5)

In the biblical texts to be examined now, the scope of self-affliction widens to envelop the whole body politic. Time and time again depictions of fast days emphasize the participation of the entire community[43] while continuing to stress the presence of societal elites. Though scholars have tended to view the rites of the communal fast day as penitential and its purpose as restoration of the moral order,[44] many depictions fail to mention anything about sin. What comes to the fore instead is prayer, which frequently constitutes the climactic culmination of the day's mourning rites.[45]

The account of a communal fast in the book of Joel is particularly illuminating. It begins with the dramatic proclamation of a fast day:

> Lament—like a maiden girt with sackcloth for the husband of her youth!... The country is ravaged, the ground must mourn; for the new grain is ravaged, the new wine is dried up, the new oil has failed.... Gird yourselves and lament, O priests, wail, O ministers of the altar; come, spend the night in sackcloth, O ministers of my God. For offering and libation are withheld from the House of your God. Solemnize a fast, proclaim an assembly; gather the elders—all the inhabitants of the land—in the House of the Lord your God, and cry out to the Lord. (1:8–14)[46]

---

43. Considering the possible role of fasting attending the many communal laments in the Hebrew Bible may help us fulfill the mandate of Gunkel and Begrich to "visualize the prominently portrayed practices of the lament festival if one wants to understand this poetry" (*Introduction to Psalms*, 85).

44. See, e.g., Sigmund Mowinckel, *The Psalms in Israel's Worship*, 2 vols. (Oxford: Blackwell, 1962), 1:193.

45. Prayer is seen as the key moment of the fast day in rabbinic law, as well. See m. Ta'an. 2:2.

46. Many scholars consider fasting here to be penitential. See, for instance, Hans Walter Wolff, *Joel and Amos*, ed. S. Dean McBride Jr., trans. Waldemar Janzen, S. Dean McBride Jr., and Charles A. Muenchow, Hermeneia (Philadelphia: Fortress, 1977), 29, 33; James L. Crenshaw, *Joel*, AB 24C (New York: Doubleday, 1995), 98, 101, 105. Their

Several important points emerge from this passage. The call to fast appears after the call to mourn and before the call to prayer: one flows naturally into the other.[47] This suggests a fluid relationship between fasting as an act of mourning and fasting as an act of petition that belies facile efforts at classification. Furthermore, the author exploits the power of visualized distress to elicit pity. He sets the evocative natural image of the land's reduced state—the environmental plight—next to the induced ritual state of its inhabitants, thus adding to the sense of plight that ultimately spills forth in prayer.

This Joel text also offers something more precise about how the fasting body reflects the reality of affliction. The proclamation in Joel gathers diverse instances of suffering that together suggest an account of affliction as a state of cessation and absence: the loss of procreative potential ("like a maiden"), the lack of food (grain, wine, and oil), and the interruption of the temple service. In many texts from the Hebrew Bible, these themes, ultimately the conditions of death, are juxtaposed with their opposites: fertility, abundance, and praise—the province of the living. The presence of this heightened polarity generates a destabilizing tension that allows individuals or groups to flip suddenly from one extreme state to another. This process of transformation is usually seen as conditioned on divine intervention, exemplified above by the case of Hannah. By forswearing sustenance and other acts of self-abnegation, the practitioner keys into this chain of associations; the cessation of normal bodily functions provides a way to ape the ultimate cessation that is the object of dread, as when fasting is used to help the living achieve ritual identification with the deceased. As for Joel, fasting allows those assembled to mirror the emaciated condition of the land upon their bodies and to hope for the reversal of the death-like state into which they have entered.

6. "And Let Everyone Turn Back from His Evil Ways" (Jonah 3:8)

Both the logic of fasting and the nature of its limitations are exploited in arguably the most powerful reflection on fasting—or, more accurately, fast days—found in the Hebrew Bible:

---

impetus, in part, derives from the call to "turn" in Joel 2:12–14. In its position and form, however, this call to "turn" is quite separate from the initial call to lament, as well as from the call to lament that appears in 2:15–17.

47. Note also the juxtaposition of fasting and lamenting in Zech 7:5.

They seek me daily ... like a nation that has acted justly...: "Why have we fasted, and you haven't seen? We have afflicted ourselves, and you haven't attended?" Because on your fast day [*yôm ṣômkem*] you pursue your business and oppress all your laborers!... Your fasting today is not such as to make your voice heard on high. Is such the fast [*ṣôm*] I desire, a day [*yôm*] for men to afflict themselves?... Like that, do you proclaim a fast [*ṣôm*], a day [*yôm*] favorable to the Lord? No, this is the fast [*ṣôm*] I desire: to unlock fetters of wickedness, and untie the cords of the yoke to let the oppressed go free; to break off every yoke. It is to share your bread with the hungry, and to take the wretched poor into your home; when you see the naked, to clothe him, and not to ignore your own kin.... Then, when you call, the Lord will answer; when you cry, He will say: Here I am. (Isa 58:2-9)

Israel fails to understand why God has not "seen" their manifest distress. But he will not alleviate their suffering because a much more horrific scene has seized his attention: the oppression of the downtrodden. Only with the relative (if temporary) elevation of those who are truly downcast can the otherwise well-off supplicants compellingly present themselves among the ranks of the afflicted. Only then will the deity attend to *their* cries.

The common interpretation of this passage proceeds from a nominalization of the object in this passage; the word *ṣôm*, which appears throughout, is thought to refer to the practice of fasting. For some, the passage thereby repudiates fasting and even ritual in general as *inherently* lacking. For others, it critiques the absence of an inner accounting or, alternately, the presence of the requisite sincerity accompanying the external rite.[48] But what this passage seems to argue with its constant reference to fast *days* (the word for "day" [*yôm*] appears throughout) is that the parameters of the proceedings overall must be enlarged beyond rites of appeal to include what we might call, for lack of a better term, social justice. The definition and continuation of fasting as a practice are not at stake. Indeed, the logical flow of this passage fits a common pattern of requiring concurrently two different sorts of rituals, those that appeal to the mercy of the deity and those that enable a rectification of injustice. In this case, allowing economic oppression within one's midst is akin to har-

---

48. Claus Westermann, *Isaiah 40-66: A Commentary*, trans. David M. G. Stalker, OTL (Philadelphia: Westminster, 1969), 335-36.

boring an object unsightly to God, and it causes the rites of appeal to fail in light of the absence of a proper rectification of injustice.[49]

The fast of the Ninevites is also commonly viewed as an exemplary "penitential" fast.[50] Indeed, the passage has deep structural similarities to Isa 58. Here, too, methods of appeal appear side-by-side with the removal of sin, even as the latter receives special emphasis:

> When the news [of impending doom] reached the king of Nineveh, he rose from his throne, took off his robe, put on sackcloth, and sat in ashes. And he had the word cried through Nineveh: "By decree of the king and his nobles: No man or beast—of herd or flock—shall taste anything! They shall not graze, and they shall not drink water! And they shall be covered with sackcloth—man and beast—and shall cry mightily to God. And let everyone turn back from his evil ways and from the injustice of which he is guilty...." God saw their deeds, that they had turned back from their evil ways, and God renounced the punishment he had planned to bring upon them, and did not carry it out. (Jonah 3:6–10)

After performing rites of royal humiliation (effectively relinquishing the throne), the king of Nineveh enjoins three acts as part of a communal fast: (1) refraining from food, (2) crying out to God, and (3) turning back from evil ways. Those who interpret fasting (no. 1) in light of the command to turn away from evil (no. 3) skip over the intervening requirement for verbal petition (no. 2). The actual sequence of the proclamation—fasting → prayer → turning away from evil—suggests that once again rites of self-affliction are most closely associated with appeals to the deity. This impression is confirmed by the herd and flock's participation in the fast and subjection to Jonah's decree along with the people.[51] There is no reason

---

49. In a preceding discussion (Lambert, *How Repentance Became Biblical*, 23–26), I discuss two separate tracks for approaching the deity. The "mercy" track involves appeal to the deity by means of prayer and sacrifice, both of which work in normal situations when significant sin is absent. The failure of appeal signals a disturbance in the "justice" track, some sort of abhorrent object present before the deity. Thus fast days often involve not only rites of appeal but also attempts to remove such wrongdoing before the deity's sight.

50. Uriel Simon, *Jonah*, JPSBC (Philadelphia: Jewish Publication Society of America, 1999), 30; James Limburg, *Jonah: A Commentary*, OTL (London: SCM, 1993), 80; Jack M. Sasson, *Jonah*, AB 24B (New York: Doubleday, 1990), 244–45, 255, 257; Brongers, "Fasting In Israel," 12; and Guthrie, "Fast, Fasting," 2:243.

51. See Joel 1:18 for the role of groaning beasts on fast days. The "possessions"

to distinguish between these animals' lowing from hunger—surely not an act of penitence—and the pleas of their more articulate human masters.

What is new here is the requirement to "turn back from evil ways" (no. 3). Notice how "turning back from evil ways" fits the visual sense of evil's presence that informs the activities encompassed by the "justice" sphere: "God *saw* their [present] deeds (for they had turned away from their evil ways), and God renounced the punishment" (Jonah 3:10). God only persists in anger when actively provoked by seeing evil done.[52] Leaving off sinful activities effectively removes sin from his sight and frees a now mollified God to experience pity: "Should not I care about Nineveh, that great city, in which there are more than a hundred and twenty thousand persons who do not yet know their right hand from their left [i.e., children], and many beasts as well!" (Jonah 4:11).

These texts share the concern to distinguish between and ultimately privilege one type of religious concern over another.[53] The common way to define the split has been to maintain that one category, generally associated with repentance, constitutes the inner, emotional experience that must accompany the other, the outer ritual display. Actually, two distinct ritual modes appear to be in play. One mode, that of "justice," is emphasized over the other not because it reflects the "real" theological concern at the "heart" of ritual practice, but rather because it must be pursued simultaneously, despite its difficulties, if the standard forms of appeal are to succeed.

7. The Day of Atonement

The most famous of all fasts, *yôm hakkippûrîm* (known as the "Day of Atonement"), is highly atypical as a regular, annual occurrence, not an ad hoc fast. The enumeration of the day's proceedings, as recorded in Leviticus, may be divided into two parts: (1) a description of the purifications the high priest performs (Lev 16:1–28) and (2) commandments to the community to afflict themselves and desist from all productive labor

---

mentioned in Ezra 8:21 may very well refer to livestock. See also Jdt 4:10. The practice of *ḥērem*, the total annihilation of one's enemy in accord with a divine mandate, included the destruction of cattle as well (1 Sam 15:3).

52. Thus, for instance, he (and his angels) must descend to Sodom to witness present wrongdoing for themselves and only then punish (Gen 18:21).

53. Further instances are Jer 36:6–7 and Joel 2:12–13.

(16:29–31). Like other representations of fast days, this priestly text presents us with a fast revolving around two foci: the activities of the leadership and the participation of the community as a whole. In reading Lev 16, one notices a rather abrupt transition: the nonpriestly community, totally absent from the first section, suddenly comes into view in the second. Accordingly, the latter section reads rather like an appendix, an impression confirmed by the presence of equivalent material in Lev 23:26–32 and Num 29:7 unaccompanied by priestly instruction. This structure has led scholars to question whether fasting originally attended the purification rites.[54] The literary disjunction between purification rites and communal fasting, however explained, undermines the common penitential reading of the day, which would view the people's fast as mirroring the actions of the priest, reflecting the proper inner disposition for outer purifications.[55] But, in fact, it underscores the paradigm we have presented whereby the removal of sin (in this case through purification) and fasting appear as parallel-but-distinct ritual tracks that may appear separately or together.

At its heart, *yôm hakkippûrîm* is a series of rituals for purifying the sanctuary and, according to the "appendix" that mandates fasting, purifying the people as well. Incorporating a communal fast reflects the day's gravity, but it also accomplishes an additional task. It provides the people with a way to signify their vested interest and even participation in the otherwise removed activities of the high priest. Mourning can function as a mechanism of participation because it tests and reveals lines of societal interconnectedness. Affliction of the body and the broader suppression of the self involved in the interruption of labor (as mandated in Lev 16:29) provide Israel with concrete acts by which to constitute themselves as a community in need and thereby benefit from the purifying process that unfolds (quite independently) within the sanctuary—a far cry from the expression of individual subjectivities bound up in the notion of fasting as penitential. Precisely for this reason, anyone who fails to fast, who does not subject themselves to the communal-wide affliction, "will be cut off from his kin" (Lev 23:29).

---

54. Israel Knohl, *The Sanctuary of Silence: The Priestly Torah and the Holiness School* (Minneapolis: Fortress, 1995), 27–34.

55. Jacob Milgrom, *Leviticus 1–16: A New Translation with Introduction and Commentary*, AB 3A (New York: Doubleday, 1991), 1066. Roy Gane also sees self-affliction as an expression of repentance (*Cult and Character: Purification Offerings, Day of Atonement, and Theodicy* [Winona Lake, IN: Eisenbrauns, 2005], 380).

8. Conclusion

A wide range of instances of fasting in the Hebrew Bible have been examined, moving from cases of individuals to kings to communities. Along the way, it has been noted that themes commonly associated with "repentance" are usually absent. This overall absence prompted a proposal for an alternative understanding of various modes of self-deprivation as forms of embodiment, ways of inscribing upon the body a disaster that would otherwise remain remote. Even when supposed "penitential" themes figure in the passages under consideration, the continued vitality of fasting as a manifestation of distress, rather than as merely an outward expression of internal feelings, seems evident. On the whole, this essay exposes a powerful tendency among readers of the Bible to favor interiorizing interpretations of ritual behavior and helps raise the question of how and whether to assign "emotion" a role as a category in the analysis of biblical texts in their ancient Israelite contexts.

Select Bibliography

Anderson, Gary A. *A Time to Mourn, a Time to Dance: The Expression of Grief and Joy in Israelite Religion*. University Park, PA: Pennsylvania State University Press, 1991.
Carasik, Michael. *Theologies of the Mind in Biblical Israel*. StBibLit 85. New York: Lang, 2006.
Di Vito, Robert A. "Old Testament Anthropology and the Construction of Personal Identity." *CBQ* 61 (1999): 217–38.
Fisher, Philip. *The Vehement Passions*. Princeton: Princeton University Press, 2002.
Lambert, David A. *How Repentance Became Biblical: Judaism, Christianity, and the Interpretation of Scripture*. New York: Oxford University Press, 2016.
———. "Refreshing Philology: James Barr, Supersessionism, and the State of Biblical Words." *BibInt* 24 (2016): 332–56.
Mirguet, Françoise. "What is an 'Emotion' in the Hebrew Bible? An Experience That Exceeds Most Contemporary Concepts." *BibInt* 24 (2016): 442–65.
Moran, William. "The Ancient Near Eastern Background of the Love of God in Deuteronomy." *CBQ* 25 (1963): 77–87.

Muffs, Yochanan. *Love and Joy: Law, Language, and Religion in Ancient Israel*. New York: Jewish Theological Seminary of America, 1992.
Taylor, Charles. *Sources of the Self: The Making of the Modern Identity*. Cambridge: Cambridge University Press, 1989.
Turner, Victor. *The Drums of Affliction: A Study of Religious Processes among the Ndembu of Zambia*. Oxford: Clarendon, 1968.
———. *The Ritual Process: Structure and Anti-structure*. Chicago: Aldine, 1969.
Van Wolde, Ellen. *Reframing Biblical Studies: When Language and Text Meet Culture, Cognition, and Context*. Winona Lake, IN: Eisenbrauns, 2009.

Emotion, Repentance, and the Question of the "Inner Life" of Biblical Israelites: A Case Study in Hosea 6:1-3

Dennis Olson

This essay seeks to do a close reading of Hos 6:1-3 as a case study on the topic of emotion and repentance in the Hebrew Bible. I will use this "return to the Lord," or *šûb*, text to interact with David A. Lambert's treatment of Hos 6 in his excellent book *How Repentance Became Biblical*.[1] I will then draw out some conclusions about larger issues involving emotion, repentance, the inner life of human beings, and future research on these topics.

1. Hosea 6:1-3 as a Text of Repentance

Our text from the eighth-century prophet, Hos 6:1-3, is embedded within the larger poetic unit in 5:8-6:6. The text begins in 5:8 with God's voice issuing a command to sound a trumpet's alarm announcing a devastating divine judgment about to come upon both the northern kingdom of Israel/Ephraim and the southern kingdom of Judah. Judah is condemned for attacking its northern brother tribe Ephraim. Ephraim in turn is condemned by God for seeking alliances with a foreign king instead of seeking help from Israel's God, YHWH—"When Ephraim saw his sickness, and Judah his wound then Ephraim went to Assyria and sent to the great king. But he [the great king of Assyria] is not able to cure you or heal your wound" (5:13). As a result, God, portrayed metaphorically as an angry lion, promises to attack. The Hebrew is emphatic. God says, "I—yes, I—will rip

---

1. David A. Lambert, *How Repentance Became Biblical: Judaism, Christianity, and the Interpretation of Scripture* (Oxford: Oxford University Press, 2016).

to pieces/tear the flesh" (5:14). The Hebrew verb *ṭrp* is used for a beast tearing at the flesh of its prey. Elsewhere in Hosea, the people are repeatedly called to "return" (*šûb*), but God the lion declares in a kind of reversal that "I will return [*šûb*] to my place until they are utterly destitute on account of their guilt.[2] In their distress, they will seek me and beg for my favor" (5:15).

This then provides the context as the poem continues with a new section marked by a change in voice. God no longer speaks in the first person but now quotes the voice of the people in indirect discourse. The speech in 6:1 is a call to return to Israel's God: "Come, let us return to the Lord, for it is he who has torn, and he will heal us; he has struck down, and he will bind us up." God had earlier promised to return when "they are utterly destitute because of their guilt" and "beg for my favor." Do these words of return or repentance in 6:1 satisfy that criterion or not? Does the implied human speaker of this repentance or return understand the depth of the wound, the extent of the guilt, and the extreme condition in which Israel finds itself? Or does the human speaker see the present wound as little more than a surface irritant that will soon be healed with little trouble? While some commentators argue that God is offering here a template for what true words of return or repentance from the people would sound like, other commentators see this call to return or repent in 6:1–3 as God's quotation of what this still-rebellious people will say just to go through the motions of an insincere return to God.

Reading through 6:1–3 carefully, the reader notices that the form and parallelism of the poetry is suddenly very regular, well rounded, without the usual jagged edges, changing lengths of lines, and other irregularities common to much of Hosea's prophetic poetry. When set off against the surrounding oracles, the almost overly polished parallel form of the poetry gives the impression of a mechanical and smoothed out formalism. Reality is a cycle of assured rhythms: spring follows winter, healing follows wounding, presence follows absence, God's saving follows humans' returning to the Lord. Like the poetry of these verses, reality is assumed to be rounded, closed, comprehensible, and mechanical. Listen to the poetry:

Come, let us return [*šûb*] to the Lord;
for it is he who has torn, and he will heal us;

---

2. I have adopted here Lambert's translation of the Hebrew verb *'āšēm*, "to be utterly destitute on account of guilt." See Lambert, *How Repentance Became Biblical*, 60–61, 80–81. All biblical translations are otherwise my own.

he has struck down, and he will bind us up.
After two days he will revive us;
on the third day he will raise us up,
that we may live before him.
Let us know, let us press on to know the Lord;
his appearing is as sure as the dawn;
he will come to us like the showers,
like the spring rains that water the earth. (6:1–3)

This tidy poem reassures its readers that the killing wound and other "unpleasantness" will last only a couple of days, three days at most. Then, assuredly, God will raise the people up. The poem links God's coming with a return to the cycles of the sun rising without fail at dawn and the rain showers coming each spring no matter what.

2. Lambert, Repentance, and Two "Return" Texts in Hosea

2.1. Overview of Lambert and the "Penitential Lens" in the Hebrew Bible

At this point in our analysis, I turn to Lambert's interesting and substantive monograph on biblical repentance. Lambert argues that we often wrongly impose anachronistic expectations or concepts on alleged Hebrew Bible repentance texts. Later postbiblical readers, both ancient and modern, tend to assume that the real focus and function of supposed acts and words of repentance (confession of sin, fasting, bodily mutilation, offering of sacrifices, and the like) is to reflect a sincere, interior transformation in the inner life of an individual human self. The interior life of the penitent is the primary concern, not the outward and public acts and words. Some scholars suggest that this notion of repentance as interior transformation of the self singularly derives from the Hebrew Bible.[3] Lambert, however, argues against this point. He maintains instead that every Hebrew Bible repentance text that later postbiblical interpreters assume is primarily about interior self-transformation in the inner life of an individual can be more accurately read (in its ancient Near Eastern context) as an exterior, material, public, out-in-the-open social transaction within a network of

---

3. Lambert (*How Repentance Became Biblical*, 193 n. 6) cites as an example Herman Cohen, *Reason and Hope: Selections from the Jewish Writings of Herman Cohen*, trans. Eva Jospe (New York: Norton, 1971), 201–2.

community relationships, both human and divine. This network serves several purposes, including: a plea for healing, realignment of community hierarchies and perceptions, release from communal shame, and other social and transactional functions.

Confessions of sin, fasting, offering sacrifices, tearing of clothing, and other acts are all external mechanisms for making one's pain, shame, or remorse publicly known so that the one experiencing the pain of public shaming or disaster can name and broadcast the pain and begin to move toward some kind of resolution. By externalizing the pain and naming it publicly, the sufferer puts leverage on other humans or on God to help to reorder relationships; make public new social power dynamics; and otherwise participate in reducing the trauma, reestablishing status, or bringing healing within the community. Lambert's book provides a series of extended readings of so-called repentance texts in the Hebrew Bible, addressing the question: what if we counter-read the details of this given repentance text not as about inner self-transformation but as about a public, externalized transaction or communication within a community of social relationships needing some kind of resolution? One of Lambert's concerns is to honor the integrity of the voices of the ancient "others" embedded within the Hebrew Bible and to allow them to have their say on their own terms within their ancient cultural world without imposing our often deeply ingrained, unconscious, or unreflective assumptions about the inner life and consciousness of the individual self. Such notions of the interiority of the self, Lambert contends, emerge only later in postbiblical Judaism and Christianity, beginning with a major shift in the works of Philo and ancient Greek philosophy and then accelerated into the modern post-Enlightenment West. One thinks here of the philosopher Charles Taylor's *The Sources of the Self: The Making of the Modern Identity* or Krister Stendahl's classic essay on "Paul and the Introspective Conscience of the West," among others.[4]

I confess that I find compelling many of Lambert's readings that intentionally run against the grain of an overly interiorized "penitential lens" in interpreting the Hebrew Bible. For example, the book of Judges contains the element of "crying out" in a repeated narrative cycle: Israel sins, God allows

---

4. Charles Taylor, *Sources of the Self: The Making of Modern Identity* (Cambridge: Harvard University Press, 1989); Krister Stendahl, "The Apostle Paul and the Introspective Conscience of the West," *HTR* 56 (1963): 199–215. See Lambert, *How Repentance Became Biblical*, 9, 195, 216, 219.

Israel to be oppressed by an enemy, Israel cries out to God, and then God sends a judge to rescue the Israelites. The "crying out" element in the cycle has been interpreted by commentators as consisting of the Israelites' expression of repentance to God for their sin. Moreover, according to this view, repentance signals an interior change in the Israelites that directly motivates subsequent divine deliverance. Lambert demonstrates, however, that repentance of sin plays no role in these cycles in Judges except with the very last one in 10:10. Everywhere else in Judges, the crying out is simply a cry of pain (not repentance), and it is this cry of pain from human sufferers that leverages a merciful God to respond. Moreover, the one actual confession of sin in 10:10 proves wholly ineffective in stimulating God's deliverance (10:13). God eventually does respond to the people, not because of their confession of sin, but rather because a merciful God "could no longer bear to see Israel suffer" (10:16). As Lambert observes, "It is clear that compassion for suffering, ... not the cessation of sin, proves to be the immediate catalyst, the efficient cause of redemption."[5] Repentance has no great effect on God; the simple cry of human pain and plea for help does.

It is also the case that the motif of human repentance plays a much less frequent role in the prophets of the Hebrew Bible than commonly assumed. The most prevalent forms or genres in prophetic books are descriptive oracles of divine judgment or descriptive oracles of deliverance with relatively few exhortations to repent. Similarly, the offerings of sacrifice within the Priestly tradition may not function primarily as external expressions of an internal state of deep personal remorse within an individual who brings the offering. The sacrifices may be better understood as public acts to rid the sanctuary and community from a communal miasmic sin perceived as an exterior, objective, and material reality that infects the community rather than a deformed inner disposition within individual selves that must be transformed.

2.2. Return (šûb) in Hosea 6:1–3 and Its Immediate Context

While I appreciate many of Lambert's insights throughout his book, I want to examine his treatment of the šûb ("turn/return") text in Hos 6:1–3 as a way to raise some larger issues about his project. Lambert notes that "undoubtedly the richest collection of early shuv material is found in the

---

5. Lambert, *How Repentance Became Biblical*, 43–44.

scroll attributed to the eighth-century prophet, Hosea."[6] The call in 6:1–3 to "turn" or "return" to God does not result in God's deliverance of the people. Was this call to return a poorly performed act of repentance? Was this call a failure to achieve a sufficiently sincere internal shift of affections and emotions within the inner life of individual Israelites? No, says Lambert: "This passage provides little that suggests improper performance, a lack of the requisite sincerity."[7] The real problem, in Lambert's view, is that Israel's "turn" away from Assyria's king and to God "comes too late, after they have already insulted the deity by appealing to Assyria," and they did not bring material gifts owed to Israel's God as part of Israel's "seeking" the Lord.[8] As an anthropopathic deity with human emotions, Lambert interprets God's refusal to respond positively to Israel's words of "turning" quite negatively. God is full of "spite." God is "self-interested" and anxious for the people to utterly fail "in order to clarify their true source of sustenance."[9] The Israelites missed the deadline for returning, and God wants to make them pay. Here a number of questions and concerns arise. I begin with three pertaining to the text and immediate context of 6:1–3.

First, Lambert's discussion includes only one of the three verses calling for return to the Lord. Curiously, Lambert presents a lengthy quotation of Hos 5:13–6:4 *except* for the two crucial verses in 6:2–3 regarding the people's repentance. Moreover, he does not mark these verses as a deletion with the customary ellipsis; rather, his citation abruptly jumps from 6:1 to 6:4. Though I am not suggesting that this lacuna was intentional, the absence of 6:2–3 considerably skews the tone of the call to return. Contrary to Lambert's conclusion about insincerity not being in evidence here, those two deleted verses clearly seem, in my judgment, to suggest a lack of sincerity and a failure to recognize the depth of Israel's sin: "After two days [the Lord] will revive us; on the third day he will raise us up, so that we may live before him. Let us press on to know the Lord; his appearing is as sure as the dawn; he will come to us like the showers, like the spring rains that water the earth." It is no big deal, says the smug voice of Israel. God will get us up and running in two or three days. God's healing is guaranteed, automatic, cyclical—as sure as the sun's rising every day and the coming of the rains every spring. The lack of sincerity, I would argue, is

---

6. Ibid., 79.
7. Ibid., 80.
8. Ibid., 80; cf. n. 33 and n. 206.
9. Ibid., 81.

expressed in both the content and the polished poetic form of Israel's call to return that I noted above.

Second, Lambert does not comment on God's explicit assessment of the insincerity and shallowness of the people's confession of wrongdoing that immediately follows Israel's call to return in 6:4. God's voice speaks in exasperation: "What can I do for you, O Ephraim? What can I do for you, O Judah? Your love/your covenant loyalty [ḥesed] is like a morning cloud, like the dew that goes away early." God seems here engaged in an internal dialogue, a conversation within the inner life of God. God condemns the people's love and loyalty as ephemeral, shallow, and short lived. God experiences Israel's love and attachment to God as insincere, without depth or breadth. God is emotionally troubled.

Third, in addition to omitting 6:2–3 from his analysis of Israel's call to return, Lambert also fails to include the final two verses of this prophetic poem, 6:5–6 (the poetic unit runs from 5:8 to 6:6). Once again, this pair of verses offers essential information on the debate whether this text focuses primarily on the internal life and emotions of the Israelites or on more externalized, material, and transactional dynamics within a network of social relationships. God speaks again, "Therefore I have hewn them [the Israelites] by the prophets, I have killed them by the words of my mouth, and my judgment goes forth as the light" (6:5). The carefully crafted poetic words of the prophet have power to shape, hew, and kill. How do poetic words of judgment do such things? Poetry is heightened human language that touches both intellect and emotion through the double play of sound and image. The poem enters the ears of its hearers as spoken words, and, the text claims, something hugely transformative, even deadly, happens as sound waves translate into language within the hearer's body. One might speak here of a language-induced inner life and inner death.

God's voice continues in 6:6, the last verse of the poem: "For I desire steadfast love/loyalty [ḥesed again] and not sacrifice, the knowledge of God rather than burnt offerings." Here Lambert's claim that every šûb ("return") text in the Hebrew Bible is all about externality, materiality, and outward social dynamics and interaction rather than the transformation of internal affections or emotions comes into question. Neither material sacrifices nor physical burnt offerings are at the heart of what God desires. Instead, God desires love, loyalty, and a deep knowing of God, all of which occur within human bodies, both individual and communal, as an essential element in relationship to God. In terms of priority of concern: inner life, yes, externality, no.

2.3. Return (*šûb*) in Hosea 14:1-7 in Comparison with 6:1-3

Lambert's analysis of Hosea's *šûb* material also ignores a decisive second call to repentance, a second call to return at the very end of the book. I consider Hos 14:1-3 to be the most important of all the *šûb*/return texts in Hosea, and yet Lambert does not mention it. This second call to return begins with an exhortation: "Return [*šûb*], O Israel, to the Lord your God, for you have stumbled because of your iniquity. Take words with you and return [*šûb*] to the Lord; say to him, 'Take away all guilt; accept that which is good, and we will offer the fruit of our lips. Assyria shall not save us; we will not ride upon horses; we will say no more, 'Our God,' to the work of our hands. In you the orphan finds mercy" (14:1-3).

Thus, we have in the book of Hosea two calls to return that we can compare and contrast. The contrast in tone, mood, and emotion between them is significant. The penitent one in chapter 14 is an orphan without material resources who has stumbled in iniquity, who seeks forgiveness of guilt, and who has only "the fruit of our lips" to offer back to God. While God rejects the call to return in chapter 6, God has a very different assessment and response to this call to repentance in 14:1-3. God responds immediately after the second repentance speech with these words: "I will heal their disloyalty; I will love them freely; for my anger has turned from them" (14:4). A few verses later God continues: "They [the Israelites] shall again live beneath my shadow" (14:7). Words can enter into the hearer and kill, but they can also make alive: "Take words with you and return to the Lord (14:2). In Hos 14, the people's repentance and return involve refraining from entanglement with external objects and relationships: no seeking of material aid from Assyria, no trust in the physical military strength of horses, no worship of human-created external objects as deities. Only words that flow from inside human bodies, the fruit of our lips.

I return now to Lambert's rather negative characterization of God in Hos 6 noted above. According to Lambert, God in Hos 6 is spiteful, self-interested, in pursuit of power, and anxious to make Israel suffer in order to pay for the dishonor and the lack of material offerings and sacrifices that God suffered when Israel went off and sought aid from Assyria.[10] If, however, we pull back and view the full characterization of God in Hosea, and especially the full texts of both of these two calls to "return" to the Lord, I

---

10. Ibid., 81.

think the portrait of God is somewhat more positive: in the end, a God of mercy, a God who desires loyalty and love rather than material offerings and sacrifices, a God whose ultimate desire is for life and not death, a God who in the end heals and loves, a God who ultimately "turns" (*šûb*) God's anger away from God's people. Given Lambert's strong and laudable desire to read these ancient texts in ways that honor how ancient audiences would have heard these texts of Hosea, I find it difficult to imagine that an ancient Israelite hearing the full content of Hosea's prophetic poetry would have construed God's character in such a negative and cynical way.

Lambert uses one other argument to support his contention that God in Hos 6 is primarily upset by the loss of Israel's *material* goods as sacrifices. Israel is going off to Egypt and Assyria with offerings in exchange for aid (11:5). God is upset because these physical offerings properly belong to Israel's God, not to Egypt or Assyria. God, after all, is the source of Israel's sustenance, and so God ought to receive offerings back in exchange. Lambert notes that the motif of Hosea's marriage to his prostitute wife involves a similar model of exchange. The prostitute Gomer, like Israel, seeks out material sustenance from other lovers. Hosea, like God, refuses to support her for a time. Ultimately, a restoration occurs in which Hosea provides material sustenance again for his formerly wayward wife. In return, she will call out the prophet's name in a relational model of exchange, although what Gomer and Israel have in the end to give to God is simply words, verbal acknowledgements that their material sustenance comes from God.[11] The relationship is about exchange of goods done publicly and openly, not about internal feelings or emotions of marital love, jealousy, and the like.

However, such an extended relational metaphor can play at multiple levels within Hosea. The issue of mutual exchange and acknowledgement of the source of material goods may well be one dimension, but relationships of courting and marriage in ancient Israel could and often did involve something more emotional and internally sustained through bonds of attachment to one another (Gen 29:20; Song of Songs). The words of God in Hos 2:19–20 play off the husband-and-wife metaphor and include God's intimate and emotional bonds to Israel as God's marital partner that seem to go beyond the mutual exchange of physical goods: "And I will take you for my wife forever; I will take you for my wife in

---

11 Ibid., 81.

righteousness and in justice, in steadfast love, and in mercy. I will take you for my wife in faithfulness; and you shall know the Lord." One also recalls a second powerful relational metaphor that operates within Hosea, and that is the parent-and-child metaphor that figures prominently in chapter 11 and includes vocabulary of intimate emotion and affection in describing God's relationship to Israel. God recalls, "When Israel was a child, I loved him, and out of Egypt I called my son…. Yet it was I who taught Ephraim to walk, I took them up in my arms; but they did not know that I healed them…. How can I give you up, O Ephraim? How can I hand you over, O Israel?" (11:1–8). Here we have another instance of God's own internal dialogue regarding the relationship with Israel, a window into a divine inner life similar to what we saw in 6:4. Such intimate attachment language applied to God sets up an expectation of similar inner emotional attachment from the human side.

3. Conclusions and Suggestions for Further Research

Based on this study of the prophet Hosea, I now offer some conclusions, hunches, lingering questions, and suggestions for further research on the topics of repentance, emotions, and notions of the inner lives of both God and humans in the Hebrew Bible.

First, how do we distinguish between more or less universal human capabilities hardwired into our brains as human beings evolved over millions of years and culturally and historically shaped frameworks of understanding that we may be unaware of or that we assume are universal when they are not? The construction of a sense of a self and of an inner life, the capacity (or lack thereof) to discern accurately the dynamics of that inner life within oneself or others, and the role of emotions in the dynamics of repentance and forgiveness in human history all call for an interdisciplinary conversation with evolutionary biology, neuroscience, psychology, anthropology, and other fields.

For example, the field of affective neuroscience offers insights on the topic of emotions and human reasoning in social relationships. Although one must be cautious in how one appropriates knowledge based in other disciplines, such interdisciplinary exploration may provide interesting "virtual parallels" that stimulate new questions in our reading and interpretation of texts, even ancient texts like the Bible.

In a 2003 paper entitled "Seven Sins in the Study of Emotion: Correctives from Affective Neuroscience," Richard J. Davidson summarized the latest findings in neuroscience prompting a rejection of several outdated views on emotion. One major incorrect assumption in past research was that "affect and cognition are served by separate and independent neural circuits" within the brain. Past researchers often identified reason and rationality with the more newly evolved parts of the human brain while emotion was linked to the more primitive, reptilian part. Davidson instead emphasized more recent research that points to a significant "overlap between circuitry involved in cognitive and affective processing" or an overlap in brain processes involved in intellect and emotion. Brain imaging and other research suggest that reasoning and decision making in the social domain (having to do with interactions with others and related moral reasoning) occur within the same regions of the brain and along the same networks as the processing of emotions. Moreover, Davidson also notes that neuroscience challenges the view that emotions are (or necessarily involve) conscious feeling states. Emotions are defined as cognitive information processes that activate dispositions for action. Feelings, on the other hand, involve conscious awareness and reflection upon such processes of activating dispositions.[12]

In a 2012 article, Michael Spezio offers an assessment of neuroscientific research on emotion and concludes similarly that "what is emerging is a complex interconnection of circuits in which emotional signals cannot be separated from adaptive reasoning and decision making, when such judgment and action are relevant for oneself and others. That this emerging account has implications for moral theology, especially any system that values human relationality, should be clear."[13] Gerald Clore concurs in his survey of psychology's contribution to understanding emotions and rationality: "Rather than thinking ... of emotion and cognition as horses pulling in different directions, we should think of them as strands of a single rope, made strong by their being thoroughly intertwined."[14]

---

12. Richard J. Davidson, "Seven Sins in the Study of Emotion: Correctives from Affective Neuroscience," *BC* 52 (2003): 129–32. See also R. Adolphs, "The Neurobiology of Social Cognition," *CON* 11 (2001): 231–39; N. Tsuchiya and R. Adolphs, "Emotion and Consciousness," *TCS* 11 (2007): 158–67.

13. Michael Spezio, "The Neuroscience of Emotion and Reasoning in Social Contexts: Implications for Moral Theology," in *Faith, Rationality, and the Passions*, ed. Sarah Coakley (Malden, MA: Wiley-Blackwell, 2012), 236.

14. Gerald Clore, "Psychology and the Rationality of Emotion," in Coakley, *Faith, Rationality, and the Passions*, 221.

One specific aspect of this integration of the brain's processing of emotion and social cognition involves "the experience of an emotion or intention in oneself and the perception of intention or emotion in another. The networks carrying out this double duty of self- and other-representation are termed 'shared circuits,' or sometimes 'mirror neurons.' These networks are then supportive of empathy, which is the ability spontaneously to reconstruct in oneself what another is feeling, thinking, and intending."[15] This hardwired ability to reconstruct thoughts and emotions within other humans enables empathy with modern fictive characters when reading a novel or with ancient biblical characters when reading the Bible.[16] Might we assume that eighth-century Israelites also had mirror neurons and were capable of imagining the inner thoughts, emotions, and intentions of other humans, of human characters in narratives, as well as themselves? Might the close overlap between emotional dispositions and cognitive processing in social relationships in brain research cause us to be cautious about assuming too strong a binary between the emotional inner life of a self and the outward, material, and objective dynamics of public social interaction? Might a better model involve a more complex and integrated view of the intertwined emotional inner life and outward social interaction of human beings with some persons leaning more or less in one direction or another (e.g., extroversion versus introversion)?

Second, the issues of how our sense of self and identity emerge remains a large area of debate in the natural sciences and philosophy of the mind, with various models ranging from a pure physicalism to a mind/body dualism or some notion of a human soul. We simply do not know how the electrochemical reactions among the 86 billion neurons that make up the human brain translate into the sense that we are a unified self with emotions, inner dialogues, and interactions with an outside world.[17] Thus, on these large questions that remain under dispute, our conclusions need to be provisional and open and perhaps even agnostic in the face of unresolved mysteries.

---

15. Spezio, "Neuroscience of Emotion," 235.

16. Suzanne Keen, "A Theory of Narrative Empathy," *Narrative* 14 (2006): 207–36; Keen, *Empathy and the Novel* (Oxford: Oxford University Press, 2007).

17. The number of 86 billion neurons packed into a mere 1,400 grams of matter in the human brain has been confirmed by the painstaking research of the Brazilian neuroscientist Suzana Herculano-Houzel, *The Human Advantage: A New Understanding of How Our Brain Became Remarkable* (Cambridge: MIT Press, 2016).

Third, a lingering question that arises from this work is the relationship of identity based on a more individualistic view versus one heavily dependent on a communal or corporate view of the self in which identity derives primarily from a network of relationships.[18] The two calls to return to the Lord in Hos 6 and 14 focus on communities as a whole, not on individuals. The verbs and pronouns have plural referents when speaking of humans. What might texts like Deuteronomy—with its interchange of second-person singular and second-person plural address—or Jeremiah—with its portrayal of the individual prophet's inner life and struggles with God alongside Jeremiah's more public role as a prophet to a community who will soon struggle in similar ways as he does—teach us about the relationship of individual and community and the identity of the self? Moreover, can one speak meaningfully of the inner life of a community, the emotions of a community (psychology has a field called social mood), or the corporate responsibility of the community? How does this intersect with notions of the inner life of individuals?

Fourth, the Hebrew Bible contains within it a diversity of images of God's body that operate within different traditions.[19] The body of God in the Priestly tradition is a cosmic, mystical, and abstract body. The notion of sin within the Priestly tradition and the process of its elimination is more objective, material, and less relationally oriented. On the other hand, texts like Hosea or Jeremiah portray God in a more anthropomorphic way with human-like emotions and an inner divine life and dialogue. Do portrayals of the relative emotionality or the possible role of an inner life involved in human sin and repentance in this stream of tradition within the Hebrew Bible correlate with the more human-like portraits of the emotionality of God? Might one need to concede that there are one or more individual streams of tradition in the Hebrew Bible that do indeed place more focus on repentance as a transformation in the inner life of individuals or a community, involving an integrative interaction of emotional dispositions, cognitive processes, and public social interactions and

---

18. See Joel Kaminsky, *Corporate Responsibility in the Hebrew Bible* (Sheffield: Sheffield Academic, 1995).

19. See Benjamin D. Sommer, *The Bodies of God and World of Ancient Israel* (Cambridge: Cambridge University Press, 2009); Mark S. Smith, *Where the Gods Are: Spatial Dimensions of Anthropomorphism in the Biblical World* (New Haven: Yale University Press, 2016); Terence E. Fretheim, *The Suffering of God: An Old Testament Perspective*, OBT 14 (Philadelphia: Fortress, 1984).

dynamics, well before the late Second Temple period? Might also Deuteronomy be included as such a stream of tradition with its language of the "heart" involved in an individual's internal dialogue ("do not say in your [singular] heart" [Deut 7:17; 8:17; 9:4]) associated with loyalty to God, in God's setting the divine heart on Israel (7:7), and in loving God with all your heart (mixing intimate familial and political covenant language [6:5])? One might also note the juxtaposition of the motif of circumcising the heart in Deut 10:16, addressed to the community as a second-person *plural* command from God to the human and assuming *human* agency ("Circumcise, then, the foreskin of your heart, and do not be stubborn any longer"), and in 30:6, promised to the individual in a second-person *singular* imperfect form with God as the subject promising *divine* agency ("YHWH your God will circumcise your heart").[20]

---

20. On the origin and meaning of the "love" of God in Deuteronomy and elsewhere in the Hebrew Bible, see Jon D. Levenson, *The Love of God: Divine Gift, Human Gratitude, and Mutual Faithfulness in Judaism* (Princeton: Princeton University Press, 2016). Levenson writes: "The love of God in the Hebrew Bible, then, is a matter of both action and affect, with each influencing the other. Efforts to separate action and affect, and conceptions of the self that disjoin the two, can lead only to a drastic misunderstanding" (xiv). Elsewhere in this work, Levenson observes that the covenantal love of God in Deuteronomy has some resonance with the language of "love" understood as loyalty to a superior in the international diplomatic realm of ancient Near Eastern treaties between a more powerful emperor and a lesser king. Levenson argues, however, that the notion of covenant "does not *originate* in international diplomacy. Instead, it borrows much of its character and force from something more primal: namely, from family relations. 'In tribal societies,' Frank Moore Cross writes, 'there were legal mechanisms or devices—we might even say legal fictions—by which outsiders, non-kin, might be incorporated within the kinship group.' He adds, 'Oath and covenant, in which the deity is witness, guarantor, or participant, is also a widespread legal means by which the duties and privileges of kinship may be extended to another individual or group, including aliens'" (*The Love of God*, 22–23, citing Frank Moore Cross, *From Epic to Canon: History and Literature in Ancient Israel* [Baltimore: Johns Hopkins University Press, 1998], 7–8). Further, Levenson responds to a claim by Dennis J. McCarthy: "McCarthy's claim that the love in question 'is simply a matter of reverence, loyalty, obedience, things subject to command and commanded,' and not one of 'tender, feeling love' (146) is not correct, as I argue later in this chapter." See Levenson, *The Love of God*, 202 n. 27; McCarthy, "Notes on the Love of the Love of God in Deuteronomy and the Father–Son Relationship between Yahweh and Israel," *CBQ* 27 (1965): 144–47. In answering yes to the question of "whether some element of feeling is also entailed in Israel's covenantal love of the LORD as portrayed in the Hebrew Bible," Levenson (*The Love of God*, 202–3 n. 28, n. 31) cites approvingly the

A close reading of Hos 6:1–3 within the larger context of the book of Hosea has suggested that at least some streams of traditions within the Hebrew Bible do indeed include some role for emotions and some notion of an inner self in texts dealing with repentance. Lambert is correct to note a scholarly overuse of the "penitential lens" in interpreting some alleged "repentance" texts in the Hebrew Bible. He is also correct to underscore the multiple ways in which the Hebrew Bible typically portrays individuals and communities as always operating within a network of public and material "others," including other human bodies, the divine "other," and the larger culture and world of a given time and space in history. I have suggested, however, that at least one text, Hos 6:1–3, may be more adequately understood within a more integrative model that includes attention to the inner life of emotion and attitude of individuals and communities as one element among others within a dynamic web of self, other selves (both human and divine), and the cultural world in which these texts are embedded.

Select Bibliography

R. Adolphs. "The Neurobiology of Social Cognition." *CON* 11 (2001): 231–39.
Clore, Gerald L. "Psychology and the Rationality of Emotion." Pages 209–22 in *Faith, Rationality, and the Passions*. Edited by Sarah Coakley. Malden, MA: Wiley-Blackwell, 2011.
Davidson, Richard J. "Seven Sins in the Study of Emotion: Correctives from Affective Neuroscience." *BC* 52 (2003): 129–32.
Herculano-Houzel, Suzana. *The Human Advantage: A New Understanding of How Our Brain Became Remarkable*. Cambridge: MIT Press, 2016.
Keen, Suzanne. *Empathy and the Novel*. Oxford: Oxford University Press, 2007.
Lambert, David A. *How Repentance Became Biblical: Judaism, Christianity, and the Interpretation of Scripture*. Oxford: Oxford University Press, 2016.

---

following articles: J. W. McKay, "Man's Love for God in Deuteronomy and the Father/Teacher–Son/Pupil Relationship," *VT* 22 (1972): 426–35; Jacqueline Lapsley, "Feeling Our Way: Love for God in Deuteronomy," *CBQ* 65 (2003): 350–69; Bill T. Arnold, "The Love–Fear Antinomy in Deuteronomy 5–11," *VT* 61 (2011): 551–69.

Levenson, Jon D. *The Love of God: Divine Gift, Human Gratitude, and Mutual Faithfulness in Judaism*. Princeton: Princeton University Press, 2016.

Smith, Mark S. *Where the Gods Are: Spatial Dimensions of Anthropomorphism in the Biblical World*. New Haven: Yale University Press, 2016.

Sommer, Benjamin D. *The Bodies of God and World of Ancient Israel*. Cambridge: Cambridge University Press, 2009.

Spezio, Michael L. "The Neuroscience of Emotion and Reasoning in Social Contexts: Implications for Moral Theology." Pages 223–40 in *Faith, Rationality, and the Passions*. Edited by Sarah Coakley. Malden, MA: Wiley-Blackwell, 2011.

Tsuchiya, N., and R. Adolphs. "Emotion and Consciousness." *TCS* 11 (2007): 158–67.

The Pride of Babylon in Isaiah 47 Revisited in Light of the Theory of Self-Conscious Emotions

Antony Dhas Prakasam

Babylon has become the symbol of "pride before a fall" due to the reception history and modern exegesis of Isa 47, among other oracles against Babylon.[1] Scholars agree that within the biblical tradition Babylon was transformed from a historical entity (the capital of the Nebuchadnezzar's empire) to an apocalyptic type (a symbol of powers hostile to God in the end times).[2] Such an apocalyptic presentation of Babylon began in Isa 13–14, continued in Daniel, and was perfected in Rev 17–18.[3] For the author of Revelation, Babylon no longer represents the ancient historical

---

1. Scholars generally concur that the motif of pride is prominent in Isaiah's Oracles against the Nations; see, e.g., Duane L. Christensen, *Transformations of the War Oracle in the Old Testament Prophecy: Studies in the Oracles against the Nations*, HDR 3 (Missoula, MT: Scholars Press, 1975), 137; G. R. Hamborg, "Reasons for Judgment in the Oracles against the Nations of the Prophet Isaiah," *VT* 31 (1981): 152.

2. E.g., Robert Martin-Achard states: "Le nom de Babel sert, au terme d'une evolution qui s'esquisse avec et après l'exil, à designer une réalité qui n'est pas simplement une cite terrestre, fût-elle la célèbre capital de l'empire de Nébucadnetsar, mais qui peut s'incarner dans n'importe quelle forme d'absolutisme, lorsque le pouvoir se prend pour fin et s'imagine être Dieu" ("Esaïe 47 et la tradition prophétique sur Babylone," in *Prophecy: Essays Presented to Georg Fohrer on His Sixty-Fifth Birthday*, ed. J. A. Emerton [Berlin: de Gruyter, 1980], 104). For a similar view, see J. Vermeylen, *Du prophète Isaïe à l'Apocalyptique, Isaïe I–XXXV, miroir d'un demi-millénaire d'expérience religieuse en Israël*, 2 vols., EBib (Paris: Lecoffre, 1977), 1:289.

3. Willem A. M. Beuken argues that the prosaic introductory verses of Isa 14:1–4a and the concluding verses of 14:22–23, in which the name of Babylon occurs, are postexilic additions to or an apocalyptic *relecture* of the original poem in 14:4b–21. See Beuken, *Jesaja 13–27*, HThKAT (Freiburg: Herder, 2007), 83.

city but symbolizes a political-economic-religious power, which is all evil, proud, and oppressive of God's people.[4]

Though Revelation does not identify "Babylon" with any particular city or nation, the church fathers routinely identified present-day enemies of God with proud Babylon of old. Tertullian links Babylon with Rome, Cyprian associates it with Jerusalem in his anti-Jewish polemic, and Tyconius goes a step further to identify the Beast and Whore (Babylon) as the mystical body of Satan.[5] This hermeneutic of identification continued into the Reformation, as Protestants extended the proud Babylon-Rome nexus to the epicenter of Catholicism.[6]

Modern scholars such as Chris A. Franke and Robert Martin-Achard, on the other hand, take keen interest in categorizing and labeling the pride of Babylon as "pride before a fall."[7] For these and many other scholars, the oracles against Babylon like Isa 47 are, in fact, oracles of salvation for Jerusalem, celebrating the reversal of Babylon's fortunes and her fall caused by her proud flaunting of political, economic, and religious power.[8] The divine intervention in Isa 47, consistent with the theology of Second Isaiah, humiliates proud Babylon and asserts divine sovereignty over all human authorities.[9]

---

4. Many New Testament commentators rightly argue that the image of Babylon in Rev 17–18 is based on the raw materials of Isa 47, Jer 51, Ezek 27–28, and Daniel. See Ian Boxall, "The Many Faces of Babylon the Great: Wirkungsgeschichte and the Interpretation of Revelation 17," in *Studies in the Book of Revelation*, ed. Steve Moyise (Edinburgh: T&T Clark, 2001), 177–93.

5. Judith Kovacs and Christopher Rowland, *Revelation: The Apocalypse of Jesus Christ*, Blackwell Bible Commentaries (Malden, MA: Blackwell, 2004), 178–79.

6. Boxall, "Many Faces of Babylon," 177–93.

7. "The address to Virgin Daughter Babylon in Isa xlvii can be seen to function as a foil or point of comparison and contrast to the figure of Daughter Zion.… The ironic tone of xlvii heightens even more the contrast between the two. The humiliations and losses of Babylon emphasize by contrast the rejoicing and elevation of Jerusalem/Zion in xliv–lv" (C. A. Franke, "The Function of the Satiric Lament over Babylon in Second Isaiah [XLVII]," *VT* 41 [1991]: 417). See also Martin-Achard, "Esaïe 47 et la tradition."

8. "La disparition de Babel est la condition de la realization du plan de Yahvé en faveur de Jérusalem" (Martin-Achard, "Esaïe 47 et la tradition," 90). See also Chris A. Franke, "Reversals of Fortune in the Ancient Near East: A Study of the Babylon Oracles in the Book of Isaiah," in *New Visions of Isaiah*, ed. Roy F. Melugin and Marvin A. Sweeney, JSOTSup 214 (Sheffield: Sheffield Academic, 1996), 110–16.

9. "Yahvé et uniquement Yahvé conduit l'histoire, il dispose souverainement des natioins et ne supporte aucun rival à des côtés" (Martin-Achard, "Esaïe 47 et la tra-

Such identification of Babylon with pride, along with the rhetorical amplification and vilification of this pride, tends to distance readers from the text, prompting an *us-versus-them* attitude. In the process, any trace of pride is easily denigrated and shunned, and humiliation of the proud is construed as just (divine?) retribution.

I will look at the pride of Babylon in Isa 47 from a new perspective provided by the psychological theory of Self-Conscious Emotions (SCE) propounded by psychologists Jessica L. Tracy, Richard W. Robins, and June P. Tangney. This theory presents pride as a reality in every human heart and argues that not all pride is bad. By analyzing the dynamics of Babylon's pride, assisted by SCE theory, this essay distinguishes between different facets of Babylon's pride and affirms that divine intervention is not as humiliating as previously presented. Before engaging the text of Isa 47 in detail, I delineate the salient features of the theory of SCE, with special attention to pride.

1. Pride as a Self-Conscious Emotion: A Theoretical Survey

SCE theory originated as the result of a revolution in the understanding of emotions: beyond mere feelings, emotions are grounded in "bodily expressions and actions, cognitive appraisals, and social interactions."[10] Some emotions are biologically based, shared with other animals, and universally experienced as so-called "basic emotions," such as anger, fear, disgust, sadness, happiness, and surprise. Other emotions, however, may be distinguished as "self-conscious emotions," including shame, guilt, pride and embarrassment.[11]

Psychologists distinguish self-conscious emotions from basic emotions on the following lines:[12]

---

dition," 92). See also Chris A. Franke, *Isaiah 46, 47, and 48: A New Literary-Critical Reading*, BJSUCSD 3 (Winona Lake, IN: Eisenbrauns, 1994).

10. Kurt W. Fischer and June Price Tangney, "Self-Conscious Emotions and the Affect Revolution: Framework and Overview," in *Self-Conscious Emotions: The Psychology of Shame, Guilt, Embarrassment, and Pride*, ed. Tangney and Fischer (New York: Guilford, 1995), 6.

11. Jessica L. Tracy and Richard W. Robins, "The Self in Self-Conscious Emotions: A Cognitive Appraisal Approach," in *The Self-Conscious Emotions: Theory and Research*, ed. Jessica L. Tracy, Richard W. Robins, and June Price Tangney (New York: Guilford, 2007), 4.

12. Ibid., 5–7.

- Self-conscious emotions require self-awareness, self-representations, and self-evaluative processes. In short, a concept of self is central to these emotions. While basic emotions like fear and sadness may involve a self-evaluative process, self-conscious emotions *must* involve such a process.
- Psychological surveys have shown that self-conscious emotions, unlike basic emotions, emerge later in childhood, from three years of age forward.[13]
- While basic emotions may promote survival goals, self-conscious emotions, besides facilitating survival goals, are directed toward social goals such as stabilizing social hierarchies and affirming social roles.[14]
- While basic emotions have universal facial expressions, self-conscious emotions vary from culture to culture in their facial markers.[15]

Although all emotions are social, self-conscious emotions "are founded in social relationships ... [and] built on reciprocal evaluation and judgment. For example, people are ashamed or guilty because they assume that someone (self and/or other) is making a negative judgment about some activity or characteristic of theirs."[16] They are also called "moral emotions," since they "arise when reflecting on one's self and evaluating that self in reference to values and standards."[17] These "emotions influence moral behavior in two distinct contexts: as anticipatory emotions that come into

---

13. For a detailed study of the development of self-conscious emotions, see the following essays in Tangney and Fischer, *Self-Conscious Emotions*: Michael F. Mascolo and Kurt W. Fischer, "Developmental Transformations in Appraisals for Pride, Shame, and Guilt," 64–113; Carolyn Zahn-Waxler and Joann Robinson, "Empathy and Guilt: Early Origins of Feelings of Responsibility," 143–73.

14. For a detailed study of the social function of self-conscious emotions, see Karen Caplovitz Barrett, "A Functional Approach to Shame and Guilt," in Tangney and Fischer, *Self-Conscious Emotions*, 25–63.

15. Though pride is universal with widely recognized nonverbal expressions, such expressions are discouraged in certain cultures and religions as marks of arrogance. Hence, discrepancies exist between felt and verbally communicated experiences of pride; see Vanda Lucia Zammuner, "Felt Emotions and Verbally Communicated Emotions: The Case of Pride," *EJSP* 26 (1996): 243.

16. Fischer and Tangney, "Self-Conscious Emotions," 3–4.

17. June Price Tangney, Jeffrey Steuwig, and Debra J. Mashek, "What's Moral

play when we review and contemplate behavioral alternatives, and as consequential emotions in the wake of actual behavior, motivating subsequent behavior such as altruism, reparation, or defensiveness."[18]

Pride is an important self-conscious emotion central to social life, since it functions to maintain and promote an individual's social status and acceptance.[19] It is noteworthy that pride has long been recognized as the root cause of all evil. Dante refers to it as the deadliest of the Seven Deadly Sins.[20] However, modern Western culture typically regards pride as a virtue. So a fundamental moral question emerges: is pride good or bad?[21]

SCE theory argues that pride is multifaceted rather than a single unified construct. Psychologists distinguish "the pride that results from a specific achievement or prosocial behavior [e.g., 'I won because I practiced'] from pride in one's global self [e.g., 'I won because I'm always great']."[22] They dub the former "authentic" or *beta* pride and the latter "hubristic" or *alpha* pride. Authentic/*beta* pride may be further unpacked in terms of one's sense of "accomplishment," "success," "achievement," "fulfillment," "self-worth," "confidence," and "productivity"; hubristic/*alpha* pride in terms of "snobbery," "pomposity," being "stuck-up," "conceit," "egotism," "arrogance," and "smugness."[23] Studies have also proved that since hubristic pride words have negative connotations, people tend to use them to describe the pride of others, while using authentic pride words to describe their own pride.[24]

These two facets have distinct personality correlates: "one facet is associated with positive personality profile and prosocial behaviors, whereas the

---

about the Self-Conscious Emotions?," in Tracy, Robins, and Tangney, *Self-Conscious Emotions*, 21.

18. Tangney, Steuwig, and Mashek, "What's Moral?," 31.

19. Jessica L. Tracy and Richard W. Robins, "The Psychological Structure of Pride: A Tale of Two Facets," *JPSP* 92 (2007): 506.

20. Dante Alighieri, *The Divine Comedy: The Inferno*, trans. John A. Carlyle (London: Bell, 1891), cantos 31–34.

21. Jessica L. Tracy and Richard W. Robins, "The Nature of Pride," in Tracy, Robins, and Tangney, *Self-Conscious Emotions*, 264.

22. Tracy and Robins, "Psychological Structure of Pride," 507.

23. Robin S. Edelstein and Phillip R. Shaver, "A Cross-Cultural Examination of Lexical Studies of Self-Conscious Emotions," in Tracy, Robins, and Tangney, *Self-Conscious Emotions*, 205.

24. Tracy and Robins, "Psychological Structure of Pride," 509.

other is associated with a more negative profile and antisocial behaviors."[25] Authentic pride is positively related to self-esteem, and the big five consensus personality factors of extraversion, agreeableness, conscientiousness, emotional stability, and openness, as well as prosocial investments of relationship maintenance and altruism. By contrast, hubristic pride contributes to aggression and hostility, interpersonal conflicts, and maladaptive and narcissistic behaviors.[26]

In the realm of causality, "attributing positive events to internal, unstable, controllable causes (e.g., effort) should lead to authentic pride, whereas attributing those same events to internal, stable, uncontrollable causes (e.g., ability) should lead to hubristic pride."[27] The two facets of pride, therefore, are not distinguished by the kinds of events (e.g., achievements) that elicit them. It is not the specific event, but rather how the event is appraised that determines the emotional experience. Moreover, it is evident that an individual's internal assessment of a *success* partly, even significantly, determines the type of pride that results.[28] Considering these factors, can we say that authentic pride and hubristic pride are two distinct emotions, like shame and guilt? The answer is not that simple. From a behavioral perspective, they seem more like two facets of a single emotion.[29]

In answer to the question "When does the emotion of pride develop in a person?" psychologists distinguish between the experience of pride and the capacity to understand it. A three-year-old may express pride for having completed a task, either alone or with someone's aid, by tilting the head back or expanding the chest. But children are not able to make clear attributions of pride before age seven, and even then they typically credit external causes like luck rather than internal causes like effort. Only by

---

25. Tracy and Robins, "Nature of Pride," 266.

26. According to Tracy and Robins, narcissism is "a defensive process in which explicit self-aggrandisement and hubris are used to protect the self from deep-seated feelings of shame and inadequacy" ("Nature of Pride," 266). For a further detailed study of narcissism and its connections to hubris, see Carolyn C. Morf and Frederick Rhodewalt, "Unraveling the Paradoxes of Narcissism: A Dynamic Self-Regulatory Processing Model," *Psychological Inquiry* 12 (2001): 177–96.

27. Tracy and Robins, "Nature of Pride," 267.

28. Ibid., 267–68.

29. Tracy and Robins, "Psychological Structure of Pride," 523.

age eleven do children learn to make positive internal evaluations, though usually in achievements rather than moral situations.[30]

Considering the distinct characteristics and dynamics of the two facets of pride and the fact that pride develops over the course of a lifetime, it is possible that the dual elements of pride evolved separately to solve unique adaptive problems via discrete motivational orientations. Authentic pride is geared toward long-term attainment and maintenance of social status, whereas hubristic pride aims for quick boosts in status through shortcuts. In the latter case, the status obtained is usually fleeting and fraught with interpersonal conflicts, as in extreme psychopathic or Machiavellian personality disorders. Often such boastful behavior operates in social scenarios where displaying superiority serves to intimidate an opponent. Accordingly, authentic pride orients toward prosocial goals motivated by mastery, whereas hubristic pride orients toward antisocial goals motivated by performance.[31]

Having delineated the salient features of pride as a self-conscious emotion, we now turn to analyzing Isa 47 in light of SCE theory, with primary concerns to determine whether the pride of Babylon is authentic or hubristic and ultimately the motif behind the divine intervention.

2. Analysis of the Pride of Babylon in Isaiah 47

Isaiah 47 is an oracle against Babylon[32] featuring the literary device of personification. However, it also integrates other stylistic forms, such as funerary lament over a city's destruction and satire, complicating definitive conclusions regarding the genre of Isa 47.[33]

---

30. For a detailed study of the development of pride, see Ekaterina N. Kornilaki and Gregory Chlouverakis, "The Situational Antecedents of Pride and Happiness: Developmental and Domain Differences," *BJDP* 22 (2004): 605–19; see also Sharon Griffin, "A Cognitive-Developmental Analysis of Pride, Shame, and Embarrassment in Middle Childhood," in Fischer and Tangney, *Self-Conscious Emotions*, 219–36; Deborah Stipek, "The Development of Pride and Shame in Toddlers," in Fischer and Tangney, *Self-Conscious Emotions*, 237–52.

31. Tracy and Robins, "Psychological Structure of Pride," 523.

32. Claus Westermann, *Isaiah 40–66: A Commentary*, trans. David M. G. Stalker, OTL (Philadelphia: Westminster, 1969).

33. For funerary lament, see Roy F. Melugin, *The Formation of Isaiah 40–55*, BZAW 141 (Berlin: de Gruyter 1976). For satire, see R. Norman Whybray proposes a combination of funeral song and satire (*Isaiah 40–66*, NCBC [London: Oliph-

The chapter is considered an autonomous and well-structured literary unit on the following grounds:

- It begins by mentioning the addressee ("virgin daughter Babylon") and continues to address her in second-person singular.
- It coheres around repeated terms: the verbs בוא (47:5a, 9a, 9b, 11a, 11b, 13b) and ישׁב (47:1aα, 1aβ, 5a, 8a, 8b, 14b); the negative particles אין (47:1a, 10a, 14b, 15b) and לא (47:1b, 3b, 5b, 6b, 7bβ, 8bα, 8bβ, 11aα, 11aβ, 11b, 14a); and the expression אני ואפסי עוד (47:8, 10).
- Besides the vocabulary and formulaic expressions, the alternation between perfect and imperfect verbs and the use of imperatives highlight the contrast between what is and what will/should be. All these expressions relate to self-knowledge (ידע), identity (אני), security (בטח), and the pain (seated on dust [עפר] and nakedness revealed [גלה]) associated with self-realization.[34]

Scholars have proposed two main structural options for the poem: either six strophes (47:1–4, 5–7, 8–9, 10–11, 12–13, 14–15) or five strophes (47:1–4, 5–7, 8–11, 12–13, 14–15).[35] Both schemes concur on the centrality of 47:8–11. As these verses are framed by בוא (47:9a, 9b, 11a, 11c), ידע (47:8, 11a, 11c; also the noun דעת in 47:10b), לא (47:8, 11a, 11b, 11c), and עליך (47:9b, 11a, 11b, 11c), they are linked internally by nominal and verbal forms of בטח (47:8, 10), the noun רעה (47:10, 11), and two expressions of אמר + (ב)לבב followed by אני ואפסי עוד (47:8, 10). With the fivefold use of the first person singular (the personal pronoun אני [2x]; two imperfects in 47:8b, 10b; and the suffix in 47:10b), the section is saturated

---

ants, 1975], 118); see also Franke, "Reversals of Fortune," 110–16. See also Edgar W. Conrad, who regards Isa 47 as an oracle proclaiming YHWH's victory on all nations that exalt themselves (*Reading Isaiah*, OBT 27 [Minneapolis: Fortress, 1991], 81–82).

34. Franke, *Isaiah 46, 47 and 48*, 145–48; For a detailed rhetorical analysis of Isa 47, see Antonino Sgrò, "*Scendi e Siedi Sulla Polvere...*": *Studio esegetico-teologico di Isaia 47*, SRSB (Assisi: Cittadella, 2014), 32–49.

35. Martin-Achard divides the text into pairs of strophes: the first with seven lines each (47:1–4, 5–7), the second with six lines each (47:8–9, 10–11), and the third with five lines each (47:12–13, 14–15) ("Esaïe 47 et la tradition," 89). However, he concedes that the break is less evident between 47:9 and 47:10. For five strophes, see Franke, *Isaiah 46, 47 and 48*, 151.

with "I."[36] Thus, even if scholars discern two units in 47:8–11 with a break at 47:10, the verbal and thematic unity between the two units remains evident. I contend, therefore, that Isa 47 has a concentric structure around the central section of 47:8–11.[37]

> A **Come down** and **sit** in the dust ... without a throne (47:1–4)
>   B **Sit** in silence.... I gave them into your hand ... you showed them no mercy (47:5–7)
>   C You **said in your heart**, "I am and there is no one besides me" (47:8–11)
>   B′ **Stand fast** ... let those ... stand up and save you (47:12–13)
> A′ **See** ... no coal for warming ... no fire ... no one to save you (47:14–15)

The speaker in the chapter is clearly the authoritative Yahweh (except in the 47:4 interlude), who opens the four sections surrounding the center with imperatives (and הנה in 47:14). Moreover, the roots ישׁב (47:1, 14c) and עבר (47:2, 15) link the first and last sections (A/A′), while the antonymous parallels of "sitting in darkness" (47:5) and "gazing into the stars" for enlightenment (47:13) correlate the second and fourth units (B/B′).

2.1. Babylon's Sense of Security and Self-Image

The concentric structure of Isa 47 calls our attention to the center of the pericope, to the heart of pride in 47:8–11. The rhetorical marker ועתה ("and now") in 47:8 calls our attention to the theme of the section. It is introduced by two expressions: לבטח היושבת ("she who sits securely") and האמרה בלבבה ("she who says in her heart"). These two expressions juxtaposed to each other make it evident that Babylon's sense of security is expressed by the thoughts in her heart, what she thinks of herself.

That the motif of "heart" is central to this section is evidenced by the use of לב in 47:8 and 47:10 and links it to the previous section (47:7: "You did not lay these in your heart or remember"). With an emphasis on the heart, the section affirms that pride is an emotion in the heart. In the context of Old Testament tradition, heart must be understood as the mind

---

36. Franke, *Isaiah 46, 47 and 48*, 156; Sgrò, *Scendi e Siedi Sulla Polvere*, 44–45.
37. All biblical quotes are from NRSV except for the highlights, which are mine.

of the person, the center of human thoughts and decisions. This section is abundant with words that Babylon speaks in her heart as evidenced by the expressions that introduce a direct quotation: "[you] who say in your heart" (47:8), "you said" (47:10), "and you said in your heart" (47:10). To this we must add "you said" in 47:7. These introductory words are followed by a direct quotation of Babylon, indicating that pride as an emotion has verbal expressions that are spoken in the secret of human hearts. The quoted speech consists of words attributed to the character, in our case, Babylon. Epistemologists and literary historians call this "represented speech."[38] Represented speech is a literary device used by the author of the poem to ridicule the character (the *self*) of the speech introduced by "you said."[39] Therefore, it is also a character speech, describing the character/self who speaks the words.

As stated above, this section is saturated with "I" and the words that this "I" (Babylon) speaks in her heart, such as: "I shall be mistress forever," "I am, and there is no other," "I will not sit as a widow," "I will not know bereavement," and "No one sees me." The poet makes it clear that this is the way that Babylon thought of herself, her self-evaluation reflective of self-awareness and self-concept. We have seen how SCE theory affirms that pride is inextricably linked with a concept of self and the various processes involved in forming that concept. The personification of Babylon is a tool in the hands of the poet to portray this pride-centered self-image.

That Babylon has a pompous, self-aggrandizing image of herself is made evident in the very expressions themselves. אהיה לעולם denotes the quality of "enduring forever," a quality that belongs to Yahweh alone ("The Lord reigns forever" [Ps 9:7]); when attributed to humans, it is clearly

---

38. Represented speech is different from direct or indirect speech, since there is no quotation or subordinating conjunction (e.g., "that," "whether") after a "saying" introit like "and you said." Unlike direct speech, represented speech expresses a third-person point of view. In others words, we can distinguish the expression's *speaker* (in our case, Yahweh or the poet) and its "subject-of-consciousness," called *self* (in our case, Babylon), who addresses no one in particular. Ann Banfield identifies the literary style of represented speech as a "speech rendered as perceived or experienced—'overheard'—expression, but with the communicative function removed" ("Where Epistemology, Style, and Grammar Meet Literary History: The Development of Represented Speech and Thought," *NLH* 9 [1978]: 431).

39. Danna Nolan Fewell applies this theory of represented speech to her analysis of 2 Kgs 18:13–19:37 in "Sennacherib's Defeat: Words at War in 2 Kings 18.13–19.37," *JSOT* 34 (1986): 79–90.

granted by God (2 Sam 7:29).[40] The term אפס,[41] featured in the twofold repetition of אני ואפסי עוד in 47:8 and 47:10, is a synonym for the usual negative particle אין and has the sense of "not being" or "cessation of." If so, the larger phrase can be literally translated: "Me, and my exclusivity still (is)," or "I, and I exclusively [= I alone] exist."[42] Once again we find similar expressions placed in the mouth of Yahweh in Deutero-Isaiah: "I am the Lord, and there is no other" (אני יהוה ואין עוד) [45:5, 6, 18, 21; cf. also 45:22]); "I am God, there is no other ... there is no one like me" (אנכי אל ואין עוד ... ואפס כמוני [46:9]). These expressions affirm the uniqueness of Yahweh in the context of idolatry. With these words in her mouth, Babylon arrogates to herself the quality of uniqueness reserved to Yahweh alone.[43]

The expressions "I will not sit as a widow, I will not know bereavement" (Isa 47:8) add another perspective to the security and self-image of Babylon, now featuring her as a lady of noble status. She has the means of pleasure such as fine clothes (2 Sam 1:24), sexual activity (Gen 18:12), and food (Jer 51:34). She abides secure with husband and children, with no fear of losing them in battles.[44] Since Babylon is a city personified, bereft widowhood can also refer to the loss of her husband-gods and her population or daughter-cities. Once again the specter of military defeat arises, against which Babylon affirms her invincibility in brazen self-assurance that "I shall be mistress [of the kingdoms] forever" (Isa 47:7; cf. 47:5). In sum, since widowhood implies material poverty and legal vulnerability, compounded by the loss of any supportive children, Babylon's counter-claims give confident expression to her pride-centered social goals.[45]

---

40. Franke, *Isaiah 46, 47 and 48*, 127.

41. Lawrence Boadt ("Internal Alliteration in Second Isaiah," *CBQ* 45 [1983]: 361) argues that the *yodh* in אפסי is a *hireq campaginis*, not a first-person suffix. This creates assonance with אני.

42. P. Joüon and T. Muraoka, *A Grammar of Biblical Hebrew*, 2nd ed., SubBi 27 (Rome: Editrice Pontificio Istituto Biblico, 2006), 572 n. 160.

43. There are other capital cities that claimed to be unique, such as Nineveh in Zeph 2:15, where the personified city is accused of making the same claim as Babylon in Isa 47: היושבת לבטח האמרה בלבבה אני ואפסי עוד; see Klaus Baltzer, *Deutero-Isaiah: A Commentary on Isaiah 40–55*, trans. Margaret Kohl, Hermeneia (Minneapolis: Fortress, 2001), 276.

44. Joseph Blenkinsopp, *Isaiah 40–55: A New Translation with Introduction and Commentary*, AB 19A (New York: Doubleday, 2002), 282.

45. Baltzer, *Deutero-Isaiah*, 276.

2.2. Reasons for Babylon's Security: War Victories and "Science"

In section BB' of the concentric structure, we find the achievements of Babylon narrated: she reigns as mistress of kingdoms due to her war victories (Isa 47:5–6) and has a well-developed "science" (47:12–13). The former makes it clear that Babylon was a powerful kingdom and seemed invincible in battle. From the time of Hammu-rapi (1792–1750 BCE), old Babylonian inscriptions attest to "the hegemony of Babylon over the entire land of Sumer and Akkad, a feat unparalleled since the days of the Ur III state."[46] Though Babylon ceased to be the center of power and domination under the Assyrian Empire "at the end of the 7th century B.C.E., power shifted back to Babylon, whose rulers inherited most of the territories formerly ruled by the kings of Assyria."[47] The expression "I gave them into your hand" in 47:6 hints at Babylon's military victory over Israel, referred to as "my people" by Yahweh during this period. That Yahweh sanctions these conquests is evident here and in Ezek 39:23 and Jer 32:4; 38:3.[48]

Moreover, inscriptions during this period attest to the prosperity of Babylon as it overcame economic stagnation and civil disorder to generate cultural and religious development: "During this relatively short but brilliant period (626–539 BCE) the kings of the Neo-Babylonian dynasty embellished their capital with numerous architectural wonders [and] rebuilt the temples of Babylon."[49] It is no wonder, then, that Isaiah calls Babylon "the glory of the kingdoms, the splendor and pride [גאון] of the Chaldeans" (Isa 13:19), and "tender and delightful" (רכה וענגה [Isa 47:1]).[50]

---

46. Douglas Frayne, introduction to "Late Old Babylonian Inscriptions," *COS* 2:256.

47. Paul-Alain Beaulieu, introduction to "Neo-Babylonian Inscriptions," *COS* 2:306.

48. The use of נתן and ביד in these references denote war victories of Babylon over the people of God; the terms appear in Isa 47:6 and Ezek 39:23 in contexts of fulfilling the prophecies of Jer 32:4; 38:3.

49. Beaulieu, "Neo-Babylonian Inscriptions," *COS* 2:306.

50. The adjective רך can mean "tender, weak, soft, timid, gentle" (as a human quality [Gen 29:17; 33:13; Deut 20:8; 28:54, 56; 2 Sam 3:39], tender meat [Gen 18:7], or soft words [Job 40:27; Prov 15:1; 25:15]) (*HALOT* 3:1230). The adjective ענג in all its Old Testament uses has the positive meaning of "delightful" (Deut 28:54, 56) or "to delight" in its verbal forms (delighting in the Sabbath [Isa 58:13], in the Lord [Job 22:26; 27:10; Ps 37:4, 11; Isa 58:14], in the abundance of Zion [Isa 66:11]); see T. Kronholm, "עָנֹג," *TDOT* 11:212–15.

Isaiah 47:12-13 presents another feat of Babylon: its "science" of sorceries and spells, wisdom and knowledge, introduced in 47:9-11 and developed further in 47:12-15. The Babylonian view of nature sought to establish connections between apparently unconnected events and circumstances as a way of reducing the sense of insecurity and randomness endemic to human life and keenly perceived in that ancient culture. From this worldview grew a vast "science" of omens or signs of good/bad portents, drawn from both casual events and celestial phenomena or obtained through specific omen-revealing techniques.[51] Ancient Mesopotamian divinatory practices spanned three millennia[52] and evolved "into a complex, literate, and highly venerated discipline. By the first millennium, Mesopotamian scholars applied much of their intellectual energy to the practice of divination and the scholarship associated with the omen collections."[53]

Associated with the study of omens were examinations of sudden ruptures or deviations in nature, such as eclipses and monstrous births. Babylonian astronomy was advanced to the point that, by the fourth century BCE, lunar eclipses could be predicted a year in advance.[54] "Celestial and meteorological events, abnormal births, behavior of animals, features of the human habitat, attributes of human physiognomy and behavior were studied not as events to be understood for their own sake, but for their cryptic power to signify."[55]

2.3. Pride of Babylon: Authentic or Hubristic?

According to the theory of SCE stated above, authentic pride distinguishes itself from hubristic pride in that the former attributes achievements to

---

51. Blenkinsopp, *Isaiah 40–55*, 282–83; Baltzer, *Deutero-Isaiah*, 277–80.

52. The various divinatory practices in Mesopotamia can be grouped into three categories: (1) *omnia oblative*: observations based on freely offered or unsolicited omens; (2) mediumistic divination, in which a human being is used as a divinatory vehicle, necromancy (consultation with the dead) being one such technique; and (3) impetrated divination, which consists of techniques of asking questions and evoking direct answers. Examples of the latter include: observing oil as it is dropped into water (lecanomancy), smoke as it rises from a censer (libanomancy), flour scattered on water (aleuromancy), and examination of entrails (extispicy); see Ann K. Guinan, introduction to "Divination," *COS* 1:421–22.

53. Guinan, "Divination," 421.

54. Blenkinsopp, *Isaiah 40–55*, 282–83; Baltzer, *Deutero-Isaiah*, 277–80.

55. Guinan, "Divination," 422.

internal, unstable, and controllable causes while the latter attributes them to internal, stable, and uncontrollable causes. Babylonian achievements such as war victories, cultural development, "science," and national security were true and real. But she *attributed* these achievements to internal, stable, and uncontrollable causes and *presumed* that these successes would last forever, as evidenced in the spate of Babylon's "I" sayings. Accordingly, Babylon merits the sharp prophetic critique: "You did not lay these things to heart or remember their end" (Isa 47:7). This emotional attitude gave Babylon a false sense of security, a deluded image of herself, and an aggrandized self-image. She even went into denial mode, rejecting the possibility of widowhood and bereavement resulting from battlefield defeats and refusing to acknowledge the instability of her material and legal protection. Such denial constitutes another psychological tool Babylon used to sit "securely" in her own mind, not knowing that this putative safety comes from false attributions and images of herself fed by deceptive wisdom and knowledge (47:10). Bottom line: Babylon has become a showcase of hubristic pride.

That Babylon is hubristic is evidenced from her unethical and oppressive behavior. The theory of SCE states that authentic pride leads to prosocial behaviors whereas hubristic pride leads to oppressive behaviors. Isaiah's indictment of Babylon extends beyond general abuse ("you showed them no mercy") to particular offences, such as oppression of the elderly (47:6). Nothing more is demanded of Babylon than basic humaneness. To lay a heavy yoke on aged persons is simply unacceptable (inhumane). At the heart of the indictment, however, is Babylon's claim to be eternal and invincible. With this claim, power absolves itself of the need to justify its legitimacy.[56] An inextricable link between hubris and unethical behavior is forged here.

We have seen how אפס is used in relation to the false image of Babylon. Notably, this term also occurs in Isa 5:8 in the first of the six "woes" (5:8–24). These verses condemn—in hyperbolic terms—the unjust practices of accumulating possessions of property, houses, and fields at the expense of the poor and other have-nots, or even of the less propertied, in such a manner that "there is room for no one [אפס] but you, and you are left to live alone!" This brings out the reality that one who is full of himself

---

56. Baltzer, *Deutero-Isaiah*, 273–74.

(no room for another) alone acts out in the moral world with injustices as if no one else exists. The moral implications of such hubris are obvious.

As the theme of wickedness emerges in 47:10, the reader may be surprised by Yahweh's comment: "You felt secure in your wickedness." How can one be secure in wickedness? The answer is given in the words of Babylon: "No one sees me" (47:10a). According to 47:8, Babylon dwells in security. Now Babylon's security is attributed to an element of evil: her wickedness makes her secure. Babylon assures herself that no one can see her evil deeds. As prospects of being seen by someone can prevent us from doing evil deeds, Babylon's words reveal the inverse point that presumed invisibility (being seen by no one) can encourage wicked behavior. Though security is the catchword in 47:8 and 47:10, it associates with two distinct ideas: dwelling in security and doing evil with supposed impunity. Taken together, the full implication is that Babylon feels she can sit on her throne securely *because* of her wicked deeds. Conversely, however, the observer knows that Babylon's evil deeds will in fact precipitate her undoing; her wickedness certifies her *insecure* throne.[57] A double witticism spices 47:10a. When Babylon is quoted as saying "no one sees me," that is actually true, since she resides in the underworld (see discussion of 47:1–5 below). But at the same time it exposes the longstanding erroneous belief of rulers that their secret intrigues remain concealed. Yet their machinations inevitably come to light with deleterious repercussions. Otherwise Babylon would not now sit in dust and darkness symbolizing the underworld (Sheol). Israelite faith professes that God sees and intervenes—a theological fundament that Babylon has overlooked for all her "wisdom and knowledge";[58] hence the stinging accusation: "you did not lay these things to heart" (47:7).

2.4. Divine Interventions: A Call to True Self-Image and Authentic Pride

Divine intervention consists of desecuritization (47:14–15) and the uncovering of Babylon's true self (47:1–4). Whatever means Babylon counted for her security are rendered insecure. Widowhood and bereavement, which Babylon denies would ever happen to her, "shall come upon you," Yahweh insists, "in a moment, in one day ... in full measure in spite of

---

57. Franke, *Isaiah 46, 47, and 48*, 133.
58. Baltzer, *Deutero-Isaiah*, 277.

your many sorceries and the great power of your enchantments" (47: 9). By denying widowhood and bereavement, Babylon had implicitly denied any battle defeats and loss of her warriors. Now she confronts the harsh truth that she will not be victorious ("mistress of the kingdoms") forever. Moreover, 47:14–15 make clear that Babylon's many sorceries, astronomy, wisdom, and knowledge are also unreliable, since their "science" experts are destroyed by fire and rendered helpless. Babylon is left with "no one to save" her (47:15). Thus the poem exposes the utter futility of the "scientific knowledge" whereby Babylon has attempted to ward off evil and disasters; incantations and spells prove useless in maintaining a good and secure life. This theme of desecuritization or destabilization permeates the poem.[59]

From the outset, Isa 47 reveals Babylon's true self. The hymn's first verse personifies Babylon as a woman: "O virgin daughter Babylon," "O daughter Chaldea." This literary device allows the poet to speak poignantly to the heart of Babylon. The series of imperatives, starting with the command "to go down" (47:1), sets the tone for the entire poem focused on Babylon's precipitous descent.

The substantives ארץ + עפר constitute a sequence common in Ugaritic literature and in the Hebrew Bible—in inverse order, as it happens, in Isa 47:1.[60] The expression "go down and sit in the dust" can (1) evoke the destruction of a city (Isa 26:5), (2) create an impression of degradation and shame (Isa 25:12), or (3) can be an expression of mourning (Isa 3:26).[61] Occurrences of these expressions elsewhere in the Hebrew Bible show that such a humiliation is not limited to Babylon. Jerusalem laments that she is flung to the ground (Lam 2:1) and reduced to dust (Lam 2:10; cf. Ps 44:25). Moreover, even a righteous person like Job is reduced to a dust-like situation (Job 2:12; 4:19; 10:9; 16:15). "Sinking down to the dust" may be taken as an expression of repentance in Ps 44:25 (and urged upon Babylon in Isa 47:1). We find the motif of "humans made of dust" in Ps 103:14.[62]

---

59. Blenkinsopp, *Isaiah 40–55*, 282. Compare this with the status of Jerusalem in exile (widowed and bereaved [Lam 1:1–8]) and how she is misled and abandoned by her priests and prophets (2:14).

60. See Deut 28:24; Job 14:8; 39:14; Pss 7:6; 22:30; Prov 8:26; Isa 25:12; 26:5; 29:4; 34:7; 49:23; Lam 2:10; Ezek 24:7; for the noun עפר in constructive with ארץ: Gen 13:16 (2x); 28:14; Exod 8:12, 13; 2 Sam 22:43; 2 Chr 1:19; Job 1:9; 14:19; Isa 40:12; Amos 2:7; see Stanley Gevirtz, *Patterns in the Early Poetry of Israel*, SAOC 32 (Chicago: University of Chicago Press, 1963), 38.

61. Blenkinsopp, *Isaiah 40–55*, 280–81; Franke, *Isaiah 46, 47, and 48*, 106–7.

62. Blenkinsopp, *Isaiah 40–55*, 280–81.

Furthermore, the pairing of "earth" and "dust" brings to mind the dead "going down [ירד]" to the grave/nether world," a "dust"-filled environment (Isa 29:4).[63]

The oracle against the arrogance or pride of people in general (Isa 2:6–22, esp. 2:17) features the gesture of covering the head with dust as a way of evoking "the earth whence the human has been taken and whither he must return."[64] In sum, the symbol of dust demonstrates the reality of humans as noneternal, weak, and sinful. Such a symbol strikes at the very heart of human pride. In our focal Isaiah context, Babylon is called upon to keep her feet on the ground (dust!) and to be realistic about herself.

The negative particles אין and לא here and elsewhere in Isa 47 (47:1, 10, 14–15) affirm that Babylon is not what she claims to be; she will be bereft of everything she relied upon for her security and identity. She will be left with nothing: no throne, no visibility, no warmth, and no salvation. The loss of the throne makes her equal to any Chaldean woman ("daughter Chaldea"), no longer called "tender and delightful." She will be one among many, an anonymous person.[65] This rhetoric attacks Babylon's personal stature rather than her international status, as in 47:5.[66] Such a charge is strengthened by the expressions "uncover your hair," "strip off your skirt," "uncover your head," and "enter into darkness," referring to the humiliation and the deprivation of land associated with exile. Even the possession of land is not stable.[67] Attributing this devastation to God's causality affirms that God controls Babylon's fate. Babylon's identity is ultimately determined by God, not by her temporary resources, however great they may seem.

---

63. Nicholas J. Tromp, *Primitive Conceptions of Death and the Nether World in the Old Testament*, BibOr 21 (Rome: Pontifical Biblical Institute, 1969), 29; Baltzer is convinced that the entire chapter describes Babylon's descent into Sheol (*Deutero-Isaiah*, 267).

64. Robert Martin-Achard, *From Death to Life: A Study of the Development of the Resurrection in the Old Testament*, trans. John Penny Smith (Edinburgh: Oliver & Boyd, 1960), 26.

65. Baltzer, *Deutero-Isaiah*, 273. See how Jerusalem comes to be described in her exile: no king, and no one to comfort her (Lam 1:9; 2:9).

66. Franke, *Isaiah 46, 47, and 48*, 112.

67. Compare the situation of Babylon with that of Jerusalem: her nakedness seen by all (Lam 1:8), and scenes of captivity are captured by many references in the Old Testament.

3. Conclusion

Isaiah 47 issues a clarion call to true self-image and authentic pride. Everything Babylon counted as stable and uncontrollable is rendered unstable and controllable from God's sovereign perspective. If she had kept these things in mind she could have become prosocial rather than "mercilessly oppressive," even when seated on the throne of power.[68]

The above analysis of the pride of Babylon calls into question the religious suspicion against pride in general that has influenced scholarship on biblical texts dealing with pride. More importantly, this essay opens the possibility of applying the theory of SCE to other biblical treatments of pride. One additional key passage is Isa 14, which exposes the pride of Babylon's king. Traditional scholarship has endeavored to identify this king either with historical figures such as Sargon, Sennacherib, Nebuchadnezzar, and Nabonidus, or with the cosmic figure of Satan. Accordingly, the reader is distanced from the text and warned against any pride as despicable, even diabolical. Isaiah 14:13–14, however, particularly calls our attention to the heart as the source of pride, making clear that hubris leads to oppressive practices (see 14:6–8). Moreover, the vocabulary of "falling from the heavens," "going down to Sheol," and the words of derision in the mouth of the inhabitants of Sheol (14:9–11, 16–17) remind the king of Babylon of his true self. Finally, the divine intervention in 14:4–5, 22–23, traditionally understood as a reversal of fortune, renders all that the king thought stable and uncontrollable *unstable* and *controllable by God*. An invitation to true self-image and authentic pride indeed! Last but not least, this study challenges scholarship to apply SCE theory to the biblical texts on the pride of *Zion* as well, since, as some scholars argue, Zion is subsumed under "all nations" judged for their pride.

Select Bibliography

Banfield, Ann. "Where Epistemology, Style, and Grammar Meet Literary History: The Development of Represented Speech and Thought." *NLH* 9 (1978): 415–54.

---

68. At this point I disagree with Theodoret of Cyrene's statement: "Because Babylon no longer was in power, it no longer sinned and gained the benefit of avoiding greater sins" (SC 315:48–50, cited in Elliott, *Isaiah 40–66*, 93).

Bodolica, Virginia, and Martin Spraggon. "Behavioral Governance and Self-Conscious Emotions: Unveiling Governance Implications of Authentic and Hubristic Pride." *JBE* 100 (2011): 535–50.

Kornilaki, Ekaterina N., and Gregory Chlouverakis. "The Situational Antecedents of Pride and Happiness: Developmental and Domain Differences." *BJDP* 22 (2004): 605–19.

McGregor, Ian, Paul R Nail, Denise C Marigold, and So-Jin Kang. "Defensive Pride and Consensus: Strength in Imaginary Numbers." *JPSP* 89 (2005): 978–96.

Morf, Carolyn C., and F. Rhodewalt. "Unraveling the Paradoxes of Narcissism: A Dynamic Self-Regulatory Processing Model." *Philosophical Inquiry* 12 (2001): 177–96.

Owen, David. "Hubris Syndrome." *CM* 8 (2008): 428–32.

Tangney, June Price, and Kurt W. Fischer, eds. *Self-Conscious Emotions: The Psychology of Shame, Guilt, Embarrassment, and Pride.* New York: Guilford, 1995.

Tracy, Jessica L., and Richard W. Robins. "The Psychological Structure of Pride: A Tale of Two Facets." *JPSP* 92 (2007): 506–25.

Tracy, Jessica L., Richard W. Robins, and J. P. Tangney, eds. *The Self-Conscious Emotions: Theory and Research.* New York: Guilford, 2007.

Zammuner, Vanda L. "Felt Emotions and Verbally Communicated Emotions: The Case of Pride." *EJSP* 26 (1996): 233–45.

God and the "Happiness Formula": The Ethos and Ethics of Happiness

Samuel E. Balentine

The road to hell may be paved with many good intentions,[1] as the saying goes, but the journey towards happiness is certainly no cakewalk, at least as Socrates seems to have understood it. A story in the Tablet of Cebes, which likely derives from the fifth-century Greek Sophist Prodicus, is instructive here.[2] Commentary on the Tablet is relatively sparse, but the pictorial and iconographic tradition it has inspired is impressive. Although visual images like Holbein's sixteenth-century woodcut do not perfectly map the details of the story they symbolize, they do offer constructive insight.[3]

---

1. The saying derives from the first-century Roman poet Virgil: "The gates of hell are open day and night; smooth the descent, and easy is the way" (*Aen.* 6.125).
2. The authorship and date of the Tablet are difficult to determine. Although credited to Cebes of Thebes, presumably a member of the Socratic circle, general consensus attributes it to an anonymous author of the Hellenistic period. For the text and translation, including translations included in this essay, see John T. Fitzgerald and L. Michael White, *The Tabula of Cebes* (Chico, CA: Scholars Press, 1983); see also Thomas M. Banchich, *Cebes' Pinax*, BMC (Bryn Mawr, PA: Thomas Library, Bryn Mawr College, 2002); Keith Seddon, *Epictetus' Handbook and the Tablet of Cebes* (London: Routledge, 2005). For discussion of provenance and Socratic connections, see M. B. Trapp, "On the *Tablet* of Cebes," in *Aristotle and After*, ed. Richard Sorabji, BICSSup 68 (London: Institute of Classical Studies, 1997), 159–80.
3. See Reinhart Schleier, *Tabula Cebetis, oder "Spiegel des menschlichen Lebens, darin Tugent und Untugent abgemalet ist": Studien zur Rezeption einer antiken Bildbeschreibung im 16. und 17. Jahrhundert* (Berlin: Mann, 1973); on the Holbein woodcut, see 76–89.

Hans Holbein, Tablet of Cebes, woodcut, 1547.

1. "Lord of Yourself, I Crown and Mitre You"

The basic story is as follows. An anonymous narrator recounts a time when he and his friends came upon a votive tablet (*pinax*) in a temple of Chronos. They saw that the painting depicted a walled city with multiple enclosures and a great number of people, but they could not understand the rest. An old man who had heard the explanation from the one who had dedicated it to the temple many years before offered to guide them through it (1–4).[4] The outer enclosure, he says, is Life; the figure standing just outside, who is giving instructions to those who wish to enter is Daimon (Deity). Immediately upon entering, however, the people first confront Deceit, personified as a woman giving out potions of ignorance that cause them to forget

---

4. Parenthetical line references are from Fitzgerald and White, *Tabula of Cebes*.

Daimon's instructions, then Chance (*Tychē*), who randomly gives good fortune to some, bad fortune to others (5–7). Having passed through this first gate, people come to a second gate marked Luxury and to a place disconnected from the larger geography, where Intemperance, Profligacy, Insatiability, and Flattery persuade some people to remain. For these folk, the only way to rejoin Life is with the help of Repentance (9–11). The third enclosure is the preserve of False Education (*paideian kalousin*), populated by poets, orators, musicians, arithmeticians, geometers, and other professionals (12–13). They believe they have found the right way, but they are deluded by their own opinions. The only way they can move beyond their present stage in Life is to accept the help of the first two of nine Virtues, Self-Control and Endurance, who encourage them to complete their journey by taking the treacherous path that leads to True Education (*alēthinēn paideian* [14–16]).

Those who take this path come upon a beautiful, grassy meadow, brilliantly lit. It is called "the dwelling place of the happy" because this is where Happiness (*eudaimonia*) and all the Virtues (*aretai*) live. Standing outside a fourth and final gate is True Education, with her two daughters Truth and Persuasion. Once she purifies those who have reached her of error and innocence, True Education directs them inside the final enclosure, where Knowledge (*epistēmēn*) and her sister Virtues (Courage, Justice, Goodness, Moderation, Propriety, Freedom, Self-Control, and Gentleness) lead them to their mother, Happiness (*eudaimonia* [17–21]). Happiness crowns them with her power in the same way as one crowns those who have won a victory in a grand contest. The Virtues, who have shared in the celebration, now return them to the place from which they first came. Those who seek Happiness may go wherever they want in Life, untroubled by pain or grief, avarice or poverty, or anything else that threatens to diminish their life (24–27). Empowered by Happiness, they are now "master [*kyrieuei*] of all things and superior [*epanō*] to everything" (26).

The journey toward life's consummate goal is of course a widely diffused trope. Dante, for example, attributes a Christianized version of the Greek philosophers' counsel to Virgil who, having led him through the fire of purification, sets him on his way with these parting words:

> I have brought you here with intelligence and art;
> Now you must let your own good pleasure be your guide....
> Wait no longer for words or signs from me.
> Your will is free, just, and as it should be,

And not to follow it would be a fault:
Lord of yourself I crown and mitre you. (Dante, *Purg.* 27.130–31, 139–43)[5]

With apologies, I now fast forward—beyond Socrates, Plato, Aristotle, the Stoics, and the Epicureans, all of whom joined in the philosophical pursuit of happiness as the highest good of life; past Roman poets like Seneca and Horace, who hailed Felicitas as a goddess; through profound Christian thinkers on this subject, especially Augustine and Aquinas—to come to modern-day contributions to the "science of happiness" from positive psychology.[6]

The genesis of positive psychology traces back to work begun in the 1990s by Martin Seligman, Professor of Psychology at the University of Pennsylvania and author of the original "happiness formula": H (happiness) = S (biological set point) + C (life conditions) + V (voluntary actions).[7] Seligman's equation for happiness is certainly more streamlined than the complicated story of Cebes, where the pursuit of happiness navigates four enclosures, multiple gates and paths, and more than thirty personified Virtues and Vices, but it is not necessarily less complex. A brief overview must suffice.

▶ Seligman's definition of "H" or "authentic happiness" recognizes a distinction between momentary pleasure, occasioned for example by purchasing a new car or receiving an award, and the enduring satisfaction that comes from a life well lived, experienced in sustained positive relationships and meaningful work. The distinction is essentially the same as the one the Greeks recognized between hedonistic pleasure and eudaimonic joy. The popular association of happiness with subjective feelings or emotions has

---

5. Quote from Dante Alighieri, *The Divine Comedy*, trans. C. H. Sisson (Oxford: Oxford University Press, 1993), 319.

6. Ed Diener, Shigehiro Oishi, and Richard E. Lucas, "Subjective Well-Being: The Science of Happiness and Life Satisfaction," in *The Oxford Handbook of Positive Psychology*, ed. Shane J. Lopez and C. R. Snyder, 2nd ed., Oxford Library of Psychology (Oxford: Oxford University Press, 2011), 187–94. For a survey, see Darrin McMahon, *Happiness: A History* (New York: Grove Press, 2006); Nicholas P. White, *A Brief History of Happiness* (Malden, MA: Blackwell, 2006).

7. Martin E. P. Seligman, *Authentic Happiness: Using the New Positive Psychology to Realize Your Potential for Lasting Fulfillment* (New York: Free Press, 2002), esp. 45–61. For antecedent and subsequent work within the general field of psychology, see Morton Hunt, *The Story of Psychology*, rev. ed. (New York: Anchor, 2007).

nonetheless been problematic for Seligman, who decries those who have construed his work as little more than a "happiology." In a revised version, he proposes a broader, more inclusive "well-being theory," where he makes clear the objective is to increase human flourishing, not simply maximize personal satisfaction.[8] In his words, "well-being cannot exist just in your head."[9] While admitting inadequacies in his previous work, he remains nonetheless certain of its overall merit:

> This book will help you flourish.
> There, I have finally said it.
> I have spent my professional life avoiding unguarded promises like this one. I am a research scientist, and a conservative one at that. The appeal of what I write comes from the fact that it is grounded in careful science: statistical tests, validated questionnaires, thoroughly researched exercises, and large representative samples. In contrast to pop psychology and the bulk of self-improvement, my writings are believable because of the underlying science.[10]

▶ The "S" variable is the biological set point, what Seligman calls the "genetic steersman"[11] that determines roughly 50 percent of our personality. Genetically fixed levels of happiness or sadness are beyond therapeutic change, but the nongenetically determined part of our emotional makeup can be adjusted like a thermostat. We can turn up our levels of happiness and turn down our levels of sadness, increase our hope and decrease our pessimism by discovering and building on our "signature strengths" (e.g.,

---

8. Martin E. P. Seligman, *Flourish: A Visionary New Understanding of Happiness and Well-Being* (New York: Atria, 2011), 5–29. "Flourishing" is in fact the term most classicists prefer to use as translation for *eudaimonia*. See H. A. Pritchard, "The Meaning of *agathon* in the Ethics of Aristotle," *Phil* 10 (1935): 27–39; J. L. Austin, "*Agathon* and *Eudaimonia* in the Ethics of Aristotle," in Austin, *Philosophical Papers*, ed. J. O. Urmson and C. J. Warnock, 2nd ed. (Oxford: Oxford University Press, 1970), 1–31.

9. Seligman, *Flourish*, 25. Seligman identifies five elements of flourishing. Two are transient and subjective: positive emotion, which includes but is not limited to happiness, and engagement. Three are objective: relationships, meaning, and achievement. Each of these elements can be clinically measured through "random-assignment, placebo-controlled studies" (32).

10. Ibid., 1. One example of Seligman's confidence: "Here is a brief exercise ["the gratitude visit"] that will raise your well-being and lower your depression.... You will be happier and less depressed one month from now" (30–31).

11. Ibid., 50.

love of learning, perseverance, leadership).[12] By self-consciously using these strengths every day, Seligman says, we can live the "good life."

▸ Happiness is affected not only by biological set points but also by external circumstances, the "C" variable. Conventional wisdom holds that people are happier if they are well paid, married, young, healthy, well educated, and religious, for example. Data from cross-national surveys, however, show only mixed and at best moderate correlations, which undermines any theory of causal connection. Wealthy people may be happy, but wealth in and of itself does not create happiness. Even if one could change external circumstances, for example, by making more money, getting more education, or joining a church, their level of happiness would probably increase no more than 8 to 15 percent.[13]

▸ Biological set points and external circumstances affect happiness, and while psychotherapy, drugs, and intentional life changes may result in moderate enhancements, there is little we can actually do in these areas to create sustainable improvement in the quality of our life. For this reason, Seligman regards the voluntary variables (V) as the most important part of his happiness formula. Certain external factors will likely always remain beyond our control, but we do have sufficient autonomy and capacity to make important changes in the way we live. Here, cognitive science provides a helpful corrective to Freudian ideology.[14] The past does not control our present or our future. We can choose to interpret the past positively

---

12. Seligman (*Authentic Happiness*, 137–60; see *Flourish*, 38–44) identifies twenty-four "signature strengths," which he groups together under six "virtue clusters": Wisdom and Knowledge (curiosity/interest in the world, love of learning, judgment/critical thinking/open-mindedness, ingenuity/originality/practical intelligence/street smarts, social intelligence/personal intelligence/emotional intelligence, perspective); Courage (valor and bravery, perseverance/industry/diligence, integrity/genuineness/honesty); Humanity and Love (kindness and generosity, loving and allowing oneself to be loved); Justice (citizenship/duty/teamwork/loyalty, fairness and equity, leadership); Temperance (self-control, prudence/discretion/caution, humility and modesty); Transcendence (appreciation of beauty and excellence, gratitude, hope/optimism/future-mindedness, spirituality/sense of purpose/faith/religiousness, forgiveness and mercy, playfulness and humor, zest/passion/enthusiasm). He provides readers a "Values-in-Action" survey (VIA; also available online) that enables self-rating. In describing the strengths of the virtuous person, he is indirectly drawing upon Aristotelian principles of virtue ethics.

13. Seligman, *Authentic Happiness*, 61.

14. Ibid., 64–70.

or negatively, and therefore we can think ourselves into either satisfaction and contentment or anger and depression. We can also learn the difference between pleasure and gratification. The former we may increase by choosing to be more mindful in each and every experience. To increase the level of gratification in our life is more difficult because this requires not only thinking the good life but also, and more importantly, living the good life by enacting personal strengths and virtues. Seligman describes such living in Aristotelian terms: "*Eudaimonia*, what I call gratification, is part and parcel of right action."[15] How then does one live *eudaimonically*? Seligman's answer, positive psychology's answer, uses language and imagery that resonates with what we have seen in the Tablet of Cebes:

> Positive Psychology takes seriously the bright hope that if you find yourself stuck in the parking lot of life, with few and only ephemeral pleasures, with minimal gratifications, and without meaning, there is a road out. This road takes you through the countryside of pleasure and gratification, up into the high country of strength and virtue, and finally to the peaks of lasting fulfillment: meaning and purpose.[16]

The history of happiness, including the snapshots of texts and movements I have discussed above, takes scant notice of religion or the Bible. The views of Christian theologians such as Augustine and Aquinas have their place in the discussion, but generally they are consigned to the dust left behind in the intellectual move from irrational to rational explanations for life. "Getting religion" may make you feel better, Seligman says, but it will have only a "moderate effect" on your long-term well-being.[17] When it comes to consideration of specific religious texts like the Old and New Testaments, the burgeoning science of happiness is indifferent, or should we say, apathetic.[18] Nonetheless, the "biblical lexicon of happiness" is extensive, and critical theological reflection on possible partnerships with cognitive science is underway, as the recent collection of essays in *The Bible and the Pursuit of Happiness* edited by Brent A. Strawn impressively demonstrates.[19]

---

15. Ibid., 112.
16. Ibid., xii.
17. Ibid., 61.
18. The literature is vast. For current work in the field, see *Journal of Positive Psychology* (2006–) and *Journal of Happiness Studies* (2000–).
19. Brent A. Strawn, ed., *The Bible and the Pursuit of Happiness: What the Old*

In what follows, I single out two particular concerns, integral to both positive psychology and the Bible, that will benefit from stronger collaboration: (1) the lure of transcendence and (2) eudaimonic ethics.

2. Aspirations to Self-Sufficiency and the Lure of Transcendence

The "aspiration to rational self-sufficiency" lies at the heart of Greek philosophy.[20] Plato exemplifies this conviction when he says that the truly good person, the person of practical reason, will not be seriously affected by external misfortune, because "he is most of all sufficient to himself for flourishing living, and exceptionally more than others he has the least need of another" (Plato, *Resp.* 387d–e).[21] In the Platonic quest for happiness, the goal of such self-sufficiency is "becoming like a god."[22] The impulse is to control, if not eliminate, external contingencies; in short, to replace divine agency with human agency.

Greek philosophers were certainly not the first to understand human nature this way. Most cosmogonies in the ancient world, from Mesopotamia's Gilgamesh Epic to Hesiod's *Theogony* and *Works and Days*, describe the human aspiration to divinity, including, of course, the creation stories in Genesis, with their "image of God" language. The Greeks, however, were likely the first to make exploration of the possibilities and limitations of self-sufficiency the subject of rigorous philosophical investigation.[23] How far into the unknown do or can we extend our cognitive capacities without

---

and *New Testaments Teach Us about the Good Life* (Oxford: Oxford University Press, 2012). Note the Appendix by Michael J. Chan, "A Biblical Lexicon of Happiness," which Strawn rightly commends as "the fullest listing of biblical terms on happiness ever amassed" (16).

20. Martha C. Nussbaum, *The Fragility of Goodness: Luck and Ethics in Greek Tragedy and Philosophy*, rev. ed. (Cambridge: Cambridge University Press, 2001), 3.

21. Tranlsation from Plato, *Republic: Books 1–5*, ed. and trans. Chris Emlyn-Jones and William Preddy, LCL 237 (Cambridge: Harvard University Press, 2013).

22. Julia Annas, *Platonic Ethics, Old and New*, CSCP 57 (Ithaca, NY: Cornell University Press, 1999), 52–71.

23. Note, however, the increasing attention to "premoral" or "prephilosophical" texts in the Hebrew Bible, especially texts addressing virtue, character, and moral formation; see, e.g., Jaco Gericke, *The Hebrew Bible and Philosophy of Religion*, RBS 70 (Atlanta: Society of Biblical Literature, 2012); John Barton, *Ethics in Ancient Israel* (Oxford: Oxford University Press, 2014); Seizo Sekine, *Philosophical Interpretations of the Old Testament*, BZAW 458 (Berlin: de Gruyter, 2014).

compromising authentic humanity? What external limits on our ingenuity, our imagination, our capacity to be creators and not only consumers, can we accept without relinquishing our autonomy and freedom?

In fifth-century Greece, the debate on these questions took the shape of a contest between *technē* and *tychē*, between rational science and indiscriminate chance. The contest played itself out on two stages that simultaneously solicited the favor of the same audience. In the corridors of medicine, Hippocratic physicians decried the "charlatans and quacks"[24] who sacralized affliction and disease by diagnosing it as sin and prescribing repentance as its cure. In a treatise entitled *The Sacred Disease*, Hippocrates polemicized that no disease is caused by divine intervention; instead, every disease has a cause that can be discovered and treated by a skilled physician who knows the organics of the four bodily humors (phlegm, blood, yellow bile, white bile). Hippocrates did not address human emotions like joy and happiness, but we can reasonably assume that he would not have viewed them as divinely given.

In the halls of medicine, *technē* claimed the conqueror's crown, but on the public stage of tragedy, all bowed in humble submission to *tychē*. Even as medicine was rationalizing disease, and by extension human misfortune, Sophocles and the Greek tragedians were dramatizing the capricious intervention of fate and chance and the heroic but futile resistance to it.[25] Whether embodied by Agamemnon or Antigone, Orestes or Oedipus, on the theater's stage the drama of life moved inexorably toward a tragic ending. Human agency is frustrated, human choice is contradictory, and human suffering is inevitable. The chorus in Sophocles's *Philoctetes* announces the inescapable verdict on the "unhappy race of mortal man, doomed to an endless round of sorrow, and immeasurable woe."[26] Paradoxically, it was the valiant struggle of the hero to regain control over the (mis)fortunes of chance that reminded Greek audiences of the true nobility of human life. "Many are the wonders," the chorus sings in *Antigone*, "but none is more wonderful than man."[27]

---

24. Jacques Jouanna, *Hippocrates*, trans. Malcolm B. DeBevoise (Baltimore: Johns Hopkins University Press, 1999), 184 (citing Hippocrates, *Morb. sacr.* 4).
25. Ibid., 187–88.
26. Translation from Thomas Francklin, trans., *The Tragedies of Sophocles, from the Greek* (London: Valpy, 1832), available only at https://tinyurl.com/SBL0396i.
27. Translation from Sophocles, *The Theban Plays*, trans. E. P. Watling (New York: Penguin, 1974), 135.

The aspiration to self-sufficiency, regally tragic as it may be, was nonetheless never invulnerable to the lure of the transcendent. The tragedians staged their plays in honor of the god Dionysus, in essence, a sacrificial solicitation considered worthy of the god's favor. Moreover, while there are no happy endings in Greek tragedy, there is by convention a dramatic reassurance that even the deepest sorrows do not eliminate the hope for something more from the transcendent beyond. Beginning with Aeschylus, Greek tragedies concluded with the appearance of a *deus ex machina*, "a god from the machine," so called because an actor dressed as a deity would be lowered onto stage by some sort of crane. Even in tragedy, where chance could appear to be sovereign, divinity hovers ... and descends.[28]

Intimations of transcendence are in fact built into the etymology of the Greek word *eudaimonia* (*eu*, "good, well" + *daimonia*, "divinity, spirit"), the scaffold on which Seligman builds the happiness formula.[29] At issue for the ancient Greeks and to a certain extent also for the positive psychologists is what role *daimonia* plays in the pursuit of happiness. Aristotle equivocates. On the one hand, he acknowledges that happiness is a gift from the gods: "If the gods give any gift at all to human beings, it is reasonable for them to give us happiness (*eudaimonia*) more than any other human good" (Aristotle, *Eth. nic.* 1.9 [1099b]);[30] on the other hand, his primary focus is not on what may be god given but instead on what humans can acquire for themselves by learning or habituation.[31] Hence his

---

28. At least by the first century CE and almost certainly long before, both *technē* and *tychē* were divinized as Hermes (science) and Fortune (chance), a subtle recognition that the contest between what can and cannot be controlled was not played out on earth's stage alone. See the discussion on science and luck in Jouanna, *Hippocrates*, 250–52.

29. See Seligman, *Authentic Happiness*, 112.

30. All citations from Aristotle, *Nicomachean Ethics*, trans. Terence Irwin, 2nd ed. (Indianapolis: Hackett, 1999).

31. See Aristotle, *Eth. nic.* 10.7 (1177b): "We ought not to follow the makers of proverbs, and 'Think human, since you are human', or 'Think mortal, since you are mortal'. Rather, as far as we can, we ought to be pro-immortal, and go to all lengths to live in accord with our supreme element." The immediate context of this sentiment (10.7–8) is one of the most contested texts in the *Nicomachean Ethics* because its tilt toward Platonic idealism is inconsistent with Aristotle's position elsewhere. See J. L. Ackrill, "Aristotle on *Eudaimonia*," *PBA* 60 (1974): 339–59; John M. Cooper, *Reason and the Human Good in Aristotle* (Cambridge: Harvard University Press, 1975). Nussbaum's commentary on Aristotle's inconsistency is apt: "We cannot have a harmonious fusion of the human and the divine" (*Fragility of Goodness*, 377).

definition of happiness as a "certain sort of activity of the soul in accord with virtue [and hence not a result of fortune (*tychē*)]" (Aristotle, *Eth. nic.* 1.9, 7; see also 3.5). Holbein's pictorial representation of the Tablet of Cebes places the *daimon* figure in a similarly ambiguous position. Depicted as a bearded, elderly sage, Daimon stands just outside the entry gate to Life, offering instruction to infants as they embark on the journey toward adulthood. However important Daimon's guidance may be, Deceit misleads with her potion and Chance (*tychē*) randomly takes away what she has given to some and gives it to others. Daimon is clearly present as the journey toward Happiness (*eudaimonia*) begins, but the significance of his contribution is only marginal.

Seligman is similarly, but more boldly, ambiguous in his assessment of the role transcendence plays in the search for happiness. On the one hand, he includes transcendence, broadly defined as spirituality, within a cluster of six groups of "ubiquitous virtues" that a person may display "by acts of will."[32] If persons want to know how much or how little they are "enacting" the virtue of transcendence, they can take the twenty-five minute "signature strengths exercise." They can rank their transcendence level on a scale of one to five and then compare their scores with others who have done the same exercise. Those who do the exercise online get immediate and detailed feedback.[33] In short, Seligman metricizes transcendence and makes it accessible to human calculation.

On the other hand, Seligman is wary of attributing much significance to transcendence, whatever a person's score may be. He does, however, permit himself to speculate:

---

32. Seligman, *Authentic Happiness*, 137, 140. Seligman lists "transcendence" as a cluster of seven "emotional strengths (appreciation of beauty; gratitude; hope/optimism/future mindedness; spirituality/sense of purpose; faith/religiousness; forgiveness and mercy; playfulness and humor; and zest/passion/enthusiasm) that reach outside and beyond you to connect you to something larger and more permanent: to other people, to the future, to evolution, to the divine, or to the universe" (*Authentic Happiness*, 154; *Flourishing*, 259). For the six virtues and their corresponding strengths, see n. 12 above.

33. According to the summary statement in the hard copy, persons will typically self-report five or fewer scores of nine or ten (highest strengths) and several scores in the four-to-six range (weaknesses). See Seligman, *Authentic Happiness*, 159–60; Seligman, *Flourishing*, 265–66.

I have wavered between the comfortable certainty of atheism and the gnawing doubts of agnosticism my entire life, but ... I feel, for the very first time, the intimations of something vastly larger than I am or that human beings are. I have intimations of a God that those of us who are long on evidence and short on revelation (and long on hope, but short on faith) can believe in.[34]

Most positive psychologists generally agree with Seligman's diffuse understanding of transcendence, as far as I can tell, but Jonathan Haidt's "happiness hypothesis" may be singled out for special attention. A professor of psychology, Haidt describes himself as a Jewish atheist whose clinical studies have led him to "conclude that the human mind *does* simply perceive divinity and sacredness, whether or not God exists."[35] He describes "intimations of sacredness" that shrink our immodest aspirations to omnipotence and expand our sense of awe before the vastness of that which is beyond us. "Awe," he says, "is the emotion of self-transcendence."[36] In this context, Haidt's notion of divinity equates with a moral dimension of life, rooted in "biological necessity," that causes us to avoid or rid ourselves of what is contaminated and unhealthy and to protect ourselves with its antidote, virtuous living.[37] Religious people believe that God is the source of happiness, but Haidt, like Seligman, believes that "our life is the creation of our mind," and in this sense, it is human nature to seek divinity "with or without God."[38]

---

34. Seligman, *Authentic Happiness*, 257–58.

35. Jonathan Haidt, *The Happiness Hypothesis: Finding Modern Truth in Ancient Wisdom* (New York: Basic Books, 2006), 183–84 (emphasis original).

36. Ibid., 202. Cf. the notion of "cosmic consciousness" formulated by William James and the techniques developed by major religions, especially Eastern religions, to attain it (*The Varieties of Religious Experience: A Study in Human Nature* [New York: Longmans, Green & Co., 1902; repr., New York: Macmillan, 1961], 313).

37. Haidt, *Happiness Hypothesis*, 187. In the immediate literary context of this discussion, Haidt does not explain what he means by "biological necessity"; however, in a subsequent chapter (p. 234) he refers to the evidence presented by geneticist Dean Hammer for a "God-gene" that is linked to self-transcendent experiences; see Dean H. Hammer, *The God-Gene: How Faith Is Hardwired in Our Brain* (New York: Doubleday, 2004).

38. Haidt, *Happiness Hypothesis*, 181. "Divinity with or without God" is the title of ch. 9, in which Haidt presents the argument surveyed here. Although he does not specifically acknowledge it, Haidt builds on a philosophical tradition that has long pondered the transcendent. Plato distinguished between matter and form (spirit) and

I take it from this survey that the ethos of the human quest for *eudaimonia*, by ancient Greek philosophers and modern-day positive psychologists alike, has always been shadowed by the lure of transcendence. I cannot say whether Seligman and his colleagues have rediscovered Aristotle's observation that a life of happiness would necessarily be "superior to the human level" (Aristotle, *Eth. nic.* 10.7.27–28 [1177b]), therefore tantamount to the divine. But to the extent they agree that contemplating transcendence and divinity are part of what makes a happy or flourishing

---

urged his followers to leave the shadow of the cave (matter) and embrace the world of eternal truths (form), the divine (*Resp.* 7.1–3 [514a–517c]). Aristotle linked happiness to the contemplation of the gods and urged his followers to go to all lengths possible to become immortal (*Eth. nic.* 10.7.8 [1177b]). Among contemporary psychologists, Haidt's views are most similar to Lawrence Kohlberg's postulation of a seventh and ultimate "religious stage" of moral development, in which a person experiences a connection with humanity and with the universe that compels moral judgments and actions (*The Psychology of Moral Development: Moral Stages and the Idea of Justice. Essays on Moral Development*, vol. 1 of *Essays on Moral Development* [New York: Harper & Row, 1981]). In the field of the cognitive science of religion (CSR), postulation of the divine or the transcendent is considered to be intuitive or "minimally counter-intuitive." See Pascal Boyer, *Religion Explained: The Evolutionary Origins of Religious Thought* (New York: Basic Books, 2001), 71–91; see also Justin L. Barrett, *Cognitive Science, Religion, and Theology: From Human Minds to Divine Minds* (West Conshohocken, PA: Templeton, 2011), 96–112. In addition to work being done in the fields of positive psychology, CSR, and moral philosophy, we can include emerging work in neurotheology, which studies the connections between brain processes and spiritual states of consciousness, in other words, "the mind's machinery of transcendence." See, for example, the conclusions of Andrew B. Newberg, Eugene D'Aquili, and Vince Rause: "The neurobiological roots of spiritual transcendence show that Absolute Unitary Being is a plausible, even probable possibility. Of all the surprises our theory has to offer—that myths are driven by biological compulsion, that rituals are intuitively shaped to trigger unitary states, that mystics are, after all not necessarily crazy, and that all religions are branches of the same spiritual tree—the fact that this ultimate unitary state can be *rationally* supported intrigues us most. The realness of Absolute Unitary Theory is not conclusive proof that a higher God exists, but it makes a strong case that there is more to human existence than sheer material existence. Our minds are drawn by the intuition of this deeper reality, this utter sense of oneness, where suffering vanishes and all desires are at peace. As long as our brains are arranged the way they are, as long as our minds are capable of sensing the deeper reality, spirituality will come to shape the human experience, and God, however we define that majestic, mysterious concept, will not go away" (*Why God Won't Go Away* [New York: Ballantine, 2001], 171–72 [emphasis original]; see further Newberg, *Principles of Neurotheology* [Surrey: Ashgate, 2010]).

life complete, they are speaking a language biblical scholars and theologians should understand. They are creating space—inadvertently or not—for dialogue that could be constructive for all parties.

3. Eudaimonic Ethics, with or without Divinity?

For Haidt, the lure of the transcendent is the abiding intuition that produces an "ethic of divinity." He refers to a "moral elevation," beyond our two-dimensional social world, to a third dimension of enlightenment, "a specifically moral dimension that I call divinity."[39] His point of reference is Hinduism. He cites, for example, what the headmaster of a Sanskrit school in Bhubaneswar, India, taught him:

> We ourselves may be gods or demons. It depends on karma. If a person behaves like a demon, for example he kills someone, then that person is truly a demon. A person who behaves in a divine manner, *because a person has divinity in him*, he is like a god.... We should know that we are gods. If we think like gods we become like gods, if we think like demons we become like demons.[40]

So, what exactly is an "ethic of divinity"? To explore this question, Haidt turns to the research of the cultural psychologist Richard Shweder, whose field studies concentrate on how different cultures moralize about suffering.[41] Cross-cultural ethnographic research indicates that when explaining and responding to suffering, people typically use three types of moral discourse, which correspond with three conceptualizations of self. Experiences of personal misfortune or victimization trigger an "ethics of

---

39. Haidt, *Happiness Hypothesis*, 183. Haidt's research generally coincides with work done in the fields of evolutionary psychology on the expanding moral horizon of ethical decision making. For a philosophical basis for this thinking, see Peter Singer, *The Expanding Circle: Ethics, Evolution, and Moral Progress* (Princeton: Princeton University Press, 1981). For popular discussions, see Robert Wright, *The Moral Animal: Why We Are the Way We Are: The New Science of Evolutionary Psychology* (New York: Random House, 1994); Michael Shermer, *The Moral Arc: How Science and Reason Lead to Truth, Justice, and Freedom* (New York: Holt, 2015).

40. Haidt, *Happiness Hypothesis*, 190 (emphasis added).

41. Richard A. Shweder et al., "The 'Big Three' of Morality (Autonomy, Community, Divinity) and the 'Big Three' Explanations of Suffering," in *Morality and Health*, ed. Allan M. Brandt and Paul Rozin (New York: Routledge, 1997), 119–67.

autonomy" that aims to protect and restore the exercise of individual will and the pursuit of personal preferences; experiences of brokenness and loss that threaten social solidarity prompt an "ethics of community" that seeks to protect and restore the integrity of groups, families, companies, or nations; and experiences perceived to breach the natural order of the world, where the mystical and the sacred are immanent, are met with an "ethics of divinity" that seeks to protect the spiritual aspects—the divinity—of the human agent and nature from degradation.[42]

The lure of the transcendent for Haidt is not the appeal of theism; it is instead a summons to recognize the higher, more moral self that is within every person. Correspondingly, an ethics of divinity is not behavior informed by or obedient to an external set of divinely sanctioned laws and commandments; rather, it is behavior guided by our perception of cosmic sacredness, which is a human universal. Paradoxically, Haidt's laboratory studies indicate that elevated states of consciousness—for example, a sense of wonder, even reverence, before extraordinary beauty—do not typically result in changed behavior. When enthralled by the mysteries of nature or enchanted by the mystique of the galaxy, we *feel* differently, we are more serene, more contemplative, but we do not *act* differently. We think more deeply, but we do not automatically sign up for altruistic volunteer work.[43]

What, then, does an ethics of divinity actually contribute to our well-being? Is a *eudaimonic* life that issues forth in *eudaimonic* judgments richer and more fulfilling than a *hedonic* one? The simple answer offered by Seligman, Haidt, and other positive psychologists is not surprising: Yes, of course; "ways of living that are compatible with divinity ... bring out the higher, nobler self."[44] Without an ethics of divinity, life in any society would be "ugly and unsatisfying."[45] Nonetheless, Haidt, like Seligman, worries about granting unfettered authority to any transcendent, external sources. It is dangerous, Haidt warns, for an ethics of divinity to supersede

---

42. Ibid., 130–40; Haidt, *Happiness Hypothesis*, 187–91.

43. Haidt's studies on the physiology of elevation indicate that the vagus nerve, the main nerve of the sympathetic nervous system, is responsible for calming people by slowing their heart rate, thus enabling them to appreciate something unusually inspiring (*Happiness Hypothesis*, 196–97).

44. Ibid., 199.

45. Ibid., 211.

an ethics of autonomy; when it does, zealous fundamentalists, religious and irreligious, use divine sanction to legitimate despotic sovereignty.[46]

As a psychologist and a scientist, Haidt is generously open to the wisdom of theologians concerning life and happiness. When he speaks of divinity with or without God, or morality and ethics with or without God, or happiness with or without God, his objective is not to reduce theism's contribution to the quest for a eudaimonic life but instead to expand the horizon of moral discourse by creating space for the empirical data that cognitive science brings to the table. Even so, his bias for psychology is understandably clear. Theologians and philosophers, he believes, have a peculiar expertise in dealing with questions about the meaning and purpose *of* life, the "Why are we here?" questions. For them, divinity is a God whose presence cannot be verified, whose power and empowerment is beyond rational explanation. Haidt cedes these sorts of "Why?" questions and the attempts to answer them to the "soft sciences." There is also, however, the question of the purpose *in* life or as Aristotle would put it, "How should I live? What should I do to have a happy, fulfilling, and meaningful life?" This question is empirical—"a question of fact that can be examined by scientific means."[47] For this question, Haidt argues, psychology is superior to but not exclusive of theology and philosophy. To clarify, I appropriate and recast one of Haidt's own analogies. If the search for the meaning of/in life were like the activity that goes on within a beehive, theologians and philosophers would be essential as worker bees; the queen, whose presence and potency subordinates all others, would be psychology.[48] No doubt such notions will cause most biblical scholars and theologians to flinch. Worker bees?

Even so, Haidt ends his study with words that direct me to my own conclusion about the possibility of constructive dialogue between cognitive science, biblical wisdom, and happiness:

---

46. As a Jewish atheist, Haidt is acutely sensitive to religious fundamentalism, especially to the culture wars in the United States waged by the religious right (ibid., 208–11).

47. Ibid., 218–19.

48. Ibid., 238. The subtle malleability of Haidt's use of the analogy is indicated by the title of a chapter subsection: "God Gives Us Hives" (230). The language may simply be playful, but the syntax suggests a causality that seems inconsistent for a psychologist who works with empirical data.

Religion and science ... are often thought to be opponents, but as I have shown, the insights of ancient religions and of modern science are both needed to reach a full understanding of human nature and the conditions of human satisfaction.... Psychology and religion can benefit from taking each other seriously, or at least by agreeing to learn from each other while overlooking the areas of irreconcilable difference.[49]

4. Concluding Thoughts: You Are (W)here!?

Pictorial representations of the Tablet of Cebes appeared on the title pages of books of various genres throughout the fifteenth century. Holbein's woodcut was published in an edition of the works of Strabo, a first-century CE Greek geographer. Other representations were included in the Greek Lexicon of Aldus Manutus of Marz, Austria, in a 1522 publication of Augustine's *City of God*, and in the third edition of Erasmus's *New Testament*.[50] This gives me license to imagine that the visual might not be out place in a modern version of the Bible. If it were, then imagine yourself opening a Bible and finding this picture with a big yellow "You are here!" sticker affixed to it (alternatively, "Where's Waldo?"). Where in this labyrinth of paths promising to lead to Happiness would we locate our work as biblical scholars? Here? There? Anywhere?[51]

Aspirations to self-sufficiency, the lure of the transcendent, eudaimonic ethics, divinity with or without God. I have culled each of these terms and concepts from the positive psychology literature I have been reading. Each of them seems to me to be polyvocal. Their immediate literary context may be psychology, but when I read them I hear echoes of the vocabulary I exegete in the Bible. I do not much care for the analogy of theologians as worker bees, but if I understand correctly their function, they are the ones who determine who the queen bee will be. It is probably best not to press the analogy beyond reasonable inferences.[52]

---

49. Ibid., 241.

50. Schleier, *Tabula Cebetis*, 35. Schleier includes reproductions of a total of 135 illustrations.

51. In Holbein's rendering, poets, musicians, arithmeticians, and other professionals (e.g., biblical scholars?) congregate in the area of False Education. They believe they have found the right way, but they delude themselves. In self-defense, I locate this information in a footnote, not in the body of the text.

52. Nonetheless, we will no doubt take some comfort from Aristotle, who con-

I do, however, believe that given the Bible's substantial lexicon of happiness, we should find our place(s) in this discussion. The stakes are large, because a "new utilitarianism"[53] rooted in happiness studies is now being embraced as the basis for constructing economic policy, health initiatives, and political strategies around the world.[54] Perhaps what we have to contribute about God, world, and humankind cannot be metricized and marketed like the clinical studies psychologists draw upon. Perhaps this is precisely why our contributions will be important. Maybe not defining, but surely important.

Select Bibliography

Barrett, Justin L. *Cognitive Science, Religion, and Theology: From Human Minds to Divine Minds*. West Conshohocken, PA: Templeton, 2011.

Boyer, Pascal. *Religion Explained: The Evolutionary Origins of Religious Thought*. New York: Basic Books, 2001.

Fitzgerald, John T., and L. Michael White. *The Tabula of Cebes*. Chico, CA: Scholars Press, 1983.

---

sidered theology to be "the most honorable (*timōtatēn*)" of the sciences (*Metaph.* 6 [1026a.20]; cf. Aquinas, *Sum. theol.* 1.1.2).

53. Ruut Veenhoven, "Happiness as a Public Policy Aim: The Greatest Happiness Principle," in *Positive Psychology in Practice*, ed. P. Alex Linley and Stephen Joseph (Hoboken, NJ: Wiley, 2004), 658–78.

54. E.g., President Obama appointed prominent happiness studies researcher Alan Kreuger as chair of the White House Council of Economic Advisors in the summer of 2012; British Prime Minister David Cameron, advised by Professor Richard Layard of the London School of Economics, a prominent advocate of well-being models for economic policy, launched the UK's Wellbeing Index in 2011, a move now adopted by various other countries, including the US, Italy, Germany, and Japan; in 2008, French President Nicolas Sarkozy commissioned the former Chief Economist at the World Bank, Joseph Stiglitz, to produce a report exploring the limits of the Gross National Product (GNP) as a statistical measure and to consider the merits of indicators of well-being, what is now being called the Gross Domestic Happiness (GDH). In April 2012, the United Nations unanimously adopted a resolution calling for a new happiness-based economic model for consideration by the international community. For a current survey and critique of how happiness is being translated into contemporary political and economic policies and practices, see the thematic issue entitled "Translating Happiness: Medicine, Culture and Social Progress," ed. K. Aubrecht, *HCS* 5 (2013).

Gericke, Jaco. *The Hebrew Bible and Philosophy of Religion*. RBS 70. Atlanta: Society of Biblical Literature, 2012.
Haidt, Jonathan. *The Happiness Hypothesis: Finding Modern Truth in Ancient Wisdom*. New York: Basic Books, 2006.
Lopez, Shane J., and C. R. Snyder, eds. *Oxford Handbook of Positive Psychology*. 2nd ed. Oxford: Oxford University Press, 2011.
McMahon, Darrin M. *Happiness: A History*. New York: Grove, 2006.
Nussbaum, Martha C. *The Fragility of Goodness: Luck and Ethics in Greek Tragedy and Philosophy*. Rev. ed. Cambridge: Cambridge University Press, 2001.
Schleier, Reinhart. *Tabula Cebetis, oder "Spiegel des menschlichen Lebens, darin Tugent und Untugent abgemalet ist": Studien zur Rezeption einer antiken Bildbeschreibung im 16. und 17. Jahrhundert*. Berlin: Mann, 1973.
Seligman, Martin E. P. *Authentic Happiness: Using the New Positive Psychology to Realize Your Potential for Lasting Fulfillment*. New York: Free Press, 2002.
———. *Flourish: A Visionary New Understanding of Happiness and Well-Being*. New York: Atria, 2011.
Strawn, Brent A., ed. *The Bible and the Pursuit of Happiness: What the Old and New Testaments Teach Us about the Good Life*. Oxford: Oxford University Press, 2012.
White, Nicholas P. *A Brief History of Happiness*. Malden, MA: Blackwell, 2006.

"Your Faith Has Made You Well" (Mark 5:34; 10:52): Emotional Dynamics of Trustful Engagement with Jesus in Mark's Gospel

F. Scott Spencer

In Western thought that idolizes the faculty of Reason, debates about Christian faith readily polarize around ardent apologists, on one end, advocating rational belief in a set of alleged historical facts and doctrinal truths about Jesus's person and work, and cynical skeptics, on the other, scorning irrational acceptance of unscientific, metaphysical claims about a supposed divine-human figure. Often ignored or undervalued, however, in such debates is the *emotional* factor of *trust* integral to faith and intertwined in a complex web of embodied mental and social experience. This essay aims to unpack this emotional dimension as a principal concern of select characters' faith (πίστις) placed in and praised by Jesus in Mark's Gospel.

From the start, I work from the premise that the πίστις lexicon in biblical Greek, along with *fides* in Latin, correlates "faith" with "trust." As Teresa Morgan confirms in her extensive investigation of πίστις/*fides* in the epigraphy and literature of the early Roman era, including the LXX and New Testament, "It is now widely accepted that they share almost all their meanings. 'Trust', 'trustworthiness', 'honesty', 'credibility', 'faithfulness', 'good faith', 'confidence', 'assurance', ... are all widely attested as meanings of both lexica."[1] Of course, this rich semantic field does not license pouring all of these nuances into every usage of πίστις/*fides*; context remains determinative of meaning. But the strong trust-faith nexus does militate against an

---

1. Teresa Morgan, *Roman Faith and Christian Faith: Pistis and Fides in the Early Roman Empire and Early Churches* (Oxford: Oxford University Press, 2015), 7; see also Erich Gruen, "Greek *pistis* and Roman *fides*," *Athenaeum* 60 (1982): 50–68.

abstract, "reified" notion of biblical "faith" as a set of orthodox beliefs: "*the faith*" once delivered and forever defended.[2] Though this more catechetical use of ἡ πίστις has roots in later New Testament letters (1 Tim 3:9, 13; 4:1; 5:8; 6:10, 21; 2 Tim 1:13; 2:18; 4:7; Tit 1:13; Jude 3), it does not predominate in the New Testament and does not exclude affective and social elements of trust alongside more cognitive and individual appraisals.

By the same token, efforts to drive a sharp wedge between Jewish traditions of covenantal-loyal faith/trust and Christian avowals of propositional-dogmatic belief have proven narrow-minded. Drawing on the pivotal work of James Barr, Morgan concludes: "The *'emunah* lexicon ... has a wide range of meaning, and 'trust' and 'belief' as concepts are just as 'Hebraic' as 'faithfulness.'"[3] Likewise, πίστις in the LXX (often translating *'emunah*)[4] and New Testament can carry notions of behavioral-relational "faithfulness/trust" as well as "belief/assent," including πίστις Χριστοῦ ("faithfulness *of* Christ") in Paul (Rom 3:22, 26; Gal 2:16; 3:22; Phil 3:9).[5]

From this semantic linkage of "faith" and "trust" in biblical and Greco-Roman thought, we proceed to investigate the more controversial *emotional* tenor of faith/trust experiences from interdisciplinary angles that remain keenly alert to primary literary and historical contexts, while also incorporating insights from contemporary theology, philosophy, and the social sciences.

1. Emotional Dynamics of Faith/Trust in Interdisciplinary Perspective

1.1. Ancient Jewish, Greek, and Roman Perspectives

As often obtains in the study of emotions, a Goldilocks factor of finding the "just right" balance comes into play in ascertaining the emotional valence of faith/trust. Morgan, for one, cautions against reading into the

---

2. Ibid., 6, 20–23, 29, 211, 291, 302, 346, 395, 503–4, 508.
3. Ibid., 9; see James Barr, *The Semantics of Biblical Language* (Oxford: Oxford University Press, 1961), 167–68, 203.
4. E.g., Deut 32:4; 1 Sam 26:23; 2 Kgs 12:16; 22:7; Ps 32:4; Prov 12:17, 22; Jer 5:1, 3; 7:28; Hos 2:22; Hab 2:4.
5. See Richard B. Hays, *The Faith of Jesus Christ: The Narrative Substructure of Galatians 3:1-4 :11*, 2nd ed. (Grand Rapids: Eerdmans, 2002); Stanley Stowers, *A Rereading of Romans: Justice, Jews, and Gentiles* (New Haven: Yale University Press, 1994), 194–226.

Hellenistic period later conceptions of faith as predominantly propositional and instrumental, epitomized in Augustine's distinction (not dichotomy) between *fides quae creditur* ("the faith which is believed") and *fides qua creditur* ("the faith by which it is believed" [Augustine, *Trin.* 13.2.5]).[6] We might characterize the former as "too hard/cold," too *rational-objective*; the latter as "too soft/hot," too *emotional subjective*. Between these two perspectives, however, Morgan identifies the main factor motivating πίστις/*fides* in the New Testament and related materials: "It is first and foremost, neither a body of beliefs nor a function of the heart or mind, but a *relationship* which creates community."[7] In other words, faith chiefly denotes *relational trust* between divine and other authority figures—political rulers, military officers, landlords, household heads—and their subjects.

In the highly stratified society of imperial Rome, it mattered little what the troops *thought* or *believed* about the résumé of their commanding officers, or how wives, children, and slaves *felt* about the sincerity or compassion of their paterfamilias. The hierarchical *relationship*, set by law and convention, simply demanded subordinates' loyalty (fidelity) and obedience as well as *trust* in leaders' exercise of oversight and responsibility. That said, however, within her relational understanding of faith/trust, Morgan resists sharp taxonomic divisions in human nature: "What modern scholars struggle to distinguish, Greek, Roman, Jewish, and early Christian sources rarely attempt to. We ... find *pistis*, *fides*, and their cognates constantly treated as simultaneously cognitive and affective, active and relational."[8] Correlating *pistis*-language in ancient romance novels, amatory poetry, and Pauline letters, David Fredrickson uncovers a vital erotic-passionate element of *longing*: "*Pistis* can no longer be thought of as a substitute for knowledge, that is, an adherence to a set of teachings.... It must instead be understood as keeping alive *longing for communion* in the face of the mortality, sinfulness, and absence of the other. In short, *pistis* is infinite faithfulness to a finite other."[9] This broad understanding of faith/trust aligns, as Morgan acknowledges, with the renewed focus of

---

6. Morgan, *Roman Faith*, 11–12, 14, 28–30.
7. Ibid., 14, emphasis added.
8. Ibid., 19; for further exposition, see ch. 11, pp. 444–72.
9. David E. Fredrickson, "The Justice of Faith," *Di* 52 (2013): 124, emphasis added; see Fredrickson, *Eros and the Christ: Longing and Envy in Paul's Christology*, Paul in Critical Contexts (Minneapolis: Fortress, 2013), 140–42.

recent multidisciplinary studies on the integral *interconnectedness* of emotions with physical (somatic), mental (psychic), volitional, and relational aspects of holistic experience, more consonant with Jewish and Aristotelian thought than with rigid Stoic and Cartesian dualisms pitting *logos* against *pathos*.

Though an unfeeling robot might be programmed to engage in approximate, perfunctory faith/trust relations, subjective passions inevitably affect the dynamics of human hierarchies in complex ways. Whatever the precise emotional makeup of faith/trust itself, it naturally synergizes with "feelings" of love, goodwill, gratitude, and confidence on the positive-pleasurable pole and fear, doubt, shame, and frustration on the negative-painful pole—always dependent on the social context. Among numerous ancient examples briefly referenced by Morgan supporting "interior" emotional components of faith/trust, I expand on two: Josephus's interpretation of Jacob's long faith journey with God and Plutarch's report of Cato the Younger's trustworthy leadership of Roman subjects.[10]

Josephus's description of Jacob's emotion-charged reaction to the belated report of his beloved Joseph's survival and success in Egypt (see Gen 45:25–28) features the old patriarch's *faith-filled* relationship with God. Though in deep throes of mourning over Joseph's absence and probable demise, Jacob does not deem this fresh account of Joseph's well-being "incredible/unbelievable" (ἄπιστον) because of his long historical experience of God's "beneficence/goodwill" (εὔνοια). This is not some automatic faith assessment on Jacob's part, however, since God's acts of goodwill have been distressingly "intermittent" (διαλείπω) of late (*Ant.* 2.169). We might say that something has not "felt" right in Jacob's faith relationship with God; he has struggled, wrestled with God, and held on for dear life (see Gen 32:22–32). It is not simply that cognitive *belief* in God must steel itself against affective swells of grief and doubt, but that "faithful feelings"[11] feeding the serious divine-human relationship swirl in kinetic tension with a range of emotions, including painful, bond-threatening ones.

But not only pangs of pain. For no sooner does Jacob hear of Joseph's salutary position in Egypt, wrought by the faithful God, than he "imme-

---

10. Morgan, *Roman Faith*, 456–57 (Josephus); 453 (Plutarch [cf. 119])—part of the chapter, "Relationality and Interiority in *Pistis* and *Fides*," integrating social, cognitive, and affective dimensions of faith/trust (444–72).

11. Appropriating the title from Matthew A. Elliott, *Faithful Feelings: Rethinking Emotion in the New Testament* (Grand Rapids: Kregel, 2006).

"YOUR FAITH HAS MADE YOU WELL" (MARK 5:34; 10:52)   221

diately" (εὐθύς) rushes out (ὁρμάω) toward Egypt with his household to see Joseph. Yet en route Jacob starts to worry again. In fact he is overcome with *fear* (φοβέομαι) about his people "falling in love" (ἐμφιλοχωρέω) with the good life in Egypt and abandoning God's land of promise, even as he also *fears* (δείδω) that he might die on the journey without reuniting with his precious son. With all these concerns "turning" (στρέφων) over in his mind, Jacob falls asleep by a well and encounters God in a dream, rehashing their long covenantal relationship and reassuring Jacob that all would continue as promised (*Ant.* 2.169–171; cf. Gen 28:10–22). Buoyed by this personal theophany embedded in his consciousness, Jacob awakes and whisks onward to Egypt "more eagerly/zealously" (προθυμότερον [*Ant.* 2.176]).

Faith, unfaith, doubt, grief, love, goodwill, fear, and zeal all churn together in the emotional cauldron of interpersonal relations, especially in strong, long-term trust relations accustomed to emotional openness, including those with God as well as with other people.

Plutarch's account of the Roman praetor Cato the Younger features conflicting emotional attitudes regarding Cato's trustworthiness as a magistrate. Because of his shabby attire and alleged excessive lunchtime libations before hearing afternoon cases (Plutarch nullifies this charge), "it was thought that he did not so much add majesty and dignity to the office by a good administration as he took away from it by disgracing [καταισχύνειν] it" (*Cat. Min.* 44.1).[12] In truth, Cato aimed to reform the corrupt judicial system riddled with bribes, sinecures, and favoritism. He made great strides to this end, even garnering praise for his integrity from legal and political officials. Ironically, however, the common citizenry, who had suffered most under the rigged regime, believed that Cato's housecleaning "caused more vexation [grief, distress (λυπέω/λύπη)] and odium [ill-will, envy (φθόνος)] than anything else; they felt that he was investing himself with the powers of senates, courts, and magistrates" (44.7).

Even as a just, trustworthy (δίκαιος) authority, Cato provoked a mixed bag of love-hate emotions: love for his fair-minded treatment of all citizens meriting the confident faith/trust of plaintiffs; hate for the vulnerable position citizens inevitably occupy before a powerful magistrate—even, and

---

12. All Plutarch translations from Plutarch, *Lives*, trans. Bernadotte Perrin, 11 vols., LCL (Cambridge: Harvard University Press, 1914–1926).

perhaps especially, one committed to deciding their fate justly, without partiality up or down the social ladder.

> For no virtue, by the fame [praise/esteem (δόξα)] and credit [faith/trust (πίστις)] which it gives, creates more envy [ἐπιφθόνους] than justice [δικαιοσύνης], because both power [δύναμις] and credit [faith/trust (πίστις)] follow it chiefly among the common folk. These do not merely honor the just [δικαίους], as they do the brave, nor admire them merely, as they do the wise, but they actually love [φιλοῦσι] the just, and put confidence and trust [θαρροῦσιν καὶ πιστεύουσιν] in them. (*Cat. Min.* 44.7-8)

On another occasion, as a military officer, Cato sought to join forces with Pompey in northern Africa only to learn upon reaching Libya that Pompey had died in Egypt. From the troops' perspective, Cato was the only trustworthy successor—an opinion they reached and Cato accepted on *emotional* grounds. As Plutarch states:

> All, of course, were *deeply distressed*, but no one, now that Pompey was gone, would even listen to any other commander while Cato was at hand. For this reason also Cato, who had *compassion* [pity/sympathy (οἰκτείρων)] on men who were brave and had given proof of *fidelity* [faithfulness/trustworthiness (πιστέως)], and was ashamed [αἰδούμενος] to leave them helpless and destitute in a foreign land, undertook the command. (*Cat. Min.* 56.2)

The soldiers' sense of Cato's compassion toward them in the midst of their grief and his deep sense of responsibility to care for their "helpless" condition in alien territory—fueled by shame that would prevail if he did not aid them[13]—reflect the bubbling emotional brew fueling the faith/trust relationship between leader and people.

As these examples situate faith/trust in a thick relational-emotional web, they highlight two particular strands: reciprocity and risk. *Reciprocity* denotes that faith/trust runs both ways, even in dominant

---

13. On the emotional dimensions of shame (associated with loss of social status) in the Greco-Roman world, see Aristotle, *Rhet.* 2.6 (1383b–1385a); David Konstan, *The Emotions of the Ancient Greeks: Studies in Aristotle and Classical Literature* (Toronto: University of Toronto Press, 2006), 91–110; Robert A. Kaster, *Emotion, Restraint, and Community in Ancient Rome*, Classical Culture and Society (Oxford: Oxford University Press, 2005), 28–65, 92–99.

(trustee)-subordinate (trustor) relations. This emotional valence can vary considerably on both sides. Just as subordinates may not like or feel (consciously) much of anything toward masters they must trust and obey, so masters may remain callous or numb toward underlings they *entrust* with various duties and orders. Indeed, some might say a military commander should maintain emotional distance when weighing national interests of ordering troops into battle. But not Cato. His manifest *compassion* for his brave soldiers, coupled with a *shameful anxiety* about letting them down, solidified their faithful/trustful bond to him and throughout the ranks as a cohesive military company.

In biblical terms, we may liken it to the *covenantal* bond between God and Israel, including the eponymous "Israel" (Jacob). This arrangement does not merely constitute a social contract of pledges and obligations that Israel must believe and obey but a dynamic relationship of *faithful love*, including God's *entrusting* God's self to the people with compassionate concern and even anger, frustration, and disappointment when Israel proves faithless, not because God is cranky, but because God is fully committed—*emotionally, passionately*—to this love affair.[14]

Love-trust matches also involve *risk* that the trusted party may, wittingly or not, fail to meet expectations, with or without feeling shame.[15] To be sure, the Hebrew Bible advocates God's unfailing, ever-faithful love, whatever the fickleness of God's people in return. Yet substrains of lament toward God by faithful Israelites—like Abraham, the psalmist, and Habakkuk during difficult periods when God seems disengaged or "intermittent" in goodwill (as toward Jacob in Josephus's reading)—inject a poignant element of *felt* risk amid faith in God. As for Greek thought, Morgan argues that "*pistis* is always freighted with risk, fear, and doubt in ways that *'emunah* is not.... Perhaps the choice of *pistis* language in many [LXX] passages to translate the *'emunah* lexicon testifies to a sense that trusting even a trustworthy God, let alone trusting his creatures, always involves

---

14. See Jon D. Levenson, *The Love of God: Dvine Gift, Human Gratitude, and Mutual Faithfulness in Judaism* (Princeton: Princeton University Press, 2016).

15. Sociologist Anthony Giddens confirms that "trust presupposes awareness of circumstances of risk," while also clarifying that "risk" is a modern secular term correspondent with ancient notions of *fortuna* ("fortune/fate"), but operating from a different worldview, less preoccupied with spiritual forces and whims of the "gods" or "fates" (*The Consequences of Modernity* [Stanford, CA: Stanford University Press, 1990], 30–31).

risk, doubt, and negotiation." It is a "fearfully risky" thing to fall into the hands of a passionate God.[16]

1.2. Modern Theological, Philosophical, and Psychological Perspectives

This review of the relational-emotional *mentalité*[17] of faith/trust in early Jewish, Greek, and Roman contexts resonates nicely with conceptions in various fields of inquiry. The theologian Paul Tillich opens his trenchant treatment of *The Dynamics of Faith* with this definition: "Faith is the state of being ultimately concerned: the dynamics of faith are the dynamics of man's ultimate concern."[18] Independently of Tillich's discussion, recent philosophers and research psychologists have stressed the core nature of emotions as "concern-based construals," reflections of our deepest goals, what matters most, what "one strongly cares about."[19] Since Tillich understands faith as "an act of the personality as a whole," he appreciates the emotional dimension operating in dynamic "tension between the cognitive function of man's personal life, on the one hand, and emotion and will, on the other hand."[20] He also keenly discerns the "existential doubt," anxiety, and risk that ineluctably attend faith relations, requiring an "act of courage" to surmount via cognitive, volitional, and affective (confidence, optimism, pride) engagements with fear and doubt. Though cautioning that "faith is more than trust in authorities ... even the most sacred authority" and is more than an impulsive "emotional outburst" without substantive foundation (blind leap), Tillich affirms *trust* and *emotion* as key elements within the holistic experience of "participation in the subject of one's ultimate concern with one's whole being."[21]

In Western academic fields of philosophy and psychology, emotions, as supposed distortions of sound reason, have not always been welcome at

---

16. Morgan, *Roman Faith*, 209–10.
17. Ibid., 3, 10–11, 24–26, 38–39.
18. Paul Tillich, *Dynamics of Faith* (New York: Harper, 1957), 1.
19. Robert C. Roberts, *Emotions: An Essay in Aid of Moral Psychology* (Cambridge: Cambridge University Press, 2003), 143, 320; see Martha C. Nussbaum, *Upheavals of Thought: The Intelligence of Emotions* (Cambridge: Cambridge University Press, 2001), 30–31; Keith Oatley, *Emotions: A Brief History* (Malden, MA: Blackwell, 2004), 3, 10, 12, 42–43, 81–82.
20. Tillich, *Dynamics of Faith*, 5, 8.
21. Ibid., 8 ("emotional outburst"), 37–38.

the seminar table.²² But recent decades have witnessed a dramatic reevaluation—and renaissance—of the affective dimension of human life and the complex role emotions play within it. Though faith/trust has not received as much attention as so-called "basic" emotions like fear and anger, it has not gone unnoticed. Philosopher and ethicist Karen Jones makes a strong case for trust as an affective "attitude of optimism that the goodwill and competence of another will extend to cover the domain of our interaction with her, together with the expectation that the one trusted will be directly and favorably moved by the thought that we are counting on her." Jones thus "cashes out" trust, as she puts it, "not primarily in terms of belief, but rather ... emotions—in terms of a distinctive, and affectively loaded, way of seeing the one trusted."²³ In this view, the reciprocity of emotion-laden trust operates not only in the trustor's hopeful sense of the trustee's "goodwill," as Josephus assessed Jacob's feelings about God's εὔνοια, but also in the potential for the trustor's trust to *move* ([e]motivate) the trustee to participate "favorably" in the trusting relationship, as Cato was moved to satisfy the troops' longing for his leadership.²⁴

By evaluating trust as an affective *attitude*, Jones properly allows for attendant cognitive and volitional engagements of mind and will with heart. Similarly, Ronald de Sousa clusters faith/trust with *epistemic feelings*—like wonder, curiosity, doubt, rightness, and certainty—that "impinge on the pursuit of knowledge."²⁵ More precisely, he situates emotional trust "between the strictly epistemic and the strategic," that is, between propositional belief and personal behavior, influenced biochemically by the "cuddle" hormone oxytocin, naturally operative in mother-child bonding and now synthetically available (for research) in a nasal spray!²⁶

---

22. George E. Vaillant, *Spiritual Evolution: How We Are Wired for Faith, Hope, and Love* (New York: Broadway, 2008), 20: "Until very recently, emotion has been an unwelcome guest at the academic table, for passion often unsettles reason and emotion seems to threaten Enlightenment science."
23. Karen Jones, "Trust as an Affective Attitude," *Ethics* 107 (1996): 4.
24. On trust as an interactive and reactive emotional attitude of *participation*, see Bernd Lahno, "On the Emotional Character of Trust," *ETMP* 4 (2001): 181–82; Richard Holton, "Deciding to Trust, Coming to Believe," *AusJP* 72 (1994): 67–72.
25. Ronald de Sousa, *Emotional Truth* (New York: Oxford University Press, 2011), 159.
26. Ibid., 162–64; see Michael Kosfeld et al., "Oxytocin Increases Trust in Humans," *Nature* 435 (2005): 673–76.

The philosopher Robert Solomon further nuances the emotive-epistemic ligaments of faith:

> Faith has been so often construed as a narrowly epistemic category (a form of belief without the usual requisites for justification) that it has been ignored as an emotion. When it has been treated as an emotion, … it has usually been *opposed* to reason and knowledge. Faith, like any emotion, is a judgment, but not a purely epistemic or "cognitive" judgment. The emotion of faith is neither an ineffable "feeling" nor a peculiar form of knowledge.[27]

"Authentic" faith/trust does not incapacitate the mind and will in some super-surge of loving feeling, but neither does it "purely" reduce to a calculated decision based on evidentiary judgments.[28] Again, emotional, rational, and volitional elements swirl together in forging bonds of faith/trust commitment.[29]

With the effervescence of this social-psychological brew comes a degree of unpredictability, even volatility, again underscoring the risk factor of faith/trust. In his extensive studies of trust, research psychologist David DeSteno has observed integral links with different emotions: "The more we examined vacillations in emotions and moral behavior, the more we realized that trust often played a central role."[30] Grateful sentiments, for example, tend to prime emotional willingness to trust others and/or reciprocate others' trust in us. Simply put, if I feel thankful for something you have done—or just feel thankful in general for some reason apart from you—I will be more inclined to trust you in a particular encounter and prove worthy of your trust in return. Also, "quick flashes of pride can signal people that they can trust your competence."[31] Or

---

27. Robert C. Solomon, *The Passions: Emotions and the Meaning of Life* (Indianapolis: Hackett, 1993), 251, emphasis original.

28. See the extended discussion of "authentic trust," including its emotional elements, in Robert C. Solomon and Fernando Flores, *Building Trust in Business, Politics, Relationships, and Life* (Oxford: Oxford University Press, 2001), 90–154; see also Solomon, *Spirituality for the Skeptic: The Thoughtful Love of Life* (Oxford: Oxford University Press, 2002), 44–57.

29. On the importance of "commitment" in trust relations, see Giddens, *Consequences of Modernity*, 27, 79–92.

30. David DeSteno, *The Truth about Trust: How It Determines Success in Life, Love, Learning, and More* (New York: Hudson Street Press, 2014), xiii–xiv.

31. Ibid., xiv; see 19–20.

counterintuitively, feelings of social anxiety actually spur one to be more cooperative and trusting. But such trust evaluations and commitments are acutely context-specific—even *moment*-specific: "simple, momentary fluctuations in emotional states can alter a person's trustworthiness."[32] In fact, cognitive science has demonstrated that trust assessment begins with near-instantaneous millisecond responses at subconscious levels that prime (preaffect) conscious deliberations. Add in instinctive-impulsive physiological reactions ("feelings")—"the pits in our stomachs, the rapid heartbeats in our chests, the calming effects of another's touch"—that charge our trust batteries (before we catch our breaths and gather our thoughts), and the dynamics of faith/trust become even more complicated.[33]

DeSteno's laboratory observations serve a practical as well as analytical function. The volatile cognitive-affective impulses of trust render it potentially deceptive and exploitative. We can be taken in by incompetent, insincere self-promoters before we know it: the insistent plea—"Trust me; believe you me"—by a charismatic figure ought to set off alarm bells, but often lulls us into surrender.[34] We *want* to trust so badly. Even if we take time to adjudicate a trustee's competence, we can still get into trouble. We tend to make emotional judgments about trustworthiness based on historical reputation, moral character, and personal familiarity: patterns of trust established by known people of goodwill ("good faith").[35]

But again, it all depends on context, particularly what we trust people to do when. My closest confidant is my wife, whom I trust with all sorts of things, including advice about literary criticism (she holds a PhD in English); but should I ever need heart surgery, she would not be my first choice. There I would trust a qualified cardiologist, likely one I have never met before; it would scarcely matter if I liked her personality, provided she has a track record of surgical success. But even then there is risk. She may be the best-rated cardiologist in the region, but the *particular time* I need to trust her medical skills may coincide with emotional stressors in her own life (say, her partner's recent death or a flare-up of anxiety attacks)

---

32. Ibid., 20.
33. Ibid., 36; see 27–34, 36–37.
34. On the "trust me" problem, see Annette C. Baier, "Trust and Antitrust," in *Moral Prejudices: Essays on Ethics* (Cambridge: Harvard University Press, 1994), 95–129; Jones, "Trust," 18–20.
35. DeSteno, *Truth about Trust*, 15–34.

that *might* compromise her abilities. Trusting is risky business anyway you go about it with inevitable blind spots.[36] It involves heart, mind, and will, but it is not for the fainthearted, feebleminded, or weak willed.

2. Emotional Dynamics of Faith/Trust in Mark's Narrative

Within these frameworks of understanding the emotional dynamics of faith/trust, we turn to investigate two salient cases in Mark: both healing stories concluding with Jesus's matching commendations of restored characters: "Go, your faith [ἡ πίστις σου] has made you well/saved you [σέσωκέν σε]" (5:34; 10:52).[37] The first infirm figure expresses faith in Jesus by quiet stealth and feel, the second by loud supplication and leaping action. But amid these distinctions, both experience emotion-charged *trust relations* with Jesus operative in *reciprocal* exchange *face-to-face*, or in "facework commitment" mode, as Anthony Giddens puts it.[38]

To the extent that the narrative allows, we pursue a range of emotive inquiries in these faith/trust encounters:

- How does faith *form*? (motivational/causative)
- How does faith *feel*? (physical/instinctive)
- How does faith *fit*? (contextual/narrative)
- What does faith *think/believe/judge*? (cognitive/evaluative)
- What does faith *want/desire*? (volitional/conative)
- What does faith *do*? (action potential/expressive)[39]
- Who/how does faith *engage*? (relational/intersubjective)

---

36. Giddens, *The Consequences of Modernity*, 33: "*All* trust is in a certain sense blind trust!" (emphasis original).

37. Biblical translations are from the NRSV, with occasional minor modifications.

38. Setting "facework commitments ... expressed in social connections in circumstances of copresence" over against "faceless commitments" (Giddens, *The Consequences of Modernity*, 80).

39. See Geoffrey Hosking, *Trust: A History* (Oxford: Oxford University Press, 2014), 27: "All three aspects of the word 'trust' ... —as feeling, attitude, and relationship—imply a social context, and they are all to do with behavior and action or the potential for action."

2.1. The Faith/Trust of a Bleeding Woman (Mark 5:24–34)

Though this encounter with Jesus ends face-to-face, it does not begin that way. The hemorrhaging woman first sneaks up behind Jesus, pushing through the crowd to touch his outer garment, without asking permission. It is a clandestine, tap-and-go operation; there's nothing like it in the gospel tradition. We might imagine a variety of emotions driving the woman's surreptitious approach: *fear* about approaching a powerful figure (which she does evince *after* her healing [5:32]), *shyness* in public settings, *shame*—even *disgust*—over her irregular "flow" (though *not* necessarily related here to purity regulations).[40] Whereas Cato's anticipated shame over letting the troops down prompted him to accept the burden of command, the bleeding woman's already realized shame relegates her to the margins of society. More positively, we might attribute the woman's back-door strategy to her *gritty determination* to contact Jesus, whatever it takes, or less seriously, to a *flippant insouciance* (like teenagers ringing a doorbell and hiding in the bushes) or *whimsical optimism* ("might as well give this a whirl; I have tried everything else"). But while we might create a plausible profile and back story supporting these emotions, Mark specifies none of these, and as always in sparse biblical narratives, we must resist overpsychoanalyzing characters. Nonetheless, given the centrality of emotions to human life unfolding in *narrative progression* (our life "story"),[41] we need not stanch all emotional impulses in interpreting biblical figures.

As it happens, Mark offers some clues into the bleeding woman's "story," focused on the protracted duration of her disorder (twelve years) and bleeding of all her financial resources by inept physicians who only made matters "worse" (5:26). Her "suffering" (παθοῦσα [5:25]) undoubtedly exacted a heavy physical-emotional (πάθος) as well as socioeconomic

---

40. "Flow of blood" (ἡ πηγὴ τοῦ αἵματος [Mark 5:29]) designates menstruation in Lev 12:7 and 20:18 LXX. In all likelihood, the woman suffered from chronic uterine bleeding. Though rendering her ritually impure with restricted temple access, this "impurity" was less a stigma for her in Galilee than her inability to have children or normal marital relations. Moreover, her constant oozing of blood closely identified her with death and decay, common cross-cultural sources of shame and disgust; cf. Martha C. Nussbaum, *Hiding from Humanity: Disgust, Shame, and the Law* (Princeton: Princeton University Press, 2004).

41. On the basic narrative structure of emotions, see Peter Goldie, *The Emotions: A Philosophical Exploration* (Oxford: Oxford University Press, 2000), 4–6, 11–16, 102–10, 181–89; Carolyn Price, *Emotion* (Malden, MA: Polity, 2015), 25–28, 50–53.

toll. Again, we are not told precisely what the woman "felt" about these past dozen years, but emotional judgments of frustration, despair, disappointment—and *mistrust*—would be perfectly natural. Having been burned by professional doctors, well intentioned or not, she is bound to be wary, if not hypervigilant, about trusting anybody, especially purported caregivers. Or maybe her mistrust toward the medical establishment sparked some openness, still tinged with caution, toward alternative methods and "folk healers" like Jesus.[42]

In any event, Mark cuts to the chase and discloses the woman's prime motivation for approaching Jesus as she does: "If I but touch his clothes, I will be made well" (5:28). Though she "says" these words, we have no idea who hears them. Jesus certainly does not amid the clamoring crowd (unless we assume Superman sonar). The setting suggests an interior comment by the woman. Regardless, her confession implies an optimistic faith/trust in Jesus's competence and goodwill to heal *her* (see Jones's definition above). It also stands out as an exceptional expression of faith/trust: a quick touch of Jesus's clothing will do the trick. Maybe she sees no need to make a fuss, to bother the great healer, or to establish any long-term relationship with him: a simple back brush is sufficient. Perhaps, then, she has no thickly tangled emotional investment in Jesus; but she has at least some spark of trustful emotional attitude toward Jesus.

So what *formed* this faith/trust? All Mark says is that the woman "had heard about Jesus" (5:27). Heard what? Our only clues are contextual. No doubt, as she mingles among the crowd, she hears about Jesus's good-willingness to make a healing house call on Jairus's ill daughter (5:21–24). If this esteemed synagogue ruler trusts Jesus's therapeutic compassion for his dying little girl, why should the woman slowly bleeding to death not also reach out to him? Or perhaps word of Jesus liberating the deranged demoniac across the lake (5:1–20)—from which he had just returned to the waiting crowd and pleading Jairus (5:21–22)—inspired the woman's faith. Perhaps, but in any case, she seems to have no prior relationship with Jesus (no covenantal bond like Jacob enjoyed with God), still less, no dossier of Jesus's medical qualifications or curative success rate. Jesus is a stranger to the woman (and she to him) and an outsider (all the more suspect by his border crossing into pig country [5:11–16]), making faith/trust

---

42. On Jesus as "folk healer," see John J. Pilch, "Sickness and Healing in Luke-Acts," in *The Social World of Luke-Acts: Models for Interpretation*, ed. Jerome H. Neyrey (Peabody, MA: Hendrickson, 1991), 197–200.

in him risky business. Also, recalling DeSteno's caution about past being prologue; just because Jesus aided a demoniac and aims to help Jairus's daughter, that does not guarantee that he can or wants to heal *this* woman of *her* condition at *this* time.

But she thinks and feels it is worth the risk, though again her sneak attack—allowing herself a safe "out"—may reflect some anxiety and doubt amid her confidence. But faith/trust wins out, moving her to act and contact Jesus. The "hearing about" Jesus, whatever the content, suggests some evidentiary basis and cognitive appraisal: she *knew* something about him that favorably disposed her toward him. But again, her movement toward him to forge a relationship with him, however momentary, should not be reduced to a dispassionate decision. Knowing-and-acting inevitably involves some cognitive-affective-volitional interface, an epistemic emotional attitude—like faith/trust—stimulating the embodied will toward active response.

So what does the bleeding woman "feel" that motivates her to push through the crowd to touch Jesus? Does she "feel" some neural tingle from the buzzing crowd or some radioactive pulse, as it were, that the charismatic Jesus emits? Maybe, but Mark does not quite go there. Still, he has no problem describing the event in deeply felt somatic, sensate, stimulating terms bordering on the thaumaturgical and electromagnetic. The woman's "touch" that both demonstrates her faith in Jesus and detonates "power" (δύναμις) from him into her carries intimations of emotional "feeling,"[43] and the "power" discharge "out from" (ἐξελθοῦσαν) Jesus's body and "into the body" (τῷ σώματι) of the woman constitutes an energy "flow" that cauterizes her debilitating "flow" of blood (5:29–30). In Mark's perspective, this laser treatment is no illusory psychosomatic manipulation, but rather an authentic psychic and somatic experience fueled by the woman's trust in Jesus, which she "*felt* in her body," as the NRSV renders it. The verb is γινώσκω, commonly translated "know," but encompassing a dense web of perception, as existential as intellectual, as affective as cognitive, but always thoroughly embodied. Though Paul might wonder whether he was "in the body or out of the body" in his third-heaven ascent (2 Cor 12:2),

---

43. See F. Scott Spencer, "A Woman's Touch: Manual and Emotional Dynamics of Female Characters in Luke's Gospel," in *Characters and Characterization in Luke-Acts*, ed. Frank E. Dicken and Julia A. Snyder, LNTS 548 (London: Bloomsbury T&T Clark, 2016), 90–92.

Mark steers clear of such metaphysical speculation. Biblical knowledge is typically "felt" knowledge in one's body, one's gut.

What a lovely "feel"-good story of faith! Brimming with optimism in Jesus's goodwill and competence—trustingly "counting on" (Jones again) him to help her if she but touches his cloak—the woman's faith, not without considerable risk, is duly rewarded with palpable healing. As the theologian Elisabeth Moltmann-Wendel aptly (and pastorally) describes this woman's experience: "This is no dogmatic faith, no church faith, no 'solid' faith as it is sometimes ascribed to the so-called faithful of our church. It is much more the *basic trust in the life-making energies of God* in this world."[44] With this faithful "vivacity,"[45] we expect an outburst of emotion: feeling whole ("saved") for the first time in twelve years calls for whooping and hollering, leaping and dancing, or at least some expression of joy and thanksgiving. But the woman is preempted from any further reaction by *Jesus's* dramatic response. She is not allowed to shout and praise, or even just hit and run, as Jesus "immediately" feels power exit his body, stops the procession, and demands to know, "Who touched my clothes?" (5:30).

His "feeling" is denoted by ἐπιγινώσκω, an intensive form of the "knowing/feeling" experienced by the woman. She has not simply drawn power from Jesus; she has *drawn him* into her life at this moment, and with that she has *drained him* to some extent, jolted him into action without his prior knowledge. She has sparked a faith/trust *relationship* with Jesus that is clearly *reciprocal*—it involves him, elicits something essential from him—and *risk-infused* because of the physical, emotional, and volitional cost (he does not *choose* this power surge) it exacts from him. Whatever risk the woman takes in approaching Jesus trustfully from behind does not subside when she is healed; in fact the risk factor ramps up with Jesus's deeper engagement in the event.

But this is the compassionate healing Jesus, right? Surely the woman has nothing to fear from him. That is not how she views the situation, however. Though the tone of Jesus's "Who touched me?" remains ambiguous in the written text, the context tilts toward *annoyance* (the woman's catalytic touch diverted his energies away from the urgent mission at Jairus's house), possibly even *anger* and *angst* (he is not entirely in control

---

44. Elisabeth Moltmann-Wendel, "Experiencing God Physically," in Jürgen Moltmann and Elisabeth Moltmann-Wendel, *Passion for God: A Theology in Two Voices* (Louisville: Westminster John Knox, 2003), 18, emphasis added.

45. Ibid.

of this situation): "Who touched me! Who tapped my power! Let the thief show him/herself!"[46] He intently "looks all around" (περιεβλέπετο), the same move that accompanies his earlier angry (μετ' ὀργῆς) and aggrieved (συλλυπούμενος) scowl at a hardhearted synagogue audience (3:5). Counterclaims that the omniscient Jesus seeks out the healed woman simply to affirm her faith and allow her to testify do not fit with her fitfully falling down *before* (not behind) Jesus in "fear and trembling (φοβεηθεῖσα καὶ τρέμουσα)" and spilling out "the whole truth." Though cured for the moment, she is scared to death (way beyond reverential "fear") because of what *she knows* (εἰδυῖα) she has done and what "has happened to her" (5:33). She is the one most "in the know" here, but heretofore she has concealed the truth she knows. Though trusting in Jesus, she has not been trustworthy in return—hence Jesus's anxiety about this mysterious power-grabber and her dread about being exposed. Emotion begets emotion in vulnerable relationships of trust, always teetering on the edge of mistrust. The woman now has little choice but to come clean, and for all her knowledge of recent events, what she does not know is how the emotional Jesus will respond to her confession. A man this powerful could do anything, especially if he has been publicly offended. Remember, the woman is not working from a long-term relationship with Jesus. She is not a disciple.

Jesus's "immediate awareness," as Mark describes it, may reflect an instinctive "protoemotion,"[47] a "pre-passion" (προπαθεία) or "mental impression" (φαντασία), according to Epictetus and other Greek moral philosophers (Epictetus, frag. 9, from Aulus Gellius, *Noct. Att.* 19.1),[48] "that first mental jolt (*primum animi ictum*) produced by the impression of an injury," as Seneca describes the trigger to anger, a "preparation for the passion" (*praeparatio adfectus*), a subconscious, involuntary response before the "second movement, which is born of deliberation (*iudicio*)" or judgment—cognitive assent or dissent (*Ira* 2.4).[49] So Jesus's stopping in his tracks, scouring the crowd, and agitatedly asking "Who touched me?" appear to represent his first feelings, his wary, protective, mistrustful

---

46. See F. Scott Spencer, *Dancing Girls, Loose Ladies, and Women of the Cloth: The Women in Jesus' Life* (New York: Continuum, 2004), 60–61.
47. David Konstan, *Pity Transformed*, CIF (London: Duckworth, 2001), 11.
48. Cited in Margaret R. Graver, *Stoicism and Emotion* (Chicago: University of Chicago Press, 2007), 85–86; see also 7–8, 85–108.
49. Lucius Annaeus Seneca, *Anger, Mercy, Revenge*, trans. Robert A. Kaster and Martha C. Nussbaum (Chicago: University of Chicago Press, 2010), 36–37.

instincts. On second *thought*, however (perhaps millisecond thought), he comes to a more considered emotional judgment toward the trembling woman, calling her "daughter" (on a par with Jairus's child), commending her trusting faith, and commissioning her to go "in peace" (5:34). Though she and Jesus never meet again in Mark, the dynamics of this poignant scene forge an *emotional relation of reciprocal faith/trust* between them, negotiating an *emotional tension of risk and vulnerability*.⁵⁰

2.2. The Faith/Trust of Blind Bartimaeus (Mark 10:46–52)

Like the bleeding woman, blind Bartimaeus reaches out in faith to the peripatetic Jesus amid a "large crowd," this time on the "road/way" (ὁδός) out of Jericho toward Jerusalem (10:46). The man's leading expression of faith, however, is forcefully verbal rather than furtively tactile. Sitting at his roadside begging station, he twice cries out, "Son of David, have mercy on me": the first time adding Jesus's name, the second time shouting "even more (μᾶλλον) [loudly]" over the crowd's sharp shushing objections (10:47–48). The infirm man and indignant mob clearly have strong opposing feelings; Jesus's role in this emotion-charged scene remains to be seen.

We again read the entire episode as a faith/trust engagement with Jesus. As Juan Carlos Ossandón comments, the blind beggar's "many actions appear as a manifestation of a single reality, his faith."⁵¹ Of course, his "actions" intertwine with his social identity and emotional attitudes. Although the Greco-Roman world credited special blind persons with heightened powers of wisdom and in-"sight," by and large it lumped the blind with the mass of unfortunate disabled and destitute persons on the lowest rung of society.⁵² Although from Mark's ideological point of view Bartimaeus proves to be a model of faith and more prescient about Jesus

---

50. They will, however, share a bond of bloody suffering, a "plague/scourge" (μάστιξ [5:29, 34], μαστιγόω [10:34]); see Barbara E. Reid, *Choosing the Better Part? Women in the Gospel of Luke* (Collegeville, MN: Liturgical Press, 1996), 142. Jesus and the woman are the only two "bleeding" characters in Mark.

51. Juan Carlos Ossandón, "Bartimaeus' Faith: Plot and Point of View in Mark 10,46–52," *Bib* 93 (2012): 391.

52. See Mary Ann Beavis, "From the Margin to the Way: A Feminist Reading of the Story of Bartimaeus," *JFSR* 14 (1998): 25–27, 36–38; Felix A. Just, "From Tobit to Bartimaeus, From Qumran to Siloam: The Social World of Blind People and Attitudes toward the Blind in New Testament Times" (PhD diss, Yale University, 1997).

than the crowd and disciples,⁵³ socially he ranks among the poor (beggar) and despised ("many" seek to silence him). A key wordplay reinforces this tension. The rare naming of an interlocutor with Jesus outside the Twelve begs for attention, and this particular moniker—ὁ υἱὸς Τιμαίου [that is] Βαρτιμαῖος—is particularly intriguing, since it means "son of *honor/worth*" (from τιμάω/τιμή), a status that the crowd deems utterly *un*worthy of this loudmouth mendicant to whom they "sternly" issue a gag order, censuring him—literally, "laying [a negative] value upon" (ἐπιτιμάω) him⁵⁴—and virtually stripping him of his "honorable" Τιμαῖος identity. A τυφλός τιμαῖος—an "honorable blind person"—was typically an oxymoron.

The vociferous public shaming (shouting down) obviously betrays vehement emotion on the part of the rabble around Jesus. What does the blind man "feel" in return? His shouting back "all the more" reflects a gutsy determination in the face of the angry mob to make contact with Jesus and also implies a notably *confident* faith/trust in Jesus's therapeutic competence. Does he also "feel" the emotional scars of his shame? This would hardly be the first time he had suffered societal ridicule, and it would be surprising if he had not internalized some emotional attitudes of shame (like the bleeding woman), making his gritty faith performance all the more remarkable.

Bartimaeus clearly has a robust desire to be healed. But why does he turn to Jesus in faith/trust? As with the bleeding woman, this man has never met Jesus before but only "heard" about him (10:47). Yet he knows more than Jesus's general healing reputation, including his Nazareth roots and Davidic heritage (10:47–48). From his spot near Judean Jericho, it is hard to see why Bartimaeus should bother at all with Jesus of *Galilean Nazareth*; if anything, such a datum should be off-putting ("Can anything good come out of Nazareth?" [John 1:46]). Apart from a few references to Jesus as Christ/Messiah (Mark 1:1; 8:29; 9:41) that may *imply* a royal Davidic connection, nothing in Mark's narrative has heretofore linked Jesus with David in any Messianic sense.⁵⁵ So it seems that in Mark's story Bartimaeus has not so much "heard" of Jesus's Davidic lineage and vocation as intuited it himself or received divine revelation; in any case, he indeed has special "prophetic" (in)sight, preparing the way for Jesus's

---

53. See Ossandón, "Bartimaeus' Faith," 382–87.
54. LSJ, s.v. "ἐπιτίμαιος."
55. The only explicit David reference before now comes from Jesus in Mark 2:25–26, alluding to David's eating sacred bread in 1 Sam 21:1–6.

ensuing entry into Jerusalem amid shouts of "Blessed is the kingdom of our ancestor David!" (11:10; cf. 12:35–37).[56]

Mark's narrative, however, values (honors!) Bartimaeus more than simply as a public relations agent for Jesus's royal procession into Jerusalem. Uniquely among those whom Jesus heals, Bartimaeus "immediately regains his sight and *follows [Jesus] on the way* [ὁδῷ]" into Jerusalem (10:52). More than itinerary and geography constitute this "way" in Mark: this is the way of God's realm, the way of discipleship, the way of *faith/ trust* as an *ongoing, progressing* relationship. This marks a new step (leap) of faith that Bartimaeus takes over the bleeding woman and other seekers of Jesus.

Whatever other dimensions of Jesus's Davidic-Messianic vocation Bartimaeus might entertain, the most salient feature is Jesus's capacity for *merciful* attention. "Have mercy/pity on me" (ἐλέησόν με) encapsulates what he needs and trusts Jesus for. Mercy/pity (ἔλεος) is a relational emotion linking one who pities with a pitied person or group; hence Bartimaeus seeks to draw Jesus passionately and actively into his pitiable life. In Aristotle's discussion of passions in the *Rhetoric*, he defines pity (ἔλεος) "as a certain pain at an apparently destructive or painful event happening to one who does not deserve it and which a person might expect himself or one of his own to suffer, and this when it seems close at hand" (*Rhet.* 2.8.2 [1385b]).[57] Key elements include: (1) some mirror feeling of pain over another's pain, that is, some degree of sympathy or compassion; (2) an assessment of the pitied party's *unmerited suffering* (if the sufferer has brought pain on himself through poor judgment or conduct, he is worthy of blame, not pity); and (3) a palpable awareness

---

56. Beavis, "From the Margin," 36–38. See also the insightful broader assessment of biblical prophets by the philosopher-theologian John D. Caputo: "We take a 'prophet' in the biblical sense, not as one who tries to see the future, which is what the blind Greek prophet and seer has his eye on, for that would confine everything to the plane of being, to predicting the future present on the basis of present being. But a prophet belongs, not to the order of being, but to the order of the event of the call, not to presence but to provocation, to one who speaks for justice" (*The Weakness of God: A Theology of Event* [Bloomington: Indiana University Press, 2006], 30–31). In the Markan "event," blind Bartimaeus's prophetic "call" to Jesus "provokes" not only the crowd's countercall, but Jesus's reciprocal call (10:49).

57. Aristotle, *On Rhetoric: A Theory of Civic Discourse*, trans. George A. Kennedy, 2nd ed. (New York: Oxford University Press, 2007), 139.

of *proximate* ("close at hand") *vulnerability* to similar pains afflicting the object of pity.[58]

Though the merit issue does not arise in Bartimaeus's story, it was not unusual in Mark's milieu to regard blindness as justified penalty for wrongdoing, whether in military (eye gouging conquered enemies [Judg 16:2; 1 Sam 10:27]) or missionary (Paul's cursing the magician Elymas with blindness [Acts 13:9–11]) settings. In another case involving a blind man, Jesus's disciples presume guilt and eschew pity: "Rabbi, who sinned, this man or his parents, that he was born blind?" (John 9:2). Jesus promptly dismisses their query as irrelevant and proceeds to give the man his sight as evidence of God's creative "works." Whether or not Jesus *feels* pity toward this blind man is never stated, but his *undeserved* suffering ("neither this man nor his parents sinned" [9:3]) allows for such emotion, though not requiring it.

Concerning the blind man in John or Bartimaeus in Mark, Jesus could theoretically judge them guiltless of their affliction and proceed to correct it in a routine, detached fashion. Moreover, Jesus's *own* sense of vulnerability to sight impairment or any other disability as a prerequisite of pity might seem not merely remote, but impossible, for such a powerful "divine man." What does he personally know about human frailty? Ditto for pagan deities whom the ancient Greeks "did not expect ... to be merciful" and for despotic rulers, commonly viewed as divine agents.[59] But the God of Israel, though sovereign and almighty, is not impassible and does evince sympathetic mercy (compassion) in biblical literature (e.g., Exod 34:6–7; Ps 117 [118]:1–4, 29; 135 [136]). The Son of God and of David, Jesus of Nazareth, displays a rich range of emotions in Mark identifying with human suffering, culminating with gut-wrenching expressions of vulnerability at Gethsemane (angst [Mark 14:33–34]) and Golgotha (abandonment [15:34]). Encountering Jesus "close at hand" to this perilous "way" of the cross, Bartimaeus's faith/trust in Jesus's passionate mercy/pity proves to be well placed.

---

58. See Konstan, *Pity Transformed*, 1–29, 49–74, 128–36; Konstan, *Emotions of the Ancient Greeks*, 201–18; Martha C. Nussbaum, *The Fragility of Goodness: Luck and Ethics in Greek Tragedy and Philosophy*, rev. ed. (Cambridge: Cambridge University Press, 2001); 383–91; Nussbaum, *The Therapy of Desire: Theory and Practice in Hellenistic Ethics* (Princeton: Princeton University Press, 1994), 86–94, 495–97.

59. Kenneth Dover, *Greek Popular Morality in the Time of Plato and Aristotle* (Indianapolis: Hackett, 1994), 156; cited in Konstan, *Pity Transformed*, 105.

Bartimaeus's faith receives a further boost when Jesus halts and insists that the crowd aiming to throttle the blind man's voice should "call [φωνήσατε] him [to Jesus]" (10:49). As in the case of the bleeding woman, Jesus's stopping and speaking constitutes a summons to reciprocal relationship with the faithful seeker. This again involves an element of risk, though less so than for the silent, secretive woman Jesus exposes. Bartimaeus hides nothing; yet Jesus's answering the blind man's call with a curt return call may not be a benevolent response (Jesus does *not* say, "Call him here *so I can restore his sight*") but more like a calling on the carpet: "Why are you making such a ruckus and impeding my way to Jerusalem?" Though we might imagine other powerful figures brusquely interrogating a bellowing beggar in this fashion, even the obstructionist crowd here thinks better of Jesus and relays his call to Bartimaeus as an encouraging gesture: "Take heart; get up, he is calling you" (10:49). "Take heart" or "Be confident" (θάρσει) is a direct *emotional* appeal to Bartimaeus to enjoy closer contact with Jesus, at his behest. Aristotle includes "confidence" (θάρσος) in his catalogue of passions, specifically as the antidote to "fear" (φόβος) (*Rhet.* 2.5.16 [1383a]). Mark's only other usage of θαρσέω confirms the confidence-fear antithesis: "Take heart [θαρσεῖτε], it is I; do not be afraid [μὴ φοβεῖσθε]" (spoken by the water-walking Jesus to his terrified disciples [6:50]). As θάρσος boldly allays φόβος, it also closely aligns with πίστις, as in the Plutarch passage above: "they actually love the just, and put *confidence and trust* (θαρροῦσιν καὶ πιστεύουσιν) in them" (*Cat. Min.* 44.8).

The antiphonal imperatives of Bartimaeus's crying out to Jesus and Jesus's calling to him set the cognitive-emotive tone for a dynamic faith/trust bond between the son of David and son of Timaeus. Within this promising framework, however, further response is required. The next move is up to Bartimaeus, who makes it with pert alacrity—and *passionate intensity*. His twin actions of "throwing off [ἀποβαλών] his cloak" and jumping up on his feet (ἀναπηδήσας) convey a wholehearted, enthusiastic, all-in commitment to meet Jesus (10:50). Just as he did not allow the crowd to shout him down, Bartimaeus allows nothing to keep him down, not even his outer garment, when Jesus calls. He takes a literal leap of fervent faith, brimming with purposeful emotion. Jesus slows him down a bit with a question requiring cognitive reflection, but it is a question about *desire*, appropriate to the man's charged emotional-volitional state: "What do *you want* [θέλεις] me to do for you?" (10:51). Jesus asked James and John precisely the same question in the preceding scene, exposing their chief desire to attain high status and glory (10:36–37). Although the other ten disciples react angrily to this pair's audacious request, it seems clear from Jesus's response that, wanting similar promotions, they are just mad that James and John beat them to the punch (10:41–45). Emotions ride high among honor-jockeying disciples of Jesus and reveal *what matters most* to them.

So what matters most to Bartimaeus, the son of "honorable" Timaeus? What is his heart's desire? Clearly not public acclaim, fancy attire, or any other trappings of social honor. He just wants desperately "to see again"—which in Mark reflects not only physical restoration, but also spiritual perception into Jesus's way: an integral mark of faith-full discipleship (along with leaving behind possessions, like clothing; see 1:16–20; 6:7–8; 8:21–33; 10:28–29).[60] That Bartimaeus's emotional faith/trust bond with Jesus moves to this extended level of *committed fellowship*, beyond a momentary miraculous encounter, is evident in his final response, as we have already seen. Though Jesus says, "Go [ὕπαγε]; your faith has made you well," far from taking his renewed vision and going away, Bartimaeus "immediately" goes *with Jesus*, "follow[ing] him on the way" to Jerusalem and the cross. And Jesus does not deter him: evidently, Jesus *wants* this honorable faith/trust relationship to continue.

3. Conclusion

The saving (whole-making) faith in Jesus exhibited by the bleeding woman and blind Bartimaeus is neither an irrational, mindless leap in the dark nor a purely rational, calculated choice motivated by logical proofs. Both characters "had heard" something about Jesus, but nothing like a complete profile, still less a catechism of orthodox beliefs about Jesus's person and work. They had formed some cognitive judgments supporting Jesus's restorative power (5:28) and merciful purpose (10:47–48), but not in some isolated calculation chamber. Cognitive judgments or appraisals percolate in dynamic interface with embodied affective, volitive, associative, and active experience at both subconscious and conscious levels. Hence the saving πίστις of the two figures in Mark is best understood as a *multiplex* of events and experiences within and among embodied persons.

---

60. See Ossandón, "Bartimaeus' Faith," 383–84.

As for the *emotional* element (again, interlinked with the full repertoire of human experiences), the faith of the woman and Bartimaeus clearly manifests as *trust*, the emotional attitude of optimistic reliance on Jesus's "goodwill" toward them at an opportune moment of encounter, which they seize by demonstrative touch (woman) or shout (Bartimaeus). The initiative is theirs, primed and "action readied" by their emotion-laden trust in Jesus which, in turn, draws him into their orbit (the woman quite literally, "electrically" draws Jesus out) with his own multifaceted "faith" responses. A tension between *hierarchy* and *reciprocity* emerges. Though patently the superior authority, Jesus does not command faith in these cases (no "Trust/believe me")[61] but rather is compelled to assess *his faith* in these passionate seekers, his willingness to *entrust himself* to them and commit himself to a *relationship of trust*, whether short or long term.

Of course, Jesus does emotionally (and physically, volitionally, verbally) engage with and affirm these faithful pursuers—*eventually*. But, as always in trust relations, a degree of *risk* enters the situation, prompting some negotiation of tension. Remember that these characters have never met before in the narrative and that both supplicants vigorously push themselves on Jesus in a volatile crowd. They trustfully "count on" Jesus to help, but the odds are not unequivocal for a favorable outcome. Attendant emotions like fear, frustration, shame, mercy, and zeal complicate the context-specific interactions—for Jesus as well as for the salvation seekers. Faith in these cases is no purely blind leap or lucky strike, but it nonetheless remains risky business—though well worth the risk from Mark's perspective.

Select Bibliography

Baier, Annette C. *Moral Prejudices: Essays on Ethics*. Cambridge: Harvard University Press, 1994.
De Sousa, Ronald. *Emotional Truth*. New York: Oxford University Press, 2011.
Desteno, David. *The Truth about Trust: How It Determines Success in Life Love, Learning, and More*. New York: Hudson Street Press, 2014.
Fredrickson, David E. "The Justice of Faith." *Di* 52 (2013): 121–27.

---

61. Mark's Jesus does command faith (πίστευε/πιστεύετε) in various places (1:15; 5:36; 11:23–24); these examples merit a separate study.

Giddens, Anthony. *The Consequences of Modernity.* Stanford, CA: Stanford University Press, 1990.
Hosking, Geoffrey. *Trust: A History.* Oxford: Oxford University Press, 2014.
Jones, Karen. "Trust as an Affective Attitude." *Ethics* 107 (1996): 4–25.
Konstan, David. *The Emotions of the Ancient Greeks: Studies in Aristotle and Classical Literature.* Toronto: University of Toronto Press, 2006.
———. *Pity Transformed.* CIF. London: Duckworth, 2001.
Lahno, Bernd. "On the Emotional Character of Trust." *ETMP* 4 (2001): 171–89.
Moltmann, Jürgen, and Elisabeth Moltmann-Wendel. *Passion for God: A Theology in Two Voices.* Louisville: Westminster John Knox, 2003.
Morgan, Teresa. *Roman Faith and Christian Faith: Pistis and Fides in the Early Roman Empire and Early Churches.* Oxford: Oxford University Press, 2015.
Solomon, Robert C. *The Passions: Emotions and the Meaning of Life.* Indianapolis: Hackett, 1993.
Solomon, Robert C., and Fernando Flores, *Building Trust in Business, Politics, Relationships, and Life.* Oxford: Oxford University Press, 2001.
Tillich, Paul. *Dynamics of Faith.* New York: Harper, 1957.

Not "Hardened Hearts" but "Petrified Hearts" (Mark 6:52): The Challenge to Assimilate and Accommodate the Vastness of Jesus in Mark 6:45-52

Ivar Vegge

To set the perspective of this article I start with a personal story typical of many overwhelming human experiences. In first through third grade, I lived in a boarding school in Addis Ababa, Ethiopia. I came home at Christmas, Easter, and throughout the summer. My parents visited me once between my holidays. At age eight I told them, "Don't come and visit me. For it is so painful when you leave me again." I vividly recall one visit when my father sat down and wanted to help me with my homework assignment of memorizing a Christian hymn. But however much he tried, words and lines went all over the place, except into my head. I just could not "get it." Because my father was leaving the next morning, I was overwhelmed by poignant emotions of anxiety and pain (hyperarousal) mixed with numbness, emptiness, and depression (hypoarousal). Most people, psychologically trained or not, will readily acknowledge that this small boy was too emotionally distraught that day to process cognitively a hymn. Few would accuse him of being stupid or willfully resisting his father (moral failure).

But such accusations are commonplace in popular and scholarly commentaries regarding the shaken and stunned reaction of the disciples to the sea-walking Jesus in Mark 6:45-52.[1] A key reason for this assessment involves the long Western tradition of incorrectly translating ἀλλ' ἦν αὐτῶν ἡ καρδία πεπωρωμένη as "but their hearts *were hardened*" (6:52), as if the

---

1. The major critical commentary by Joel Marcus is representative, characterizing the disciples in this scene as "thickheaded" moral failures (*Mark 1-8: A New Translation with Introduction and Commentary*, AB 27 [New York: Doubleday, 2000], 434).

disciples were beset by unbelief, obduracy, moral faithlessness, or "hard-heartedness." The term πωρόω, however, generally refers to a process of petrification and/or its concomitants, such as insensibility, numbness, and blindness. Hence, in this context where the disciples are overwhelmed by Jesus, πωρόω connotes a state of severe emotional-cognitive distress, throttling their ability to process and integrate who Jesus is and what he says and does.

In what follows, I first sketch the history of research on awe and fear in Mark. Then I investigate descriptions of awe (and fear) in modern psychological and neuroscience research. Hermeneutically, these new insights have been crucial for my interpretation of Mark, particularly prompting doubt about rendering πωρόω as "hardened" in 6:52. Positively, the same material led me to discover fresh lexical and narrative connections in Mark and in other ancient texts. More specifically, I prepare the ground for my new reading of Mark 6:45–52 (and πωρόω especially) by examining how trauma and terrifying awe reactions are described in the Hebrew Bible and how characters in Mark struggle to assimilate and accommodate the vastness of Jesus.

My methodological approach to Mark is narrative critical, focusing on emotions as a vital component of characterization. Furthermore, I analyze how Mark as narrator offers readers privileged information in and through the way he tells the story, and how this may enable "the competent reader"[2] to assimilate and accommodate the vastness of Jesus beyond the internal perspective of the disciples in 6:45–52.

1. Awe, Wonder, and Fear in the History of Research in Mark

Mark uses four main verbs and their cognates to express awe, wonder, and amazement: (1) θαυμάζω, θαυμαστός; (2) ἐξίστημι, ἔκστασις; (3) ἐκπλήσσω; and (4) θαμβέω. Various other words (φοβέω, φόβος, τρόμος, and ταράσσω) express fear and terror, with possible related nuances of awe and wonder (1:22, 27; 2:12; 3:21; 4:41; 5:15, 20, 33, 42; 6:2, 6, 20, 50, 51; 7:37; 9:6, 15, 32; 10:24, 26, 32; 11:18, 32; 12:11, 12, 17; 14:33; 15:5, 44; 16:5, 6, 8). These terms apply to the crowds, disciples, Jesus's enemies (scribes, priests, elders, Herod, Pilate), minor characters like the hemorrhaging woman

---

2. I use the concept of "the competent reader" as one who understands and respects signals in the text, following Wolfgang Iser, *The Act of Reading: A Theory of Aesthetic Response* (Baltimore: Johns Hopkins University Press, 1978).

(5:33), the Old Testament psalmist (12:10-11), and, rarely, to Jesus himself (6:6; 14:33). Usually, awe and fear emerge as responses to what Jesus does, says, and experiences. Often Mark intensifies awe and fear responses with prefixes and/or adverbs (4:41; 6:51; 7:37; 9:6, 15; 10:26; 12:17; 14:33).

Research on awe, wonder, and fear in Mark can be grouped into five major positions.

(1) Some claim that awe, wonder, and fear represent a *conventional motif in miracle stories* in the ancient world and the New Testament. As such, this motif serves to dramatize and emphasize the significance of the miracles' effects on witnesses.[3]

(2) Others see awe, wonder, and dread as *typical components of revelatory experiences* (such as theophanies) in Mark. By characterizing responses to Jesus as both amazement and fear, the evangelist signals his intent for readers to see Jesus in a divine light. The motif thus serves a *Christological purpose*, or even a *theophanic purpose* of numinous awe.[4]

(3) Timothy Dwyer has pointed out that some texts in the Old Testament and early Jewish literature link wonder and amazement with God's eschatological action. In light of this usage, Dwyer argues that wonder and fear in Mark reflect *signs of God's in-breaking rule* in the miracles, teaching, and person of Jesus.[5] This approach joins the first two in seeing fear and awe as generally appropriate responses to the miraculous, numinous manifestation of God's realm. They all struggle, however, to explain the puzzling connection between the disciples' awe in 6:51 and their so-called "hardening" in 6:52.

(4) Since (a) Mark's Jesus exhorts his disciples to have faith and fear not (4:40), (b) the disciples' amazement is related to their "hardened hearts" (6:51-52), and (c) even Jesus's enemies (not only the disciples and crowds) experience fear and amazement (6:20; 11:18; 12:17; 15:5, 44), *fear and amazement appear opposed to faith and trust*. Accordingly, fear and amazement in Mark seem to be typical responses of unbelievers or

---

3. E.g., Gerd Theissen, *The Miracle Stories of the Early Christian Tradition*, trans. Francis McDonagh (Edinburgh: T&T Clark, 1983), 47-72.

4. See two important monographs: Maksimilijan Matjaž, *Furcht und Gotteserfahrung: Die Bedeutung des Furchtmotivs für die Christologie des Markus*, FB 91 (Würzburg: Echter, 1999); Joan L. Mitchell, *Beyond Fear and Silence: A Feminist-Literary Approach to the Gospel of Mark* (New York: Continuum, 2001), esp. 66-75, 114-15.

5. Timothy Dwyer, *The Motif of Wonder in the Gospel of Mark*, JSNTSup 128 (Sheffield: Sheffield Academic, 1996).

doubters. This perspective supports a portrait of disciples in Mark as total failures and foils to Mark's theology.[6] Some scholars moderate this position somewhat, evaluating the disciples as fallible, but not irremediable, followers of Jesus, who display both positive and negative traits. Their fear, amazement, and "hardened hearts" fit the negative profile. Readers are thus challenged to avoid these deleterious responses and to evince more faithful attitudes.[7]

(5) Douglas Geyer focuses on what he calls "the anomalous frightful" in Mark 4:35–6:56 and two of its aspects: perplexing uncertainty and fear. Since the anomalous is bewildering, confusing, and uncertain, it creates perceptual problems in need of interpretation: "No matter what the religious or intellectual orientation, it was *necessary that there be some sort of mental conclusion* about perceptual uncertainty, indetermination, or objects that seemed vaguely attested."[8] Such "mental conclusions" do not come easily, however, as 6:52 further confirms.

2. Awe (and Fear) in Psychology and Neuroscience

In our Western cultural and philosophical heritage, a dichotomy has existed between reason and passion, thinking and feeling, judgment and emotion. In recent decades, however, such a dichotomy has been strongly opposed and challenged. Scholars advocating somatic theories of emotion, based on new neurological research, see emotions as older forms of reason that operate automatically in response to certain classes of circumstance.[9] This new emphasis on the interrelationship of emotion and cognition has had a profound impact on our understanding of awe, fear, and related emotions.

---

6. See esp. Theodore J. Weeden, *Mark: Traditions in Conflict* (Philadelphia: Fortress, 1971); Werner H. Kelber, *The Kingdom in Mark: A New Place and a New Time* (Philadelphia: Fortress, 1974).

7. Ernest Best, "The Role of the Disciples in Mark," *NTS* 23 (1977): 377–401; David Rhoads, Joanna Dewey, and Donald Michie, *Mark as Story: An Introduction to the Narrative of a Gospel*, 2nd ed. (Minneapolis: Fortress, 1999), 92–97, 122–29; Elizabeth Struthers Malbon, *In The Company of Jesus: Characters in Mark's Gospel* (Louisville: Westminster John Knox, 2000), 41–69.

8. Douglas W. Geyer, *Fear, Anomaly, and Uncertainty in the Gospel of Mark*, ATLAMS 47 (Lanham, MD: Scarecrow, 2002), 27, emphasis added.

9. See, for example, Antonio Damasio, *Self Comes to Mind: Constructing the Conscious Brain* (London: Heinemann, 2010).

2.1. Prototypical Awe

In 2003 Dacher Keltner and Jonathan Haidt published a seminal article on awe. Reviewing earlier treatments of awe in religion, sociology (Max Weber, Emile Durkheim), philosophy (Edmund Burke), and psychology (Charles Darwin, William McDougall, Abraham Maslow), they find a consensus understanding that awe "involves being in the presence of something powerful, along with associated feelings of submission. Awe also involves a difficulty in comprehension, along with associated feelings of confusion, surprise, and wonder."[10] A range of objects and events may trigger awe, such as religious encounters, charismatic political leaders, and natural objects. Correspondingly, a number of awe-related states may arise, including milder feelings of beauty, astonishment, fear, admiration, elevation, and adoration. Furthermore, awe can be both profoundly positive and terrifyingly negative.

Though languages (and cultures) may differ widely in how they define (translate) various emotional experiences into specific terms, these linguistic distinctions do not necessarily imply differences in emotion-related experience or behavior.[11] Accordingly, Keltner and Haidt approach awe from a prototypical perspective focused on core features, themes, and components. In this vein, they posit two central appraisals for awe: (1) *perceived vastness* and (2) *required accommodation*, defined as an inability to assimilate an experience into current mental structures.

Vastness in most cases strongly correlates awe with power. Yet, in many aesthetic experiences of awe, power seems less operative. The more perceptually oriented term "vastness" thus proves more apt. Vastness refers to "anything that is experienced as being much larger than the self, or the self's ordinary level of experience or frame of reference."[12] Vastness can involve physical and/or social size (authority, power, fame, or prestige). The effects on the self can vary from feelings of smallness to subordination, humbleness, creature-feeling, amazement, wonder, confusion, fear, being overwhelmed, and being overpowered. Since vastness expands the

---

10. Dacher Keltner and Jonathan Haidt, "Approaching Awe, a Moral, Spiritual, and Aesthetic Emotion," *CE* 17 (2003): 303.
11. Jonathan Haidt and Dacher Keltner, "Culture and Facial Expressions: Open-Ended Methods Find More Expressions and a Gradient of Recognition," *CE* 13 (1999): 225–66.
12. Keltner and Haidt, "Approaching Awe," 303.

observer's usual frame of reference in some dimension or domain, a need for accommodation emerges.

Accommodation is understood in line with the Piagetian process of adjusting mental structures that cannot assimilate a new experience. Whereas assimilation involves incorporating present stimuli into existing schemas, accommodation focuses on deviations of stimuli from established schemas, revising these structures or creating new ones to absorb the deviations.[13] For example, a small child may easily assimilate a dog as a "dog" based on earlier experiences of canine creatures. But upon encountering a cat for the first time, that child will typically require education from older persons to help the little one *accommodate* this new feline phenomenon, to update and create a new category called "cat" distinct from "dog."

This concept of accommodation brings together many insights about awe:[14] First, descriptions of awe experiences typically highlight *confusion*, as stimuli become so overwhelming and different from existing mental schemas that awe-filled persons struggle to interpret and describe the wonders they are beholding.

Second, since prototypical awe challenges or negates existing mental structures and makes the self feel small, powerless, and confused, such experiences may be not only disorienting but downright *frightening*. When attempts at understanding and accommodation falter or fail, cognitive breakdown may result in emotional fear, even terror.

Third, when mental structures expand to accommodate previously unknown data and stimuli, awe may involve feelings of *enlightenment* and *rebirth*. Maslow's emphasis on the *transformative power* of "peak experiences," which clearly involve awe, is well known.[15] From a sociological perspective, Weber has likewise emphasized how a charismatic leader in times of crisis awes the masses by performing miracles or acts of heroism that bring about revolutions by internally changing people, who then proceed to change society.[16] Awe-inducing events may thus

---

13. Jean Piaget and Bärbel Inhelder, *The Psychology of the Child*, trans. H. Weaver (New York: Basic Books, 1969).

14. For the following, see Keltner and Haidt, "Approaching Awe," esp. 304.

15. Abraham H. Maslow, *Religions, Values, and Peak-Experiences* (Columbus: Ohio State University Press, 1964).

16. Max Weber, *Economy and Society: An Outline of Interpretive Sociology*, ed. Guenther Roth and Claus Wittich (Berkeley: University of California Press, 1978).

be one of the most rapid and dynamic methods of personal and social change and growth.[17]

Even though Keltner and Haidt (and most subsequent scholarship on awe) acknowledge the possibility of failure in the accommodation process, hardly any of the phenomena of awe they discuss includes the element of fear, let alone terror.[18] This approach seems to be a product of modern Western cultural and conceptual biases toward awe as a positive aesthetic emotion related to vast, inspiring stimuli deriving from perceptions of landscapes, art, music, and the like.[19] Situations involving emotional fear, helplessness, and horror, in which cognitive processes are disabled and disrupted, are more usually implicated in experiences of *trauma*. I now turn to the question of similarities and differences between trauma and terrifying awe.

2.2. Trauma and Terrifying Awe

Two examples from Mark illustrate differences and similarities between trauma and terrifying awe. Events associated with the life-threatening storm on the sea (4:35–41) and the suffering, death, and burial of Jesus (15:1–47) meet the criteria of trauma established in the American Psychiatric Association *Diagnostic and Statistical Manual of Mental Disorders–5* (DSM–5): "Exposure to actual or threatened death, serious injury, or sexual violence."[20] By definition, traumatic events are unbearable and overwhelming, resulting in subjective responses of intense fear, helplessness, and horror.[21]

---

17. Keltner and Haidt, "Approaching Awe," 312.

18. Though note the important exception of Louise Sundararajan, "Religious Awe: Potential Contributions of Negative Theology to Psychology, Positive or Otherwise," *JTPP* 22 (2002): 174–97.

19. See Michelle N. Shiota et al., "Transcending the Self: Awe, Elevation, and Inspiration," in *Handbook of Positive Emotions*, ed. Michele M. Tugade, Michelle N. Shiota, and Leslie D. Kirby (New York: Guilford, 2014), 362–77.

20. American Psychiatric Association, *Diagnostic and Statistical Manual of Mental Disorders: DSM-5*, 5th ed. (Arlington, VA: American Psychiatric Publishing, 2013). These criteria apply to both Acute Stress Disorder (with trauma symptoms lasting no more than a month) and Post-Traumatic Stress Disorder (chronic symptoms).

21. See the telling title of Bessel A. van der Kolk, Alexander C. McFarlane, and Lars Weisaeth, eds., *Traumatic Stress: The Effects of Overwhelming Experience on Mind, Body, and Society* (New York: Guilford, 2007).

However, Jesus's stilling of the storm (4:35–41) and being raised from the dead (16:1–8), are clearly not traumatic events in Mark. Yet such phenomena normally elicit awe. When such awe is so overwhelming that those witnessing are unable to assimilate and accommodate it, fear, even terror, may be the outcome (see Mark 4:41, "they feared a great fear," and 16:8, "trembling and astonishment had come upon them ... for they were afraid"). Thus, while trauma and the awe events are distinct, the emotional responses may be similar.

Modern neuroscience further clarifies this relationship.[22] To simplify, we may locate the brain's alarm system in the amygdala (gauging emotional significance) and the hypothalamus (secreting stress hormones) and its regulation system in the hippocampus (categorization and memory) and prefrontal cortex (conscious elaboration). All sensory information initially routes through the thalamus, which "stirs all the input from our perceptions into a fully blended autobiographical soup, an integrated, coherent experience of 'this is what happens to me.'"[23]

Two neural pathways egress from the thalamus. The so-called "low road" to the amygdala and hypothalamus is extremely fast. If the amygdala interprets the emotional significance of a sensory input as a threat, a message transmits to the hypothalamus to secrete stress hormones. Intensified threats trigger a progressive action-response sequence: (1) *fight or flight*, experienced as fear; (2) *freeze*, associated with terror; and (3) *fold/collapse*, prompting helpless/hopeless horror.[24] Survival reactions of fight and flight are related to emotional *hyper*arousal, while those of freeze and fold/collapse are related to *hypo*arousal.[25]

The other neural pathway, the so-called "high road," takes some milliseconds longer but offers a conscious and much more refined interpretation. The hippocampus categorizes the sensory information according to earlier experiences and memory, while the prefrontal cortex elaborates the

---

22. For the effects of trauma on the brain, see the instructive presentation by Bessel A. van der Kolk, *The Body Keeps the Score: Brain, Mind, and Body in the Healing of Trauma* (New York: Penguin, 2015), 39–104.

23. Ibid., 60.

24. See Stephen W. Porges, *The Polyvagal Theory: Neurophysiological Foundations of Emotions, Attachment, Communication, and Self-Regulation*, NSIN (New York: Norton, 2011).

25. Pat Ogden, Kekuni Minton, and Clare Pain, *Trauma and the Body: A Sensorimotor Approach to Psychotherapy*, NSIN (New York: Norton, 2006), 85–107.

present event, predicts future results, and informs conscious deliberations and decisions.

Neuroscience operates from the fundamental premise that "what is wired together, fires together." For example, when someone hears a door slam shut, the amygdala may initially interpret it as a threat, causing stress hormones in the hypothalamus to kick the body into survival mode (fight, flight, or freeze). Soon, however, the prefrontal cortex may reason, "It was only a door!" while the hippocampus classifies the experience from its memory base, "Doors are not normally dangerous." The hippocampus and prefrontal cortex may thus function as an integrated network regulating the emotional arousal caused by the alarm system.

On the other hand, when the amygdala goes on overdrive, the person becomes so emotionally and somatically overwhelmed (hyper- and/or hypoarousal) that the hippocampus (categorization and memory) and the prefrontal cortex (conscious elaboration) may be disabled or disrupted.[26] Moreover, traumatic events often fail to "make sense" (as in the book of Job). When the sensory input from these events defy classification in terms of prior experiences and memories in the hippocampus, assimilation falters; likewise, when the prefrontal cortex struggles to comprehend and integrate traumatic realities into new or adjusted perceptual schemas, accommodation aborts. In short, traumatic experiences plunge the victim into a vicious cognitive-affective-somatic spiral.

Keltner and Haidt theorize that assimilation and accommodation initially fail with terrifying awe. Such a cognitive breakdown subsequently affects the person emotionally and bodily.[27] In terms of neuroscience, this implies that terrifying awe is also tracked on the brain's intersecting "high" and "low roads." However, while traumatic events initially attack the low road, terrifying awe events first affect the high road of the brain. Yet, due to the wiring and firing together of neural pathways, both experiences may plunge the victim into a vicious cognitive-affective-somatic spiral, a volatile haywire act along tremulous neural pathways. Consequently, terrifying awe manifests many of the same symptoms associated with trauma, such as *emotional* hyper- and/or hypoarousal; *physical* fight, flight, freeze, or fold/collapse reactions; and *cognitive* disruptions. The freeze reaction to traumatic and awe-full events will be of special interest to my analysis

---

26. See further Ogden, Minton, and Pain, *Trauma and Body*, 3–40, 139–61.
27. Keltner and Haidt, "Approaching Awe."

of Mark 6:52 and selected Hebrew Bible texts. In this "frozen" state, the *body* reacts with increased muscle tension and reduced heart rate (becoming "like a stone"), *emotions* become flat and numb, and *cognitive faculties* suffer paralysis and stupefaction.[28]

3. Trauma and Terrifying Awe Reactions in the Hebrew Bible

The Hebrew Bible offers a variety of reactions describing the response to traumatic events. Of special interest are texts that focus on the emotional, bodily, and cognitive implications. Job 17:6–7 reads:

> He has made me a byword of the peoples,
>   and I am one before whom people spit.
> My eye has grown dim from grief,
>   and all my members are like a shadow.[29]

Job's disastrous sufferings have overwhelmed him emotionally in the form of "grief." The statement "All my members are like a shadow" describes a hypoaroused bodily and emotional state of immobilization and numbness. The parallel comment "My eye has grown dim" must be understood along the same line, although the "dimming" factor may relate more closely to cognitive diminishment (dimwittedness). This text marks the only occurrence of πωρόω in the LXX, here rendering כהה ("eye *has grown dim*"), a fact we will bear in mind below in examining the semantic range of πωρόω overall and in Mark 6:52 in particular.

Two additional Hebrew Bible texts describe the freeze reaction to terrifying awe and/or threat as bodies becoming like "stone." First, the Song of Moses exclaims:

> Who is like you, O LORD, among the gods?
>   Who is like you, majestic in holiness,
>   awesome in splendor, doing wonders?
> You stretched out your right hand,
>   the earth swallowed them....
> The peoples heard, they *trembled* [B];
>   *pangs/fear* [B + E, חיל] seized the inhabitants of Philistia.

---

28. Muriel A. Hagenaars, Melly Oitzl, and Karin Roelofs, "Updating Freeze: Aligning Animal and Human Research," *NBR* 47 (2014): 165–76.

29. Unless otherwise noted, all quotations of biblical texts are from NRSV.

> Then the chiefs of Edom were *dismayed* [E + C + B, בהל];³⁰
> *trembling* [B] seized the leaders of Moab;
> all the inhabitants of Canaan *melted away* [B + E + C, מוג].³¹
> *Terror and dread/trembling* [E + B, פחד] fell upon them;
> by the might of your arm, *they became still as a stone* [כאבן]
> until your people, O Lord, passed by,
> until the people whom you acquired passed by. (Exod 15:11–16)

The deadly fate of the Egyptians and God's awesome wonders in saving the Israelites through the Red Sea are the elicitors of all these action responses. Hebrew terms like חיל, בהל, מוג, and פחד have a semantic range in which emotional, bodily and/or cognitive dimensions are interrelated, as is also true for a freeze reaction ("becoming still as a stone").

First Samuel 25 tells the story of David, Nabal, and Abigail. When Nabal refuses to compensate David and his followers for protecting his three thousand sheep and goats, David threatens to kill Nabal and all his men. After a drinking party, Nabal's wife Abigail informs him about the lethal threat: "In the morning, when the wine had gone out of Nabal, his wife told him these things, and *his heart died within him*; *he became like a stone* [לאבן]. About ten days later the Lord struck Nabal, and he died" (1 Sam 25:37–38). Though many commentators have argued that these verses describe a "heart attack," no such medical diagnosis was known in antiquity.³² But neither is this text ascribing to Nabal a morally and spiritually "hardened heart."³³ Nabal's seizing heart and "becoming like a stone" are *action responses to the lethal threat* communicated by Abigail. Furthermore, empirical studies of freeze reactions emphasize that two readily observable somatic reactions occur: reduced heart rate ("heart died") and increased muscle tension ("like a stone"; see also Gen 45:26; Exod 12:16).³⁴

Though not using "stone" imagery, the Joseph story in Gen 45 further elucidates the "freeze" response to stunning events. When Joseph finally reveals himself to his brothers, they are utterly shocked: "But his brothers could not answer him, so dismayed [בהל (horrified, out of their

---

30. *HALOT*, s.v. "בהל": be horrified/out of one's senses/out of breath or to rush.
31. BDB, s.v. "מוג": be in a state of commotion/being helpless and disorganized through terror/melt in fear.
32. Majorie O'Rourke Boyle, "The Law of the Heart: The Death of a Fool (1 Sam 25)," *JBL* 120 (2001): 403–12.
33. Contra ibid., 412–27.
34. Hagenaars, Oitzl, and Roelofs, "Updating Freeze."

senses); LXX: ταράσσω] were they at his presence" (Gen 45:3–4). The reality seemed too overwhelming to sink in, prompting Joseph to repeat: "I am your brother, Joseph" (45:3, 5). Only after Joseph's lengthy monologue and much hugging and weeping are the brothers able to respond verbally or "come to their senses," so to speak (45:15).

Father Jacob, who earlier suffered the trauma of believing (falsely) that his favorite son Joseph had been killed by wild animals, now experiences a dramatic "revival" upon learning of Joseph's survival and high position in Egypt.

> So they went up out of Egypt and came to their father Jacob in the land of Canaan. And they told him, "Joseph is still alive! He is even ruler over all the land of Egypt." He was stunned [lit., his heart froze/became solid/paralyzed/numbed (פוג)]; *he could not believe them*. But when they told him all the words of Joseph that he had said to them, and when he saw the wagons that Joseph had sent to carry him, *the spirit of their father Jacob revived*. Israel said, "Enough! My son Joseph is still alive. I must go and see him before I die. (45:25–28)

Jacob's "stunning" (פוג)[35] experience no doubt describes a classic freeze reaction, even though it entails an action response not to threat but to *good news* that was simply too overwhelming for Jacob to assimilate and accommodate. In neuroscience terms, Jacob's taxonomic and memory functions in the hippocampus and conscious elaborative faculties in the prefrontal cortex broke down, even as his capacity to interpret emotional significance in the amygdala was impaired, prompting the hypothalamus to secrete bodily stress hormones. The basic physical dimension of פוג ("freeze/become solid") highlights the integral *bodily* aspect of the freeze reaction. Semantic nuances of "paralyze" or "numb" in the same term stress *emotional* and *cognitive* elements.[36] The narrator's further report that Jacob "could not believe [אמן; LXX: πιστεύω] them" (45:26), though perhaps intimating that the patriarch could not *trust* his sons, more strongly suggests in this context a cognitive inability to *comprehend* the overwhelming

---

35. See the extensive analysis of the rare word פוג by Marshall D. Johnson, "The Paralysis of Torah in Habakkuk I 4," *VT* 35 (1985): 257–66.

36. A number of other ancient sources interrelate bodily freeze reaction with emotional numbness and/or cognitive paralysis: Horace, *Ep.* 1.6.9–16; Philo, *Legat.*, 189; Plutarch, *Cor.* 31.3; Statius, *Theb.* 6.735–40; Calpurnius Siculus, *Buc.* 35; Prudentius, *Psych.* 585.

good news. In any case, a rendering along the lines of "Jacob's heart froze/ was petrified" (45:27, my trans.) nicely incorporates bodily, emotional, and cognitive dimensions of the Hebrew phrase.[37]

The story also brilliantly illustrates the *transforming* experience of accommodating the overwhelming new reality. After further hearing "the words of Joseph" and seeing confirming signs, "the spirit of their father Jacob *revived* [חי] (recovered/returned to life); LXX: ἀναζωπυρέω (take on new life/kindle into flame)]" (45:27). Jacob's climactic expression— "Enough! My son Joseph is still alive. I must go and see him before I die" (45:28)—further evidences feelings of "enlightenment" and "rebirth," described by Keltner and Haidt, resulting from successful accommodation of awe-experiences. Nothing in Gen 45:25–28 ascribes moral blame to Jacob for a frozen/numbed/paralyzed heart concerning the good news he has just received. Nevertheless, Jacob's stunned reaction is *counterproductive* to his "revived spirit" and accommodation action responses to the new reality.

4. The Challenge to Assimilate and Accommodate the Vastness of Jesus in Mark

Repeatedly, Mark portrays Jesus as an overwhelmingly vast and powerful figure whom various characters must struggle to assimilate and accommodate. Characters are alternately amazed, stunned, confused, petrified, terrified, and tongue-tied. Notably, many of Mark's stories *end* with such befuddled responses (1:27; 2:12; 4:41; 5:15, 20, 42; 6:51–52; 7:37; 9:6; 10:26). Indeed, the entire Gospel narrative ends on a "fearful" note (ἐφοβοῦντο [16:8]). Thus, reminiscent of Jacob's climactic reaction in Gen 45:25–28, Mark punctuates awesome experiences of Jesus with reports of characters being "petrified" (פוג), so to speak, and unable to "believe" (אמן/πιστεύω) what they saw or heard; in other words, they found themselves hard pressed to assimilate or accommodate Jesus's incredible vastness. As with Jacob's experience discussed above, we should scarcely blame the characters in Mark for their immobilized and incredulous action responses,

---

37. Mark S. Smith argues persuasively that "heart" in the Hebrew Bible often has both bodily and emotional (and cognitive) components ("The Heart and Innards in Israelite Emotional Expressions: Notes from Anthropology and Psychobiology," *JBL* 117 [1998]: 427–36).

even as we appreciate their counterproductive consequences. Only if the characters *remain* in a state of "unbelief" are they to be blamed morally.

For example, I think that Jesus's retort to the disciples, in the wake of his stilling the storm—"Have you still [οὔπω] no faith [πίστις]?" (4:40)— must be balanced. On the one hand, he is not accusing them of being "nonbelievers." They continue to follow Jesus. On the other hand, he warns them not to *remain* (οὔπω) in their state of "unbelief." Furthermore, a pastoral intention of Mark 4:35–41 is likely that readers should know that they can *trust* ("have faith in") God/Jesus in all kinds of "storms." I am critical, though, to push the argument further and claim that Mark expects readers never to be afraid in "storms" nor to be overwhelmed by awe. Nonetheless, readers of this story informed by Mark's entire narrative are in a better position to accommodate the vastness of Jesus than the disciple characters engulfed in the fraught moment of fear, amazement, and confusion.

In most "amazing" Markan stories, stunned characters do not altogether accommodate the vastness of Jesus or fully experience a "revival of the spirit" (like patriarch Jacob) or feeling of enlightenment. Possible exceptions include the crowd "being amazed" and "praising God" when Jesus heals the paralyzed man (2:12) and the cured bleeding woman ultimately falling before Jesus "in fear and trembling" and "telling the whole truth" (5:33). The most patent case of cognitive enlightenment features the blind man's progression from partial and confused vision to clear vision in 8:22–26. For the most part, however, figures in Mark who encounter the vastness of Jesus remain lost throughout the stunning scene in a maze of amazement.

This repeated failure to assimilate and accommodate Jesus's vastness rhetorically stresses that no common category or schema of thought can contain Jesus. Accordingly, if and when readers start to think that they now "get it," before long another episode ends with more uncontrollable awe that further shatters expectations.

4.1. A Lexical Analysis of πωρόω and Its Semantic Range

A search in *Thesaurus Linguae Graecae* shows every usage of πωρόω and πώρωσις. Among Second Temple Jewish texts, it is found only in Job 17:7 in the LXX and nowhere in Philo or Josephus. When the LXX translates the Hebrew notion of a "hardened heart" related to unbelief and/or a moral state of faithlessness, stiffness, stubbornness and obduracy, it typically

NOT "HARDENED HEARTS" BUT "PETRIFIED HEARTS" 257

uses cognates of βαρέω, κατισχύω, and especially σκληρύνω—but never πωρόω. Originally, as J. Armitage Robinson argued early in the last century, ancient Greek medical writers used πωρόω and πώρωσις in reference to stones forming in the bladder, to calluses rejoining fractured bones, or to any hard, thickened, or coagulated bodily substance.[38] In short, πωρόω/πώρωσις denoted some process of petrification. The terms also applied to insensibility and numbness (results of petrification), with no particular relation to hardness, as the story of Dionysius the tyrant of Heraclea (d. 306/305 BCE) illustrates:

> But the consequence of his physical size and corpulent body was difficulty in breathing. As a cure for this complaint the doctors, it is said, gave instructions to prepare very long, thin needles, which were then to be pushed into his ribs and belly when he had fallen into a deep sleep. Their object was to have the needle pass right through the flesh—it was *insensitive* [πωρόω] and in a sense not part of him—while he lay there just like a stone. If the needle reached a point that was still healthy and part of his system, not transformed by the excess of fat, then he would notice and wake up. (Aelian, *Var. Hist.* 9.13)[39]

Athenaeus tells the same story: "As long as the needle was in a part of his body that had been *deadened* [or *numbed* (πωρόω)] by the fat, he felt nothing; but once it passed through there and came in contact with an undamaged area, he woke up" (*Deipn.* 12.549b).[40]

In Job 17:7 LXX πωρόω renders the Hebrew כהה: "My eye *has grown dim* from sorrow." The verb thus connotes insensibility, dullness, or obscuration of the faculty of sight. As discussed above, this text describes the deleterious cognitive impairments of trauma.

In sum, πωρόω/πώρωσις develops from an original sense of the process of petrification (turning to stone) to its resultant state of emotional insensibility and numbing and, further, to an optical image of obscuration or blindness.[41] Prior to the New Testament, no evidence directly links the rare πωρόω/πώρωσις with σκληρύνω and its cognates that refer to unbe-

---

38. J. Armitage Robinson, "ΠΩΡΩΣΙΣ and ΠΗΡΩΣΙΣ," *JTS* 3 (1902): 81–96.
39. Translation from Aelian, *Historical Miscellany*, trans. N. G. Wilson, LCL 486 (Cambridge: Harvard University Press, 1997).
40. Translation from Athenaeus, *The Learned Banqueters: Books 12–13.594b*, trans. S. Douglas Olson, LCL 327 (Cambridge: Harvard University Press, 2010).
41. Robinson, "ΠΩΡΩΣΙΣ and ΠΗΡΩΣΙΣ," 81–93, esp. 92–93.

lief, moral stiffness, or obduracy. Accordingly, New Testament interpreters should be wary of associating πωρόω/πώρωσις with "hardness of hearts/minds." Robinson's survey of Latin, Armenian, and Syriac translations of πωρόω/πώρωσις in Mark 3:5; 6:52; 8:17; John 12:40; Rom 11:7, 25; 2 Cor 3:14; and Eph 4:18 turned up no nuances of "hardheartedness." One Syriac version of Mark 6:52 renders "fattened" (stupefied) hearts, while another has "blind" hearts. Latin translations of Mark 6:52 and 8:17 read *obcaecatum* (blindness) and *obtusum* (dullness, obtuseness). Armenian texts have "'stupefied' as with a deep sleep" (6:52) and "'stupefied' as with amazement" (8:17). All these versions may allude to insensible understanding, but not to willful obduracy or moral faithlessness per se.

How does Mark 3:5 fit into this semantic schema? The English "callous," from the Latin *callosus/callus* (closely parallel to the Greek πώρωσις), metaphorically designates "lack of feeling" and emotional numbness.[42] However, "having no feeling," in the sense of having no sympathy for others, has a moral twist in English of "callous indifference to suffering," which is precisely the case in Mark 3:5. The Pharisees and Herodians' lack of sympathy toward the man with the withered hand accounts for Jesus's anger toward them (3:5a). Hence, "callousness of heart" aptly translates πώρωσις τῆς καρδίας here. Alternatively, "hardheartedness toward suffering" (see Deut 15:7) captures the idea. But the subtly, yet significantly, distinct "hardened hearts" in the absolute sense goes too far with its sclerotic connotations of unbelief, obduracy, and moral faithlessness associated with σκληροκαρδία in the LXX. "Callousness of heart" describes the Pharisees and Herodians *in a specific situation*. "Hardened heart," on the other hand, is *an overall moral characteristic* of them. Much too often, Christian theologians have made such an illegitimate move in analyzing Jewish characters.

The semantic range of πωρόω/πώρωσις thus aptly describes *freeze reactions* with (1) *bodily* effects of becoming stiff, solid, or stone-like (petrification; see Gen 45:26; Exod 15:16; 1 Sam 25:37); (2) *emotional* experiences of hypoarousal, numbness, and insensibility; and (3) *cognitive* impairments of obscuration and blindness (see Job 17:7). J. K. Rowling has popularized similar notions in "petrifying" freeze reactions in her accounts of Hogwarts wizardry.

---

42. See ibid., 81.

4.2. The Action Responses of the Disciples to the Vastness of Jesus in Mark 6:45–52

The struggle of the disciples to assimilate and accommodate the vastness of Jesus's walking on the sea is described at the end of the scene:

> But when they saw him walking on the sea, they thought it was a ghost and cried out; for they all saw him and were in a terrified turmoil [ταράσσω]. But immediately he spoke to them and said, "Take heart, it is I; do not be afraid." Then he got into the boat with them and the wind ceased. And they were completely at the extreme outside of themselves [λίαν ἐκ περισσοῦ ἐν ἑαυτοῖς ἐξίσταντο], for they did not understand about the loaves, but their hearts were petrified [ἀλλ᾿ ἦν αὐτῶν ἡ καρδία πεπωρωμένη]. (Mark 6:49–52 [my trans.])

Here the natural and preternatural orders seem to coalesce for the disciples (6:49).[43] Their action response designated by ταράσσω reflects cognitive confusion and turmoil swirling with other hyperarousing emotions like fear and horror (see Matt 2:3; Luke 1:12; 24:36–39; John 12:27–28a; 14:1, 27; and Gen 42:28; 45:3; Deut 2:25; Ps 6:3, 4 in the LXX).[44] Hence, I translate ταράσσω in Mark 6:50 as "terrified turmoil."

As the disciples' fear and failure to recognize Jesus go hand in hand in 6:49–50a, so Jesus's exhortation "not to fear" links with his aim to reveal himself in 6:50b–51a. Despite his best efforts, however, the disciples are not able to assimilate and accommodate Jesus. Instead, their cognitive density and emotional intensity escalate: "They were utterly at the extreme outside of themselves" (6:51b). The verb ἐξίστημι, qualified here by the adverb λίαν ("very much, exceedingly") and probably also by the prepositional phrase ἐκ περισσοῦ ("abundantly"),[45] has both an emotional and a cognitive component. In transitive usage, ἐξίστημι denotes "to cause to be in a state in

---

43. George W. Young, "Surprised by the Eye: Charting the Fantastic in Mark 6.49–50," *Neot* 34 (2000): 225–35.

44. For confusion and turmoil as essential to ταράσσω, see further LSJ, s.v. "ταράσσω"; BDAG, s.v. "ταράσσω."

45. For the question of the originality of ἐκ περισσοῦ (in brackets in UBS[5] and NA[28]), see Bruce M. Metzger, *A Textual Commentary on the Greek New Testament: A Companion Volume to the United Bible Societies' Greek New Testament (Fourth Revised Edition)*, 2nd ed. (Stuttgart: Deutsche Bibelgesellschaft; New York: United Bible Societies, 1994), 79.

which things seem to make little or no sense, confuse, amaze, astound." In intransitive cases describing an emotional state of "amazement and astonishment," it connotes a state of "inability to reason normally, lose one's mind, be out of one's senses."[46] In other words, the disciples' experience of Jesus's self-revelation as the one walking on the sea strikes them as so cognitively vast and overwhelming that it renders them utterly incapacitated, unable to expand and stabilize their mental schemas and categories to comprehend (accommodate) Jesus.

In 6:52a, the Markan narrator associates the disciples' action responses to Jesus's walking on the sea (6:51b) with his feeding the multitudes in 6:30–44: "For [γάρ] they did not understand about the loaves." Though most scholars speculate concerning *what* "they did not understand about the loaves,"[47] the point is simply *that* the disciples were unable to understand the loaves incident, just as they were unable to understand the sea-walking feat. In both cases, encounters with supernatural events involving Jesus proved too vast for the disciples to comprehend.

Immediately following the "loaves" comment, the narrator concludes in 6:52b: ἀλλ᾽ ἦν αὐτῶν ἡ καρδία πεπωρωμένη. I argued above that the widespread contemporary translation "but their hearts were hardened" has no lexical support at the time of Mark. Even more importantly, nothing in the narrative context indicates that the disciples suffered from unbelief, obduracy, stubbornness, or moral faithlessness on this occasion. On the contrary, notions of petrification, numbness, dullness, insensibility, and blindness, so well documented for πωρόω, make perfect sense in tandem with the disciples' extreme cognitive affective distress ("outside of themselves") in 6:51b. In other words, they "freeze up" *emotionally* with numbness and insensibility, *cognitively* with blindness and obscurity (see 6:52a: "they did not understand/comprehend [συνίημι]), and *bodily*

---

46. BDAG, s.v. "ἐξίστημι."

47. Numerous explanations have been offered. Quentin Quesnell has written an entire monograph claiming that the disciples in 6:52 specifically misunderstand the eucharistic implications of the feeding miracle (*The Mind of Mark: Interpretation and Method Through the Exegesis of Mark 6,52*, AnBib 38 [Rome: Pontifical Biblical Institute, 1969]). Suzanne Watts Henderson argues that the disciples' failure consists in not exercising authority over the sea given to them by Jesus ("'Concerning the Loaves': Comprehending Incomprehension in Mark 6.45–52," *JSNT* 83 [2001]: 3–26). Frank J. Matera contends on the basis of 6:52 that faithful discipleship hinges on proper Christological understanding ("The Incomprehension of the Disciples and Peter's Confession [Mark 6,14–8,30]," *Bib* 70 [1989]: 164).

with stone-like feeling. In English, one word brilliantly captures all these dimensions: "Their hearts were *petrified*" (6:52b).⁴⁸

4.3. Readers Accommodating the Vastness of Jesus in Mark 6:45–52

The way Mark narrates the story in 6:45–52 privileges the reader with considerably more information than that perceived by the disciple characters within the story, specifically, information portraying Jesus in a divine light.

▶ First, scholars have noted Jesus's own supernatural "seeing" and insight. In the darkness, Jesus sees that the disciples "were straining at the oars against an adverse wind" in the middle of the sea (6:47–48).⁴⁹
▶ Second, the fact that only God and God's wisdom "walk on the sea" in the Hebrew Bible (Job 9:8; Ps 77:19; Isa 43:16; 51:9–10; Hab 3:15; cf. Sir 24:5–6) makes it likely that the same action by Jesus implies divinity.⁵⁰
▶ Third, the curious phrase "he wanted to pass by them" (ἤθελεν παρελθεῖν αὐτούς [6:48c]), is best interpreted in light of God's "passing by" Moses and Elijah in theophanies (Exod 33:19, 22; 34:6; 3 Kgdms 19:11). Thus, the phrase pictures Jesus as God himself.⁵¹
▶ Fourth, the multiple theophanic features in the narrative may give Jesus's simple "It is I (ἐγώ εἰμι)" self-identification to the disciples (6:50b) another layer of meaning, echoing God's "I am" formula (Exod 3:14; Deut 32:39; Isa 41:4; 43:10–11; 45:18).⁵²

---

48. In a forthcoming monograph, I will argue that Mark 8:17 should likewise be translated "Are your [the disciples'] hearts petrified?" with significant consequences for interpreting the entire scene in 8:14–21.
49. So also Rudolf Pesch, *Das Markusevangelium*, 2 vols., HThKNT 2 (Freiburg: Herder, 1977), 1:360; Marcus, *Mark 1–8*, 423.
50. So most commentators, such as Adela Yarbro Collins, *Mark: A Commentary*, Hermeneia (Minneapolis: Fortress Press, 2007), 333.
51. Ernst Lohmeyer, "'Und Jesus Ging Vorüber': Eine exegetische Betrachtung," *NThT* 23 (1934): 206–24, esp. 216–19; see also John Paul Heil, *Jesus Walking on the Sea: Meaning and Gospel Functions of Matt. 14:22–33, Mark 6:45–52, and John 6:15b–21*, AnBib 87 (Rome: Biblical Institute Press, 1981), 69–71.
52. Pesch, *Das Markusevangelium*, 1:362; Robert A. Guelich, *Mark 1–8:26*, WBC 34A (Dallas: Word, 1998), 351. Robert H. Stein goes too far when he takes this as

▶ Fifth, when Jesus calms the contrary wind (6:51a), the competent reader can scarcely ignore that in the Hebrew Bible and Jewish tradition only God can rescue people on the sea (Ps 107:23-32; Jonah 1:1-16; Wis 14:2-4).

Mark never explicitly identifies Jesus as divine in 6:45–52 or elsewhere. However, the disciples are portrayed as being lost in a maze of amazement due to the overwhelmingly vastness of Jesus. Furthermore, competent readers are provided with key narrative clues expanding their categories and schemes of thinking (accommodation), making them *intuitively* identify Jesus with the God of the Hebrew Bible. Moreover, the multiple passages in Mark ending with characters lost in a maze of amazement, fear, and terror *perpetually expand* the categories and schemes of thinking of the reader concerning Mark's Jesus. To assimilate the vast Jesus presented in Mark ultimately requires nothing less than divine frameworks of thought. Readers may thus become caught up in a "saturated phenomenon," as Jean-Luc Marion envisions an *excess of intuition* over and above the *concept*, an intuition that no singular concept (like "Messiah," "son of David," "Son of Man," or "Son of God") adequately captures, but rather demands a multiplicity of quasi concepts or "narratives" in Mark's case.[53] Compared to other canonical gospels, Mark's Christology may appear less prescriptive and more allusive, but Mark still offers a "divine" Christology.[54]

Mark 6:45–52 dramatically illustrates the Second Gospel's uncanny ability to involve its readers in endless and expansive wonder and awe concerning the identity of Jesus, who simply cannot be contained within narrow, rigid schemas and categories. Such a narrative strategy persis-

---

a reference to Jesus's "divine *nature*" (*Mark* [Grand Rapids: Baker Academic, 2008], 326). R. T. France sees no such echo or reference in "It is I" (6:50b), since "a declaration of divinity does not seem appropriate at this point in the narrative where the focus is on the initial failure to recognise Jesus and his consequent self-identification" (*The Gospel of Mark: A Commentary on the Greek Text*, NIGTC [Grand Rapids: Eerdmans, 2002], 273 n. 71). Unfortunately, France does not distinguish between the confused perspective of the disciples and the privileged perspective of the reader informed by the theophanic features in the narrative.

53. Jean-Luc Marion, "Banality of Saturation," in Marion, *The Visible and the Revealed*, trans. Christina M. Gschwandtner, Perspectives in Continental Philosophy (New York: Fordham University Press, 2008), 130–31.

54. I will address this highly-debated christological issue more fully in my forthcoming monograph.

tently challenges readers to retell and forthtell again and again the glorious gospel of Jesus Christ, the Son of God.

Select Bibliography

Antonio Damasio. *Self Comes to Mind: Constructing the Conscious Brain.* London: Heinemann, 2010.
Hagenaars, Muriel A., Melly Oitzl, and Karin Roelofs. "Updating Freeze: Aligning Animal and Human Research." *NBR* 47 (2014): 165–76.
Haidt, Jonathan, and Dacher Keltner. "Culture and Facial Expressions: Open-Ended Methods Find More Expressions and a Gradient of Recognition." *CE* 13 (1999): 225–66.
Keltner, Dacher, and Jonathan Haidt. "Approaching Awe, a Moral, Spiritual, and Aesthetic Emotion." *CE* 17 (2003): 298–303.
Ogden, Pat, Kekuni Minton, and Clare Pain. *Trauma and the Body: A Sensorimotor Approach to Psychotherapy.* NSIN. New York: Norton, 2006.
Porges, Stephen W. *The Polyvagal Theory: Neurophysiological Foundations of Emotions, Attachment, Communication, and Self-Regulation.* NSIN. New York: Norton, 2011.
Shiota, Michelle N., Todd M. Thrash, Alexander F. Danvers, and John T. Dombrowski. "Transcending the Self: Awe, Elevation, and Inspiration." Pages 362–77 in *Handbook of Positive Emotions.* Edited by Michele M. Tugade, Michelle N. Shiota, and Leslie D. Kirby (New York: Guilford, 2014).
Smith, Mark S. "The Heart and Innards in Israelite Emotional Expressions: Notes from Anthropology and Psychobiology." *JBL* 117 (1998): 427–36.
Sundararajan, Louise. "Religious Awe: Potential Contributions of Negative Theology to Psychology, Positive or Otherwise." *JTPP* 22 (2002): 174–97.
Van der Kolk, Bessel A. *The Body Keeps the Score: Brain, Mind, and Body in the Healing of Trauma.* New York: Penguin, 2015.
Van der Kolk, Bessel A., Alexander C. McFarlane, and Lars Weisaeth, eds. *Traumatic Stress: The Effects of Overwhelming Experience on Mind, Body, and Society.* New York: Guilford, 2007.

Reflexivity and Emotion in Narratological Perspective: Reading Joy in the Lukan Narrative

Michal Beth Dinkler

It is difficult to wrap words around "joy." The author of 1 Peter recognizes this difficulty when he writes that belief in Christ leads to a joy that is "inexpressible" (ἀνεκλάλητος [1 Pet 1:8]).

Still, we try.

This very impulse to try to express in words our affects, emotions, and experiences is fundamentally human. Indeed, our attempts to reflect—and reflect *on*—our ways of being in the world are what make the human a *homo narrans* (storytelling self).[1]

There are many ways in which one might consider the topic of joy in biblical literature. One might take a comparative approach, exploring intersections between biblical texts and other ancient discourses on emotion, as represented in some chapters of *Stoicism in Early Christianity*.[2] Yet another avenue of exploration would be thematic, as in a collection entitled *The Bible and the Pursuit of Happiness: What the Old and New Testaments Teach Us about the Good Life*.[3]

My own interests are literary and rhetorical: I am concerned with the ways that ancient narratives—qua narrative—shape the emotional repertoires of their intended audiences, partly by representing emotional

---

1. John D. Niles, *Homo Narrans: The Poetics and Anthropology of Oral Literature* (Philadelphia: University of Pennsylvania Press, 1999).

2. Tuomas Rasimus, Troels Engberg-Pedersen, and Ismo Dunderberg, eds., *Stoicism in Early Christianity* (Grand Rapids: Baker Academic, 2010).

3. The papers were generated by a conference at Emory in 2009 funded by the John Templeton Foundation. Brent Strawn, ed., *The Bible and the Pursuit of Happiness: What the Old and New Testaments Teach Us about the Good Life* (Oxford: Oxford University Press, 2012).

experiences like joy within the story itself and partly by engendering experiences of emotion like joy in their implied audiences.[4] As Patrick Colm Hogan writes, "Narrative is intimately bound up with emotion."[5] These interests lead me to ask: What are the relationships between narration, emotion, and interpretation in ancient narratives broadly, and in New Testament narratives more specifically?

This question gestures toward four assumptions that will be helpful to clarify at the outset. After outlining these points of departure, I will pose a more focused version of the question above and offer a suggested answer with respect to a New Testament narrative that makes extensive use of vocabulary related to joy: the Gospel of Luke (dubbed by some the "Gospel of Joy")[6] and the book of Acts.[7]

---

4. I adopt the approach of narrative and reader-response critics who avoid pinpointing specific, monolithic profiles of the gospels' "real readers" in favor of situating their implied audiences in a general first-century CE Jewish and Greco-Roman milieu. See David Rhoads, "Narrative Criticism: Practices and Prospects," in Rhoads, *Reading Mark: Engaging the Gospel* (Minneapolis: Fortress, 2004), esp. 32; Robert Fowler, *Let the Reader Understand: Reader-Response Criticism and the Gospel of Mark* (Minneapolis: Fortress, 1991). "Implied readers" are the narrative's intended recipients, who cooperate with and share the "implied author's" assumptions, as distinct from an actual, historical audience. I base my use of these concepts on the foundational work of Wayne Booth, *The Rhetoric of Fiction*, 2nd ed. (Chicago: University of Chicago Press, 1983); Umberto Eco, *The Role of the Reader* (Bloomington: Indiana University Press, 1979); Wolfgang Iser, *The Act of Reading: A Theory of Aesthetic Response* (Baltimore: Johns Hopkins University Press, 1978); Iser, *The Implied Reader: Patterns of Communication in Prose Fiction from Bunyan to Beckett* (Baltimore: Johns Hopkins University Press, 1974); on the latter, see Zoltán Schwáb, "Mind the Gap: The Impact of Wolfgang Iser's Reader-Response Criticism on Biblical Studies—A Critical Assessment," *JLT* 17 (2003): 170–81. Importantly, the concept of "implied reader" can include *auditors*, which—as is by now well established—was the case for most of the original recipients of the Gospels.

5. Patrick Colm Hogan, *The Mind and Its Stories: Narrative Universals and Human Emotion* (Cambridge: Cambridge University, 2003), 5.

6. John Painter, "Joy," in *Dictionary of Jesus and the Gospels*, ed. Joel Green and Scot McKnight (Downers Grove, IL: Inter Varsity Press, 1992), 394; William Morrice, *Joy in the New Testament* (Grand Rapids: Eerdmans, 1984), 96, inter alia.

7. Implicit in my reference to a singular New Testament narrative is, of course, the view that the Gospel of Luke and Acts were written by the same author (whomever that might have been) as a coherent narrative (at least in some sense). Those interested in the still-debated unity and composition of the Gospel and Acts might consult, e.g., Henry J. Cadbury, *The Making of Luke-Acts* (London: Macmillan, 1927); Joseph Ver-

1. Four Points of Departure

First, I assume, with constructivists, that *vocabularies of emotion—and the experiences and conceptions they elicit—are not universal*. Despite Darwinian and recent cognitivist claims that emotions are trans- or precultural, there is ample evidence that various cultures conceive of and linguistically describe emotions differently.[8] For instance, the Greek terms ἵμερος or πόθος express a love laced with longing or grief; as classicists routinely note, these words can be difficult to translate into English. Or consider the terms αἰδώς and αἰσχύνη, which are both typically rendered in English as "shame" but differ subtly in Greek. In addition to differences between source languages and the receptor languages into which they are translated, even ancient thinkers using the same language did not all share a common taxonomy of emotions. Diogenes Laertius's four main classes of emotion are grief (λύπη), fear (φόβος), desire (ἐπιθυμία), and pleasure (ἡδονή) (*Vit. Phil.* 7.111), whereas Aristotle's list of πάθη in *Rhetoric* does not include grief at all.[9]

---

heyden, ed., *The Unity of Luke-Acts* (Leuven: Leuven University Press, 1999); Robert O'Toole, *The Unity of Luke's Theology: An Analysis of Luke-Acts* (Wilmington, DE: Glazier, 1984); Robert Tannehill, *The Narrative Unity of Luke-Acts: A Literary Interpretation*, 2 vols. (Philadelphia: Fortress, 1986–1990); Mikael Parsons and Richard I. Pervo, *Rethinking the Unity of Luke and Acts* (Minneapolis: Fortress, 1992); Patricia Walters, *The Assumed Authorial Unity of Luke and Acts: A Reassessment of the Evidence* (Cambridge: Cambridge University Press, 2009); Michael Wolter, *Das Lukasevangelium*, HNT 5 (Tübingen: Mohr Siebeck, 2008).

8. Several treatments of emotions in classical antiquity have influenced my thinking in this regard. E.g., Carlin Barton, *The Sorrows of the Ancient Romans: The Gladiator and the Monster* (Princeton: Princeton University Press, 1993); *Roman Honor: The Fire in the Bones* (Berkeley: University of California Press, 2001); John M. Cooper, *Reason and Emotion: Essays on Ancient Moral Psychology and Ethical Theory* (Princeton: Princeton University, 1999); David Konstan and N. K. Rutter, eds., *Envy, Spite, and Jealousy: The Rivalrous Emotions in Ancient Greece* (Edinburgh: Edinburgh University Press, 2003); Robert A. Kaster, *Emotion, Restraint, and Community in Ancient Rome* (Oxford: Oxford University Press, 2005); Konstan, *The Emotions of the Ancient Greeks: Studies in Aristotle and Classical* (Toronto: University of Toronto Press, 2006); Ruth R. Caston and Robert A. Kaster, eds., *Hope, Joy, and Affection in the Classical World* (Oxford: Oxford University Press, 2016).

9. Referring to *pathē*, Konstan simply asserts, "It is better to employ the Greek word here." Konstan, *Emotions of the Ancient Greeks*, xii.

Variations in vocabulary are not merely matters of linguistic symbolization. It is well known by now that culturally-constructed linguistic systems actually lead people to experience the world differently.[10] Along with using lexical terminology in specific ways, cultures also develop various valuations of and moral exhortations about emotions. In antiquity, for example, Peripatetics argued that good action could result from anger, while Stoics insisted that anger should be kept inside and controlled. As David Konstan puts it, events and actions are judged "as positive or negative in valence, *depending on the value system of the population in question.*"[11] Indeed, many ancient discussions and representations of emotion belie modern emotion-related binaries, blurring boundaries between σῶμα and ψυχή, volition and intuition, and so-called "positive" emotions like happiness and "negative" emotions like humiliation or shame. My first assumption, in short, is that *conceptions and experiences of emotions are not transhistorical or invariant.*[12]

My second premise is more specific and follows from the first: *concepts of joy in ancient Christian texts and their communities are not uniform.*[13] Although most New Testament scholars recognize in theory that we should not assume a monolithic continuity between modern and ancient conceptions of emotions, many still treat all references to joy in the New Testament as reflective of a unified early Christian worldview. Yet, even

---

10. For example, affective neuroscientists Jaak Panksepp and Lucy Biven argue that humans have innate "primary affect systems" of fear, lust, rage, seeking/curiosity, care, play, and grief. Hunger and thirst they call "homeostatic affects"; sweetness, bitterness, disgust, and certain kinds of physical pain are "sensory affects" See Panksepp and Biven, *The Archaeology of Mind: Neuroevolutionary Origins of Human Emotions* (New York: Norton, 2012), 18.

11. Konstan, *Emotions of the Ancient Greeks*, 24, emphasis added.

12. Douglas Cairns offers an important caveat: "If it is proper for us to pay particular attention to the ways in which the construction of emotion varies from culture to culture, it is also necessary for us to accept that we cannot expect that variation to be free and unconstrained, [given] our nature as a physically embodied, social species" ("Ethics, Ethology, Terminology: Iliadic Anger and the Cross-Cultural Study of Emotion," in *Ancient Anger: Perspectives from Homer to Galen*, ed. Susanna Morton Braund and Glenn Most [Cambridge: Cambridge University Press, 2003], 14).

13. Virginia Burrus highlights the simultaneity of shame and joy in early Christian texts: "It is also in shame that flesh is conceived as the passionate site of pleasure inseparably wedded to pain, joy bound up with its own thwarting" (*Saving Shame: Martyrs, Saints, and Other Abject Subjects* [Philadelphia: University of Pennsylvania Press, 2008], 46).

within the limited corpus of the New Testament, writers espouse distinct (not necessarily incompatible, but distinct) reasons for joy, and these have different rhetorical effects and various theological implications.

Often, New Testament writers use joy-related terms in association (or as synonymous) with the kingdom of God and/or heaven (e.g., Matt 13:44; 25:21, 23; Luke 15:7, 10; Rom 14:17; Heb 12:2). Relatedly, joy appears, on the one hand, to be a gift bestowed by divine figures; in both gospels and epistles, the passive form of πληρόω (people *are filled* with joy) is used, often with God named as the active "filling" agent (e.g., John 3:29; 15:11; 16:24; 17:3; Acts 13:52; 14:17; Rom 15:13; 2 Tim 1:4). Divine messengers also deliver news and/or prophecies that engender joy (e.g., Luke 1:14; 2:10). On the other hand, Jesus and Paul use the imperative form of χαίρω ("rejoice"/"be joyful" [e.g., Matt 5:12; Luke 6:23; 10:20; Phil 2:18; 3:1; 4:4 (2x); 1 Thess 5:16; similarly, Phil 2:2]), and Paul lists χαρά with other apparently intentional behaviors like being generous (e.g., Gal 5:22; Phil 2:29). These latter references imply that joy is an active choice, not an involuntary impulse or feeling caused by an external source or circumstance.

The reasons for joy differ across New Testament texts as well. In John's Gospel, Jesus's teachings and the act of prayer are meant to produce joy (χαρά [e.g., John 15:11; 16:24; 17:13]). In 2 Corinthians, however, Paul rejoices because of his recipients' grief (because it led to repentance [7:7–9]). At times, New Testament authors depict joy as the absence of suffering, but at other times, joy and suffering are not readily distinguishable. Joy can be a futuristic promise of salvation *from* suffering[14] and, simultaneously, the right response *in the midst of* suffering (e.g., Acts 5:41; Rom 5:3–5; Col 1:24; Jas 1:2–4; 1 Pet 4:13). So Paul can say in Col 1:24 that he is "now" (νῦν) rejoicing "in [his] sufferings" (ἐν τοῖς παθήμασιν), and the author of 1 Peter can call Christians to rejoice while "sharing in the sufferings of Christ" (κοινωνεῖτε τοῖς τοῦ Χριστοῦ παθήμασιν χαίρετε [4:13]).[15] Luke

---

14. E.g., Believers are assured in apocalyptic terms that their earthly suffering is, as 1 Peter says, only for a short time (1:6; 5:10; see similarly 2:12), and will turn into eternal joy at the eschaton (e.g., Jesus promises his disciples their grief [λύπη] will turn into joy [χαρά] in John 16:20–23). If one assumes that suffering accompanies illness and demon possession, then joy is contrasted with suffering implicitly when Jesus performs healings and exorcisms that lead to joy (even "great joy" [πολλὴ χαρά] in Acts 8:8).

15. See also ἀγαλλιάω in 1 Pet 1:6. Relatedly, psychologists, sociologists, and affect theorists challenge dichotomies between apparently discordant emotions. See, e.g., Silvan Tomkins, *The Positive Affects*, vol. 1 of *Affect, Imagery, Consciousness* (New

writes that Peter and John rejoiced (χαίροντες) because they were worthy of being dishonored for the sake of the name (Acts 5:41).

Looking only at vocabulary that is associated with joy or happiness in the modern Western world can obscure these complicated dynamics. For instance, the index of Greek lexemes related to happiness in the *Bible and the Pursuit of Happiness* lists κορέννυμι ("to satisfy/to have enough") as a word associated with happiness.[16] Yet attention to context shows that when Paul uses κορέννυμι in 1 Cor 4:8, it is in a sarcastic contrast between the Corinthians' state and his own debased (but preferable) circumstances; he is not implying that they are happy or satisfied. All of this is to say that the New Testament invokes, evokes, represents, and recommends joy for multiple reasons and in complicated ways. Joy should not be understood as merely the absence or opposite of apparently negative emotions or circumstances; in many cases, they are mutually constitutive—so closely bound as to be inseparable.

Thus, my second point of departure is this: *New Testament texts employ joy in different ways*. As with recent scholarly efforts to differentiate between various ancient views on suffering, we also should be wary of assuming that all New Testament writers—let alone all ancient Christians or all ancient thinkers—agreed about the nature of, reasons for, and/or sources of joy.[17] In keeping with this assumption, I will focus on the corpus of the author we call Luke in the remainder of this essay.

My third basic point is that *verbal persuasion shapes emotional experience*.[18] Even as emotions are not transhistorical, it is fairly noncontroversial to assert that most human societies have espoused the view that words

---

York: Springer, 1962); Tomkins, *The Negative Affects*, vol. 2 of *Affect, Imagery, Consciousness* (New York: Springer, 1963).

16. Brent A. Strawn, ed. *The Bible and the Pursuit of Happiness: What the Old and New Testaments Teach Us about the Good Life* (New York: Oxford University Press, 2012), 345.

17. In recent years, New Testament and ancient Christianity scholars have given a great deal of attention not only to the rhetorical potency of early Christians' references to their own suffering but also to differentiating concepts of suffering in the ancient world. On this, see Michal Beth Dinkler, "Suffering, Misunderstanding, and Suffering Misunderstanding: The Markan Misunderstanding Motif as a Form of Jesus' Suffering," *JSNT* (2016): 1–23 and citations therein. Fewer scholars have worked to differentiate between conceptions of joy.

18. On the noncontradiction of particularist and universalist study of emotions and texts, Hogan concludes that "the study of universals and the study of cultural and

affect people's emotions;[19] certainly, diverse thinkers from across centuries and cultures have made such claims. The fifth-century BCE Sophist Gorgias, for example, writes:

> [λόγος] is able to dispel fear, to assuage grief, to inculcate joy [χαρὰν ἐνεργάσασθαι], and to evoke pity.... [W]hen the audience hears it ... the soul experiences its own emotion [πάθημα] at the actions and feelings of others in their fortunes and misfortunes, produced through words. (*Hel.* 8)[20]

Moreover, Konstan has traced how, for ancient Greeks generally, "persuasion was central to the idea of an emotion, whether in the law courts, in political assemblies, or in the various therapies that relied on verbal interactions to change the judgments that are constitutive of the passions."[21] Theorists in the Hellenistic period also believed words had the power to shape the soul. Roman Stoic and Epicurean philosophers in particular were concerned with ψυχαγωγεῖν, or the leading of the soul through words (e.g., Plato, *Phaed.* 260e–272b).[22]

Concern for the soul-forming, persuasive power of words was an important trope in Hellenistic Judaism, made its way into New Testament texts, and remained significant into later centuries as well. We find a telling account in Achilles Tatius's second-century CE novel *Leucippe and Clitophon*. Leucippe, we read, was "caught in emotional chaos ... shame, grief, and anger are three waves rising in the soul.... Speech is the father of all three: like arrows aimed at a target and hitting it dead center, words pierce the soul and wound it in many places.... The only remedy for them

---

historical particularity are mutually necessary ... not contradictory, but complementary" (*Mind and Its Stories*, 10).

19. Though cognitive theorists regularly make universal claims about humans' emotional responses, I have not done the comparative work to make a universal claim. For our purposes, it is enough to recognize that this is the majority view of most contemporary thinkers as well as those from the time periods of the texts we are considering here.

20. Gorgias, *Encomium of Helen*, trans. Douglas M. MacDowell (Bristol: Bristol Classical Press, 1982).

21. Konstan, *Emotions of the Ancient Greeks*, xii, 40.

22. See Elizabeth Asmis, "*Psychagogia* in Plato's *Phaedrus*," *ICS* 11 (1986): 153–72; Pedro Laín Entralgo, *The Therapy of the Word in Classical Antiquity*, ed. and trans. L. J. Rather and John M. Sharp (New Haven: Yale University Press, 1970).

is counterattack with the same weapons. The wound caused by one sharp tongue is healed by the razor edge of another" (Achilles Tatius, *Leuc. Clit.* 2.29).[23] The view that words can either cause or ameliorate emotions like anger or shame was common in the ancient world, as it is today.

My fourth assumption again is more specific and follows from the previous one: *narrative is a particular form of verbal persuasion*. This is true of both written and oral narratives. As James Phelan writes, "Narrative *is* a rhetorical action in which somebody tries to accomplish some purpose(s) by telling somebody else that something happened."[24] A key corollary is that narratives can be persuasively productive by invoking emotional reactions in their audiences. Karl Kuhn is correct: "Not only is affect crucial to the construction and experience of narrative, it is also essential to the rhetorical function and force of narrative."[25] Therefore, as affect theorist Sara Ahmed advocates, "Rather than asking 'What are emotions?,'" we should be asking "What do emotions *do*?"[26] One answer may be that in and through narrative texts, emotions lead listeners/readers to engage with the narrated world—and, by extension, the "real" (extratextual) world—in new ways. Narratives are not merely demonstrative and/or evocative of emotion; they are also formative.

To summarize my points of departure: Conceptions and experiences of emotions are culturally particular; indeed, early Christian writers were not always consistent amongst themselves with respect to emotion. Yet, humans from many times and places also appear to share the view that verbal persuasion can evoke recipients' emotions; more specifically, if narrative is a form of verbal persuasion, it is important to attend to the various ways in which New Testament narratives depict characters' emotions and facilitate affective responses in their implied audiences.

---

23. Translation from John Winkler, "Achilles Tatius: Leucippe Clitophon," in *Collected Ancient Greek Novels*, ed. Brian Reardon (Berkeley: University of California Press, 1989), 202–3.

24. James Phelan, "Rhetoric/Ethics," in *The Cambridge Companion to Narrative*, ed. David Herman (Cambridge: Cambridge University Press, 2007), 209, emphasis added.

25. Karl Kuhn, *The Heart of Biblical Narrative: Rediscovering Biblical Appeal to the Emotions* (Minneapolis: Fortress, 2009), 3. Kuhn describes his analysis as "affective-rhetorical."

26. Sara Ahmed, *The Cultural Politics of Emotion*, 2nd ed. (New York: Routledge, 2014), 4, emphasis added.

The consequent challenge arising from these observations is how we might answer the question (with some adaptation) posed by the classics scholar Robert Kaster:

> How can we understand, as fully and authentically as possible, the emotion talk of another culture['s narratives] removed in time in a way that does not entail either simplification—by reducing the emotion to a convenient lexical package in our own language—or projection—by answering the question according to the emotion *we* might feel (whoever "we" might be) in [response to] the same [narrative]?[27]

Toward that end, I offer below a conviction, an additional question, and a suggestion.

2. Joy in/and the Lukan Narratives

The *conviction* is this: The Lukan narratives—like all narratives—reflect and reshape the emotional repertoires of their implied audiences by depicting characters' emotions and by inviting recipients' emotional responses. Thus, the *question*: do Luke and Acts offer clues about how they might engender emotional responses, and can we discern them without simplification and projection?

A growing number of scholars considering the intersections of emotion and New Testament narratives spark a *suggestive* answer to that question.[28] One recent work is especially relevant: David Wenkel's published Aberdeen dissertation, *Joy in Luke-Acts: The Intersection of Rhetoric, Narrative, and Emotion*.[29] As customary in a dissertation, Wenkel must make the case that his work contributes something new to Lukan scholarship;

---

27. Robert A. Kaster, *Emotion, Restraint, and Community in Ancient Rome* (Oxford: Oxford University Press, 2005), 7.

28. On joy in Luke-Acts more broadly, see, e.g., Paul J. Bernadicou, "The Lucan Theology of Joy," *ScEs* 25 (1973): 75–88; Morrice, *Joy in the New Testament*; Stephen Barton, *The Spirituality of the Gospels* (Eugene, OR: Wipf & Stock, 1992), 71–112; Kindalee Pfremmer De Long (who distinguishes between praise and joy), *Surprised by God: Praise Responses in the Narrative of Luke-Acts* (Berlin: de Gruyter, 2009); Anke Inselmann, *Die Freude im Lukasevangelium: Ein Beitrag zur psychologischen Exegese* WUNT 2/322 (Tübingen: Mohr Siebeck, 2012).

29. David Wenkel, *Joy in Luke-Acts: The Intersection of Rhetoric, Narrative, and Emotion*, Kindle edition (Crownhill, UK: Paternoster, 2015).

consequently, he critiques John Painter's entry on "Joy" in the *Dictionary of Jesus and the Gospels* for "not explain[ing] how emotions such as joy may be used rhetorically to influence and persuade the reader."[30] Yet Wenkel limits his self-described "socio-rhetorical examination of joy" (an adaptation of Vernon Robbins' methodological school) to the question of "how the rhetoric of reversal works in the context of the logos, ethos, and pathos"—in spite of the fact that he claims that his own "study does not use technical Greco-Roman rhetorical categories," since he prefers to "focus on the persuasive nature of the whole narrative."[31]

Distinguishing between classical Greek rhetorical tropes as evidenced in the Lukan speeches and the rhetoricity of the whole narrative is important.[32] Wenkel repeats the point, but fails to take full advantage of the considerable theoretical resources (ancient or modern) on narrative: what it is, how it works, and the complex ways in which emotions and narrative relate to one another.[33] Instead, Wenkel studiously avoids what he dubs "radical postmodern readings and other reader response methods."[34] This strategy is unfortunate, since Wenkel's treatment of joy in Luke-Acts would have benefitted from engaging with methodological advancements that have sharpened literary approaches to the New Testament over the past several decades.

I agree with Wenkel on several counts, not least that the Lukan narrative is meant to be persuasive.[35] Even Luke's Jesus assumes that narrative can persuade, as when he refers to the story of David to explain his behavior (Luke 6:3), and when he tells parables to his interlocutors throughout the gospel.[36] I also agree with Wenkel that the theme of joy functions

---

30. Ibid., loc. 731. John Painter, "Joy," in *Dictionary of Jesus and the Gospels*, ed. Joel Green and Scot McKnight (Downers Grove, IL: InterVarsity Press, 1992), 394–95. Wenkel's critique is likely justified, since Painter's dictionary entry is (necessarily) short.

31. Wenkel, *Joy in Luke-Acts*, loc. 345, 688.

32. See Michal Beth Dinkler, "New Testament Rhetorical Narratology: An Invitation toward Integration," *BibInt* 24 (2016): 203–28; Dinkler, "Rhetorical Studies," *BRP* (forthcoming 2017).

33. Wenkel, *Joy in Luke-Acts*, loc. 345, 5015, 5029. Wenkel's main conceptual lens is intertextuality, by which he means Lukan citations of Hebrew Bible texts (loc. 441).

34. Ibid., loc. 797.

35. On narrative as a mode of persuasion, see Dinkler, "New Testament Rhetorical Narratology," and the citations therein.

36. On the persuasiveness of the parables in Luke, see Lauri Thurén, *Parables*

rhetorically in Luke and Acts and in close connection with the theme of reversals. I would insist, however, that these dynamics are much more complicated than Wenkel's conclusions allow (see further below).

Another recent publication, Michael Whitenton's "Feeling the Silence: A Moment-by-Moment Account of Emotions at the End of Mark (16:1–8)," provides an example of a theoretically informed and appropriately nuanced treatment of emotion and New Testament narrative.[37] Working with ancient theories about emotion, as well as contemporary performance criticism and cognitive theory, Whitenton aims to present "the most plausible emotional responses to the abrupt ending of the Gospel of Mark."[38] After affirming the heterogeneity of the gospel's intended audience, Whitenton recognizes that recipients of a narrative identify with and/or empathize with characters differently depending on a multitude of factors, including "audience members' education and socioeconomic levels, ethnicity, gender, and religion, the infinitely diverse set of personal experiences that make up one's identity," as well as "audience elevation and the inferences made from that elevated perspective."[39] Whitenton rightly suggests many potential emotional responses to the end of Mark, including confidence, superiority, pity, sympathy, fear, ironic hope, and/or urgency to preach the gospel.[40] Certainly, these responses are plausible. Still, Whitenton's treatment could be developed in the following way.

Whitenton's reading assumes a *cognitive* form of engagement with the narrative. His proposals of possible emotional responses to the women's silence are all contingent on audience members' identification with the characters—identification that is refracted through their perceptions of

---

Unplugged: Reading the Lukan Parables in Their Rhetorical Context (Minneapolis: Fortress, 2014).

37. Michael Whitenton, "Feeling the Silence: A Moment-by-Moment Account of Emotions at the End of Mark (16:1–8)," *CBQ* (2016): 272–89. Whitenton writes about joy, though not narrative, in "Figuring Joy: Gratitude as Medicine in 1 Thessalonians 2:1–20," *PRSt* 39 (2012): 15–23.

38. Whitenton, "Feeling the Silence," 272.

39. See especially the sections "Inherent Audience Heterogeneity" (275–77, quote from 276) and "Audience Identification and Accompanying Emotional Responses" (277–85, quote from 285) in Whitenton, "Feeling the Silence." Regarding identification and empathy, see Kirsten Marie Hartvigsen, *Prepare the Way of the Lord: Towards a Cognitive Poetic Analysis of Audience Involvement with Characters and Events in the Markan World* (Berlin: de Gruyter, 2012), esp. 78–80.

40. Whitenton, "Feeling the Silence," 289.

their own role(s) vis-à-vis the gospel narrative. For example, Whitenton proposes that some "who viewed the women as equals due to shared experiences as 'co-witnesses' to the crucifixion … would probably have sympathy for them," while others might consider themselves to be "the only ones who [could] keep the young man's commission" and thus feel "superiority" over the women.[41]

To be fair, Whitenton explicitly states that he reads the text through recent advancements in cognitive science, including theories of embodied cognition and cognitive appraisal.[42] To highlight how heavily he leans toward cognitive assessment is not a criticism per se; indeed, Whitenton is in line with several New Testament scholars who have shown how fruitful cognitive theories can be for considering ancient views of emotion.[43] As noted above, ancient theorists did not always agree about emotions, but many did hold the view that reason plays a constitutive role in human emotion.[44] For Aristotle, it is through πάθη that "people come to differ in their judgments" (*Rhet.* 2.1.8 [1378a]), while for Diogenes Laertius, "reason supervenes as the craftsman of impulse" (*Vit. Phil.* 7.86). Closely related are discussions of virtue or morality as giving rise to certain affects, like Philo's claim that virtue leads to joy (*Mut.* 167) or Seneca's point that doing good for others is pleasurable (*Ep.* 81.20). Multiple ancient writers assert that cognitive judgment and rational evaluation can control (and elicit new) embodied emotional experiences.[45]

---

41. Ibid. 288–89.

42. Foundational for modern appraisal theory is Richard Lazarus and Susan Folkman, *Stress, Appraisal, and Coping* (New York: Springer, 1984).

43. Recently, e.g., Frederick Tappenden, *Resurrection in Paul: Cognition, Metaphor, and Transformation*, ECL 19 (Atlanta: SBL Press, 2016); Risto Uro, "Cognitive Science in the Study of Early Christianity: How it is Helpful—and Why?" (paper delivered at the SNTS General Meeting, Montreal, Canada, 4 August 2016); Joel Green, *Conversion in Luke-Acts: Divine Action, Human Cognition, and the People of God* (Grand Rapids: Baker Academic, 2015); Colleen Shantz, *Paul in Ecstasy: The Neurobiology of the Apostle's Life and Thought* (Cambridge: Cambridge University Press, 2009); Petri Luomanen, Ilkka Pyysiäinen and Risto Uro, eds., *Explaining Early Judaism and Christianity: Contributions from Cognitive and Social Science*, BibInt 89 (Leiden: Brill, 2007).

44. See the helpful framework of emotion as cognitive, motivational, relational, and value laden in F. Scott Spencer, "Why Did the 'Leper' Get Under Jesus' Skin? Emotion Theory and Angry Reaction in Mark 1:40–45," *HBT* 36 (2014): 112.

45. Matthew A. Elliott's claim that Plato's views were noncognitive while Aristotle's were cognitive leads him to oversimplify: "There was a choice in the world of

At the same time, however, impulses toward or away from character identification—and correlatively, audience members' responses to a narrative more generally[46]—are not always (entirely) rational.[47] Surely, some of Mark's hearers would have been more or less likely to identify with the women based on factors outside of conscious processes, such as their own gendered and/or socioeconomic status. Might some male audience members have had a harder time considering the women "as equals," even if they were "'cowitnesses' of the crucifixion"? Or, if these women were known to have financial means (see Luke 8:1–3), might some hearers of lower economic status be more reticent to relate to them?[48] What of those who are skeptical about the story? Might they be more likely to agree with the Jewish or Roman authorities in the gospel who considered Jesus a threat and the women foolish? These varying responses also occur in degrees; some will be more or less likely to sympathize, while others will be more or less likely to identify with the characters.[49] The intersectionality of audience members' various identity markers (e.g., race, ethnicity, gender, age, education, enslaved/free, and/or marital or familial status)

---

the New Testament between a cognitive and non-cognitive understanding of emotion" (*Faithful Feelings: Emotion in the New Testament* [Leicester: Inter-Varsity Press, 2005], 240).

46. Neither do emotion and narrative always or solely intersect at the point of identification with characters. Focusing on human relationality alone can be problematically anthropocentric, a point beyond the scope of this chapter. See, e.g., Jennifer Koosed, ed., *The Bible and Posthumanism* (Atlanta: Society of Biblical Literature, 2014).

47. Scholarly claims to have proven a gospel writer's authorial intention often miss this crucial point. Stephen Moore thus highlights an ironic weakness in such arguments when he asks, "If it is a wholly cognitive role of reading that has been charted, can it be said … to have adequately connected with this ancient narrator's intent?" (*Literary Criticism and the Gospels* [New Haven: Yale University Press, 1989], 97).

48. Jennifer Glancy advances similar questions with respect to female enslaved persons in "Obstacles to Slaves' Participation in the Corinthian Church," *JBL* 117 (1998): 481–501.

49. Whitenton uses these terms interchangeably (see "Feeling the Silence"), but I prefer Mark Currie's distinction: "Sympathy [is] a feeling of goodwill towards a character. Identification suggests self-recognition [and] touches my own subjectivity in a more profound way, because I have seen myself in the [narrative], projected my identity into it, rather than just made a new friend" (*Postmodern Narrative Theory*, 2nd ed. [New York: Palgrave Macmillan, 2011], 36).

plays an important—but often irrational—role in determining the degree to which they identify with narrative characters.⁵⁰

Here, we might draw on developments in that congeries of post-poststructuralists across a variety of disciplines who have been foregrounding the complicated interstices between affect, emotion, embodiment, and cognition—known to many as affect theorists.⁵¹ Many affect theorists differentiate between *emotion*, which is perceived and understood cognitively, and *affect*, which precedes cognition and is, in Brian Massumi's well-known formulation, "irreducibly bodily and autonomic."⁵² Certainly, some notion of affect that precedes or exceeds expressibility appears in ancient texts. We need think only of Aristotle's sensations or perceptions (αἰσθήσεις or φαντασία [*De an.* 1.1 (403a)]) or Epictetus's impressions (πρόληψεις [*Diatr.* 1.27.6]). Reading Roman comedies, Ruth Caston remarks that joy in particular appears to be "an exuberance not easily contained."⁵³

The precise relationship between conscious and un-/preconscious affect/emotion is an ongoing debate in affect theory.⁵⁴ But generally, as Margaret Wetherell puts it: "To attend to affect is to stress the limits of

---

50. Whitenton recognizes that character identification, mental simulations of a story, and empathetic engagement are "often automatic and unconscious" ("Feeling the Silence," 277). Nevertheless, his "account of the plausible spectrum of emotions" remains squarely within the cognitive (i.e., conscious, rational) domain.

51. It is common to note that the singular "affect theory" is problematic; there are many iterations of this conglomeration of concerns. See Patricia Ticineto Clough, ed., with Jean Halley, *The Affective Turn: Theorizing the Social* (Durham, NC: Duke University Press, 2007).

52. Brian Massumi, *Parables for the Virtual: Movement, Affect, Sensation* (Durham, NC: Duke University Press, 2002), 28. Massumi is indebted to Gilles Deleuze. See, e.g., Deleuze, *Negotiations, 1972–1990*, trans. Martin Joughin (New York: Columbia University Press, 1995).

53. Caston means joy is "irrepressible," though I would add that joy also is "not easily contained" in language—that is, it is inexpressible ("The Irrepressibility of Joy in Roman Comedy," in Caston and Kaster, *Hope, Joy, and Affection*, 95). Closely related, but outside the scope of this chapter, are discussions of humor in Lukan narrative. See, e.g., Kathy Chambers, "'Knock, Knock—Who's There?' Acts 12:6–17 as a Comedy of Errors," in *A Feminist Companion to the Acts of the Apostles*, ed. Amy-Jill Levine (London: T&T Clark, 2004), 89–97.

54. Ruth Leys insists that the distinction "cannot be sustained" ("The Turn to Affect: A Critique," *CI* 37 [2011]: 434 n. 2).

reason and the limits of the immediately knowable and communicable."⁵⁵ Paradoxically, then, the affectivity with which we are concerned is both inexpressible and expressed in words. But this can also be affect theory's unique contribution to textual interpretation insofar as it facilitates "a dynamic understanding of the text as generating *new* affect patterns and thought structures."⁵⁶ (Re)cognized emotion and irrational affectivity both play roles in narratives' rhetorical functions. Therefore, we ought to allow space in our narrative interpretations for those affective reactions that exceed or precede cognitive capacities but nevertheless catalyze readers'/hearers' responses to stories and shape their emotional repertoires.⁵⁷

I suggest that a concept from contemporary literary theory—narrative reflexivity—can be a fruitful way to draw together Wenkel's goal of exploring the narrative rhetoricity of joy in Luke-Acts, Whitenton's allowance for varied emotional responses to a Gospel narrative, and the noncognitive dimensions of affect highlighted above.⁵⁸ As I have written about reflexivity elsewhere, let me offer but a brief description here.⁵⁹ *Reflexivity*, as its etymology suggests (from the Latin *reflexivus*, *re* [again] + *flectere* [to bend]) is a turning or bending back on oneself.⁶⁰ Jeffrey Williams defines *narrative* reflexivity as those moments "when narrative refers to itself, to its own medium, mode, and process, rather than simply to other (nonlinguistic) 'events,' that we normally assume constitute a narrative."⁶¹

---

55. Margaret Wetherell, "Affect and Discourse—What's the Problem? From Affect as Excess to Affective/Discursive Practice," *Subjectivity* 6 (2013): 351. Samuel Powell appears unaware of this point and affect theory in general in *Impassioned Life: Reason and Emotion in the Christian Tradition* (Minneapolis: Fortress, 2016).

56. Isobel Armstrong, *The Radical Aesthetic* (Oxford: Blackwell, 2000), 124, emphasis added.

57. Hogan discusses this as perceptual emotion triggering (*Affective Narratology*, esp. 46–47).

58. Other terms include self-reference, self-figuration, textual narcissism, self-consciousness, "breaking the frame," obtrusiveness of the narrator, metafiction, and metanarrative.

59. I explain why I find it appropriate to use a contemporary concept like narrative reflexivity to discuss ancient narratives in Michal Beth Dinkler, "Acts of Interpretation: Acts 8.26–40 and Ancient Narrative Pedagogical Scenes," *NTS* 63 (2017): 411–27.

60. For foundational work on reflexivity in the field of linguistics, see Oswald Ducrot, *Dire et ne pas dire* (Paris: Hermann, 1972).

61. Jeffrey Williams, *Theory and the Novel: Narrative Reflexivity in the British Tradition* (Cambridge: Cambridge University Press, 1998), 7.

Narrative reflexivity foregrounds the fact that stories frequently depict the acts of reading and/or interpreting stories. I contend that such scenes function pedagogically to commend particular hermeneutical principles for their audience.[62] One way in which these narrative scenes do so is to proffer models of proper (or improper) emotional responses to narratives. Instances of narrative interpretation *within* narratives function rhetorically to promote a particular experience *of* narratives, and those experiences often have an emotional dimension to them.[63] Put another way: narrated scenes of characters interpreting narratives often function as active agents, generating affective responses and forming the emotional repertoires of those who interpret them.

3. Reflexivity and Luke's Effective, Affective Scenes of Narrative Interpretation

Several times Luke depicts characters reading, either by mentioning the text itself or by employing the usual Greek verb for "reading," ἀναγινώσκω;[64] often, these scenes of reading are accompanied by references to characters' emotional responses. For Luke, receiving texts (written or delivered orally) is a matter of hospitality,[65] and the characters' relative degrees of hospitality are often described in terms of their πάθη. In Luke 4:16–30, for instance, after Jesus reads and interprets the

---

62. I make this case in Dinkler, "Acts of Interpretation." Acts 8:26–40, for instance, implicitly teaches that because reading is not synonymous with understanding, one ought to have an authoritative interpretive guide and embrace a hermeneutic of hospitality toward the received narrative.

63. Patrick Colm Hogan, *What Literature Teaches Us about Emotion*, SESI (Cambridge: Cambridge University Press, 2011); Hogan, *Affective Narratology: The Emotional Structure of Stories* (Lincoln: University of Nebraska Press, 2011).

64. Uses of ἀναγινώσκω include Luke 4:16; 6:3; 10:26; Acts 8:28, 30, 32; 13:27; 15:21, 31; 23:34. Acts 13:15 uses the noun form: "After reading the law and the prophets" (μετὰ δὲ τὴν ἀνάγνωσιν τοῦ νόμου καὶ τῶν προφητῶν). Acts 17:11 refers to "examining" the Scriptures using the verb ἀνακρίνω. On the Greek verbs associated with reading, see the now-classic Pierre Chantraine, "Les verbes grecs significant 'lire' (*anagignōskō, epilegomai, entunkhanō, analegomai*)," in *Pagkarpeia: Mélanges Henri Grégoire*, vol. 2, AIPh 10 (Brussels: Secretariat des Éditions de l'Institut, 1950), 115–26.

65. The verb δέχομαι typically refers in Luke to welcoming a person (2:28; 9:5, 48, 53; 10:8–10; 16:4, 9), whereas in Acts the usage shifts to references to welcoming "living messages" (7:38), the "word of God" (8:14; 11:1), the "message" (17:11), and "letters" (22:5; 28:21).

Isaiah scroll in Nazareth, his hearers initially receive the message as "words of grace" (τοῖς λόγοις τῆς χάριτος [4:22]) but ultimately "are filled with rage/anger" (ἐπλήσθησαν ... θυμοῦ [4:28]) and attempt to drive him off a cliff. Just a short time later, Jesus warns against being one of those who "receive the word with joy" (μετὰ χαρᾶς δέχονται τὸν λόγον) but "fall away" (ἀφίστημι) when tested (8:13).

In Acts, we find several narrative instantiations of Jesus's admonition to receive the word with joy. The Ethiopian eunuch receives Philip's interpretation of Isaiah and leaves "rejoicing" (χαίρων [8:39]), while the Antiochene believers rejoice (ἐχάρησαν) after "having read" (ἀναγνόντες [15:31]) the letter from the Jerusalem Council, and the jailor and his household rejoice (ἠγαλλιάσατο [16:34]) after receiving "the word of the Lord" (τὸν λόγον τοῦ κυρίου [16:32]). Though the generic form and delivery of these texts differ (Scripture, letter, oral proclamation), the process and end result are the same: the recipients welcome the message and respond by rejoicing.

The notion of reflexivity prompts us to attend to the fact that these pericopes are depictions of textual interpretation that are themselves being interpreted. The Lukan narrative draws attention to this point, bookended as it is by references to the importance of right readerly reception.[66] Read as instances of narrative reflexivity, scenes of characters reading or interpreting narratives advance a kind of hermeneutical theory that applies not only to the texts in those scenes, but also to the Lukan narrative itself.[67] As Philip guides the Ethiopian eunuch to interpret the story of Israel in a particular way,[68] Luke also aims to guide Theophilus (and, by extension, other recipients) in interpreting the Jesus traditions to which he refers in Luke 1:4 and Acts 1:1. That he considers himself an able authoritative guide is

---

66. If one takes Luke and Acts as a unified whole, that is. Cf. Luke 1:1–4 and Acts 28:26–27 (citing Isa 6:9–10).

67. Joel Green agrees: "Luke's purpose is hermeneutical" ("Internal Repetition in Luke-Acts: Contemporary Narratology and Lukan Historiography," in *History, Literature, and Society in the Book of Acts*, ed. Ben Witherington III [Cambridge: Cambridge University Press, 1996], 288).

68. Philip interprets the Isaiah text Christologically, as Jesus does in Luke 4; both exemplify H. Gregory Snyder's point: "The interpreter who finds meaning in a text not known to its prophetic authors is making a striking claim to interpretive authority" (*Teachers and Texts in the Ancient World: Philosophers, Jews, and Christians* [London: Routledge, 2000], 227).

evident in his self-reference as one who has "researched" or "been trained" (παρακολουθέω [Luke 1:3]) regarding the narrative he proceeds to tell.[69]

Importantly, the Lukan attempts to guide—indeed, to *persuade*—the implied audience are not only cerebral. In the ancient world no less than our own, "it was recognized that emotional appeals are extremely important in the shaping of opinion."[70] That Luke's narratives would have been read aloud in community means that the lector/performer's emotional emphases during delivery also would have influenced an audience. As Whitney Shiner points out: "Emotional impact was considered an essential aspect ... of verbal performance in Greek culture ever since classical times. The success of verbal art was often judged by the way it affected the emotions of the listeners."[71] The Lukan Jesus's admonition "Watch how you listen" (βλέπετε πῶς ἀκούετε [8:18]) should not be read apart from these ancient conceptions and experiences of emotion's rhetorical impact.[72]

If moments of narrative reflexivity underscore the Lukan narrator's role as interpretive guide, they also constitute appeals to recipients to respond to the narrative in particular ways. Narratologist Gerald Prince discusses this dynamic in terms of metanarrativity: "Metanarrative signs," Prince writes, "constitute the answer of a text to the question 'How should we interpret you?' "[73] A story like that of the eunuch rejoicing at Philip's interpretation of Isaiah subtly places Luke's audience into the same learning framework as the eunuch; read reflexively, the scene nudges the Lukan audience to emulate the eunuch as they interpret the Lukan narrative.[74]

---

69. Though most English translations of παρακολουθέω gesture toward the author's apparent historical "research" or investigation, David Moessner ("Luke as Tradent and Hermeneut," *NovT* 58 [2016]: 297) argues that it refers to Luke's "long-standing involvement in 'the way.'"

70. Whitney Shiner, *Proclaiming the Gospel: First-Century Performance of Mark* (Philadelphia: Trinity Press International, 2003), 58.

71. Ibid., 58.

72. On which, see John Darr, "'Watch How You Listen' (Lk. 8.18): Jesus and the Rhetoric of Perception in Luke-Acts," in *The New Literary Criticism and the New Testament*, ed. Elizabeth Struthers Malbon and Edgar V. McKnight, JSNTSup 109 (Valley Forge, PA: Trinity Press International, 1994), 87–107.

73. Gerald Prince, *Narratology: The Form and Functioning of Narrative* (Berlin: Mouton, 1982), 126.

74. Emulation is distinct from, but often also entails, identification. Perhaps the narrative invites readerly identification with the eunuch, even as the eunuch potentially identifies with the humiliated servant of whom he reads in Isa 53. On the latter,

Acts 8:26–40 invites recipients to accept the Lukan narrative hospitably, to embrace "the Way," and to respond with joy. Narrating joy can in this way be a means of inculcating joy.

Conversely, Acts 13:27 provides a negative example. There the residents of Jerusalem and their leaders "did not recognize" (ἀγνοήσαντες) Jesus in the Scriptures that "had been read every Sabbath" (κατὰ πᾶν σάββατον ἀναγινωσκομένας). This description of the Jerusalem Jews as failed interpreters is couched within a speech in which Paul incorporates Jesus into a retelling of Israel's story; he ends with an explicit warning:

> Beware, therefore, that what the prophets said does not happen to you:
> Look, you scoffers!
> … in your days I am doing a work,
> a work that you will never believe,
> even if someone tells you. (Acts 13:40–41; citing Hab 1:5)

The irony on one level is obvious: Paul warns them not to be like those who have contempt for (καταφρονέω) what they are told about a work of God, even as he himself claims in that very moment to be telling his audience about a work of God. On another level, read as a moment of narrative reflexivity, the scene functions as an implicit warning to Luke's audience not to scoff at *his* telling about a work of God either.

Further, as noted above, not all responses or hermeneutical choices will be cognitive or conscious. Maia Kotrosits recently has emphasized the "non-conscious, affective aspects" of early Christian experience in order to read the book of Acts as a "chronicle of the desperate brokering of fragile agency and inclusion in increasingly broken diasporic conditions."[75] Depicting figures like Paul negotiating the traumas of living in an imperial world, the Lukan narrative attests to early Jesus followers' precarious relationship to the "fraught and ambivalent" question of social belonging.[76]

Kotrosits's insights regarding the "non-conscious, affective" experiences of the characters apply to Luke's implied audience as well. Even if the timing of Luke's narrative delivery was decades—or, according to

---

see the discussion of the eunuch's likely identification with the Isaianic servant in F. Scott Spencer, *Acts*, RNBC (Sheffield: Sheffield Academic, 1997), 93–94.

75. Maia Kotrosits, *Rethinking Early Christian Identity: Affect, Violence, and Belonging* (Minneapolis: Fortress, 2015), 100, 113 n. 61; on Acts, see esp. 85–116.

76. Ibid., 86.

some, up to a century—later than the time narrated in the story, Kotrosits's description of the characters' desperation and "fragile agency" most likely describes the earliest Lukan audiences as well. That is to say that Luke's intended recipients' embodied experiences of the narrative would have been marked by an affectivity—and a plurality—that exceeds the clean linearity suggested by many cognitive accounts of emotion and/in narrative.

Of course, just as in the Parable of the Sower some who hear the word fail to mature while others bear fruit (8:14–15), and just as in Acts the Ethiopian eunuch and Jerusalem Jews respond differently to readings of the Bible, so will members of Luke's audience respond to the Lukan narrative differently, depending on a variety of factors. Moments of narrative reflexivity can be read as constituting subtle interventions—narrative attempts to reign in the chaos of potential responses—and perhaps even as giving rise to joy in the "one who has ears to hear" (ὁ ἔχων ὦτα ἀκούειν [Luke 8:8]).

4. Conclusion

In sum, the foregoing discussion has proposed that we read scenes of characters interpreting narratives as moments of narrative reflexivity. Doing so underscores the ways in which these scenes can function as rhetorical appeals to Luke's audience to emulate (certain) characters' joyful hospitality as they receive the Lukan narrative.

At the same time, as rhetorical narratologist Michael Kearns rightly notes (adopting Prince's concept of the metanarrative sign), "Even if the illocutionary force of a metanarrative sign can be predicted (readers will notice the sign), its effect on interpretation cannot be."[77] Recipients of a narrative's invitations and warnings are never coerced or forced into particular ways of making sense of the narrative; they might be encouraged, prompted, or urged to respond in certain ways through the rhetoric of the narrative, but whether they do so in reality is contingent on so many uncontrollable variables.

Let me conclude by noting that scholars of early Christianity, drawing on developments in affect theory (e.g., Stephen Moore, Maia Kotrosits, Jennifer Knust, Jennifer Koosed),[78] have recently been asking a provoca-

---

77. Michael Kearns, *Rhetorical Narratology* (Lincoln: University of Nebraska, 1999), 71–72.

78. See the special issue of *Biblical Interpretation*, introduced in Stephen Moore

tive question: how might New Testament scholarship change if we were to recognize and inquire about the various ways in which affectivity and emotion influence our scholarly endeavors? The ideas about narrative reflexivity enumerated in this chapter lead me to add that *narratives about narrative interpretation* engage the affects and emotions in particularly prescient ways. If we consider such narratives to be emotionally evocative for their earliest audiences, there is no reason to presume that they would not also give rise to various embodied responses (conscious or otherwise) in those who interpret them today.

In the end, we may find that attending to the literary aesthetics of affect shapes and sharpens our articulations of joy's rhetorical functions. Or we may find that joy in/and narrative remains ever elusive and—as the author of 1 Peter puts it—ultimately "inexpressible" (ἀνεκλάλητος [1:8]). Still, we try.

Selected Bibliography

Ahmed, Sara. *The Cultural Politics of Emotion*. 2nd ed. New York: Routledge, 2014.
Armstrong, Isobel. *The Radical Aesthetic*. Oxford: Blackwell, 2000.
Clough, Patricia Ticineto, ed., with Jean Halley. *The Affective Turn: Theorizing the Social*. Durham, NC: Duke University Press, 2007.
Herman, David, ed. *The Cambridge Companion to Narrative*. Cambridge: Cambridge University Press, 2007.
Hogan, Patrick Colm. *Affective Narratology: The Emotional Structure of Stories*. Lincoln, NE: University of Nebraska Press, 2011.
———. *What Literature Teaches Us about Emotion*. SESI. Cambridge: Cambridge University, 2011.
Sandywell, Barry. *The Beginnings of European Theorizing: Reflexivity in the Archaic Age*. 3 vols. London: Routledge, 1996.

---

and Jennifer Koosed, "Introduction: From Affect to Exegesis," *BibInt* 22 (2014): 381–87. Some New Testament scholars interested in affect draw more from the social sciences than from literary theory, e.g., Stephen Barton, "Eschatology and the Emotions in Early Christianity," *JBL* 130 (2011): 571–91; Louise J. Lawrence, "Emotions in Protest in Mark 11–13: Responding to an Affective Turn in Social-Scientific Discourse," in *Matthew and Mark Across Perspectives: Essays in Honour of Stephen C. Barton and William R. Telford*, ed. Kristian A. Bendoraitis and Nijay K. Gupta (New York: Bloomsbury T&T Clark, 2016), 83–107.

Siegle, Robert. *The Politics of Reflexivity: Narrative and the Constitutive Poetics of Culture*. Baltimore: Johns Hopkins University Press, 1986.

Wetherell, Margaret. "Affect and Discourse—What's the Problem? From Affect as Excess to Affective/Discursive Practice." *Subjectivity* 6 (2013): 349–68.

Why the Johannine Jesus Weeps at the Tomb of Lazarus

Stephen D. Moore

The cluster of interconnected disciplines known for convenience as "literary and cultural studies" is the extrabiblical academic field that has catalyzed the present essay. More precisely, the catalyst has been a certain turn in "theory"—which functions within literary and cultural studies primarily as a cipher for poststructuralism and, now additionally, post-poststructuralism (an inelegant but necessary term). In the early twenty-first century, theory has turned away from *language* and *representation*, the twin preoccupations of classic poststructuralism, and simultaneously turned toward *the nonhuman* (epitomized by materiality and animality) and *affect* (emotion but also sensation and still more diffuse states). A more detailed recitation of the history of affect theory is, however, in order, together with an explication of the competing concepts of affect that have animated it.

1. Feeling Theory

The now canonical etiology of affect theory conjures up two incongruent origins. The earlier origin—including the coinage of the term *affect theory* itself—is associated with US psychologist Silvan S. Tomkins (1911–1991), whose biologically based research distinguished nine allegedly innate affects: distress-anguish; interest-excitement; enjoyment-joy; surprise-startle; anger-rage; fear-terror; shame-humiliation; disgust; and, related to the latter but subtly distinct from it, "dismell."[1] An affect, in Tomkins's special sense of the term, is not an emotion, but rather a biological response to

---

1. See Silvan S. Tomkins, *Affect, Imagery, Consciousness*, 4 vols. (New York: Springer, 1962–1992). Vol. 1: *The Positive Affects*; vol. 2: *The Negative Affects*; vol. 3: *The Negative Affects: Anger and Fear*; vol. 4: *Cognition: Duplication and Transformation of Information*. For a more accessible entrée to Tomkins's psychology, see Tomkins,

a stimulus, whether internal or external, and as such is the biological basis of emotion. But emotion proper, for Tomkins, also entails memory and biography, the layered intricacy of a multifaceted life unfolding in time. Feeling, meanwhile, in Tomkins's understanding of the term, mediates between affect and emotion. Feeling is the incipient psychological processing of bodily affect—the conscious registering of affect—prior to its full assimilation as emotion.

Tomkins's pre-poststructuralist work on affect assumes post-poststructuralist significance in the contemporary theoretical scene through its championing and channeling by seminal queer theorist Eve Kosofsky Sedgwick.[2] In retrospect, her 1995 essay coauthored with Adam Frank, "Shame in the Cybernetic Fold: Reading Silvan Tomkins," may be said to have marked a significant early moment in turning poststructuralist attention from the linguistic to the extralinguistic—more specifically in this case, from the human body as discursive construction to the human body as extradiscursive entity.[3] Sedgwick and Frank write: "'Theory' has become almost simply coextensive with the claim (you can't say it often enough) *It's not natural,*" a stance they dub "reflexive antibiologism."[4] Consequently, Sedgwick and Frank's turn to Tomkins transgresses one of theory's most cherished dogmas: "You don't have to be long out of theory kindergarten to make mincemeat of, let's say, a psychology that depends on the separate existence of eight (only sometimes it's nine) distinct affects hardwired into the human biological system."[5] Yet this biopsychology is, in their estimation, calibrated to take the precise measure of affect in situations in which classic poststructuralist theory (Derridean, Foucauldian, or Lacanian, say) would be a clumsy tool at best.

Exploring Affect: The Selected Writings of Silvan S. Tomkins, ed. E. Virginia Demos, SESI (Cambridge: Cambridge University Press, 1995).

2. See Eve Kosofsky Sedgwick and Adam Frank, eds., *Shame and Its Sisters: A Silvan Tomkins Reader* (Durham, NC: Duke University Press, 1995). Still more important for the Tomkins trajectory of affect theory as it has impinged on literary and cultural studies has been Sedgwick's *Touching Feeling: Affect, Pedagogy, Performativity* (Durham, NC: Duke University Press, 2003).

3. Eve Kosofsky Sedgwick and Adam Frank, "Shame in the Cybernetic Fold: Reading Silvan Tomkins," in Sedgwick and Frank, *Shame and Its Sisters.*

4. Sedgwick and Frank, "Shame and Its Sisters," 109, emphasis original. Page references to this essay, which originally served as the introduction to Sedgwick and Frank, *Shame and Its Sisters*, are from the reprint in Sedgwick, *Touching Feeling*, 93–121.

5. Sedgwick and Frank, "Shame and Its Sisters," 94.

Yet it is not as though nothing pertinent to the analysis of affect has emerged from "French theory," broadly conceived. Affect theory's other point of origin is associated with French philosopher Gilles Deleuze (1925–1995). Even though Tomkins coined the term "affect theory," it should not be imagined that his biopsychology is a major driver of this theory as it has developed in literary and cultural studies. Sedgwick's "discovery" of Tomkins has impelled many literary and cultural studies folk to dip into his work—to live "a theoretical moment not one's own," as she and Frank put it[6]—though relatively few have lingered there. Far more consequential for affect theory has been the para-poststructuralist oeuvre of Deleuze, including Deleuze's extraordinary thought experiments with Félix Guattari.

Unlike Tomkins's biopsychology, Deleuze's philosophy developed in contiguity with structuralism and poststructuralism—but strategically to the side of them; for Deleuze was primarily interested in sensation and only secondarily in language. Like Baruch Spinoza, Henri Bergson, or Alfred North Whitehead, Deleuze was a philosopher of becoming, and his concept of affect was a concept of incessant, irreducible becoming.[7] More precisely, Deleuzian affect is the ineffable, preprocessed, visceral, visual, aural, tactile, olfactory, kinetic, rhythmic, chaotic encounter with the material world prior to structured sensory perception, prior to conscious cognition, prior to linguistic representation—and also prior to emotion or feeling. "Affects aren't feelings," Deleuze insisted in an interview; "they're becomings that spill over beyond whoever lives through them (thereby becoming someone else)."[8] Deleuzian affects are transpersonal but also prepersonal.

Just as the Tomkins brand of affect theory has been mediated and further elaborated by Sedgwick, so has the Deleuze brand of affect theory been mediated and further elaborated by Brian Massumi, initially in a 1995 article, "The Autonomy of Affect" (in eerily symmetrical counterpoint to Sedgwick and Frank's "Shame in the Cybernetic Fold"), and

---

6. Ibid., 117.

7. "Affects are becomings" (Gilles Deleuze and Félix Guattari, *A Thousand Plateaus: Capitalism and Schizophrenia*, trans. Brian Massumi [Minneapolis: University of Minnesota Press, 1987], 256).

8. Gilles Deleuze, "On Philosophy," in Deleuze, *Negotiations, 1972–1990*, trans. Martin Joughin (New York: Columbia University Press, 1995), 137.

subsequently in a significant book, *Parables for the Virtual*.⁹ Massumi's distinction between affect and emotion has often been quoted:

> An emotion is a subjective content, the sociolinguistic fixing of the quality of an experience, which is from that point onward defined as personal. Emotion is qualified intensity [for Massumi, "intensity" is a synonym for "affect"], the conventional, consensual point of insertion of intensity into semantically and semiotically formed progressions, into narrativizable action-reaction circuits, into function and meaning. It is intensity owned and recognized. It is crucial to theorize the difference between affect and emotion.¹⁰

This second, Deleuzian trajectory we have been tracing makes for an implacably austere, immensely elusive concept of affect. Yet it is this construal that has been most influential for affect theory in recent literary and cultural studies. Deleuzian affect explicitly permeates much of Patricia Ticineto Clough's pivotal collection *The Affective Turn*, while it implicitly permeates Gregory Seigworth and Melissa Gregg's introduction to their field-consolidating volume *The Affect Theory Reader*.¹¹ Deleuze is everywhere present even if nowhere named, for example, in Seigworth and Gregg's opening definition: "Affect is found in those intensities that pass body to body ..., in those resonances that circulate about, between, and sometimes stick to bodies and worlds.... Affect ... is the name we give to those forces—visceral forces beneath, alongside, or generally *other than* conscious knowing, vital forces insisting beyond emotion—that can serve to drive us toward movement, toward thought."¹² Meanwhile, prominent

---

9. Brian Massumi, "The Autonomy of Affect," *CC* 31 (1995): 83–109; Massumi, *Parables for the Virtual: Movement, Affect, Sensation*, PCI (Durham, NC: Duke University Press, 2002). Like Sedgwick and Frank's "Shame in the Cybernetic Fold," Massumi's "The Autonomy of Affect" (reprinted in Massumi, *Parables for the Virtual*, 23–45) also took aim at "the varieties of social constructivism currently dominant in cultural theory" (38).

10. Massumi, *Parables for the Virtual*, 28. See also Massumi, *Politics of Affect* (Cambridge: Polity, 2015), 5: "An emotion is a very partial expression of affect."

11. Patricia Ticineto Clough, ed., with Jean Halley, *The Affective Turn: Theorizing the Social* (Durham, NC: Duke University Press, 2007); Gregory J. Seigworth and Melissa Gregg, "An Inventory of Shimmers," in *The Affect Theory Reader*, ed. Gregg and Seigworth (Durham, NC: Duke University Press, 2010), 1–25.

12. Seigworth and Gregg, "An Inventory of Shimmers," 1, emphasis original.

affect theorists like Lauren Berlant, Kathleen Stewart, and Jasbir Puar also work with concepts of affect that are essentially Deleuzian.[13]

Affect theory is not a two-party system, however, as certain notable affect theorists, including Sara Ahmed and Ann Cvetkovich, fail to fit neatly into the Tompkins or Deleuze camps.[14] Indeed, Cvetkovich's comments on both "the affective turn" and the affect/emotion distinction fruitfully problematize much of the (oversimplifying) tale I have been telling thus far. Cvetkovich questions the common notion that the affective turn in the humanities is a recent phenomenon, declaring it already implicit in "the [early] feminist mantra that 'the personal is the political.'"[15] More broadly, Cvetkovich argues that many different domains of inquiry, few of them new, have been animated by an interest in affect: cultural memory studies; explorations of the role of emotions in political discourse; analyses

> of the politics of negative affects, such as melancholy and shame, inspired in particular by queer [theory]; new forms of historical inquiry … that emphasize the affective relations between past and present; the turn to memoir and the personal in criticism…; histories of intimacy, domesticity, and private life; the cultural politics of everyday life; histories and theories of sensation and touch informed by phenomenology and cultural geography

—and so on.[16] Cvetkovich also resists any rigid distinction between affect and emotion or affect and feeling: "I tend to use *affect* in a generic sense, rather than in the more specific Deleuzian sense, as a category that encompasses affect, emotion, and feeling, and that includes impulses, desires, and feelings that get historically constructed in a range of ways

---

13. See, e.g., Lauren Berlant, *Cruel Optimism* (Durham, NC: Duke University Press, 2011); Kathleen Stewart, *Ordinary Affects* (Durham, NC: Duke University Press, 2007); Jasbir Puar, *Terrorist Assemblages: Homonationalism in Queer Times*, Next Wave: New Directions in Women's Studies (Durham, NC: Duke University Press, 2007); Ann Pellegrini and Jasbir Puar, "Affect," *Social Text* 27 (2009): 35–38.

14. See Sara Ahmed, *The Cultural Politics of Emotion*, 2nd ed. (London: Routledge, 2014); Ahmed, *The Promise of Happiness* (Durham, NC: Duke University Press, 2010); Ann Cvetkovich, *An Archive of Feelings: Trauma, Sexuality, and Lesbian Public Cultures*, Series Q (Durham, NC: Duke University Press, 2003); Cvetkovich, *Depression: A Public Feeling* (Durham, NC: Duke University Press, 2012).

15. Cvetkovich, *Depression*, 8.

16. Ibid., 3.

(whether as distinct specific emotions or as a generic category often contrasted with reason)."[17]

Ahmed, another influential theorist commonly associated with the affective turn, is no less skeptical about "the affective turn" as a concept—arguing that it elides the feminist and queer work that made it possible[18]—and about the theoretical elevation of affect over emotion. "A contrast between a mobile impersonal affect and a contained personal emotion suggests that the affect/emotion distinction can operate as a gendered distinction," Ahmed contends. "It might even be that the very use of this distinction performs the evacuation of certain styles of thought (we might think of these as 'touchy feely' styles of thought, including feminist and queer thought) from affect studies."[19] Such objections to the dominance of Deleuzian affect within contemporary affect theory have prompted Pansy Duncan to propose the term *feeling theory* instead for the field "in order to encompass both work on affect and work on emotion."[20]

2. Interpreting after the End of Interpretation

However renamed, affect theory remains a complex and conflicted field, not least because it is not one field but several intersecting fields, as we have seen. What might this heterogeneous field yield for biblical interpretation? Can affect theory yield strategies for analyzing biblical texts, even for close reading biblical texts? Apparently it can because it already has. Erin Runions, Maia Kotrosits, Amy Cottrill, Jennifer Knust, Jennifer Koosed, Alexis Waller, and I myself have all published exegetical analyses of biblical texts that draw on affect theory.[21] Our interpretive appropriations of affect

---

17. Ibid., 4.
18. Sara Ahmed, "Afterword: Emotions and Their Objects," in Ahmed, *Cultural Politics of Emotion*, 205–6. This afterword, specially written for the second edition, provides a survey and critique of the field of affect theory whose emergence the first edition of the book helped to catalyze.
19. Ibid., 207.
20. Pansy Duncan, *The Emotional Life of Postmodern Film: Affect Theory's Other*, RRCMS 81 (New York: Routledge, 2015), 3. See also her "Taking the Smooth with the Rough: Texture, Emotion, and the Other Postmodernism," *PMLA* 129 (2014): 205.
21. See Erin Runions, "From Disgust to Humor: Rahab's Queer Affect," in *Bible Trouble: Queer Reading at the Boundaries of Biblical Scholarship*, ed. Teresa J. Hornsby and Ken Stone, SemeiaSt 67 (Atlanta: Society of Biblical Literature, 2011), 45–74; Runions, "Prophetic Affect and the Promise of Change: A Response," in *Jeremiah*

theory were, however, highly anomalous in the larger interdisciplinary context. In relation specifically to the field we call "literary studies," one mainly populated by denizens of modern language and comparative literature departments, our affective interpretations of biblical literature were doubly anomalous: not only were they affective interpretations of *biblical* literature, but they were affective *interpretations* of biblical *literature*. In the land of literary studies, literature is no longer king and interpretation is no longer queen.[22]

What has replaced literary interpretation in literary studies, in particular close reading? What has replaced it, mainly, is cultural studies. Close reading was the trademark practice of leading-edge literary studies from the 1930s through the 1980s, which is to say from the hegemony of the New Criticism, which invented and patented literary close reading, through the heyday of deconstructive criticism and reader-response criticism, with new historicism straddling the now and the not yet and foreshadowing the

---

(Dis)Placed: New Directions in Writing, ed. A. R. Pete Diamond and Louis Stulman, LHBOTS 529 (New York: T&T Clark, 2011), 235–42; Maia Kotrosits, "The Rhetoric of Intimate Spaces: Affect and Performance in the Corinthian Correspondence, *USQR* 62 (2011): 134–51; Kotrosits, "Romance and Danger at Nag Hammadi," *BCT* 8 (2012): 29–52; Kotrosits, *Rethinking Early Christian Identity: Affect, Violence, and Belonging* (Minneapolis: Fortress Press, 2015); Maia Kotrosits and Hal Taussig, *Re-reading the Gospel of Mark Amidst Loss and Trauma* (New York: Macmillan, 2013). See also Jennifer L. Koosed and Stephen D. Moore, eds., *Affect Theory and the Bible*, *BibInt* 22 (2014), which has articles by Jennifer Knust, Jennifer Koosed, Amy Cottrill, Alexis Waller, Maia Kotrosits, and Stephen Moore. For an exhaustive survey of biblical-scholarly engagements with affect theory, see Kotrosits, "How Things Feel: Biblical Studies, Affect Theory, and the (Im)personal," *BRP* 1 (2016): 1–53.

22. Reviewing the current literary studies scene, Jeffrey T. Nealon notes: "The decisive conceptual difference separating the present from the era of big [postmodern] theory is not so much a loss of status for theoretical discourses..., but the waning of literary interpretation itself as a viable research ... agenda" (*Post-Postmodernism: or, The Cultural Logic of Just-in-Time Capitalism* [Stanford, CA: Stanford University Press, 2012], 133). Nealon's position is in line with "the significant negative conclusion" at which Andrew Goldstone and Ted Underwood arrive in their joint survey article: "Neither interpretation, nor criticism, nor form, nor texts, nor language itself can be thought of as the invariant core of the discipline of literary studies" ("The Quiet Transformations of Literary Studies: What Thirteen Thousand Scholars Could Tell Us," *NLH* 45 [2014]: 375). Statements of this kind are now relatively common. For two further examples, see Simon During, "The Postcolonial Aesthetic," *PMLA* 129 (2014): 498; Rita Felski, *The Limits of Critique* (Chicago: University of Chicago Press, 2015), 70.

future of the discipline. In the 1990s, literature began to slide altogether from the center of US "literary studies." Now any high-cultural icon or low-cultural artifact was fair game for theory-infused analysis. We learned to stop saying "literary studies" and to say "literary and cultural studies" instead. But as literature slid to the side, so too did close reading.[23] To put it another way, contemporary literary studies is postliterary and post-methodological.[24] "Method" in the biblical studies sense—that is to say, a quasi-formulaic and easily repeatable interpretive procedure—began to hemorrhage from literary studies at precisely the same moment when close reading began to bleed from it.

Affect theory, too, has been notably uninterested in literature, by and large, in method narrowly defined (or as definable at all) or in close reading. Most affect theory huddles comfortably under the umbrella of "cultural studies" rather than "literary studies." Literary interpretation plays no significant role in *The Affect Theory Reader* or its predecessor *The Affective Turn*. Neither does literary interpretation play a prominent role, or any role whatsoever, in many of the most admired monographs of affect theory, ranging from Brian Massumi's *Parables for the Virtual*, Teresa Brennan's *The Transmission of Affect*, and Sianne Ngai's *Ugly Feelings*, to Denise Riley's *Impersonal Passion*, Kathleen Stewart's *Ordinary Affects*, and Nigel Thrift's *Non-representational Theory*.[25] The case need not be overstated. Lauren Berlant's *Cruel Optimism* does analyze some literary works alongside artistic works in other media, and the same can be said for Ann Cvetkovich's *An Archive of Feelings*, while Eve Kosofsky

---

23. See Jane Gallop, "The Historicization of Literary Studies and the Fate of Close Reading," *Profession* (2007): 181–86; Gallop, "Close Reading in 2009," *ADEBull* 149 (2010): 15–19.

24. I wrote an article some years ago entitled "A Modest Manifesto for New Testament Literary Criticism: How to Interface with a Literary Studies Field That Is Post-Literary, Post-Theoretical, and Post-Methodological," *BibInt* 15 (2007): 1–25. I was right about "Post-Literary" and "Post-Methodological," but wrong, it now seems, about "Post-Theoretical."

25. Teresa Brennan, *The Transmission of Affect* (Ithaca, NY: Cornell University Press, 2004); Sianne Ngai, *Ugly Feelings* (Cambridge: Harvard University Press, 2005); Denise Riley, *Impersonal Passion: Language as Affect* (Durham, NC: Duke University Press, 2005); Nigel Thrift, *Non-representational Theory: Space, Politics, Affect*, International Library of Sociology (New York: Routledge, 2008). Publication details for the other books listed have been provided in earlier footnotes.

Sedgwick's *Touching Feeling* devotes two chapters to Henry James and the Victorian novel. Yet none of these works sent me scurrying excitedly to my Bible to reread such-and-such a text and have it mean more and other than before. This is a highly subjective judgment, I realize. Knust and Waller, for example, upon reading Sedgwick's *Touching Feeling* and Cvetkovich's *An Archive of Feelings*, respectively, saw sparks fly onto the dusty pages of Genesis and Mark and instantly set them alight.[26] That happened for me only when I read Ahmed's *The Cultural Politics of Emotion*: the book of Revelation began to smolder as I read Ahmed's chapters on pain, hate, fear, disgust, and shame and saw how Revelation was inflamed by all these feelings.[27] Yet even Ahmed is not reading literature, but rather "web sites, government reports, political speech, and newspaper articles,"[28] which is to say that *The Cultural Politics of Emotion* too is a work of cultural studies.

But the main reason I gravitated to Ahmed is that her book, although part of the affect theory canon, does not deal with affect as such, or at least with affect in the Deleuzian mode. Ahmed renounces the Deleuzian-Massumian distinction of affect and emotion, as we saw earlier—she is, indeed, content to grapple centrally with emotion, as the title of her book suggests—and so Ahmed's theory was readily applicable to Revelation, across whose surface powerful emotions ripple and crackle audibly.

Before turning to Ahmed, however, I pondered how affect in the preprocessual, hypercorporeal, Deleuzian mode might relate to the Bible and its interpretation. I turned to *Kafka: Toward a Minor Literature*, the most celebrated Deleuzian/Deleuzoguattarian instance of literary analysis.[29] I had often dipped into this mesmerizing book over the years and let its eddying currents carry me along, but I emerged from it this time wondering whether even Deleuze and Guattari are able to translate Deleuzian affect successfully into literary analysis. Symptomatically, whereas the

---

26. Jennifer Knust, "Who's Afraid of Canaan's Curse? Genesis 9:18–29 and the Challenge of Reparative Reading," *BibInt* 22 (2014): 388–413; Alexis G. Waller, "Violent Spectacles and Public Feelings: Trauma and Affect in the Gospel of Mark and *The Thunder: Perfect Mind*," *BibInt* 22 (2014): 450–72.

27. Stephen D. Moore, "Retching on Rome: Vomitous Loathing and Visceral Disgust in Affect Theory and the Apocalypse of John," *BibInt* 22 (2014): 503–28.

28. To cite Ahmed's own list (*Cultural Politics of Emotion*, 14).

29. Gilles Deleuze and Félix Guattari, *Kafka: Toward a Minor Literature*, trans. Dana Polan, THL 30 (Minneapolis: University of Minnesota Press, 1986).

concept of "intensities," which is intimately intertwined with the concept of affect, does feature in *Kafka*,[30] the term *affect* as such is entirely absent from the book,[31] in contrast to other Deleuze-Guattari collaborations—none of them, however, works of literary analysis—in which the term and concept of affect feature explicitly and prominently.[32]

3. Jesus in the Shower

All of this brings me to Eugenie Brinkema's *The Forms of the Affects*, a book that sets out to model affect theory as close reading and to do so in critical dialogue with the Deleuzian trajectory of affect.[33] The book's manifesto-like preface takes aim at Deleuze-driven versions of affect theory that privilege ineffable affect—affect that "cannot be written," affect that is only ever "visceral, immediate, sensed, embodied, excessive," affect that "as the capacity for movement or disturbance" can never settle or congeal as any specifiable textual operations or describable formal properties.[34] Such notions of affect, Brinkema complains, are incapable of accounting for "textual

---

30. See especially Deleuze and Guattari, *Kafka*, 72–80 passim. At certain moments in Kafka's prose, Deleuze and Guattari find opening up before them "a world of pure intensities where all forms come undone, as do all the significations, signifiers, and signifieds, to the benefit of an unformed matter of deterritorialized flux, of nonsignifying signs" (13).

31. The term *affect* is also absent from Deleuze's (admittedly early) book on Proust, and even the terms *intensity* or *intensities* barely feature in it. See Gilles Deleuze, *Proust and Signs: The Complete Text*, trans. Richard Howard (London: Athlone, 2000). The danger here, I realize, is that of reductively representing Deleuze as a single-theme philosopher—a philosopher of affect—as though affect is always going to appear explicitly and centrally in every aspect of his work. Deleuze's oeuvre is more heterogeneous than that. But the fact remains that his literary engagements, whether solo or with Guattari, provide only oblique models at best for an affect-oriented literary criticism—but suggestive models, nonetheless. See further Deleuze, "On the Superiority of Anglo-American Literature," in Gilles Deleuze and Claire Parnet, *Dialogues II*, trans. Hugh Tomlinson and Barbara Habberjam, rev. ed. (New York: Columbia University Press, 2007), 36–76.

32. See, for example, Gilles Deleuze and Félix Guattari, *What Is Philosophy?*, trans. Graham Burchell and Hugh Tomlinson (London: Verso, 1994), 163–99.

33. Eugenie Brinkema, *The Forms of the Affects* (Durham, NC: Duke University Press, 2014).

34. Ibid., xii–xiii.

particularities."³⁵ Moreover, if affect is conceived as raw force, or unprocessed intensities, or the mere capability for mutability or movement, then "why turn to affect at all?" she asks, since, "in the end, ethics, politics, aesthetics—indeed, lives—must be enacted in the definite particular."³⁶

In response to this impasse, Brinkema calls for a coupling of affect theory and close reading. "There is a perversity to this," she admits; "if affect theory is what is utterly fashionable," the prescribed "corrective" of close reading is what is "utterly unfashionable."³⁷ Over against the formulaic, the predictable, the mechanical confirmation of prior theoretical models, close reading at its most effective, for Brinkema, offers "the vitality of all that is not known in advance" of the "hard tussle" with texts, along with "slow, deep attention" not just to the presence of formal features in texts but to "absences, elisions, ruptures, gaps, and points of contradiction" and to all the surprising, often unsettling complexity that is not simply "uncovered by interpretation but ... brought into being as its activity."³⁸

Did I mention that Brinkema is a film theorist? Her "texts," then, are cinematic texts, and so the models of analysis she supplies are not applicable to biblical texts without a labor of translation. Her primary text is the shower scene in Hitchcock's *Psycho* (1960):

> The black-hole vacuum of the first scream; the striating diagonals of the shower spray; the cool white grid of the cold white tile against which Marion's hand, stretched out and spread, like a claw, grasps, scratches, in bent digitate branches.... And after that, so much water. It rushes, famously mixing with the darkened blood, filling the empty drain.... The liquid rush moves in a fast counterclockwise, delimiting the contours of the hungry aperture.³⁹

The shuddering intensity of the *Psycho* shower scene is as good an indication as any of why affect theory, whether named as such or *avant la lettre*, has been at home in film theory for almost two decades. The visual, aural, and emotional bombardment that is cinematic experience might have

---

35. Ibid., xiv.
36. Ibid., xv.
37. Ibid., xv.
38. This sentence compresses ibid., xiv, 37–39.
39. Ibid., 1.

catalyzed the invention of affect theory even if Tompkins or Deleuze had never come up with it.[40]

But the *Psycho* shower scene also prompts medium-specific questions about affect and biblical texts, or affect and literature in general. Film is a bisensory medium, limited to sight and sound. So too is literature, which may be read silently or aloud. But whereas cinematic worlds are objects of *direct* visual and aural representation, literary worlds, including biblical worlds, are objects of *indirect* visual and aural representation. Moreover, whereas a cinematic text like the *Psycho* shower scene is designed for maximum visceral impact, a biblical text seldom is—even such a text as the Johannine flogging or crucifixion scene, potentially no less horrific, no less shocking. We do not read of "the black-hole vacuum of the first scream" as the whistling scourge or the hammered nail strikes home, or of "the striating diagonals of the shower" of blood, or of the warm rough wood against which Jesus's hand, "stretched out and spread, like a claw, grasps, scratches, in bent digitate branches." The Johannine Jesus does not scream, and so neither do we on reading the bloodless account of his bloody demise.

Yet the Johannine Jesus does weep, even if not when the lash is descending or the nails are being driven home. It is actually Brinkema who reminds us of his tears, and so it is no accident that we stepped out of the *Psycho* shower only to find ourselves, naked and bewildered, in the Johannine torture chamber. Brinkema's analytic lens has come to rest on the final image of the shower scene: Marion's frozen face plastered to the bathroom floor and under her now dead but open eye an ambiguous water drop that may or may not be a "small, fat tear." This "small spherule" demands to be read, indeed close read, insists Brinkema, and read it she does, first situating it "in the long history of the philosophy of emotion" that stretches back at least to Aristotle's *Poetics*, and in which "the tear has been the supreme metonym for the expressivity of interior states." "It is fitting," she adds, "that the shortest verse in … the New Testament is … 'Jesus wept' (John 11:35), *and no more needed to be said.*"[41]

---

40. Not that film was unimportant to Deleuze; he devoted two singular books to it: *Cinema 1: The Movement-Image*, trans. Hugh Tomlinson and Barbara Habberjam (London: Athlone, 1984); *Cinema 2: The Time-Image*, trans. Hugh Tomlinson and Robert Galeta (Minneapolis: University of Minnesota Press, 1989).

41. Brinkema, *Forms of the Affects*, 2, emphasis original.

4. As If the Ship Were a Folding of the Sea

Brinkema herself says no more about the Johannine Jesus weeping, but she provides tools that enable, indeed impel, us to reframe that affective display not as the expression of an internal state, self-sufficient in its signification and not requiring the supplement of speech, but rather as an external link in a causal chain that holds the text together, but so tightly as to rupture its delicate logic. Although Brinkema is scathingly dismissive of the way in which Deleuzian affect is deployed in contemporary affect theory—"every time the same model of vague shuddering intensity"[42]— Deleuze is nonetheless a crucial resource for the neoformalist model of affective criticism she is attempting to develop.

Brinkema is drawn to Deleuze's concept of *the fold*, a prominent facet of Deleuze's relentless critique of the notion of interiority in all its forms, including human subjectivity conceived as an internal self separate and distinct from an external body and an external world. Deleuze subsumes every concept of interiority into a depthless and unbounded exteriority. The inside, for Deleuze, can only ever be the inside of an outside, "an operation of the outside, ... merely the *fold* of an outside, as if the ship were a folding of the sea."[43]

How might the concept of the fold relate to the concept of character, whether cinematic or literary? For Brinkema, following Deleuze, the depthless counterepistemology of the fold forces a movement from emotion to affect in the analysis of character. The etymological trajectory of *emotion*—from Latin *emovere*, "move" or "move out"[44]—evokes expressive transmission from the interiority of a sender to the interiority of a receiver. The etymological trajectory of *affect*, however—at least for Deleuze—does not evoke transmission from depth to depth, internal subject to internal subject, but from surface to surface, body to body, action to action. *Affectus* for Deleuze, as glossed by Massumi, is "a prepersonal intensity corresponding to the passage from one experiential state of the body to

---

42. Ibid., xv.
43. Gilles Deleuze, *Foucault*, trans. Seán Hand (Minneapolis: University of Minnesota Press, 1988), 97, quoted in Brinkema, *Forms of the Affects*, 23, emphasis added. Deleuze develops his concept of the fold in dialogue with Foucault, but even more so in dialogue with Leibniz. See Deleuze, *The Fold: Leibnitz and the Baroque*, trans. Tom Conley (Minneapolis: University of Minnesota Press, 1993).
44. As Ahmed also notes (*Cultural Politics of Emotion*, 11).

another,"[45] which, as we saw earlier, is precisely the concept of affect that, in the hands of contemporary affect theorists, tends to dissolve into the unrepresentable, the ineffable, the apophatic. But Brinkema is having none of it. She is intent on locating Deleuzian affect in textual form, thereby rendering it readable, even close readable. She writes: "This book regards any individual affect as a self-folding exteriority that manifests in, as, and with textual form."[46]

5. Deep Emotion, Flattened Affect

All of this also resonates with me. In recent years I have become fascinated with postclassical narratology, so called, and particularly with certain poststructuralist inflections of it that interrogate the traditional and still-prevalent concept of literary character as an unproblematized channeling of the Cartesian concept of interiorized human subjectivity.[47] Oceans of ink have been spilled on the inner lives of paper people. Many of these paper personages have been biblical.[48] Turning to Stephen Voorwinde's *Jesus' Emotions in the Fourth Gospel*, for instance, we encounter repeated ascription of inner lives to biblical characters.[49] The adjective "deep" punctuates declarations about characters' emotional states in Voorwinde's study with a symptomatic repetitiveness. God experiences "deep sorrow," while Jesus experiences "deep distress" and "deep emotional disturbance."[50]

---

45. Brian Massumi, translator's introduction to Deleuze and Guattari, *Thousand Plateaus*, xvi. Deleuze in turn is glossing Spinoza, from whom he takes (and retools) the terms *affectus* and *affectio*.

46. Brinkema, *Forms of the Affects*, 25. Brinkema also wants to detach Deleuzian affect from its tight attachment to the body (24–25), but I am not yet ready to follow her there. The body has established too tentative a toehold in biblical studies, all told, to be beaten back quite so quickly.

47. This narratological trajectory began in earnest with Mark Currie's *Postmodern Narrative Theory*, Transitions (New York: Palgrave, 1998). See more recently Jan Alber and Monika Fludernik, eds., *Postclassical Narratology: Approaches and Analyses*, TIN (Columbus: Ohio State University Press, 2010).

48. For an incisive critique of biblical narrative criticism from the vantage point of postclassical narratology, see Scott S. Elliott, *Reconfiguring Mark's Jesus: Narrative Criticism after Poststructuralism*, BMW 41 (Sheffield: Sheffield Phoenix, 2011).

49. Stephen Voorwinde, *Jesus' Emotions in the Fourth Gospel: Human or Divine?*, JSNTSup 284 (New York: T&T Clark, 2005). The Fourth Gospel also receives a chapter in Voorwinde, *Jesus' Emotions in the Gospels* (New York: T&T Clark, 2011), 151–214.

50. Voorwinde, *Jesus' Emotions in the Fourth Gospel*, 39, 51 n. 64, 177.

"Deep human emotions ... repeatedly come over [Jesus] on his way to the cross."[51] Deep pools of emotion occur in the Lazarus narrative in particular, as Voorwinde reads it.[52] There "Jesus is portrayed as a man of deep feeling."[53] Jesus holds "deep affection" for Lazarus and experiences "deep emotion" at Lazarus's death.[54] Jesus's affection for Mary and Martha is also "deep and close."[55] Martha in particular "arouse[s] very deep feelings in Jesus," while Mary, for her part, has a "deep devotion" to Jesus.[56] How does Voorwinde understand what, ostensibly at least, is the most emotionally fraught detail in the Fourth Gospel, "Jesus burst into tears" (ἐδάκρυσεν ὁ Ἰησοῦς [11:35])?[57] For Voorwinde, Jesus's tears well up from an assumed interiority, are expressed (in both senses of the term) as outward signs of a deep hidden pool of emotion. Jesus' tears are "the outward expressions of his sorrow," Voorwinde asserts. Jesus's grief "openly express[es] itself in the shedding of tears."[58]

Deleuze and Brinkema impel a different construal of the Johannine Jesus's emotions. They prompt us to see these apparent pockets of interiority as folds in the surface of the text, pockets of an exteriority that extends uninterruptedly to the horizon of the text. The ostensible inside becomes the fold of an outside, "as if the ship were a folding of the sea"[59]—the ship in question being a certain boat laboring strenuously across the Sea of Galilee but to which Jesus comes "walking on the sea" (John 6:19), which, after all, as a textual sea is surface without depth. Jesus himself

---

51. Ibid., 221, quoting Herman N. Ridderbos, *The Gospel According to John: A Theological Commentary*, trans. John Vriend (Grand Rapids: Eerdmans, 1997), 468.

52. Voorwinde is not alone in this regard. Many interpreters would concur with the pronouncement of Dennis Sylva on the Lazarus episode: "The otherwise virtually implacable Johannine Jesus has his *deepest* emotions involved in the plight of Lazarus and his sisters (11.33, 35, 38)" (*Thomas—Love as Strong as Death: Faith and Commitment in the Fourth Gospel*, LNTS 434 [London: Bloomsbury T&T Clark, 2013], 132, emphasis added).

53. Voorwinde, *Jesus' Emotions in the Fourth Gospel*, 139.

54. Ibid., 114, 152.

55. Ibid., 155.

56. Ibid., 148, 169.

57. As Voorwinde notes (ibid., 182), some lexicons translate δακρύω in the aorist as an inceptive, hence "burst into tears" (BDAG, s.v. "δακρύω"). Subsequent biblical translations in this essay follow NRSV, except where noted.

58. Voorwinde, *Jesus' Emotions in the Fourth Gospel*, 181.

59. Deleuze, *Foucault*, 97.

folds and refolds continuously in John, but not always as a human body. He—or, better, it—also refolds as a nonhuman animal ("Behold the lamb of God!" [1:36; cf. 1:29; 3:14]), as an inanimate object ("I am the door/gate [ἡ θύρα]" [10:9; cf. 10:7]), as a plant ("I am the true vine" [15:1; cf. 15:5]), as a processed plant ("I am the bread of life" [6:35; cf. 6:41, 48, 51]), even as electromagnetic radiation ("I am the light of the world" [8:12; cf. 9:5]). The Johannine Jesus is not a human being, but not only for the reasons ordinarily adduced.[60]

Jesus's tears, then, far from welling up expressively from a deep, hidden, internal pool of emotion—bursting up from imagined depths to splash the surface of the page—are better seen as yet further folds in the Johannine text, tiny but highly consequential pockets of insideness within its paper-thin, infinitely extensible outside. Each folding and refolding, each tear, sends forceful ripples across the surface of the text, impelling further folds and engendering further agents, events, and objects. Consider the consequential causal ripple that comes into view when we approach Jesus's tears not as an expressive outward sign of an abruptly unleashed (e)motion surging up from an imagined human interior but as an impersonal affective force impelling horizontal movement across the plane of the text. Jesus wept. Because Jesus wept, Lazarus lived. Because Lazarus lived, Jesus died (see 11:45–53).[61] Because Jesus died, all who believe in him will live. Why then does Jesus weep?[62]

6. Refusing Rot

To begin to ponder this question is to reckon with forces in the Fourth Gospel that only come to oblique expression in it. The Johannine narrative is replete with understated—indeed, unstated—affect, one affect in

---

60. I explore this theme elsewhere; see Moore, "What a (Sometimes Inanimate) Divine Animal or Plant Has to Teach Us about Being Human: John's Jesus and Other Nonhumans," *JLT* (forthcoming).

61. Structurally, Jesus's symbolic raising of Lazarus plays the same catalytic role in the Fourth Gospel that Jesus's symbolic action in the Jerusalem temple plays in the Synoptic Gospels: it consolidates the indigenous Judean elite's opposition to him (11:45–53) and so precipitates his arrest, trial, and execution.

62. Jesus is represented as intending to raise Lazarus from the dead even before Lazarus has managed to die (11:3–4; cf. 11:11–15), which suggests that factors other than an abrupt welling of grief felt by a suddenly human Jesus have conspired to produce his textual tears.

particular, as we are about to see. That affect is not love, I would argue, despite the frequency of love language in the narrative.[63] The benign face of the Johannine God, in particular ("God so loved the world" [3:16]), masks the real locus of affect in the narrative. "No one has ever seen [that] God" (1:18; cf. 5:37; 6:46; Exod 33:20), but they have seemed to see his compassionate smile, a Cheshire cat smile that is visible even though its owner is invisible.[64] Jesus's face, although equally undescribed in the narrative, eventually cracks. Something shatters its composure. The "disturbance" that creases Jesus' preternaturally serene countenance in John 11:38—"Jesus ... greatly disturbed [ἐμβριμώμενος ἐν ἑαυτῷ], came to the tomb" (see also 12:27)—a disturbance that is a fold within the fold that is his face, together with his abrupt weeping in 11:35, fleetingly makes visible the electrifying affect that has been rippling across the surface of the narrative all along and generating its innumerable folds. That affect is disgust.

What makes Jesus's eyes water in 11:35 is a certain smell, indeed a certain unmistakable stench, as yet only wafted on the breeze, for he is still some distance from Lazarus's tomb. "Lord, by now he stinks [ἤδη ὄζει] because he has been dead four days," Martha will demur when Jesus marches up to the tomb and demands that it be opened (11:39). The text, qua text, can represent this stench but not reproduce it. "Odor, and not blindness, is vision's true other," as Brinkema notes, and never more than in the case of literary odor. In literature as in cinema, smell is the absolutely excluded, a sensory prohibition intrinsic to the medium.[65] In the Fourth Gospel, the smell that is excluded, the smell that cannot be smelled except by the figures enfolded in the text, is that of rotting flesh. As literary smell it cannot properly be spoken. It is hermetically sealed up within the surface pockets of the text. It represents the ultimate unrepresentability of the object of disgust around which the Fourth Gospel is organized. Better put, putrescence is the adhesive that holds this moldering text together.

The Fourth Gospel, then, is structured by disgust, by its convulsive, heaving movements of revulsion, expulsion, and exclusion. For of all the

---

63. On which see Voorwinde, *Jesus' Emotions in the Fourth Gospel*, esp. 150–61, 195–210, 222–23, 232–52. Voorwinde takes love to be the dominant emotion in the narrative. See also Matthew A. Elliott, *Faithful Feelings: Rethinking Emotion in the New Testament* (Grand Rapids: Kregel, 2006), 149–53.

64. "Certain assemblages of power ... require the production of a face, others do not," Deleuze and Guattari argue (*Thousand Plateaus*, 175).

65. Brinkema, *Forms of the Affects*, 121, 144.

objects that elicit disgust—bodily secretions and excretions, things that wriggle, squirm, and swarm—putrefaction and decay take pride of place.[66] Brinkema defines disgust as "the worse than the worst."[67] That is why putrefaction is the ultimate object of disgust. Death, while tragic, and even the worst, is not in itself disgusting. What is worse than the worst, and the quintessence of disgust, is that the corpse refuses to be still. "In death … the body is furiously *too much*.… It churns, it moves, it froths" in a ghastly fecundity.[68] The ultimate, utterly obscene desecration of the flesh, even after death, is as certain as death itself.[69] Which is what causes the Johannine Jesus finally to weep—or, more precisely, causes the Johannine textual logic, a machinic logic operating independently of the intentions of any human textual producer,[70] to fold its protagonist so that he assumes the form of a weeping figure.

Brinkema quotes disgust theorist Winfried Menninghaus: "Every book about disgust is not least a book about the rotting corpse."[71] Conversely, every book about the rotting corpse is not least a book about disgust. As we are beginning to see (and perhaps even to smell), the Fourth Gospel is a book about the rotting corpse—or, rather, a book about the refusal of the rotting corpse. Brinkema writes: "The form of disgust is the form of the excluded as such."[72] In the Fourth Gospel, the excluded as such is *flesh* as such. The Fourth Gospel insistently aligns flesh with death. Within the text's odorless folds, flesh is always already rotting, even in life. "It is the spirit that gives life; the flesh is worthless, worse than useless [ἡ σὰρξ οὐκ ὠφελεῖ οὐδέν]," declaims the Johannine Jesus (6:63 [my trans.]), he who took on decaying flesh, encased himself in its fetid folds, to live among us.

---

66. So ibid., 164, following Aurel Kolnai, *On Disgust*, ed. Barry Smith and Carolyn Korsmeyer (Chicago: Open Court, 2004), 53–62.

67. Brinkema, *Forms of the Affects*, 130, here taking her lead from Jacques Derrida, "Economimesis," trans. Richard Klein, *Diacritics* 11 (1981): 23. Derrida's article gradually builds up, via Kant on good taste, to an extended meditation on distaste, vomit, and hence disgust.

68. Brinkema, *Forms of the Affects*, 171, emphasis original.

69. See ibid., 177.

70. "A book exists only through the outside and on the outside. A book itself is a little machine" (Deleuze and Guattari, *Thousand Plateaus*, 4).

71. Brinkema, *Forms of the Affects*, 130, quoting Winfried Menninghaus, *Disgust: Theory and History of a Strong Sensation*, trans. Howard Eiland and Joel Golb (Albany: State University of New York Press, 2003), 1.

72. Brinkema, *Forms of the Affects*, 131.

Life cannot come of death, he insists. "What is born of the flesh is flesh, and what is born of the Spirit is spirit" (3:6). To be reborn so as never to die, never to decay, is to be born "not of blood or of the will of the flesh" (1:13). The Johannine Jesus is that which *preexists* rotting flesh ("In the beginning was the Word" [1:1]), which *becomes* rotting flesh ("And the Word became flesh" [1:14]), and which *overcomes* rotting flesh ("'Lazarus, come out!' The dead man came out, his hands and feet bound with strips of cloth, and his face wrapped in a cloth" [11:44; cf. 5:25, 28–29]). With rotting flesh, however vehemently refused, the Johannine Jesus's entire existence is intimately interfused.

7. Always Already Risen, Always Already Rotten

The Johannine Jesus does not refuse his own death, but he does refuse his own decay. In raising Lazarus, Jesus is refusing not only Lazarus's putrefaction but also his own. For although the worst does comes to pass for the Johannine Jesus—"Then Pilate took Jesus and had him flogged.... Then he handed him over to them to be crucified" (19:1, 16)—the worse than the worst does not come to pass for him. Jesus dies but apparently does not decay. Peter, the Beloved Disciple, and Mary Magdalene all boldly stick their heads into the tomb in which the shredded, blood-drained corpse of Jesus has been laid (20:3–12). But there is no stench of putrefying flesh from which to recoil, and not only because the corpse has been cocooned in aromatic spices (19:39–40). There is, indeed, no flesh of any kind in the tomb.

The tomb of the Johannine Jesus is a pocket of insideness in the outsideness of the text, a concealing fold in its surface, into which flesh vanishes and reemerges as something else. That something else is not simply spirit. The not-flesh, yet also not-spirit, that is the liminal body of the risen Johannine Jesus passes through physical barriers (20:19, 26) but also bears physical wounds: "Put your finger here.... Reach out your hand and put it in my side" (20:27). The marks of a torturous death are now eternally inscribed on a body that, we are to assume, can no longer die and hence no longer decay. These unerased and unerasable marks, however, preclude any simple separation of the risen body and the rotting body in the Fourth Gospel—and not just on the other side of the peculiar portal that is Jesus's tomb. Even when Jesus is engaged in his long, meandering journey to that tomb, the flesh he has become ("And the Word became flesh") is rotting flesh and rot-resistant flesh at one and the same time; for the pre-Easter Johannine Jesus is not yet risen, yet always already risen.

Flesh is the locus of intense and immense paradox in the Fourth Gospel.[73] Countervailing affective forces swirl around flesh in this text, producing convoluted folds in its narrative logic. Flesh is what must be renounced in the Fourth Gospel, as we have seen. It must be disowned and expelled as the ultimate object of disgust. It must be pushed outside. But the Fourth Gospel also spectacularly enacts *the paradox of disgust*, that affective ambivalence whereby intense aversion to an object coexists with intense attraction to it.[74] Turn disgust over, with a tentatively extended digit, and what is revealed, wriggling away from the light, is, more often than not, an obscene craving: an irrational desire for proximity and intimacy with the abhorrent thing. In the Fourth Gospel, flesh is not only what must be strenuously renounced, flesh is also what must be intimately embraced. It must be pushed outside but it must also be pulled inside. It must be masticated and swallowed; it must be ingested and digested (see 6:50–58).

What renders the paradox of disgust spectacular in the Fourth Gospel is that it is enacted not in a corner, not in a darkened room ("There are many rooms in my Father's house" [14:2]), but out in the open. There is no intimate huddle at a private meal, no patently ritualistic gesture to leech the ghastly act of its horror ("He took a loaf of bread, and after blessing it he broke it, gave it to them, and said, 'Take, this is my body" [Mark 14:22; cf. Matt 26:26; Luke 22:19; 1 Cor 11:23–24]), but only a raw and shocking public announcement ("The one who gnaws on my flesh [ὁ τρώγων μου τὴν σάρκα] and drinks my blood has eternal life…; for my flesh is true food and my blood is true drink" [John 6:54–55 [my trans.]; cf. 6:51–58) to a suitably shocked and scandalized audience ("How can this man give us his flesh to eat?" [6:52]).[75] The high Johannine christology is also a high

---

73. As has long been recognized. Among critical commentators on John, none wrestled more diligently with this paradox than Rudolf Bultmann. He wrote: "This is the paradox which runs through the whole [Fourth G]ospel: the δόξα is not to be seen *alongside* the σάρξ, nor *through* the σάρξ as through a window; it is to be seen in the σάρξ and nowhere else" (*The Gospel of John: A Commentary*, trans. G. R. Beasley-Murray [Eugene, OR: Wipf & Stock, 2014], 63, emphasis original). To this paradox Bultmann returns again and again in his commentary.

74. See Kolnai, *On Disgust*, 42–43; Brinkema, *Forms of the Affects*, 164–65. Ahmed also makes much of this paradox (*Cultural Politics of Emotion*, 84–100).

75. For an analysis of John 6:51–58 that absolutizes its differences from the synoptic and Pauline eucharistic narratives, see Meredith J. C. Warren, *My Flesh Is Meat Indeed: A Nonsacramental Reading of John 6:51–58* (Minneapolis: Fortress, 2015).

gastronomy. More precisely, it is *haut goût*, as we are about to see, the *haute cuisine* practice of preparing and consuming decomposing food.[76]

"Your ancestors ate the manna in the wilderness, and they died," the Johannine Jesus reminds "the Jews," contrasting "the living bread" that will enable the eater to live forever (6:49–51; cf. 6:31, 58). The ancestors ate the manna and they died and decayed, but the manna itself was also subject to decay: "It bred worms and became foul" (Exod 16:20), like Lazarus in his tomb. Ostensibly, "the living bread that [comes] down from heaven" in the Fourth Gospel, the bread that is actually flesh ("the bread that I will give for the life of the world is my flesh" [6:51]), is incapable of decay; it cannot breed worms, it cannot rot.

The guarantor of this incorruptibility is the risen body of Jesus. Even on the prolonged path to his own tomb, always dimly visible in the distance, the Johannine Jesus is always already risen, as we noted earlier, is always himself "the resurrection and the life," as he announces outside Lazarus's tomb (11:25). But Jesus's risen body in the Fourth Gospel is an uncertain guarantor of incorruptibility. The marks of death, and hence of corruption, persist indelibly on the risen body, as we also saw, and not as faint scars but as horrific puncture wounds capacious enough to enfold a finger or even an entire hand (20:25, 27). These gruesome wounds silently bespeak the unspeakably atrocious indignities to which all flesh is heir, human flesh no less than animal flesh. Indeed, the traumatic marks on the risen body bloodily smudge, even erase altogether, the human animal/nonhuman animal distinction. The risen body is an animal body,[77] and as an animal body the risen body is always dying, is always decaying. As marks of death, and hence of decomposition, the wounds on the risen body are, in effect, gangrenous, and incurably so. Even risen, then, the flesh of the Johannine Jesus bears the marks of corruption. In consequence, death clings to Jesus

---

76. See Brinkema on *haut goût* (*Forms of the Affects*, 165–66). By now Brinkema is savoring Peter Greenaway's film *The Cook, the Thief, His Wife, and Her Lover*.

77. It is hardly surprising, therefore, that the wounded risen body appears outright in animal form in Rev 5:6: "I saw a lamb standing as though it had been slaughtered (ὡς ἐσφαγμένον)" (my trans.; cf. John 1:29, 36). Elsewhere I attempt to focus Revelation's heavenly butchered sheep through the lens of posthuman animality studies; see my "Ruminations on Revelation's Ruminant, Quadrupedal Christ; or, the Even-Toed Ungulate That Therefore I Am," in *The Bible and Posthumanism*, ed. Jennifer L. Koosed, SemeiaSt 74 (Atlanta: Society of Biblical Literature, 2014), 301–26.

throughout the Fourth Gospel; necrosis subtly infects his always already risen body.

In the Fourth Gospel, which is also the Flesh Gospel, flesh remains a thing of horror, even when it is Jesus's flesh, which is why it precipitates the paradox of disgust: "the flesh is worthless" (6:63); "eat my flesh" (6:56). The affective logic of the Fourth Gospel enjoins the eating of Jesus precisely because its narrative logic, culminating in a not entirely successful resurrection,[78] has made him an indirect object of revulsion. The scent of death sits lightly on the Johannine Jesus; it is not the stench of Lazarus. But it is a scent that cannot be scrubbed clean. And that, more than anything, is why the Johannine Jesus weeps at the tomb of Lazarus.

Select Bibliography

Ahmed, Sara. *The Cultural Politics of Emotion*. 2nd ed. New York: Routledge, 2014.
Berlant, Lauren. *Cruel Optimism*. Durham, NC: Duke University Press, 2011.
Brinkema, Eugenie. *The Forms of the Affects*. Durham, NC: Duke University Press, 2014.
Chen, Mel Y. *Animacies: Biopolitics, Racial Mattering, and Queer Affect*. Perverse Modernities. Durham, NC: Duke University Press, 2012.
Clough, Patricia Ticineto, ed., with Jean Halley. *The Affective Turn: Theorizing the Social*. Durham, NC: Duke University Press, 2007.
Cvetkovich, Ann. *Depression: A Public Feeling*. Durham, NC: Duke University Press, 2012.
Deleuze, Gilles, and Félix Guattari. *A Thousand Plateaus: Capitalism and Schizophrenia*. Translated by Brian Massumi. Minneapolis: University of Minnesota Press, 1987.

---

78. Jesus's risen body is less than glorious in the Fourth Gospel, and not only because of its gaping wounds. It no longer looks like Jesus, but not because it is gloriously transfigured. It can be mistaken for the body of a gardener (20:14–15) or some other ordinary looking stranger (21:4; cf. Luke 24:15–16). For an extended philosophical meditation on the paradoxical resurrection bodies of John, Luke, and Paul, see John D. Caputo, "Bodies Still Unrisen, Events Still Unsaid: A Hermeneutic of Bodies without Flesh," in *Apophatic Bodies: Negative Theology, Incarnation, and Relationality*, ed. Chris Boesel and Catherine Keller, TTC (New York: Fordham University Press, 2010), 94–116.

Gregg, Melissa, and Gregory J. Seigworth, eds. *The Affect Theory Reader*. Durham, NC: Duke University Press, 2010.
Koosed, Jennifer L., and Stephen D. Moore, eds. *Affect Theory and the Bible*. *BibInt* 22 (2014).
Kotrosits, Maia. *Rethinking Early Christian Identity: Affect, Violence, and Belonging*. Minneapolis: Fortress, 2015.
Massumi, Brian. *Parables for the Virtual: Movement, Affect, Sensation*. PCI. Durham, NC: Duke University Press, 2002.
Schaefer, Donovan O. *Religious Affects: Animality, Evolution, and Power*. Durham, NC: Duke University Press, 2015.
Sedgwick, Eve Kosofsky. *Touching Feeling: Affect, Pedagogy, Performativity*. Durham, NC: Duke University Press, 2003.
Tomkins, Silvan S. *Exploring Affect: The Selected Writings of Silvan S. Tomkins*. Edited by E. Virginia Demos. Cambridge: Cambridge University Press, 1995.

When Enough Is Never Enough: Philosophers, Poets, Peter, and Paul on Insatiable Desire

David E. Fredrickson

Consider two very different evaluations of desire. The first, that of the Stoic philosopher Epictetus, puts humans in the shadow of Zeus's infinite capacity for self-satisfaction and the god's complete rejection of desire. Epictetus believes humans ought to imitate Zeus's power to be alone with himself, never to be forsaken, never to feel the need for another's aid or to feel any compulsion to answer anyone's call for help and recognition:

> Why, if being alone is enough to make one forlorn, you will have to say that even Zeus himself is forlorn at the World-Conflagration, and bewails himself: "Wretched me! I have neither Hera, nor Athena, nor Apollo, nor, in a word, brother, or son, or grandson, or kinsman." There are even those who say that this is what he does when left alone at the World-Conflagration; for they cannot conceive of the mode of life of one who is all alone, starting as they do from a natural principle, namely, the facts of natural community of interest among men, and mutual affection, and joy in intercourse. But one ought none the less to prepare oneself for this also, that is, to be able to be self-sufficient, to be able to commune with oneself; even as Zeus communes with himself, and is at peace with himself, and contemplates the character of his governance, and occupies himself with ideas appropriate to himself, so ought we also to be able to converse with ourselves, not to be in need of others, not to be at a loss for some way to spend our time. (*Diatr.* 3.13.4–8)[1]

---

1. Epictetus, *Discourses, Books III and IV, Fragments, the Encheiridion*, trans. W. A. Oldfather, LCL 218 (Cambridge: Harvard University Press, 1925; repr., 1978).

The other portrait of desire comes from the sixth-century CE poet Paulus Silentiarius, famous for his architecturally themed poetry as well as his erotic compositions:

> I saw the lovers [ποθέοντας]: in the ungovernable fury of their passion they glued their lips together in a long kiss, but they could not be satisfied [οὐ κόρον εἶχον] with unsparing love [ἔρωτος ἀφειδέος]. Yearning, if possible, to plunge into one another's hearts, they almost, *almost* alleviated their inexpressible [ἀμφασίης] compulsion by interchanging their soft clothing. Then he was just like Achilles in the chambers of Lycomedes, and the girl, girded in a tunic falling to just above her silvery knee, counterfeited the form of Phoebe. Again they pressed their lips together, for the inappeasable hunger of love madness still devoured them [γυιοβόρου]. One would more easily pry apart two intertwined stems of a twisted vine that have long merged their tendrils, than those lovers, with their opposed [ἀντιπόροισι] arms knotting their pliant limbs in a close embrace. Thrice blessed is he, my dear, who is wrapped in such bonds, thrice blessed! But *we* must burn [καιόμεθα] separately. (Anth. Gr. 5.255)[2]

Instead of promoting self-satisfaction, by which I do not mean smugness but the conviction that one is and has enough, Paulus's poem embraces insatiate desire as an ineradicable characteristic of human life.[3] There is no thought in this poem of eliminating desire by retreating to a circle drawn tightly around oneself, as Zeus does every ten thousand years in order to protect his monological communion, an oxymoron neither Epictetus nor centuries of theistic, metaphysical Christian theologians seem to have thought through. Rather, the lovers' impossible wish *to plunge into one another's hearts*, which the poet narrates and does not condemn, inflames their desire all the more.

This essay explores the poetics inspiring Paulus Silentiarius and the philosophy standing behind Epictetus. My hunch is that we might divide the New Testament between those writings that, on the one hand, emulated the philosophic approach to desire exemplified by Epictetus's picture of Zeus's self-satisfaction and, on the other, those that would have been intrigued with the glimpses Paulus provides of the lovers' vain experiments

---

2. All translations of *Anthologia Graeca* are from W. R. Paton, trans., *The Greek Anthology*, 5 vols., LCL (Cambridge: Harvard University Press, 1916–1918).

3. See also Aeschylus, *Ag.* 1331; Euripides, *Iph. taur.* 414–15; Anth. Gr. 5.275; 12.145; Musaeus, *Her. Leand.* 284; Apollonius of Rhodes, *Argon.* 460–61.

to satisfy their longing.[4] To ask each New Testament writing "What do you think of insatiable desire?" is, of course, too large a project to undertake here, but it is manageable to put the question to the pseudonymous Peter of 1 Pet 3:6-7 and Paul in 1 Cor 13:12. My scaled-down hunch is that Paul sides with the poetic evaluation of desire while the first letter written under Peter's name echoes the philosophic attitude toward desire.[5]

I have another purpose in following up on this hunch about the contrasting evaluations of desire in the New Testament. My impression is that the history of New Testament interpretation has been far more influenced by Epictetus's vision of Zeus's self-communion in protective isolation from desire than Paulus's story of two lovers never quite reaching the beloved other, yet always wanting to, desperately. So if Epictetus's enthusiasm for the aloneness of god recalls to the reader's mind the Christian doctrine of divine *apatheia* and the correlate motto adopted by the saved—*blessed assurance*—then what I have been writing between the lines so far will not have gone unnoticed. I intend to call attention to Epictetus's philosophic construction of the self as monitor, even disciplinarian, of the body it inhabits and to suggest another way to think about persons, not condemning them to projects of self-perfection imaging Zeus's/God's at-oneness with Himself but freeing them for a *desire beyond desire*, a phrase borrowed from Jacques Derrida that Paulus Silentiarius would, I think, have been proud to invent.[6]

---

4. Note the poet is looking at lovers looking at one another. This is itself reminiscent of Sappho, *Fr.* 31. For this peculiarity and other fascinating aspects of Sappho's poetry, see Anne Carson, *Eros the Bittersweet: An Essay* (Princeton: Princeton University Press, 1986). A similar shift in perspective from observer to participant occurs at the end of Paulus's poem.

5. My playing the real Paul off against the pseudonymous Peter runs the risk of oversimplifying a complex situation, but with this admission I am not suggesting that the author of 1 Peter ever located his theology within the emotion of desire as I believe Paul did. While Rom 1:24-27 shows that Paul was capable of repeating philosophy's aversion to desire, yet in this instance he does so for a specific, rhetorical purpose not in line with the general direction of his thinking. See David E. Fredrickson, "Natural and Unnatural Use in Romans 1:24-27: Paul and the Philosophic Critique of Eros," in *Homosexuality, Science, and the "Plain Sense" of Scripture*, ed. David L. Balch (Grand Rapids: Eerdmans, 2000), 197-222.

6. For citation of Derrida's phrase, see John D. Caputo, *The Insistence of God: A Theology of Perhaps* (Bloomington: Indiana University Press, 2013), 5 n. 15.

Proud because the two lovers do not seem to know what they desire, only that they really desire it, whatever it is, and their nonknowing persistence playing itself out to a *dis*satisfactory ending is what makes the poem, to my way of thinking, so riveting. John D. Caputo, whom I will engage throughout this essay, explains the idea of what he and Derrida call an *event*, the incoming of an unimagined and unimaginable future that, if it ever came to pass, would not be an *event*. Derrida's *desire beyond desire* is crucial for Caputo's project of rethinking religion and the question I want to put to the New Testament texts. Caputo writes,

> I am distinguishing two orders of desire. In the first place, I mark a straightforward or first-order desire, which is conscious and present to itself, which desires something identifiably itself, whether in "terrestrial" goods, like money or prestige, or even in "celestial" ones, like "heaven" or "eternal salvation." This desire has proper names with which it can name its desire and so up to a point can know what it desires and desire what it knows. I distinguish such a desire from a "desire beyond desire," the mark of which is that it lacks any proper names, that it does not know what it desires, or who is desiring or how, that it desires something *je ne sais quoi*, something going on *in* what I desire. That is the trouble. The reason that I do not know what I desire is that there is always something *coming* in what I desire, always a radical exposure to the future, something *promised* that is disturbing my present desire.[7]

I hope in this essay to bother Zeus's *peace with himself* with the two lovers' *could not be satisfied*, a phrase I interpret as an instance of Derrida's/Caputo's *desire beyond desire*, and to make a small start at what might turn into a very big project: to read the New Testament with a keen eye on what its individual writings convey about insatiable desire.

1. The Poetics of Desire

Of what possible use, it might be asked, could a sixth-century CE poem be for interpreting first-century documents like the New Testament? None, of course, if it were my intention to prove literary dependence of the New Testament, or parts of it, on Paulus Silentiarius. But that is not why Paulus plays such an important role in this essay. It is rather the case that his poem is a remarkable collection of amatory motifs, a kind of primer on

---

7. Ibid., 83–84.

the ancient poetics of love. It teaches modern readers the ways insatiable desire was inscribed beginning with Sappho in the seventh century BCE, later by Latin poets and Greek novelists, and by a few Christian writers well into the Middle Ages. The point of reading this poem with its literary ancestry in mind is to prepare ourselves to appreciate how Paul and his first readers might have written/read his letters, to witness how the irrepressible force of desire shook Paul and how the first letter written in Peter's name betrayed the trembling heart of Paul's theological vision, which, unlike the self-imposed blindness of Epictetus's Zeus, did not look away from the other to tranquilize the self.

The English translation of the first words of this poem unfortunately blunts the force of the surprising scene the poem begins to describe. "I saw the lovers" (εἶδον ἐγὼ ποθέοντες) might better be translated "I saw the longing ones." Worse poetry to be sure, but a sacrifice worth making for the moment, since the rest of the poem hinges on a distinction observed by many ancient writers, both poets and philosophers, between lovers' feelings of ἔρος and πόθος. Love when the beloved is present is ἔρος; love when the beloved is absent is πόθος (see Plato, *Crat.* 420a; Plutarch, *Amat.* 759b). Hence the paradox of this poem: the more the lovers enter each other's presence the more they experience an absence inflaming their desire. Since elements of grief, mourning, and sadness inhere in πόθος, this poem begins by provocatively locating the cause of insatiability in the very thing normally supposed to be its cure, the presence of the beloved.[8]

Neither does a kiss cure the longing of desire, not even a long kiss. This would not have surprised the lovers had they first studied the literary motifs from which the poet composed their kissing. Kissing is a great thing: "There is nothing more terribly potent than this at kindling the fires of passion. For it is insatiable and holds out seductive [sweet] hopes [ἄπληστον καὶ ἐλπίδας τινὰς γλυκείας]" (Xenophon, *Symp.* 4.25.4).[9] But those hopes need not be

---

8. This is a theme running throughout Achilles Tatius, *Leuc. Clit.* See, for example, 2.36: "'You know not, Clitophon,' said Menelaus, 'the sum of all pleasure: the unsatisfied is the most desirable of all [ποθεινὸν γὰρ ἀεὶ τὸ ἀκόρεστον]. The longer a thing lasts, the more likely is it to cloy by satiety; that which is constantly being ravished away from us is ever new and always at its prime—delight cannot grow old and the shorter its time the greater is its intensity.'" All translations of *Leucippe and Clitophon* from Achilles Tatius, *Leucippe and Clitophon*, trans. S. Gaselee, LCL 45 (Cambridge: Harvard University Press, 1969).

9. Xenophon, *Memorabilia; Oeconomicus; Symposium; Apology*, trans. E. C. Merchant and O. J. Todd, LCL 168 (Cambridge: Harvard University Press, 1979).

carnal, we discover, as Paulus's poem progresses or as the young hero of Achilles Tatius's novel *Leucippe et Clitophon* testifies:

> "What," I [Clitophon] said, "can be sweeter than her [Leucippe's] kiss? Love's full enjoyment comes to an end and one is soon sated with it [ὅρον ἔχει καὶ κόρον]—it is nothing, if you take away the kisses from it; the kiss does not come to an end, never brings satiety, and is always fresh [ἀόριστον ἐστι καὶ ἀκόρεστον καὶ καινὸν ἀεί]. Three very charming things come from the mouth; the breath, the voice, and the kiss; we kiss those whom we love with the lips, but the spring of the pleasure comes from the soul." (*Leuc. Clit.* 4.8)

Kissing, which induces the soul to perch on each lover's lips, leads naturally to the next motif, an impossible wish *to plunge into one another's hearts*.[10] In a poem by Bion of Smyrna, Aphrodite holds in her arms the mortally wounded Adonis, desiring to welcome him into her heart with an impossible hospitality: "Stay, Adonis, stay, ill-fated Adonis, so that I may possess you for the last time, so that I can embrace you and mingle lips with lips. Rouse yourself a little, Adonis, and kiss me for a final time; kiss me as much as your kiss has life, until you breathe your last into my mouth, and your spirit flows into my heart, and I drain your sweet love" (*Epitaph. Adon.* 42–49).[11]

The *compulsion* (ἀνάγκη) pressed upon Paulus's lovers is quite inexplicable. Why they should wish to plunge into each other's heart is an *inexpressible* (ἀμφασίης) secret known to no one, not even to themselves.[12] The motif of Eros rendering its victims speechless in this way, secretly burning deep within, goes back to Sappho's famous and frequently imitated description of the physical effects of falling in love.[13] Since this

---

10. Kissing leads to an impossible wish in this brief epigram attributed to Plato: "When I kissed Agathon, I held my soul at my lips. Poor soul! She came hoping to cross over to him" (*Anth. Gr.* 5.78).

11. Neil Hopkinson, ed. and trans., *Theocritus; Moschus; Bion*, LCL 28 (Cambridge: Harvard University Press, 2015). See also *Anth. Gr.* 12.65; Achilles Tatius, *Leuc. Clit.* 1.9.4–5.

12. Not unlike the secret carried by Abraham in Derrida's interpretation of the sacrifice of Isaac. See Jacques Derrida, *The Gift of Death*, trans. David Wills, 2nd ed. (Chicago: University of Chicago Press, 2008), 54–81.

13. For just two examples, see Catullus 51 and in the tenth century the allusion of Theodoros Kyzikos to Sappho's trembling and her turning green in his *Ep.* 7.

description plays an important role in the rest of this essay (as it has in the ancient history of erotic verse), I cite the fragment:

> He seems as fortunate as the gods to me, the man who sits opposite [ἐνάντιός] you and listens nearby to your sweet voice and lovely laughter. Truly that sets my heart trembling [ἐπτόαισεν] in my breast. For when I look at you for a moment, then it is no longer possible for me to speak; my tongue has snapped, at once a subtle fire has stolen beneath my flesh, I see nothing with my eyes, my ears hum, sweat pours from me, a trembling seizes me all over, I am greener than grass, and it seems to me that I am little short of dying. (Sappho, *Fr.* 31.)[14]

Four centuries later in the *Argonautica* of Apollonius of Rhodes, the snapped tongue of Sappho becomes Medea's *speechless amazement* (ἀμφασίη, the same word Paulus Silentiarius will use for his lovers' silence), when Eros shoots her with an arrow and she falls in love with Jason. Apollonius's depiction of the event imitates Sappho's fragment, and since the former like the latter plays an important role in this essay, I cite the relevant passage:

> He [Eros] crouched down small at the feet of Jason himself, placed the arrow's notches in the center of the bowstring, pulled it straight apart with both hands, and shot at Medea; and speechless amazement [ἀμφασίη] seized her heart. He darted back out of the high-roofed hall, laughing out loud, and the arrow burned deep down in the girl's heart like a flame. She continually cast bright glances straight [ἀντία] at Jason, and wise thoughts fluttered from her breast in her distress. She could remember nothing else, for her heart was flooding with sweet pain. And as when a woman piles twigs around a flaming brand, a working woman whose task is wool-spinning, so as to furnish light under her roof at night as she sits close by, and the flame rises prodigiously from the small brand and consumes all the twigs together—such was the destructive love that curled beneath her heart and burned in secret. And her tender cheeks turned now pale, now red, in the distraction of her mind. (*Argon.* 3.284)[15]

---

14. David A. Campbell, ed. and trans., *Greek Lyric: Sappho; Alcaeus*, LCL 142 (Cambridge: Harvard University Press, 1982).

15. Apollonius Rhodius, *Argonautica*, ed. and trans. William H. Race, LCL 1 (Cambridge: Harvard University Press, 2009).

The literary ancestry of Paulus's two lovers' dissatisfaction is becoming clearer.

Then comes a bold move. The lovers' insatiable desire to come near one another impels them to experiment, to see if their intercourse might pass through the exchange of gender markers. We see them *interchanging their soft clothing*. What were they thinking? What relief from their *inexpressible compulsion* could possibly come from cross-dressing? One explanation might be that draping the other's clothing around oneself is like holding a memento or gazing at the image of an absent beloved's face.[16] It is more likely, however, that in Paulus's poem the exchange of clothing alludes to a traditional wedding ritual in which bride and groom disrupt ordinary life and begin a transition.[17] In anthropological terms, the bride and groom cross-dress to mark their experience of liminality, a time without measure in which the usual flow of life and its rule-bound organization, including male/female categories, no longer apply.[18]

Yet their experiment deconstructing the boundaries of gender failed to rid them of desire. (And it is intriguing that the poet does not tell us they returned to their original dress!) They go back to kissing, even though they now know it has no effect on their desire other than to increase "the inappeasable hunger of love madness [that] still devoured them" (γυιοβόρον γὰρ εἶχον ἀλωφήτου λιμὸν ἐρωμανίης [Anth. Gr. 5.255]). Hesiod's misogynistic account of the creation of the first woman introduced the theme of limb-devouring (γυιοβόρος) love to erotic poetry's thesaurus of *painful desire's* (πόθον ἀργαλέον, also Hesiod's language) effects on the human body (*Op.* 66.).[19] The poets' resolve to live with insatiable desire, with all its limb-devouring, shaking, grieving, inexpressible, and liminal consequences, is

---

16. This is the explanation given for clothing exchange in Achilles Tatius, *Leuc. Clit.* 6.1, but it does not explain the playful cross-dressing in Longus, *Daphn.* 1.24.1–2.

17. Monica Silveira Cyrino, "Heroes in D(u)ress: Transvestism and Power in the Myths of Herakles and Achilles," *Arethusa* 31 (1998): 207–41; P. J. Heslin, *The Transvestite Achilles: Gender and Genre in Statius' Achilleid* (Cambridge: Cambridge University Press 2009), 237–76.

18. For the concept of liminality, see Arnold van Gennep, *The Rites of Passage*, trans. Monika B. Vizedom and Gabrielle L. Caffee (Chicago: University of Chicago Press, 1960).

19. See also Anth. Gr. 5.264. For similar expressions of Eros consuming the flesh of the lover, see Sappho, *Fr.* 96.15–17; Theocritus, *Id.* 30.21; Musaeus, *Her. Leand.* 87. For *love madness*, see Catullus 15.14; Theocritus, *Id.* 2.48–51; 11.11; 13.72; Anth. Gr. 5.266; 12.31.

summed up in the concluding words of the poem, which conclude nothing but cause the reader to wonder about other events of longing: "But *we* must burn separately" (Anth. Gr. 5.255). The poem's final word, "separately," in the English word order (it holds the penultimate position in Greek), takes us back to the theme of longing at the poem's outset. Longing is desire plus absence, and the sum is perpetual dissatisfaction. Thus, in this poem insatiable desire begins, ends, and begins again, pressing and probing throughout a simple question: What happens when strategies to satisfy desire fail?

Yet the poetic narrative is also infinitely diverse, since the "we" of "we must burn" changes its reference each time we read the poem. *We* readers are always free to invent our own doomed-to-fail strategies along with the poet, the poet's distant beloved, and the two lovers burning for one another before our eyes. The final word (in Greek word order) is "burn" (καιόμεθα), a fitting ending to a poem about insatiable desire, since heat, the melting of flesh, and the emptying of the liquefied self are all expressions of a single trope: love is a fire that liquefies lovers' innards as Sappho and Medea and hosts of other victims of love experienced.[20] Or as Meleager put it, "Love is an admirable cook of the soul" (Anth. Gr. 12.92).

One last observation about Paulus's poem before we first ask the philosophers and then Peter and Paul: *What do you think of insatiable desire?* Paulus includes a detail about the lovers' posture that could easily be missed as we read about the impossibility of separating the two lovers who still long for one another despite their proximity and whose limbs are "intertwined stems of a twisted vine that have long merged their tendrils" (Anth. Gr. 5.255).[21] This is the detail: they sit facing one another with "opposed [ἀντιπόροισι] arms." Prior to Paulus there was a long history of lovers gazing at each other face-to-face. An early example occurs at the beginning of Sappho's description in *Fr.* 31 quoted above: "He seems as fortunate as the gods to me, the man who sits opposite [ἐναντίος] you and

---

20. In another of Paulus' poems we read: "But if burning love is melting you, I hope you are melting for me" (Anth. Gr. 259). For the connection of fire, melting, and emptying, see David E. Fredrickson, *Eros and the Christ: Longing and Envy in Paul's Christology*, Paul in Critical Contexts (Minneapolis: Fortress Press, 2013), 45–65. For examples of what was perhaps the most frequently employed erotic motif in ancient literature, see Anth. Gr. 5.279, 281, 288, 290, 303; 12.22, 49, 81, 83, 99.

21. For this motif, see Ovid, *Am.* 2.16.41–42 and J. C. B. Petropoulos, *Eroticism in Ancient and Medieval Greek Poetry* (London: Duckworth, 2003), 32–36, 61–73.

listens nearby to your sweet voice and lovely laughter" (see also *Fr.* 23). Or note Apollonius's use of ἀντία in imitation of Sappho: Medea "continually cast bright glances straight at Jason" (ἀντία δ' αἰεὶ βάλλεν ἐπ' Αἰσονίδην ἀμαρύγματα [*Argon.* 3.284]).[22] Later in the story Medea and Jason meet again and face each other:

> So did Jason come to her, beautiful to behold, but by appearing he aroused lovesick distress. Then her heart dropped out of her breast, her eyes darkened with mist of their own accord, and a hot blush seized hold of her cheeks. She had no strength to raise her knees and go backwards or forwards, but her feet were stuck fast beneath her.... The two stood facing each other in speechless silence, like oaks or lofty pines that stand rooted quietly side by side in the mountains when there is no wind, but then, when shaken by a gust of wind, they rustle ceaselessly—thus were these two about to speak a great deal under the force of Love's breezes. (*Argon.* 3.960–972)

The lovers indicate by their posture not the end of desire but desire's renewal.

Two more points about this posture should be underscored. First, desire in ancient poetry was seldom described in terms of mutuality and reciprocity implied by the two lovers facing each other. Desire in the ancient imagination was mostly a one-sided affair. Greek vases, for example, frequently show a young man or a god in pursuit of a young woman.[23] The motif of pursuit, which implies that the groom is a hunter and the bride a wild animal requiring capture and domestication, pervaded ancient poetry as well.[24] So it must be emphasized that Sappho's one little word "opposite" (ἐνάντιός) stood up to the violence of male pursuit of females and opened relationships up, at least in dreams inspired by Sappho's poetry, to the kind of mutual hospitality we have seen in Paulus's poem.[25]

---

22. See also Apollonius of Rhodes, *Argon.* 1009–1010; 1065–1067; Musaeus, *Her. Leand.* 100–107; Chariton, *Chaer.* 1.1.6; Ovid, *Her.* 16.103–104.

23. See John H. Oakley, "Nuptial Nuances: Wedding Images in Non-wedding Scenes of Myth," in *Pandora: Women in Classical Greece*, ed. Ellen D. Reeder and Sally C. Humphreys (Baltimore: Walters Art Gallery, 1995), 63–73.

24. See Claude Calame, *The Poetics of Eros in Ancient Greece*, trans. Janet Lloyd (Princeton: Princeton University Press, 1999), 23–24.

25. See Ellen Greene, "Subjects, Objects, and Erotic Symmetry in Sappho's Fragments," in *Among Women: From the Homosocial to the Homoerotic in the Ancient World*, ed. Nancy Sorkin Rabinowitz and Lisa Auanger (Austin: University of Texas Press, 2002), 82–105.

The second point is simply this: the face-to-face motif points to insatiable desire and infinitely deferred knowledge. It did not refer to perfect knowledge and the end of desire, as the vast majority of Paul's interpreters read into the πρόσωπον πρὸς πρόσωπον posture in 1 Cor 13:12. As we have seen, poetic examples suggest that to know someone *face-to-face* is not yet to know them as one desires (see Anth. Gr. 12.21). Otherwise, for Sappho there would have been no need for listening "nearby to your sweet voice and lovely laughter." What makes a voice sweet and laughter lovely if not faith in the promise of surprise and the desire for something inexplicable? Or, if *face-to-face* signified perfect knowledge, there would have been no occasion for Sappho's heart to be set to "trembling/fluttering" (ἐπτόαισεν).[26] For the ancient love poets, perfect knowledge of the other was as boring a thought as a self-satisfied Zeus.

2. Philosophers against Fluttering

Of course, the philosophers would not have agreed that boredom is such a bad thing if the alternative is uncontrolled fluctuation within the soul. Plato especially had it out for Sappho's fluttering, and he paired it with the madness of the body (*Resp.* 404a; cf. *Symp.* 206d; *Phaed.* 108b). Possibly alluding to her *Fr.* 31, Plato has Socrates lay out the fundamental difference between rational and desiderative parts of the soul, and fluttering goes to the heart of the distinction:

> We claim that they are two separate forces, differing from each other, on the one hand in calling that part of the soul which does the calculating the reasoning faculty, and on the other where desires such as love, hunger, and thirst are found and which is aroused over [ἐπτόηται] other passions too, the irrational and appetitive, related to certain gratifications and pleasures. (*Resp.* 439d; cf. *Leg.* 783d; Dio Chrysostom, *1 Glor.* 1)[27]

Plato expressed an opposition between self-control and fluttering that philosophers from the various schools would later promote. This opposition ultimately made its way into the New Testament as we will

---

26. For more instances of fluttering, see Euripides, *Iph. aul.* 586; Callimachus, *Hymn. Dian.* 191; Apollonius of Rhodes, *Argon.* 1.1232.

27. Plato, *Republic: Books 1–5*, ed. and trans. Christopher Emlyn-Jones and William Preddy, LCL 237 (Cambridge: Harvard University Press, 2013).

see below. Plato has Socrates say, "Self-restraint [σωφροσύνη]—that which is commonly called self-restraint, which consists in not being excited [μὴ ἐπτοῆσθαι] by the passions and in being superior to them and acting in a seemly way—is not that characteristic of those alone who despise the body and pass their lives in philosophy?" (*Phaed.* 68c).[28] Although moving away from the Platonic division of the soul into rational and irrational/appetitive parts, the Stoics continued Plato's war on fluttering. Their founder Zeno incorporated fluttering into the definition of emotion itself: "Pathos is a fluttering of the soul" (πάθος ἐστὶ πτοία ψυχῆς [*SVF* 1.51.2; cf. 3.92.13–14; Stobaeus, *Flor.* 2.7.10]). It is difficult to overestimate the importance of Zeno's definition since for the Stoics *pathos* is the overarching term governing the four major passions (fear, desire, grief, and pleasure) and dozens of variations on this quartet. Fluttering therefore inhabits every emotion (Stobaeus, *Flor.* 2.7.10).

The fluttering brought on by insatiable desire, it was thought, plagued women far more than men. Women fail to limit the number of their friends (Plutarch, *Amic. mult.* 93c). They speak endlessly (Plutarch, *Garr.* 504d). Mourning females are insatiable in grief, never knowing when to stop keening the death of husbands and children (Aeschylus, *Pers.* 545; Euripides, *Suppl.* 79; Plutarch, *Cons. ux.* 609b). Women find no satisfaction in modest clothing, a common complaint about women and their insatiability in later New Testament writings (e.g., 1 Tim 2:9–10; 1 Pet 3:2–5).[29] Taking aim to dampen the alleged natural disposition of females to passion, philosophers taught that the virtue to which women should most aspire was self-control as the pseudonymous Neo-Pythagorean writer Perictione states: "It is necessary that a woman should sufficiently possess a harmony full of prudence and temperance. For it is requisite that her soul should be vehemently inclined to the acquisition of virtue; so that she may be just, brave, and prudent, and may be adorned with frugality [αὐταρκείη] and hate vainglory" (Perictione, *Fr.* 142 apud Stobaeus, *Flor.* 4.28.19).[30] Note that the ideals of αὐταρκεία (more accurately translated

---

28. Plato, *Euthyphro; Apology; Crito; Phaedo; Phaedrus*, trans. Harold North Fowler, LCL 36 (Cambridge: Harvard University Press, 1914).

29. See also Annette Bourland Huizenga, *Moral Education for Women in the Pastoral and Pythagorean Letters: Philosophers of the Household*, NovTSup 147 (Leiden: Brill, 2013); Galen, *Aff. dig.* 5.46.

30. Thomas Taylor, trans., *Political Fragments of Archytas, Charondas, Zaleucus and Other Ancient Pythagoreans* (Chiswick: Whittingham, 1822), 57–58.

"self-sufficiency") and the eradication of empty expectation or vainglory make the self-disciplined woman resemble Epictetus's Zeus. Self-control will lead her into tranquility and protect her from perturbation.

Not only did philosophers construct gender along the axis of self-discipline (male) and insatiability (female), but they employed the same extremes to conceptualize sexual desire (see Aristotle, [*Probl.*] 879b; Philo, *Leg.* 2.38; *Agr.* 34; *Legat.* 14). Unlike the modern system of sexuality that classifies desire with the prefixes "hetero" or "homo," the ancient concept of *the things pertaining to Aphrodite*—sex in other words—focused on the amount of desire present in the subject's soul.[31] Musonius Rufus connects luxury to insatiability and the fluctuation between desire for male and female sexual objects:

> Not the least significant part of the life of luxury and self-indulgence lies also in sexual excess; for example those who lead such a life crave a variety of loves not only lawful but unlawful ones as well, not women alone but also men; sometimes they pursue one love and sometimes another, and not being satisfied with those which are available pursue those which are rare and inaccessible, and invent shameful intimacies, all of which constitute a grave indictment of manhood. (*Diss.* 12)[32]

Dio Chrysostom echoes Musonius's view:

> The second man and the attendant spirit of that man is the one which proclaims the orgies of Pleasure and admires and honours this goddess, a truly feminine being. He is of many hues and shapes, insatiable [ἀπλήρωτος] as to things that tickle nostril and palate, and further, methinks, as to all that pleases the eye, and all that affords any pleasure to the ear.... He is passionately devoted [ἐπτοημένος] to all these things, but especially and most unrestrainedly to the poignant and burning madness of sexual indulgence, through intercourse both with females and

---

31. Dale B. Martin observes that the issue in Rom 1:24–27 is not "*disoriented* desire" but "*inordinate* desire" (*Sex and the Single Savior: Gender and Sexuality in Biblical Interpretation* [Louisville: Westminster John Knox, 2006], 57). For the inflamed appetite of Rom 1:27 as a reference to insatiable desire, see Fredrickson, "Natural and Unnatural Use," 210–15. For the formation of the concept of *sexuality* in the nineteenth century, see Arnold I. Davidson, *The Emergence of Sexuality: Historical Epistemology and the Formation of Concepts* (Cambridge: Harvard University Press, 2001).

32. Cora E. Lutz, trans., *Musonius Rufus: The Roman Socrates*, YCS 10 (New Haven: Yale University Press, 1947), 87. See also Julian, *Mis.* 347.

with males, and through still other unspeakable and nameless; after all such indiscriminately he rushes and also leads others, abjuring no form of lust and leaving none untried. (4 *Regn.* 101)³³

Note how Dio equates women, insatiable desire, fluttering (here inexplicably translated "devoted"), lack of self-restraint, and burning madness. They all lead to what some scholars today anachronistically call *homosexuality* or *homosexual behavior*, but in first-century terms would have been viewed as acts of excessive desire.

3. Fluttering in 1 Peter 3:6–7

Some New Testament writers appropriated ancient philosophy's critique of desire.³⁴ One text crucial for understanding this critique in relation to the binary construction of gender in early Christianity is 1 Pet 3:6–7: "It was in this way long ago that the holy women who hoped in God used to adorn themselves by accepting the authority of their husbands. Thus Sarah obeyed Abraham and called him lord. You have become her daughters as long as you do what is good and never let fears alarm you" (NRSV). The philosophic assumption that women's insatiate desire manifests itself in showy clothing is clear. But rendering the last words of 3:7 "never let fears alarm you" obscures the close connection to philosophy's aversion to fluttering. The Greek wording runs: μὴ φοβούμεναι μηδεμίαν πτόησιν. The wife is encouraged not to fear "fluttering," or "perturbation," as Wycliffe's Bible puts it. Might the author of 1 Peter be telling the wife not to be concerned about the onslaught of insatiate desire, since the male author of this letter knows all about the problem and knows that fluttering is put to rest by the wife's subordination to her husband? I think so. It seems that the author has familiarized himself with the philosophers' opinions on the essential difference between males (representing self-control) and females (representing insatiable desire). Furthermore, he knows the philosophic principles of household management and self-discipline and a theory of the emotions tying all these doctrines together.³⁵

---

33. Dio Chrysostom, *Discourses 1–11*, trans. J. W. Cohoon, LCL 257 (Cambridge: Harvard University Press, 1932). Cf. Anacharis, *Ep.* 4; Timaeus, *Fr.* 222; and especially Dio Chrysostom, *Ven.* 149.

34. See, e.g., Tit 3:3–7; Heb 4:1–11; 2 Pet 1:3–11.

35. For the identification of masculinity with self-control, see Eph 4:13–14. Note

Thus, he is well positioned to advise her.³⁶ She need not be concerned about fluttering because her husband knows how to live together with her according to knowledge (συνοικοῦντες κατὰ γνῶσιν). In other words, he knows how to quench the tumult of her desire with the orderliness of male rule over her, which in connection with master ruling slave and father ruling children constitutes the system of household management (see 1 Pet 2:1–3:7; cf. Eph 5:21–6:9; Col 3:18–4:1).

There is another reference to insatiable desire in 1 Pet 3:7: "Husbands, in the same way, show consideration for your wives in your life together, paying honor to the woman as the weaker vessel [ἀσθενέστερῳ σκεύει]" (NRSV, modified). Aristotle helps us see that the weakness mentioned here is the inability to control desire, a trait the philosopher believed to be present more in females than in males: "But we are surprised when a man is overcome by pleasures and pains which most men are able to withstand, except when his failure to resist is due to some innate tendency, or to disease: instances of the former being the hereditary effeminacy of the royal family of Scythia, and the inferior endurance of the female sex as compared with the male" (*Eth. nic.* 7.7.12–17 [1150b]).³⁷ First Peter's phrase "weaker vessel" doubles down on the insatiability theme, since "vessel" might allude to the popular *leaky jar* motif, as in Plato's famous comparison of the licentious orderly person:

> Consider if each of the two lives, the temperate and the licentious, might be described by imagining that each of two men had a number of jars, and those of one man were sound and full…: well, one man, when he has

---

here the striking phrase ἀνήρ τέλειος ("perfect male," mistranslated by the NRSV as "maturity"; see also 1 Cor 7:37; Heb 2:10; 5:9, 14; 6:1; 7:28; Jas 3:2) where masculine self-control is the opposite of instability. The ἀνήρ τέλειος was a technical term among the philosophers, and it clearly betrays their sexist bias; see *SVF* 3.147.5–8; Plutarch, *Stoic. rep.* 1047a; Arius Didymus, *Lib. phil. sect.* 78.1; Dio Chrysostom, *Virt.* (*Or.* 8) 16; Charondas, *Fr.* 60; Galen, *Aff. dig.* 5.14. In changing circumstances, the soul of the perfect male remains stable (see Eph 4:14). Furthermore, his own eradication of *pathos* made him a model for others' moral improvement if not perfection (Philo, *Spec.* 4.140; Galen, *Aff. dig.* 5.34–36, 55; Plutarch, *Virt. prof.* 84d–e).

36. For the philosophic treatises that transmitted the knowledge of how to manage the household (and this includes the sexual relations of husband and wife), see David L. Balch, *Let Wives Be Submissive: The Domestic Code in I Peter*, SBLMS 26 (Chico, CA: Scholars Press, 1981).

37. Aristotle, *Nicomachean Ethics*, trans. H. Rackham, LCL 73 (Cambridge: Harvard University Press, 1926).

taken his fill, neither draws off any more nor troubles himself a jot, but remains at ease on that score; whilst the other finds, like his fellow, that the sources are possible indeed, though difficult, but his vessels are leaky and decayed. (Plato, *Gorg.* 493d–494a)[38]

The philosophers and the writer of 1 Peter thought that, left to herself, the wife is a weak, leaky vessel. Insatiable desire not only prompts her to wear luxurious clothing but flutters her soul with sexual desire. Her only salvation is to subordinate herself to her husband's knowledge-based control.

3. A Conclusion of Sorts

A conclusion, the satisfying ending offered by an author when enough has been said, turns an essay into a package of knowledge to be rejected or accepted by its readers. In that respect conclusions are more to Zeus's liking than to Paulus's two lovers'. I would rather imitate their spirit of experimentation and pin my hopes for a new way of reading the New Testament on an unusual interpretation of 1 Cor 13:12 that some might find unconvincing. If so, they would be aligned with the vast majority of interpreters who for two millennia have construed the phrase "*face-to-face*" as a reference to full knowledge. They believe that Paul refers to a future time when partial knowledge of God will be replaced with perfect knowledge: "For now we see in a mirror, dimly, but then we will see face to face. Now I know only in part; then I will know fully, even as I have been fully known" (NRSV).[39] A day will come, so Paul supposedly claims, when all questions will be answered, the plan of God fully revealed, and pointless suffering shown to have had a point after all in God's all-encompassing wisdom.

I suggest a very different reading that takes into account the poetic motif of lovers' insatiable desire to cure desire with a *face-to-face* posture

---

38. Plato, *Lysis; Symposium; Gorgias*, trans. W. R. M. Lamb, LCL 166 (Cambridge: Harvard University Press, 1925). Cf. Lucian, *Dial. mort.* 21.4; Plutarch, *Prov. Alex.* frag. 7; Pollux, *Onom.* 6.43.

39. See Harm W. Hollander, "Seeing God 'in a Riddle' or 'Face to Face': An Analysis of 1 Corinthians 13.12," *JSNT* 32 (2010): 395–403. John D. Caputo adopts the traditional interpretation of 1 Cor 13:12 (*The Prayers and Tears of Jacques Derrida: Religion without Religion* [Bloomington: Indiana University Press, 1997], 6, 60). This does not, however, dissuade me from making use of his analysis of the face in Caputo, *Radical Hermeneutics: Repetition, Deconstruction, and the Hermeneutic Project* (Bloomington: Indiana University Press, 1987), 268–78.

that in fact incites *even more desire*. Rather than a perfect knowing of God and God's intentions, Paul imagines a time when knowledge itself passes away (what else could "as for knowledge, it will come to an end" in 13:8 mean?). First Corinthians 13:12, I think, is Paul's protest against patterning human life in terms of Zeus's enjoyment of blessed self-communion as the cosmos burns away. Instead Paul envisioned the cosmos and God facing one another more like the restless, insatiated lovers of Paulus Silentiarius's poem than like the solipsistic, self-satisfied Zeus of Epictetus's imagination.

An objection to my claim that the verse is about infinite deferral of knowledge arises from Paul's own words (in English translation): "Now I know [γινώσκω] only in part [ἐκ μέρους]; then I will know [ἐπιγινώσομαι] fully, even as I have been fully known [ἐπεγνώσθην]." That appears to be damning evidence, but notice that the NRSV fails to distinguish between γινώσκειν (to know) and ἐπιγινώσκειν (to recognize, discern). Recognition is not re-cognition, a simple matter of knowing again. Rather, it has the sense of picking out a friend's face in a crowd and honoring its difference from all other faces. Recognition is the very thing women, slaves, and the poor were not accorded in antiquity. Furthermore, the NRSV inserts *only* and *fully* without textual support, presumably to emphasize the idea of partial knowledge now but complete knowledge later, the idea I am contesting. Finally, to translate ἐκ μέρους as *in part* has scant lexicographic support other than the fact that it has been translated this way since the KJV. In fact, the only example of this meaning LSJ cites is 1 Cor 13:12. It might have meant "from my perspective," which is indeed partial, but what the "*my*" emphasizes in this alternate translation is the Western habit of thought to split reality into knower and that which is known, in other words into subject and object. It is precisely that split reality that insatiable desire dreams of overcoming even as it knows its dream is just that—a dream.

While most interpreters indeed stand against my reading of "face-to-face" in 13:12, one salient exception should be noted. Gregory of Nyssa comments on Moses's desire to see God face-to-face: "And this bold request which goes up the mountains of desire asks this: to enjoy the Beauty not in mirrors and reflections, but face to face.... The munificence of God assented to the fulfillment of his desire, but did not promise any cessation or satiety of the desire" (*Vit. Mos.* 2.232).[40] Gregory goes on to correlate the

---

40. All translations of *De vita Mosis* from *Gregory of Nyssa: The Life of Moses*, trans. Abraham J Malherbe and Everett Ferguson (New York: Paulist, 1978).

infinity of God with a spirituality in which the one who makes progress never comes to an end of desire. "This truly is the vision of God: never to be satisfied in the desire to see him" (2.239). A little later in the text, Gregory puts his theory of eternal progress into the mouth of God: "Whereas Moses, your desire for what is still to come has expanded and you have not reached satisfaction in your progress and whereas you do not see any limit to the Good, but your yearning always looks for more, the place with me is so great that the one running it is never able to cease from progress" (2.242). Gregory reasoned that progress is a matter of *always* not yet seeing or having God, of stretching out but never attaining God's infinity. If Augustine sought God to rest in God, Gregory imagined a desire for God without rest and without end, living in expectation of the unexpected.

So much for love poets and a famous Christian exegete favorable to my cause. I propose one more way, however, to appreciate *face-to-face* as an allusion to insatiable desire. It arises from contemplating what a marvelous and ambiguous combination of truth telling, lying, hiding, and revelation a human face is. Think of the face as a surface for the display of signs. Ancient practitioners of physiognomy believed the face gave clear indications (if one has been trained to read the signs) of the character of the person behind the face.[41] Thoughts, feelings, intentions are all there to be read. Special attention was given to the eyes, often said to be portals of the soul. If these common notions were the only things true about faces, however, then *face-to-face* would certainly not refer to an infinite deferral of knowledge as I am suggesting. Instead, face reading would hold out a possibility of perfectly knowing the other as Christian interpreters, certainly unaware of their dependence on the ancient science of physiognomy, have generally assumed.

But is the reading of another's face really so straightforward? Is the face only the mind's tool for expressing its thoughts? Eyes are indeed portals to the soul as some ancients thought, and then again they are not, as the victims of wounding or captivating glances discover.[42] What is it, then, about faces that frustrates perfect knowledge and fans the flame of

---

41. See Simon Swain, ed., *Seeing the Face, Seeing the Soul: Polemon's Physiognomy from Classical Antiquity to Medieval Islam* (Oxford: Oxford University Press, 2007).

42. For eyes communicating the soul's thoughts and feelings, see Philostratus, *Ep.* 8, 32. For the far more common motif in erotic literature of eyes snaring, burning, capturing, and wounding, see Pindar, *Fr.* 123; Achilles Tatius, *Leuc. Clit.* 1.4.2–4; Musaeus, *Her. Leand.* 90–99; *Anth. Gr.* 12.10; Philostratus, *Ep.* 10; 56; Ovid, *Am.* 11.46–47.

desire? If there is such a thing as reading faces, and there must be or we would have no relationships at all, gazing on another's face is nevertheless far more complicated than a subject's observation of an object—unless you insist that the face looking back freezes its expressions, allowing you to decode them at your leisurely convenience. As your face changes in response to what you read on the other's face, you become a different text soliciting from the other further interpretation, and as she begins to makes sense of your new facial expressions, your responses to her face scramble what she had been reading. So it goes ... never to arrive at perfect knowledge. No wonder Paulus's lovers never stop burning for one another, never put their so-called gender-appropriate clothing back on, and never stop holding each other with opposing arms. No wonder faith, hope, and love, especially love, abide.

Select Bibliography

Calame, Claude. *The Poetics of Eros in Ancient Greece*. Translated by Janet Lloyd. Princeton: Princeton University Press, 1999.

Caputo, John D. *The Insistence of God: A Theology of Perhaps*. Bloomington: Indiana University Press, 2013.

———. *The Prayers and Tears of Jacques Derrida: Religion without Religion*. Bloomington: Indiana University Press, 1997.

———. *Radical Hermeneutics: Repetition, Deconstruction, and the Hermeneutic Project*. Bloomington: Indiana University Press, 1987.

Carson, Anne. *Eros the Bittersweet: An Essay*. Princeton: Princeton University Press, 1986.

Davidson, Arnold I. *The Emergence of Sexuality: Historical Epistemology and the Formation of Concepts*. Cambridge: Harvard University Press, 2001.

Derrida, Jacques. *The Gift of Death; and, Literature in Secret*. Translated by David Wills. 2nd ed. Chicago: University of Chicago Press, 2008.

Fredrickson, David E. *Eros and the Christ: Longing and Envy in Paul's Christology*. Paul in Critical Contexts. Minneapolis: Fortress, 2013.

———. "Natural and Unnatural Use in Romans 1:24–27: Paul and the Philosophic Critique of Eros." Pages 197–222 in *Homosexuality, Science, and the "Plain Sense" of Scripture*. Edited by David L. Balch. Grand Rapids: Eerdmans, 2000.

Heslin, P. J. *The Transvestite Achilles: Gender and Genre in Statius' Achilleid*. Cambridge: Cambridge University Press, 2009.

Huizenga, Annette Bourland. *Moral Education for Women in the Pastoral and Pythagorean Letters: Philosophers of the Household*. NovTSup 147. Leiden: Brill, 2013.

Petropoulos, J. C. B. *Eroticism in Ancient and Medieval Greek Poetry*. London: Duckworth, 2003.

Swain, Simon, ed. *Seeing the Face, Seeing the Soul: Polemon's Physiognomy from Classical Antiquity to Medieval Islam*. Oxford: Oxford University Press, 2007.

The Missing Emotion:
The Absence of Anger and the Promotion of Nonretaliation in 1 Peter

Katherine M. Hockey

This essay investigates the puzzling absence of any explicit reference to anger in 1 Peter, a text that depicts its audience undergoing troubling, unjust persecution and yet maintains throughout a positive emotional tone. However, before delving into this emotional conundrum, it will be helpful to outline this essay's approach to investigating emotions in an ancient text.

1. Methodological Approach[1]

This essay takes a cognitive approach to emotions.[2] By this I mean to position myself alongside those who argue that emotions are not irrational or devoid of logical reasoning; they are not mere feelings. In fact, an emotion is a psychological *process* that contains a strong cognitive component.[3]

---

1. The following methodological approach is derived from my position on emotions elaborated in §1.2–5 of "Seeing Emotionally: An Investigation of the Role of Emotion in the Rhetorical Discourse of 1 Peter" (PhD diss., Durham University, 2016).

2. Since the 1960s, the psychologist Richard Lazarus has been a key proponent of the view that emotions contain cognition; see Richard S. Lazarus, James R. Averill, and Edward M. Opton Jr., "Towards a Cognitive Theory of Emotion," in *Feelings and Emotions: The Loyola Symposium*, ed. Magda Arnold (New York: Academic Press, 1970), 207–32. This has now become a majority position; see Agnes Moors, "Theories of Emotion Causation: A Review," *CE* 23 (2009): 625–62.

3. For various articles on the nature and definition of emotion, see *EmotRev* 4 (2012) and *SSI* 46 (2007): 381–443. For a helpful delineation of the different aspects that make up the process of an emotion, see Moors, "Theories of Emotion Causation," 626; see also Kevin Mulligan and Klaus R. Scherer, "Toward a Working Definition of

Having said this, it must be acknowledged that emotions are complex phenomena on account of being embodied: we are indeed aware of our emotions because we feel them. Yet entwined with the physicality of emotions is the cognitive process that influences it. I mention the physicality of emotions to avoid an overly reductionist approach.[4]

Nevertheless, what has been lost in the modern era of interpretation is not the visceral aspect of emotions but their cognitive/reasoning element. Emotions have been sidelined in interpretation, deemed universal, irrational, bodily, subjective, chaotic, even feminine or childish, and thus of little value to serious exegetical endeavors.[5] However, progress in the field of emotion studies has questioned this outdated perspective. Influenced by psychologists such as Richard Lazarus and Nico Frijda, and philosophers such as Martha Nussbaum and Robert Solomon, this essay understands emotions to be evaluative judgments about the salience of an object[6] to one's personal goals.[7] Fundamentally, this evaluation is an appraisal of the beneficial or detrimental effect of the object (and the object's behavior) to one's flourishing:[8] is the object good or bad for me?

Emotion," *EmotRev* 4 (2012): 346, 352; Richard S. Lazarus, "Progress on a Cognitive-Motivational-Relational Theory of Emotion," *AP* 46 (1991): 822.

4. Of course, the physical aspects of a New Testament author's or audience's emotional experience, unless explicitly stated, cannot be accessed and are therefore difficult to incorporate into exegesis. The result usually reveals more about the interpreter than the text itself.

5. See Catherine A. Lutz, *Unnatural Emotions: Everyday Sentiments on a Micronesian Atoll and Their Challenge to Western Theory* (Chicago: University of Chicago Press, 1988), 53–80. Lutz highlights the often-unspoken, embedded biases toward emotions present in Western Anglo-American approaches; see Robert C. Solomon, *The Passions: Emotions and the Meaning of Life* (Indianapolis: Hackett, 1993), 9–12, for the historical-philosophical opposition of emotion and reason.

6. As "object-directed," emotions are *about something*. See Martha C. Nussbaum, *Upheavals of Thought: The Intelligence of Emotions* (Cambridge: Cambridge University Press, 2001), 27; Solomon, *Passions*, 111–16. Solomon and Nussbaum rightly note that the object is an "intentional object" seen through the subjective lens of the person experiencing the emotion.

7. See Lazarus, "Progress," 819; Nussbaum, *Upheavals of Thought*, 19, 30–31, 52–53; Solomon, *Passions*, xvii, 15, 19–20.

8. Richard S. Lazarus argues that the appraisal of the object happens at the start of an emotion ("Cognition and Motivation in Emotion," *AP* 46 [1991]: 361–64). For a definition of appraisal, see Agnes Moors et al., "Appraisal Theories of Emotion: State of the Art and Future Development," *EmotRev* 5 (2013): 120.

Such an assessment then drives behavior. As such, emotions have associated action tendencies.[9] Thus, we cannot separate emotional life from ethical behavior because emotions motivate one towards a particular end. This evaluative-active aspect of emotions can be analyzed because it has an inherent logic that can be articulated in basic propositions; in other words, emotions contain cognitive content that tell us something about our world and help us to navigate it, including what course to pursue in given situations.[10] These dual evaluative and behavioral aspects help us assess the presence and function of an emotion in an ancient text that seeks to communicate to its audience and shape its behavior.

However, this understanding of emotions raises further questions. Most notably, what is an emotion's evaluation based on? How does this relate to the context in which it arises? These are difficult questions, and we do not have the scope to unpack them fully here. What we can determine is that, in assessing good/bad, beneficial/detrimental elements, emotions interrelate with and rely on a person's value system or worldview.[11] Consequently, because people are socialized into a value system,[12] we can understand that an emotion's occurrence in a particular context is not necessarily innate and universal, but rather depends on one's learned perspective to see things a certain way. Accordingly, the unavoidable *cultural* shape of emotions and emotional experience[13] demands that we resist investigating emotions in an ancient text in an atomized fashion; rather, we must appreciate their thoroughgoing embeddedness within a worldview whose outlook and values may alter an individual's (or a

---

9. See Nico H. Frijda, Peter Juipers, and Elisabeth Schure, "Relations among Emotion, Appraisal, and Emotional Action Readiness," *JPSP* 57 (1989): 212–28 (esp. 213). Frijda in fact goes further and makes the distinct action tendency the defining feature of each emotion; cf. Lazarus, "Progress," 822.

10. For more on the logic of emotions and thus why emotions can be analytically investigated, see Solomon, *Passions*, 193–96.

11. See Nussbaum, *Upheavals of Thought*, 67–79; Lazarus, "Progress," 820–21.

12. See the classic work by Peter L. Berger and Thomas Luckmann, *The Social Construction of Reality: A Treatise in the Sociology of Knowledge* (New York: Doubleday, 1966; repr., New York: Anchor, 1967).

13. See Catherine A. Lutz, who concludes from her anthropological work with the Ifaluk people that "emotion experience ... is more aptly viewed as the outcome of social relations and their corollary worldviews than as universal psychobiological entities" (*Unnatural Emotions*, 209); see also Batja Mesquita, "Emotions are Culturally Situated," *SSI* 46 (2007): 410–15.

group's) emotional life. For example, in the Stoic's perspective (see more below), seeing the world differently profoundly shapes one's own emotional response and consequent ethical behavior.

Furthermore, the interrelationship between emotion and worldview means that we need to understand the *narrative* that makes the occurrence of an emotion appreciable. If we encounter an emotional reaction that seems odd to us, it is usually because the emotional occurrence does not fit the nature of the event or emotion episode as we perceive it from the outside. Yet, if we converse with the person(s) experiencing the emotion and understand their personal goals and interpretive appraisals, the emotion episode becomes more comprehensible to us.[14] When approaching an ancient text in its distant cultural and historical context, we can expect to sense some oddity in its use of emotion terms. However, instead of disregarding the ancient text as unenlightened, we need to engage the text on its own ideological terms and seek to understand why, in this particular setting, an emotion seems apposite to an author. The same principle applies in the face of an oddly *absent* anticipated emotion.

So, since emotions are cultural and contextual, it follows that emotional life, even emotional repertoire (naming distinct emotions), varies between cultures, as anthropologists like Catherine Lutz have argued.[15] It is precarious to evaluate a distinctive group's emotional life from within our own cultural emotional expectations, which typically leads to a dismissive or denigrating appraisal of the other's "strange" emotional life.[16] This tendency also applies at a linguistic level. Catherine Lutz, Anna Wierzbicka, and others have argued that the usage of an emotion term imports an array of cultural data, including value systems, into the scenario where this emotion typically occurs.[17] As Lutz comments:

---

14. On how social paradigms of emotions influence a person's interpretation of her own and others' emotions, see James R. Averill, "The Social Construction of Emotion: With Special Reference to Love," in *The Social Construction of the Person*, ed. Kenneth J. Gergen and Keith E. Davis (New York: Springer, 1985), 89–109.

15. See Lutz, *Unnatural Emotions*. Lutz is influenced by the work of Jean Briggs, Robert Levy, and Michelle Z. Rosaldo. See also Nussbaum, who recognizes the innateness of emotional ability while asserting that different cultures have different "emotional repertoires" (*Upheavals of Thought*, 141).

16. See Lutz's cautionary words (*Unnatural Emotions*, 54).

17. Ibid., 7, 10; Anna Wierzbicka, *Emotions across Languages and Cultures: Diversity and Universals* (Cambridge: Cambridge University Press, 1999), 32, 240; see also Nussbaum, *Upheavals of Thought*, 150–51, 163–64.

The complex meaning of each emotion word is the result of the important role those words play in articulating the full range of a people's cultural values, social relations, and economic circumstances. Talk about emotions is simultaneously talk about society—about power and politics, about kinship and marriage, about normality and deviance.[18]

Thus, it is too simplistic to exchange emotion terms between languages and cultures and assume full mutual understanding of emotion concepts.[19] First, we should seek to understand the emotion—its use and typical scenario—within its own culture. *Then* we can make responsible cultural comparisons. This point is particularly important for us when we approach emotions in an ancient text that arises from a different cultural and linguistic environment. The burden falls on us exegetes to do the hard, critical (including self-critical) cultural and historical work to interpret ancient emotion terms and scenarios. To this end, this essay aims to investigate how anger was defined in its Greco-Roman linguistic and historical contexts before assessing its absence in 1 Peter.

Moreover, when we return to 1 Peter, we will carefully endeavor to understand the emotional outlook of the letter *on its own terms*, even if at points this may grate against our own cultural expectations and preferences. Thus, the ethical assessment of the letter's outlook will be left for a future discussion.

2. Frameworks for Assessing the Absence of Anger in 1 Peter

Emotion[20] terms pervade 1 Peter and appear at significant points of emphasis, climax, and even transition (see 1:3, 8–9, 13, 17; 2:17–18; 3:6, 8, 13–15; 4:7, 12–13). Such terms include fear (φόβος), hope (ἐλπίς), shame (αἰσχύνη), joy (χαρά), distress (λύπη), and love (ἀγάπη). However, there is no explicit reference to anger, either ὀργή or θυμός. This omission is surprising for two reasons: (1) among the emotions, anger commanded great ethical interest, even concern, from ancient philosophers; and (2) due to

---

18. Lutz, *Unnatural Emotions*, 5–6.
19. See Wierzbicka, *Emotions across Languages and Cultures*, 24; Nussbaum, *Upheavals of Thought*, 149.
20. Here I have elected to use the word *emotion* for the ancient concepts of πάθος (and *animi motus/affectus*), knowing that there are anachronistic difficulties, but still finding it the most useful English term. For more discussion, see Hockey, "Seeing Emotionally," §1.2.

the audience's situation, as presented by the letter, one could reasonably expect that the audience would experience anger as an obvious and legitimate emotional reaction. These points require unpacking.

The first reason suggests that two negative corollaries regarding anger's absence in 1 Peter are unsustainable: (1) anger is *not* part of the letter's contemporary cultural emotional repertoire and (2) anger was of little interest to the ancient world. But in fact, available works on emotions from Greco-Roman philosophers and rhetoricians provide abundant material devoted to anger, including the Epicurean Philodemus's *De ira*, the Stoic Seneca's *De ira*, and Plutarch's *De cohibenda ira*.[21] This volume of material suggests that not only was anger a frequent and observable emotion in ancient Greco-Roman society, but, moreover, knowing how to deal with one's anger was a key philosophical and ethical concern. We will return to philosophical views on anger below.

The second reason also needs elaboration. After determining what situations commonly produced the arousal of anger, we can decide whether the situation of 1 Peter's addressees fits this anger scenario.

2.1. Anger's Typical Scenario

Helpfully, a number of philosophers provide a definition of anger.[22] These definitions explore both the nature of anger and give a basic scenario in which anger was thought to arise. In *Rhetoric* Aristotle comments: "Let anger [ὀργή] be defined as a desire, accompanied by [mental and physical] distress, for apparent retaliation because of an apparent slight against a man himself or his own, when such a slight is underserved" (*Rhet.* 2.2.1 [1378a]).[23] Aristotle highlights that anger is typically aroused by an undeserved slight. Subsequently, as David Konstan has noted regarding Aristotle's understanding, anger requires a high level of social reasoning; one has to evaluate not only the other's actions, but also

---

21. Plutarch is considered more Platonic in persuasion.

22. The term is ὀργή in Greek and *ira* in Latin. I have restricted myself to these two terms, which appear to be used for parallel concepts among Greek and Latin philosophers.

23. My translation is influenced by both John Henry Freese and George A. Kennedy; see Aristotle, *The "Art" of Rhetoric*, trans. Freese, LCL 193 (Cambridge: Harvard University Press, 1926; repr., 1959); Aristotle, *On Rhetoric: A Theory of Civic Discourse*, trans. Kennedy, CAS (New York: Oxford University Press, 1991), 124.

the other's intentions.²⁴ The subject has to interpret the situation in such a way that the object is thought to have caused or aims to cause intentional harm.²⁵ Thus, anger is peculiar to social relationships: one must be angry "at some particular individual" (τῶν καθ' ἕκαστόν τινι [*Rhet.* 2.2.2 (1378b), trans. Kennedy]). In Seneca's terms, though "there can be no doubt that anger is aroused by the direct impression of injury," it exists only by the mind's assent (*Ira* 2.1.3).²⁶

Aristotle describes anger as a type of desire (ὄρεξις), which suggests that it is forward looking and drives someone towards a particular end, here retaliation.²⁷ Though anger has a sensation of distress (λύπη), this pain is mixed with pleasure (ἡδονή) due to the hope of revenge (ὀργῇ ἕπεσθαί τινα ἡδονὴν τὴν ἀπὸ τῆς ἐλπίδος τοῦ τιμωρήσασθαι [*Rhet.* 2.2.2 (1378b)]). Revenge, which aims "to restore the opinion of one's worth by an act of reprisal," is one way a person might seek to redress the loss (or personal harm, here felt as personal worth) that she has incurred. Anger is simply the "desire to restore the state of affairs prior to the insult by depreciating the offender in turn."²⁸ (It is worth noting here 1 Peter's comment not to repay "evil for evil or abuse for abuse" [NRSV], that is, equivalent harm for

---

24. David Konstan, *The Emotions of the Ancient Greeks: Studies in Aristotle and Classical Literature* (Toronto: University of Toronto Press, 2006), 43, 45.

25. Thus, as Konstan notes and as discussed above, if anger is an assessment of harm, it depends on values (*Emotions of the Ancient Greeks*, 45–46). But the type of perceived harm (belittlement, spite, or hubris) limits the occasions in which anger arises; accordingly, it occurs at different points to other emotions such as hatred or hostility that also respond to perceived harm. For Philodemus, the perception of *intentionality* is of key importance in arousing anger (*Ir.*, col. 46.28–35, cited in John Procopé, "Epicureans on Anger," in *The Emotions in Hellenistic Philosophy*, ed. Juha Sihvola and Troels Engberg-Pederson, NSyHL 46 [Dordrecht: Kluwer Academic, 1998], 177).

26. Translations of *De ira* from Seneca, *De Providentia; De Constantia; De Ira; De Clementia*, vol. 1 of *Moral Essays*, trans. John W. Basore, LCL 214 (Cambridge: Harvard University Press, 1928).

27. The Stoics also list anger (ὀργή) as a kind of "desire" (ἐπιθυμία); See Stobaeus, *Ecl.* 2.90–91 = *SVF* 3.394–95. The key terminology mirrors Aristotle. See also Andronicus, [*Pass.*] 4 = *SVF* 3.397; Diogenes Laertius, *Vit. phil.* 7.113 = *SVF* 3.396; Margaret R. Graver, *Stoicism and Emotion* (Chicago: University of Chicago Press, 2007), 56. See also Philodemus, *Ir.*, col. 47.18–41, cited in Elizabeth Asmis, "The Necessity of Anger in Philodemus' On Anger," in *Epicurus and the Epicurean Tradition*, ed. Jeffrey Fish and Kirk R. Sanders (Cambridge: Cambridge University Press, 2011), 155–56.

28. Konstan, *Emotions of the Ancient Greeks*, 55.

the felt offence [1 Pet 3:9].) Anger makes one keenly aware of the personal tally sheet.[29] Consequently, for Seneca, anger appears when the impression of injury is followed by two propositions: first, that one ought not to have been wronged, and second, that one ought to avenge (*Ira* 2.1.4). As we will see, however, Seneca does not endorse this perspective, unlike the Peripatetics (following Aristotle) who considered revenge the solution to anger and the route to regaining peace of mind.[30]

Given this understanding of anger's arousal by a perception of harm, what types of behavior are deemed especially harmful? Aristotle primarily stresses *belittling* through contempt, spite, or insult (*Rhet.* 2.2.3 [1378b]). Other philosophers, however, note that for the irascible person, even trivial events and inanimate objects can inspire outburst of rage (Philodemus, *Ir.*, col. 26.4–7).[31] For Philodemus, one's biological susceptibility and innate response to physical pain naturally produce anger.[32] Perhaps insult best suits our current inquiry, since the author of 1 Peter frequently depicts the audience's persecution in terms that suggest verbal reproach (e.g., 2:12; 3:16). Aristotle explains further, "insult [ὕβρις] is doing and speaking in which there is shame to the sufferer" (*Rhet.* 2.2.5 [1378b], trans. Kennedy; cf. 1 Pet 4:14–16).[33] By dishonoring the other, the insulter can harm by making one appear worthless (*Rhet.* 2.2.6 [1378b]). Here, the insulted person has not lost anything physically, but socially and perhaps psychologically. Such harmful dishonor is particularly important in a society where honor is a prized commodity. In this scenario, we can see that interpersonal power dynamics are in play; slander arouses anger because it unduly diminishes one's self-worth.[34] Additionally, a person can be stirred

---

29. For Phildomeus anger considers the losses one has incurred and the punishment one should exact on those who harm (*Ir.*, col. 37.20–39, cited in Asmis, "Necessity of Anger," 161).

30. Voula Tsouna, "Philodemus, Seneca and Plutarch on Anger," in *Epicurus and the Epicurean Tradition*, ed. Jeffrey Fish and Kirk R. Sanders (Cambridge: Cambridge University Press, 2011), 185–86.

31. Tsouna, "Philodemus, Seneca and Plutarch on Anger," 191. Here we see the difference between experiencing the *emotion* of anger, which has a limited time frame and responds to a particular situation, and having a more generalised and diffuse angry *mood*.

32. Asmis, "Necessity of Anger," 160–61.

33. In doing so the insulter thinks that "they themselves become more superior by ill-treating others" (*Rhet.* 2.2.6, trans. Kennedy).

34. This phenomenon is communal as much as individual, as Aristotle's point

to anger if she experiences something unexpected, since the unexpected hurts more (*Rhet.* 2.2.11 [1379a] [Kennedy]). Seneca adds: "What is unexpected we count as undeserved.... And so we are mightily stirred by all that happens contrary to hope and expectation" (*Ira* 2.31.1–2). Having highlighted these two typical scenarios in which anger is aroused—*undeserved slander* and *unexpected harm*—we can turn to 1 Peter.

2.2. First Peter's Audience and Situation

In 1 Peter, the audience is cast as a community experiencing persecution at the hands of a hostile other, variously specified as the master (2:18) or husband (3:1) or simply an unspecified non-Christian other (e.g., 2:12, 15; 3:15–16). Although the source (local or official) and level of persecution remains debatable, it is clear that a range of hostile experiences are represented, from the physical maltreatment of slaves (2:18–19) to the emotional and psychological intimidation of wives (3:6; cf. 3:14).[35] Yet verbal accusation and reproach emerge as particularly prominent aspects of the audience's beleaguered experience (2:12; 3:16). Terms such as καταλαλέω (2:12; 3:16), ὀνειδίζω (4:14), λοιδορία (3:9; cf. 2:23; 3:10), and ἀπειλέω (2:23), all relating to negative verbal actions, occur throughout the letter. Furthermore, the need for believers to "silence" (φιμόω [2:15]) malevolent opponents supports a context of verbal abuse.[36] For the author, this persecution is a direct consequence of the believers' Christian identity (ἐν ὀνόματι Χριστοῦ; ὡς χριστιανός [4:14–16]) and the behavior or "good works" (2:20; 3:6, 14, 16–17; 4:19) that flow from it.[37] Yet, despite

---

about anger's slighting effects reminds us. One's honor (like guilt and shame) can be raised or diminished by association.

35. For in-depth discussion of sources and types of persecution reflected in 1 Peter, see Travis B. Williams, *Persecution in 1 Peter: Differentiating and Contextualizing Early Christian Suffering*, NovTSup 145 (Leiden: Brill, 2012), 4–16, 299–326. The reference in 1 Pet 2:19 to pain (λύπη) can infer mental anguish, but given that the author explicitly mentions being beaten (κολαφιζόμενοι [2:20]), it likely connotes physical violence. That 4:1 specifically speaks of "suffering in the flesh" (ὁ παθὼν σαρκί), though it initially refers to Christ, might infer that physical suffering extends beyond the slaves to the community as a whole. The wives are exhorted not to fear any intimidation (μὴ φοβούμεναι μηδεμίαν πτόησιν [3:6, cf. 3:14]). It is likely that there would be a physical element to this too.

36. Williams, *Persecution in 1 Peter*, 300.

37. Here I side with Williams in seeing good works as referring to "a call to

the resulting persecution, the believers are deemed "righteous" (δικαιοσύνη [3:14]) and urged to continue to act in line with their (literally) "good-in Christ conduct" (τὴν ἀγαθὴν ἐν Χριστῷ ἀναστροφήν [3:16; cf. 4:19]). Thus, for the author of 1 Peter, association with Christ is a positive thing,[38] and suffering—being persecuted on account of it—is necessarily unwarranted and subsequently unjust (εἰ καὶ πάσχοιτε διὰ δικαιοσύνην [3:14; cf. 3:17; 4:16]; λύπας πάσχων ἀδίκως [2:19]). Moreover, the letter suggests that the believers might be surprised (ξενίζω [4:12]) that their Christianity would bring such unjust persecution.

We have just outlined that anger arises when one perceives an unjust and/or unexpected harm by another. Accordingly, it would be perfectly understandable and culturally reasonable to expect the audience of 1 Peter to have an angry response to their persecution. In this scenario, the accusations and reproaches of hostile others—which may have included not only superiors, but also family members, friends, and even fellow slaves[39]—would have shamed the believers, causing them emotional and social harm.[40] Such experiences would probably have felt like tangible losses. Moreover, if we take Philodemus's conception of natural anger that arises in response to physical pain, then, for some, experiences of unwarranted physical violence could naturally arouse anger and a desire to act in various ways to avoid future harm. Nevertheless, we find only hints that the author anticipates his audience to have an angry, vengeful response.

---

undertake distinctively Christian conduct," i.e., the thing that is causing conflict, not a "response" to conflict; see Williams, *Persecution in 1 Peter*, 296, fuller discussion at 258–75. See also Williams, *Good Works in 1 Peter: Negotiating Social Conflict and Christian Identity in the Greco-Roman World*, WUNT 337 (Tübingen: Mohr Siebeck, 2014).

38. See 1 Pet 2:1–10. In fact, to remind the believers of the value of association with Christ seems to be one of the letter's primary thrusts, particularly because it is *this* very thing which is bringing their suffering. At various points the author encourages his audience that, paradoxically, if they suffer for righteousness's sake, they are blessed (3:14; 4:14; cf. 5:10).

39. So, we cannot simply discount the nonappearance of anger by saying that the audience comprises subordinates (wives and slaves) in no social position to exhibit anger. Regardless, exhibiting or acting in anger is not the same as experiencing it.

40. John H. Elliott, *1 Peter: A New Translation with Introduction and Commentary*, AB 37 (New Haven: Yale University Press), 607; Karen H. Jobes, *1 Peter*, BECNT (Grand Rapids: Baker Academic, 2005), 216–17.

For example, he exhorts: "Do not repay evil for evil or abuse for abuse, but on the contrary blessing for to this you were called" (1 Pet 3:9).

The writer thus concurrently dissuades the believers from actions commonly linked with anger and encourages them toward nonretaliation (see 2:22–23; 3:16).[41] Yet while he directly addresses other emotions such as fear and shame and links them to the audience's experience, he does not follow suit with anger. Since we therefore have a patent contextual situation in which anger would be appropriate, yet is *not* addressed, it seems apposite to investigate anger's nonappearance.

A number of reasons might account for this absence of anger in 1 Peter. Perhaps the audience simply was not inclined to anger, though 3:9 cautions against this facile assumption. The author's neglect to mention anger when highlighting themes of self-control and sympathy could indicate a tacit disapproval of anger. Or maybe a subjugated audience blithely accepted its position in a spirit of resignation rather than indignation. But, as noted above, we cannot assume that all the hostility the audience is experiencing comes from lordly authorities. Finally, and this to me seems most likely, the larger outlook of the letter interprets the audience's situation in such a way that it naturally reduces the appropriateness of anger. As such, the author might not need to address anger directly but can disarm anger by working at a more foundational level. This may be an astute maneuver, since experience tells us that warning an angry person that they should not be angry rarely leads to peace! I suspect it was the same in the ancient world.

To deepen our understanding of this phenomenon, it will be helpful to explore further the views of ancient philosophers concerning the place of anger in one's emotional life and suggested therapies for treating anger's ill effects.

2.3. Ancient Philosophers' Conceptions of Anger

I focus briefly on three philosophers: Aristotle, Seneca, and Philodemus, who range from seeing certain types of anger as useful to advocating the

---

41. Here I read 1 Pet 3:9 as relating to the believers' relationships with outsiders (cf. 2:12, 15); see J. Ramsey Michaels, *1 Peter*, WBC 49 (Nashville: Nelson, 1988), 177; Jobes, *1 Peter*, 216; Reinhard Feldmeier, *The First Letter of Peter: A Commentary on the Greek Text*, trans. Peter H. Davids (Waco, TX: Baylor University Press, 2008), 186.

complete eradication of anger. Having outlined the nature and occasion of anger, we can turn to assess its pragmatic or ethical value.

Aristotle takes the most overtly positive stance, stating that "a person is praised if he gets angry in the circumstances one should and at the people one should, and in the way one should, and when, and for the length of time one should" (*Eth. nic.* 4.5.3 [1125b]).[42] Strangely, however, he calls this type of person "mild" (mildness being the intermediate form of anger); but to be *overly* mild is deficient. Those who do not get angry when they should are foolish, insensate, and slavish (*Eth. nic.* 4.5.5-6 [1126a]). One should have the ability to feel pain and one should defend oneself and one's own (*Eth. nic.* 4.5.6 [1126a]). As John Procopé states of the Aristotelian account: "What justifies outbursts of anger…, what makes it possible to speak of being angry 'rightly', is a certain consonance with moral realities. There are things to which anger is the right reaction."[43] Because anger alerts one to real harm and drives one to revenge (defense, restoration of loss, and presumably, justice), it is useful. But to be "irascible" is to exhibit anger in excess.

Seneca, conversely, advocates the complete eradication of anger; it only causes harm to oneself and others.[44] Anger is not in accordance with nature, which is evidenced by how it physically distorts the person. Seneca also refuses to allow that anger may be useful in war (*Ira* 1.11.1-3), that it is a necessary response to harm befalling a loved one (1.12.1-2),[45] or that a good man should be angry with bad men (1.14).[46] In his account, anger is an unmitigated violent, uncontrollable, and destructive force. However, Seneca does not discount all punishment, for he says, "The man who exacts punishment, not because he desires punishment for its own sake, but because it is right to inflict it, ought not to be counted an angry man" (*Ira* 1.9.4). Reason rather than anger is the best guide to action and

---

42. Aristotle, *Nicomachean Ethics: Translation, Introduction, and Commentary*, trans. Christopher Rowe, comm. Sarah Brodie. (Oxford: Oxford University Press, 2002).

43. Procopé, "Epicureans on Anger," 172.

44. Seneca argues against Aristotle's intermediate approach, saying that if something is inherently good, then the amount you have (more/less) should not affect its quality. If something in excess turns bad, then it cannot truly be a good in its moderate form (*Ira* 1.10.4, 13.1-2).

45. However, this does not mean he will not avenge them, but he will do so in an "undisturbed and unafraid" manner (*Ira* 1.12.1-2).

46. For if this is the case, the more evil one sees the more one will be angry and in fact go mad. Moreover, a good person's virtue should not be tied to another's vice.

justice (*Ira* 1.17.1). Prohibiting anger, therefore, does not necessarily mean a disregard for the loss a person has incurred or a failure to recognize the need for recompense.

Philodemus represents a slightly different perspective, in which anger can either be natural and necessary, or empty and futile.[47] As Elizabeth Asmis explains, for Philodemus, natural anger "is rooted in the biological 'nature' of all humans (and indeed all animals) as susceptible to death and pains," and it "rests on a recognition of what happens by nature." She goes on to say, "Accordingly, 'natural anger' fits the 'nature' of humans as rational animals, who have both biological vulnerability (as animals) and the power to use reason (as rational beings)." This type of anger is inevitable.[48] Thus, the pain of anger for an Epicurean may be negative, but anger "in combination with one's [good cognitive] disposition" can be a positive thing (Philodemus, *Ir.*, col. 37.20–29).[49] The difference between natural and futile anger is the ability to recognize the true nature of affairs, to interpret events and deeds correctly.[50] This specifically relates to "the comparative assessment of losses" and the requisite "punishments of those who harm us" (col. 37.20–39).[51] Natural anger makes correct measurements, but futile anger "arises 'from an utterly wicked disposition and draws with it countless troubles'" (cols. 37.39–38.5).[52] Philodemus also argues that the wise man experiences intentional harm as a bad thing and so acts in order to deter the harm or punish it.[53] Consequently, according to Asmis, Epicurean anger is not a desire to inflict revenge but

---

47. The following discussion depends on Asmis, "Necessity of Anger." However, Tsouna ("Philodemus, Seneca and Plutarch on Anger") also provides a similar reading of Philodemus' conception of anger. See also, Procopé, "Epicureans on Anger," 174–82. The contrast between natural and futile is rooted in Epicurus's differentiation of natural and empty desires; see Procopé, "Epicureans on Anger," 173.

48. Asmis, "Necessity of Anger," 160; see also Procopé, "Epicureans on Anger," 180.

49. Cited in Asmis, "Necessity of Anger," 161; see also Procopé, "Epicureans on Anger," 180–81.

50. As Procopé comments, Philodemus, like the Stoics and Peripatetics, uses a "principle of correspondence" stipulating that emotional reactions should correspond to the true nature of things ("Epicureans on Anger," 172). Of course, the different schools disagreed on the precise "nature of things."

51. Cited in Asmis, "Necessity of Anger," 161. The wise person will only in the last instance resort to punishment and will find no pleasure in it (see 163).

52. Ibid., 164.

53. Ibid., 168; see also Procopé, "Epicureans on Anger," 177.

a drive to "prevent future harm by the reluctant use of punishment."[54] The goal is personal safety (ἀσφάλεια), which is a natural good (see Epicurus, *Princ.* 7).[55]

Therefore, from three different schools we have three alternative perspectives on the worth of anger. For some, a controlled form of anger helps in moving one toward achieving a desired end: either the restoration of goods or deterrence of future harm; for others, anger is solely negative and has no ethical or functional value. All, however, agree that excessive anger is detrimental to the person. Where the author of 1 Peter stood is impossible to know, since he does not expressly state his opinion. Regardless, Philodemus's distinction between two types of anger, natural and futile, proves helpful for our investigation. Which type of anger one has rests on one's ability to understand events. A correct perception of goods and losses produces right and natural anger; futile anger arises from a faulty perception of the same. As we turn to examine Stoic therapy for anger, we discover that the health of one's emotional life likewise requires having the correct outlook.

The Stoics view emotions as value judgments: what is required is to judge correctly. For Seneca, we must fight against the primary causes of anger, especially not giving credence to the impression of harm (*Ira* 2.22.2). However, Seneca does not take the standard Stoic route in reevaluating harm within a logical system that perceives the right value of things and therefore judges true harm appropriately. This strategy usually entails recognizing that commonly esteemed things such as health and wealth are really indifferent matters (of no positive or negative worth), the loss of which is not really harmful after all. Instead, Seneca stunningly starts with our expectations of the other: we must first attack our evaluation of intentionality and responsibility. We must focus, then, not on what we have lost, but on how we understand the actions of the hostile other. Seneca presents humans as universally weak and prone to sinning and acting out of compulsion and ignorance; therefore, one should not be angry at their mistakes. This is simply *the nature of things*.[56] For the Stoic, "No fellow

---

54. Asmis, "Necessity of Anger," 174.

55. Procopé, "Epicureans on Anger," 177.

56. For Seneca, there is no use being angry at universal sin, since a person is not born wise, but becomes so (*Ira* 2.10.2–6). If we were angry at such things, we would have to be permanently angry.

human-being is truly hateful or worthy of your anger."[57] Instead, we should allow our reason to counsel patience (*Ira* 2.14.3) and delay our response. One should be directed not toward revenge but to the other's well-being, aiming to remedy his/her sickness. Clearly, Seneca, like Aristotle, recognizes that anger is a social phenomenon that requires an assessment of the other's intentions. If one can absolve the other of their malevolent intent and agency, then the foundations of anger start to be destabilized.

The second readjustment undermines one's impression that the experienced injury was unjust. Initially, we should assess ourselves and see whether we have ever injured another person, in which case injury may in fact constitute just repayment for our own faults. But next, and more importantly, we must acknowledge that we are not superior to other people and therefore deserving of no pain. Instead, we should expect that some blow will hit us in the course of life (*Ira* 2.31.5). This argument fits with Stoic fatalism, which encourages one to accept with tranquility whatever nature dictates, knowing that nature and the gods tend toward our benefit (see *Ira* 2.27).[58] In reality, however, the Stoic wise man does not really feel injury in any case; his mind has become impervious to external "harms," and he remains calm and tranquil (*Ira* 3.5.8). With this latter statement, we return to standard Stoic territory in which the only true good is virtue.

With the above philosophical frameworks in view, we return to 1 Peter.

3. The Absence of Anger to Promote Nonretaliation in 1 Peter

From the typical scenario of anger outlined above, we understand that an angry response on the part of believers requires their acceptance of a certain interpretation of events, namely: (1) they have been intentionally harmed unjustly, and (2) it is fitting to exact revenge or punishment. Thus, anger's absence from the letter perhaps owes to the fact that these two propositions cannot be maintained within the letter's wider outlook.

3.1. Reevaluating Harm

The primary situation that could be assessed as harmful is the audience's experience of persecution. Thus, unsurprisingly, we discover that 1 Peter

---

57. Procopé, "Epicureans on Anger," 172.
58. See ibid., 172.

works hard to encourage reevaluation of suffering. This occurs first in 1:6-7 where trials (πειρασμοί)—that is, the believers' current distressing and unanticipated experience of persecution (4:12)—are presented as proving the quality of their faith.[59] Such proven faith, which leads to salvation (1:9), is much more valuable than gold and results in the believers receiving praise, glory, and honor when Christ is revealed (1:7). Thus, the harm of trials is removed. Instead of seeing their persecution as causing them loss, the accounting is reversed via the theme of faith/faithfulness, and the believers find that they receive desirable goods (see 1:3-5), even blessing and honor.[60] From an eschatological perspective, the slander of the other, which is on account of Christ, will not result in the shame (harm) it aims to inflict; on the contrary, faithfulness to Christ will end in honor (benefit). Furthermore, the benefits the believers already have (yet await full consummation) on account of their new birth (1:3-5, 9)[61] are described in eternal and heavenly terms (κληρονομίαν ἄφαρτον καὶ ἀμίαντον καὶ ἀμάραντον [1:4]). Thus, like the inner virtue of the sage, such goods cannot be altered by any human force; they are beyond the spatial and temporal reach of the hostile other. As such, if one prizes these goods, then persecution cannot remove them and one does not have to assume a position of loss, even in the face of reproach/abuse.

Of course, one major way the author reevaluates persecution is by the example of Christ, whose suffering is presented as unjustified. He is the blameless, spotless lamb (1:19) who has suffered on behalf of the unrighteous (3:18; cf. 2:21-25). The narrative of Christ's righteous suffering and vindication has a number of effects. First, it reminds the hearers that they too were once unrighteous sinners (see more below).[62] Second, it provides an exemplary pattern (2:21)[63] and an expectation (1:11, 21; 3:18). Christ is explicitly described as suffering in his body on the tree (2:24) and in

---

59. I do not see fiery trials here as purifying, *pace* Norbert Brox, *Der Erste Petrusbrief*, EKKNT 21 (Zurich: Benziger/Neukirchen-Vluyn: Neukirchener Verlag, 1979), 64–65; Feldmeier, *First Letter of Peter*, 83–84. Rather, I think that they prove (δοκιμάζω) the true quality of the believers' faith (= faithfulness); see Michaels, *1 Peter*, 30; Paul J. Achtemeier, *1 Peter: A Commentary on First Peter*, Hermeneia (Minneapolis: Fortress, 1996), 102.

60. For more on the reevaluation of trials, see Hockey, "Seeing Emotionally," §4.2.4.

61. Elliott, *1 Peter*, 329.

62. Michaels, *1 Peter*, 202.

63. As Elliott notes, Christ's example is a moral one that "includes innocent

the flesh (4:1). Those who follow Christ should also anticipate that they will likely suffer for their allegiance to him (see 4:12).[64] However, though one's natural response might regard such physical suffering as negative, the letter does not do so. Instead, Christ's suffering is consistently bound to his glorification (1:11).[65] Since God the faithful judge vindicates Christ and raises him to a state of glorification, Christ's suffering does not stop at death (1:21; 2:18, 23). Third, Christ's suffering is a purposeful sacrifice that opened the way for believers to return to the shepherd and overseer of their souls (2:24–25). In Christ's example, the believers can start to understand that their present suffering is part of a much larger story, one in which Christ is their forerunner and pattern.[66] As John H. Elliott comments, "Jesus' resurrection and glorification is a demonstration of his acceptance, honoring, and vindication by God despite human rejection.... This honor and glory of the suffering Christ is thus a surety of the glory and honor in store for believers who remain faithful in adversity."[67]

Christ's example shows that physical and temporal loss can look different from an eternal perspective. Perhaps Philodemus's encouragement to look at the *true* nature of affairs is comparable here. For 1 Peter, the reality of the present must be viewed through an eschatological lens. Consequently, the letter asks the believers to hope in God who is able to transform the lowliness of suffering into vindication and glory.[68] As a result, the author challenges the audience to reassess what they value. From the letter's perspective, it is better and more honorable to suffer for righteousness than to secure physical safety or social esteem by question-

---

behavior, suffering without retaliation, and commitment of self to God, the just judge" (*1 Peter*, 526).

64. See Matt 5:11–12; 10:25; Mark 13:9–13; John 15:18–20. See Brox, *Der Erste Petrusbrief*, 213–14; Michaels, *1 Peter*, 260; Achtemeier, *1 Peter*, 304–5.

65. Jacques Schlosser, *La Première Épître de Pierre*, CBNT 21 (Paris: Cerf, 2011), 259.

66. Thus, it is more than a Cynic-like consolatory technique that since "suffering is to be expected," it should not be distressing (see Paul A. Holloway, *Coping with Prejudice: 1 Peter in Social-Psychological Perspective*, WUNT 244 [Tübingen: Mohr Siebeck, 2009], 214–20); rather, it entails appreciating a larger narrative of God's action in Christ that shapes one's entire worldview. See also Gordon M. Zerbe, *Non-Retaliation in Early Jewish and New Testament Texts: Ethical Themes in Social Contexts*, JSPSup 13 (Sheffield: JSOT Press, 1993), 280–84.

67. Elliott, *1 Peter*, 379; see also Feldmeier, *First Letter of Peter*, 95.

68. Feldmeier, *First Letter of Peter*, 120.

able means.[69] This reorientation of values also affects the goals that anger's action tendency might aim at—physical safety and restoration of social esteem—by transcending them. Thus we see that the author consistently works to remove the perception that suffering on account of one's Christian identity is truly harmful. In fact, it explicitly presents the opposite: suffering is an indication of blessing, God's presence, and, when understood as a participation in Christ's suffering, even a cause for rejoicing (3:14; 4:13–14). This reevaluation of suffering, indeed, *expected* suffering, reinterprets the audience's current situation and undermines key elements that would typically arouse anger.

3.2. Reassessing the Intentionality of the Other

We noted above that one of Seneca's strategies for removing anger was to nullify the intentionality of the other by emphasizing her ignorance. First Peter also depicts the hostile other's pattern of life as one of ignorance, futility, and senselessness (see 1:14, 18; 2:14; cf. 4:2–4). One wonders whether this rhetoric is not seeking to bring decisive separation between the audience and their previous community, as some have argued,[70] but instead is functioning to help the audience understand, perhaps even anticipate, that the hostile other's ignorance contributes to their faulty treatment of the believer. The hostile other inevitably misinterprets the believers' actions and mistreats them because the non-Christian simply does not see things correctly. Hostile others are indeed slandering and accusatory, physically abusive and harmful, but is it perhaps not their fault? Perhaps, due to their ignorance, their behavior is inevitable? One would not be angry at such a person because their harm is not strictly intentional; rather, one would pity her. This perspective, then, could allow the reproached believers to have a sense of superiority over their persecutors. The Christian does not

---

69. This perspective could be paralleled with what Holloway identifies as one form of "emotion-focused coping strategy," where "persons facing negative outcomes in a given value domain" cope "by 'restructuring their self-concept' so as not to be vulnerable to these outcomes" (*Coping with Prejudice*, 122, 125). One disidentifies with the troublesome domain in favor of another where one can be evaluated more positively (see 125–27).

70. See, Michaels, who understands 1:18, for example, as demonstrating that the author saw the pagan way of life as "a mortal threat" to the community (*1 Peter*, 64–65); see also Elliott, *1 Peter*, 370–71, 726; Achtemeier, *1 Peter*, 123–24.

have to engage in power plays, as anger might dictate, with those who work from the wrong game plan. Instead, in the face of hostility, the believer can choose nonretaliation rather than vengeance.

In this framework, nonretaliation is not resigning oneself to subjugation or subordination but rather fortifying oneself against domination by refusing to play by the other's rules.[71] Such nonretaliation is a choice of those empowered by an alternative perspective which appreciates the *true* nature of things.[72] However, like Seneca suggests, the audience's previous sinfulness should not be far from its memory, lest the believers distance themselves too much from the hostile other; after all, they too used to be ignorant, following human desires (1:14; 2:1; 4:2–4). Thus, with a sympathetic outlook, the cycle of conflict is removed, and the way is opened for bridge building.[73]

3.3. Removing the Need to Avenge

So far we have seen how the author has removed the evaluation of harm and reduced the intentionality of the other; lastly, we need to assess the appropriateness of vengeance (or punishment). First Peter clearly presents human ruling authorities as having the power to punish evildoers (2:13–14).[74] Ultimately, however, the letter depicts God as the chief judge of all humanity (1:17). The quotation of Ps 34:12–16 (33:13–17 LXX) in 1 Pet 3:10–12 is helpful here.[75] It directly follows the prohibition to return evil for evil (1 Pet 3:9) and appears to provide justification for this command.[76] The psalm issues a call to turn away from deceitful speech and evil and to do good and seek peace—which reinforces the command to bless one's

---

71. See Achtemeier, *1 Peter*, 223; William M. Swartley, *Covenant of Peace: The Missing Peace in New Testament Theology and Ethics* (Grand Rapids: Eerdmans, 2006), 263–64.

72. Here, then, nonretaliation operates on a different level than expecting that "meeting hostility with kindness will prove … the only possible way to survive as a Christian community in a hostile world" (Achtemeier, *1 Peter*, 222). It involves a decision to act from a life oriented around a different narrative. As such, it may even be a "nonverbal" witness to outsiders; see Feldmeier, *First Letter of Peter*, 187.

73. See Jobes, *1 Peter*, 217–18; Feldmeier, *First Letter of Peter*, 187–88.

74. See Rom 13:1–7. See also Swartley, *Covenant of Peace*, 264–66.

75. For the use of Ps 33 (LXX) throughout 1 Peter see Jobes, *1 Peter*, 221–23.

76. See Rom 12:17, which evidences an almost identical prohibition of retaliation (cf. 1 Thess 5:15). See Michaels, *1 Peter*, 177; Feldmeier, *First Letter of Peter*, 186.

abusers (1 Pet 3:9). The assurance follows: "Because the eyes of the Lord are on the righteous and his ears [are attentive] to their prayer, but the face of the Lord [is] against those who do evil" (3:12; cf. NIV).

The emotional ethic promoted by the author sits within a larger scheme of reference. The accounting of goods, "repaying evil for evil," is not to be considered solely with one's human social relationships in view. One must also consider one's actions from a cosmic viewpoint.[77] The believers are responsible for doing good and pursuing peace, which they can do with confidence that, if they act in this righteous (or just) manner, God will be on their side.[78] In this context, to act justly is not to take matters of justice into one's own hands, but to continue to do good. The believers are assured that, if they bless their persecutors, they will inherit a blessing (3:9–10).[79] This is particularly counterintuitive if Elliott (following B. J. Malina and J. H. Neyrey) is right that "successful defense of honor normally required an immediate and crafty verbal riposte."[80] Yet, the second parallel statement in 3:12 is also comforting; God not only sees those who do evil—the believers' persecutors—but sets his face against them.[81] Given the overall tone of the letter, this warning carries a sense of judgment.[82] It infers that

---

77. Achtemeier's (*1 Peter*, 124) comments regarding 1:17–21 hold here: "The readers are summoned to understand ... the importance of the events of which they are participants ... and to respond in a way appropriate to the gravity of the situation God has brought about: the impending judgement and closing of the age."

78. As Achtemeier notes, "The theme of the psalm as a whole is God's deliverance of the oppressed" (*1 Peter*, 226).

79. See Matt 5:43–48; Luke 6:27–36. As Michaels rightly comments, blessing is more than speaking well of someone; it extends favor to her (*1 Peter*, 178, 180). It is interesting, however, that 1 Peter uses a "speech" action here as a counter to abuse (3:10). It would suggest the author has a context of verbal reproach in mind; see also Elliott, *1 Peter*, 613; Jobes, *1 Peter*, 218.

80. Elliott, *1 Peter*, 607.

81. See Achtemeier, *1 Peter*, 227. The term κύριος in 3:12 relates to God, not Jesus; see Achtemeier, *1 Peter*, 226. Though ἐπί (3:12) could be read positively as "on" or "toward," it is better understood here as "against," as the contrast between God's response to the righteous and those doing evil suggests (Michaels, *1 Peter*, 181).

82. The framework of the letter assumes the reality of an ultimate, eternal judgment of all people according to their conduct (1 Pet 1:13, 17; 2:23; 4:5, 17–19), though the specific fate of the believers' persecutors is never explicitly stated (2:7–8; 3:16); see Michaels, *1 Peter*, 60–61, 181; Zerbe, *Non-Retaliation*, 287–88. See Feldmeier (*First Letter of Peter*, 108–15) for more on the theme of God as judge and the assurance this can bring victims of abuse.

those who pursue a course of harm in this present life can expect negative consequences later; for what good can come from God's face being set against you?

Consequently, 1 Peter's use of the psalm presents God as the final arbiter of goods. The following verse directly questions: "For who will harm you, if you are zealous to do good?" (3:13). Then, "If you should suffer for righteousness, you are blessed" (3:14). The former query, which initially sounds a note of encouragement, appears to be undermined by the latter statement. However, when we keep the whole passage in view, 3:13 helps the believer appreciate that God is the one who ultimately bestows goods and honor. Thus, it is of primary importance to remain in good standing with God, to be righteous. As Paul J. Achtemeier recognizes, separation from God is "a far more grievous harm" than "social rejection or even persecution."[83] Consequently, if one is righteous, then one can expect, from an eternal perspective, not to encounter true harm.[84] First Peter 3:13 provides a true and definitive *eschatological* perspective, reinforced rather than undermined by 3:14: even if believers suffer presently, because they do for a righteous cause, the eternal reality is that they are blessed (μακάριοι).[85]

So, in this section of 1 Peter we see two aspects at work that would reduce the arousal of anger: (1) again, the removal of the assessment that one has been harmed (to the contrary, the persecuted are "blessed") and (2) the reminder that God is the ultimate judge and final accountant, providing recompense to persecutors who pursue an evil course.[86] Therefore, there is no need to exact one's own revenge. As Gordon M. Zerbe comments, "because of the certainty of God's righteous judgement, which includes the punishment of the community's persecutors, Christians can defer their cause to God."[87] This eschatological outlook, which allows a reinterpretation of the parameters of the present situation, alters the believers' emotional orientation: instead of seeking revenge, they are

---

83. Achtemeier, *1 Peter*, 229.

84. For examples of other biblical passages that convey the same idea, see Michaels, *1 Peter*, 185; Feldmeier, *First Letter of Peter*, 193–94.

85. This paradox is affirmed by the example of Christ in 3:18–22; see Achtemeier, *1 Peter*, 228–29; Michaels, *1 Peter*, 185.

86. See Achtemeier, *1 Peter*, 227. See Rom 12:19, which explicitly encourages its audience to leave room for God's wrath.

87. Zerbe, *Non-Retaliation*, 288.

urged to treat even those questioning them with gentleness (3:15–16). Of course, this means that the absence of anger and the emotional ethic of nonretaliation only make sense if one accepts the letter's eschatological and theological outlook. Without this understanding, there is little hope for ultimate justice.

4. Conclusion

I have argued that the overall outlook of 1 Peter undermines the propositions required to arouse anger: that one has been intentionally harmed and that it is right to avenge. Rather, the Christian response to personal loss and harm is one that recognizes the true eschatological and theological state of affairs. This includes understanding that one's ultimate goals and goods remain unaffected by persecution, that Christ's example gives positive assurance of the good, that the other may be acting out of ignorance, and that earthly and eternal systems are in place to punish evil and reward good. Such a vision reduces the occasions for anger and opens the door to peace making and bridge building. We cannot say that the author would wholly see anger as problematic. But we can see that on this occasion, within the letter's theocentric-eschatological perspective, anger and retaliation by no means secure the ends one desires and therefore are not conducive to a flourishing Christian existence.

We have yet to explore fully why the author pursues this strategy, what this emotional ethic might imply for the social dynamics of the community, or how prohibiting anger might affect the psychological well-being of the individual. However, this essay has aimed to show that even "missing" emotions should cause us to stop and ask, "What's going on here?," so that we might better understand the world of the text and its audience.

Select Bibliography

Averill, James R. "The Social Construction of Emotion: With Special Reference to Love." Pages 89–109 in *The Social Construction of the Person*. Edited by Kenneth J. Gergen and Keith E. Davis. New York: Springer, 1985.

Frijda, Nico H., Peter Juipers, and Elisabeth Schure. "Relations among Emotion, Appraisal, and Emotional Action Readiness." *JPSP* 57 (1989): 212–28.

Lazarus, Richard S. "Cognition and Motivation in Emotion." *AP* 46 (1991): 352–67.

———. "Progress on a Cognitive-Motivational-Relational Theory of Emotion." *AP* 46 (1991): 819–34.

Lazarus, Richard S., James R. Averill, and Edward M. Opton, Jr. "Towards a Cognitive Theory of Emotion." Pages 207–32 in *Feelings and Emotions: The Loyola Symposium*. Edited by Magda B. Arnold. New York: Academic Press, 1970.

Lutz, Catherine A. *Unnatural Emotions: Everyday Sentiments on a Micronesian Atoll and Their Challenge to Western Theory*. Chicago: University of Chicago Press, 1988.

Mesquita, Batja. "Emotions are Culturally Situated." *SSI* 46 (2007): 410–15.

Moors, Agnes. "Theories of Emotion Causation: A Review." *CE* 23 (2009): 625–62.

Moors, Agnes, Phoebe C. Ellsworth, Klaus R. Scherer, and Nico H. Frijda. "Appraisal Theories of Emotion: State of the Art and Future Development." *EmotRev* 5 (2013): 119–24.

Mulligan, Kevin, and Klaus R. Scherer. "Toward a Working Definition of Emotion." *EmotRev* 4 (2012): 345–57.

Nussbaum, Martha C. *Upheavals of Thought: The Intelligence of Emotions*. Cambridge: Cambridge University Press, 2001.

Solomon, Robert C. *The Passions: Emotions and the Meaning of Life*. Indianapolis: Hackett, 1993.

Wierzbicka, Anna. *Emotions across Languages and Cultures: Diversity and Universals*. Cambridge: Cambridge University Press, 1999.

Afterword

David Konstan

It would seem to be high time for a collective study of emotions in the Bible, and the collection you have just read testifies to the rewards of such an investigation and also to the challenges it poses. The problems are well known. The contributors are working with two, or sometimes three, ancient vocabularies that may not always correspond to ostensibly comparable terms in modern English.

1. Anger and Fear

In my own research on classical Greek emotions, I was initially struck by Aristotle's claim that one could not be angry at someone whom one feared. This seemed to me, and has seemed to others, a bizarre statement. Rather than dismiss it as the eccentric view of an academic philosopher, however, I sought to determine what anger might have meant to Aristotle and his contemporaries, such that the incompatibility of anger and fear might follow logically.[1] Aristotle defines anger as "a desire, accompanied by pain, for a perceived revenge, on account of a perceived slight on the part of people who are not fit to slight one or one's own" (*Rhet.* 2.2.1 [1378a]). Someone who is afraid of the individual who behaved insultingly will repress the desire to seek vengeance; as Aristotle observes, "No one gets angry at someone when it is impossible to achieve revenge, and with those who are far superior in power than themselves people get angry either not

---

1. See David Konstan, "Aristotle on Anger and the Emotions: The Strategies of Status," in *Ancient Anger: Perspectives from Homer to Galen*, ed. Susanna Braund and Glenn W. Most, YCS 32 (New Haven: Yale University Press, 2003): 99–120; Konstan, *The Emotions of the Ancient Greeks: Studies in Aristotle and Classical Literature* (Toronto: University of Toronto Press, 2006).

at all or less so" (*Rhet.* 1.11.9 [1370b]). Aristotle's account makes sense, then, on his conception of anger, and what is more, it alerts us to the risk of unreflectively equating the word or words for anger in ancient Greek—Aristotle's uses *orgē*, but there are other terms as well—with "anger" as we understand it, assuming a more or less uniform conception of anger among speakers of English even today.

2. Pity and Mercy

Similar difficulties arise with respect to other emotions. For example, English distinguishes between "pity" and "mercy," the former an emotion, perhaps (most modern inventories of the emotions omit it, in fact), while the latter seems more like a disposition or even a virtue, comparable to "clemency." Yet the corresponding word in ancient Greek, the language of the LXX and New Testament, is simply *eleos*, which is variously, one might even say arbitrarily, rendered as "pity" or "mercy" in modern translations. Here, it is not merely a question of whether modern pity corresponds precisely to the Greek *eleos* or Latin *misericordia*, though in fact there are distinct nuances: ancient definitions tend to stress that pity is felt for those who are suffering undeservedly and thus distinguish the sentiment from what we might call "sympathy" or, more recently, "empathy." It is rather a matter of whether *eleos*, in its various usages in the Bible, qualifies as an emotion at all.[2]

The very idea of emotion, however, may not translate readily across cultures. The Greek term commonly rendered as "emotion" is *pathos*, but it is well known that this term has a wide range of meanings, basically signifying anything that one undergoes or experiences, often in a negative sense, captured in the English "pathology" but also "pathetic," a sense the term also had in ancient Greek. It may well have been Aristotle himself who first endowed the word with a significance approximating that of "emotion." The definition that he provides in the *Rhetoric*, immediately before launching on his descriptions of the various emotions, sounds rather strange and was evidently concocted with the idea of persuasion in mind: "Let the emotions [*pathē*] be all those things on account of which people change and differ in regard to their judgments, and upon which

---

2. See further discussion in David Konstan, *Pity Transformed* (London: Duckworth, 2001), esp. ch. 4.

attend pain and pleasure, for example anger, pity, fear, and all other such things and their opposites" (2.1.8 [1378a]). The examples that follow the definition serve to define the specific sense of *pathos* in this context (cf. Aristotle, *Eth. nic.* 2.5.21 [1105b] and *De. an.* 1.1.16–17 [403a], where the lists vary slightly). Aristotle goes on to discuss, in addition to the three mentioned, love and hatred, shame, envy, gratitude, confidence (the opposite of fear), rivalry, and even the appeasement of anger, which does not sound like an emotion to modern ears.[3] The terminology for emotion is equally vexed in biblical Hebrew. Roman theorists of emotion, like Cicero and Quintilian, were influenced by Greek philosophical traditions, especially the Peripatetic and Stoic, but there, too, significant variations obtain in vocabulary and meaning.

3. Sexuality

The problem is not simply that ancient writers lacked a suitable term for what we may take to be a natural category. If we ignore the ways in which they grouped notions and impose our own selection, we may miss essential features of their conceptual world. Although it lies outside the sphere of emotions proper, let me offer the example of incest. We tend to regard incest taboos as pertaining specifically to the family and arising out of tension between endogamy and exogamy: endogamy looks to preserve wealth within the family; exogamy insures the solidarity of the larger community through marriage ties. The particular needs of a given community, both practical and ideological, result in a wide variation in the nature of incest prohibitions, from the fairly extensive code in the Hebrew Bible to the more limited restrictions in ancient Greece, where marriage between half brothers and sisters was permitted if they shared the same father (but not mother). In Roman Egypt, indeed, wedlock between full brothers and sisters was allowed and even encouraged.

But a closer look at the sources brings this ready anthropological account into question. Leviticus lists among prohibited sexual relations, all described from the perspective of the male, sex with one's mother, stepmother, mother-in-law, aunt, sister, stepdaughter, daughter-in-law, and granddaughter (Lev 18:8–18; 20:11–21; cf. Deut 22:30). It is notable that

---

3. See David Konstan, "The Concept of 'Emotion' from Plato to Cicero," *Méthexis* 19 (2006): 139–51.

the list omits daughter, which may be accidental or else because the prohibition on sex with a daughter was taken for granted or was implicitly subsumed under other bans.[4] But these injunctions are part of a larger sequence in which sex with a woman during menstruation or with a neighbor's wife, as well as sex with animals and "with a male as with a woman" (Lev 18:22), are indicted as sources of defilement. It may thus be that isolating a subset under the label "incest" is misleading and that incest should rather be seen as part of a larger category of pollution.

In the patriarchal period, references to marriages or sexual relations apparently violate some of these rules, for example, Abraham's marriage with Sarah, his half sister by the same father (Gen 20:12). Cain is said to have had a wife, who may have been a sister but could have been a descendant of Adam and Eve further down the line (they lived for nine centuries, after all; as Lévi-Strauss observed, myths of human origins always run the risk of incest). The case of Lot's daughters, who seduce their father while he is asleep, differs in that their behavior is clearly condemned (it is probably irrelevant that sex between father and daughter is not explicitly prohibited in Leviticus).

After the patriarchal period, such violations were seen as a sign of extreme moral corruption. Thus, Ezekiel condemns Jerusalem for its sins: "In you they uncover their fathers' nakedness; in you they violate women in their menstrual periods. One commits abomination with his neighbor's wife; another lewdly defiles his daughter-in-law; another in you defiles his sister, his father's daughter" (Ezek 22:10–11).[5] Yet Ezekiel, too, like the list of proscribed behaviors in Leviticus, combines incest with adultery and sex during a woman's menstrual period. What is more, Ezekiel's censures follow denunciations of those who fail to care for parents, widows, foreigners, and orphans, as well as of slanderers (22:7–9). The ethical offense is contempt for divinely authorized rules, and infractions of the sexual code are lumped in with immoral behavior generally. Such indiscriminate charges of viciousness are common in all periods; in the Hebrew Bible, however, incestuous acts are treated predominantly as a sign of disobedience of God's law and a symptom of general depravity.

One of the motives for violating sexual prohibitions is erotic passion, a theme well developed in Greek and Roman literature, beginning with

---

4. See b. Yebam. 3a; *RAC*, s.v. "Incest."
5. All translations of biblical texts are from NRSV unless otherwise noted.

Helen's elopement with Paris that was the cause of the Trojan War. Classical Greek distinguished between *erōs* and love in the broader sense, *philia*, which did not necessarily carry sexual connotations. In Hebrew and Latin, as in modern English, a single term covered the range of both Greek words, making it difficult sometimes to tease out the precise sense in a given context. The Hebrew Bible does not express hostility to sex as such, but erotic passion, whether on the part of men or women, generally leads to no good. Examples are Potiphar's wife's desire for Joseph (Gen 39), Samson's passion for Delilah (Judg 16:4–21), and David's desire for Bathsheba (2 Sam 11–12), though whether David is truly in love or merely wishes to have sex with her is perhaps moot (he sends her back to her husband's house after sleeping with her [2 Sam 11:11]). Amnon rapes his half sister Tamar, professing love as the reason (2 Sam 13), and is killed in turn by his brother Absalom in a series of violent sexual episodes (Absalom rapes David's wives) that seem to play out the consequences of David's sinful lust. Other instances in which the word *'āhab* ("love") is found seem to carry a less strictly erotic sense, though by no means excluding sex from the desired relationship. Thus, Jacob loves Rachel (Gen 29:20) and Isaac loves Rebekah (24:67). Shechem rapes Jacob's daughter Dinah but then professes to love her and asks for her hand (Gen 34). Solomon is said to have loved many women (1 Kgs 11:1–2), while Rehoboam is said to have loved Maacah most among his wives (2 Chr 11:21), just as Elkanah prefers Hannah to the rest (1 Sam 1:5). Ahasuerus loves Esther above all the other women offered to him (Esth 2:17; the context suggests sexual attraction). In none of these cases does the text give fuller expression to the nature of the passion. It is only in the Song of Songs that love takes center stage, and here it assumes something of a romantic or even exalted quality. Love and sensuality are celebrated, and both the man and the woman are subjects of passion. The magnification of the beloved's qualities is one of the signs of erotic infatuation.

In Greek literature, by contrast, erotic passion plays a substantial role, giving rise to theories about the construction of sexuality that do not necessarily correspond to the structure of feeling that we can infer from biblical texts. In the scholarship on Greek sexuality, the asymmetry of sexual roles has caused a shift from an emphasis on gender to one on active vs. passive roles. As A. E. Housman observed over a century ago, "Between *philopaidia* [love of boys] and *philogynia* [love of women] the Romans saw no incongruity at all, but they did see incongruity between *to paschein* [to undergo] and *to dran* [to do]."[6] Sexual identities, on this view, were not constructed around the opposition between homosexuality and heterosexuality. Men were understood to be the subjects of erotic desire: they were the lovers or *erastai* and actively sought sexual fulfillment with women or boys. Women and boys, in turn, were the objects of desire or "beloveds" (*erōmenos* [masc.]/*erōmenē* [fem.]). It is they rather than their lovers who are characterized as possessing beauty, and they either yielded to a lover or resisted his advances.[7] But these roles were themselves fraught with contradiction. For *erōs* or erotic passion and the desire for sex (*aphrodisia*) were imagined as powerful forces, whether external or internal, that dominated people and obliged them to behave irrationally.[8] Submitting to passion was thus a kind of enslavement, in contrast to the dominant position that free adult males were imagined as occupying. Women, in turn, were regarded (by men) as less capable of self-mastery and hence more vulnerable to domination by *erōs*. In this context, sexual ethics was perceived as a matter of self-control or temperance (*sōphrosunē* or *enkrateia* in Greek; *moderatio* or *continentia* in Latin), one of the fundamental virtues in the classical Greek and Roman moral vocabulary, by which reason maintained authority over the lower appetites. Men excessively given to sex were thus regarded as effeminate.

By way of illustration, we may look briefly at fragment 1 of Mimnermus, whose verses, according to Propertius, were worth more in matters of love than those of Homer (*plus in amore ualet Mimnermi uersus Homero* [1.9.11]):

> What life is there, what pleasure without golden Aphrodite? May I die when I no longer care about secret intrigues, persuasive gifts, and the

---

6. A. E. Housman, review of *A. Persi Flacci et D. Iuni Iuvenalis Saturae*, ed. S. G. Owen, *CR* 17 (1903): 393.

7. See, e.g., Kenneth Dover, *Greek Homosexuality*, rev. ed. (Cambridge: Harvard University Press, 1989 [orig. 1978]); Michel Foucault, *L'usage des plaisirs*, vol. 2 of *Histoire de la sexualité* (Paris: Gallimard, 1984); John J. Winkler, *The Constraints of Desire: Essays in the Anthropology of Sex and Gender in Ancient Greece* (New York: Routledge, 1989); David M. Halperin, *One Hundred Years of Homosexuality and Other Essays on Greek Love* (New York: Routledge, 1990). For a recent critical survey, see Thomas K. Hubbard, ed., *A Companion to Greek and Roman Sexualities* (Malden, MA: Wiley Blackwell 2014).

8. For a view of ancient *erōs* that emphasizes its negative aspect, see Bruce S. Thornton, *Eros: The Myth of Ancient Greek Sexuality*, rev. ed. (New York: Avalon, 1998).

bed, those blossoms of youth that men and women find alluring. But when painful old age comes on, which makes even a handsome man ugly, grievous cares wear away his heart and he derives no joy from looking upon the sunlight; he is hateful to boys and women hold him in no honour. So harsh has the god made old age. (1.1–5)⁹

Aphrodite is for the young: beyond a certain age, men lose a capacity for sex (or an interest in it), although it alone provides joy in life (contrast Cephalus's more positive view in Plato's *Republic* [329c] that old age brings freedom from passion, though he concedes that others of his age do not agree). The erotic pleasures Mimnermus has in mind, moreover, are furtive and obtained by gifts; there is no question of marriage here: it is all about passion and sex. Both sexes find the charms of youth alluring; as Kenneth Dover put it in his book *Greek Homosexuality*, "The attributes which made a young male attractive to *erastai* were assumed to make him no less attractive to women."¹⁰ Girls, however, unlike boys, remain attractive even when mature; as Theocritus observed, "A boy's beauty [*kallos*] is a fine thing [*kalon*], but it endures a short while" (*Id.* 23.32), a theme repeated in rhetorical disquisitions about whether boys or women are preferable as beloveds.¹¹ Women, however, like boys, lose interest in a man when he grows old.

4. Beauty

What inspires *erōs* above all is physical beauty, and here, remarkably enough, there is an analogy with the language of the Hebrew Bible, and one that may help us to discriminate between affection in general and passionate love. The Greek term most commonly taken to mean "beautiful" in classical Greek is the adjective *kalos*, but in fact it has a much wider semantic range and may signify "honorable," "noble," and "good." Adding the definite article to the adjective yields the phrase "*to kalon*"; here too, the sense is broad, ranging from "the beautiful" or "beauty" to "virtue" to "honor," which is far more often the meaning intended. But classical Greek also had a noun that more nearly approximates the

---

9. Douglas E. Gerber, ed. and trans., *Greek Elegiac Poetry*, LCL 258 (Cambridge: Harvard University Press, 1999).
10. Dover, *Greek Homosexuality*, 172.
11. Translations are mine unless otherwise indicated.

modern sense of beauty, namely *kallos*, with a double lambda and accent on the first syllable.[12] We just saw the contrasting senses of the noun and adjective in the verse quoted from Theocritus. There is a similar contrast in the Greek text of 1 Esd 4:18. The NRSV translates:

> If men gather gold and silver or any other beautiful [*horaion*] thing, and then see a woman lovely [*kalē*] in appearance [*eidos*] and beauty [*kallos*] ...[13]

"Lovely in beauty" seems as redundant as affirming that "beauty is beautiful"; it would appear preferable, accordingly, to take *kalē* (feminine of *kalos*) in the sense of "outstanding" or the like and render the phrase: "excellent in stature [or appearance] and in beauty."

Saul Olyan has examined the qualities that characterize beautiful males in the Hebrew Bible, and he notes that Saul "is described as 'a handsome young man' (*baḥur waṭôb*), an expression drawing together the notions of youth and physical attractiveness. In fact, the text goes on to state that 'there was no man of the children of Israel more handsome (*ṭôb*) than he; from his shoulder upward he was taller than all the people.'"[14] Broadly speaking, the features that indicate attractiveness in a male are "exceptional height; youth; ruddy, clear skin; beautiful eyes; plumpness; thick hair on the head; a beard in the case of a mature man; rapid, agile movement; and physical strength.... These are the qualities that define technical expressions such as 'handsome' (*ṭôb*) and 'beautiful' (*yāpeh*)."[15]

Now, the word *ṭôb*, which is most often translated as "good," has an application comparable to that of the Greek *kalos*, and so there may be some doubt as to whether it signifies beauty in any given context. For example, in Isa 5:9 we read:

> The LORD of hosts has sworn in my hearing:
> Surely many houses shall be desolate,
> large and beautiful houses, without inhabitant.

---

12. For discussion, see David Konstan, *Beauty: The Fortunes of an Ancient Greek Idea* (Oxford: Oxford University Press, 2014).

13. Both nouns (*eidei* and *kallei*) are in the dative case.

14. Saul M. Olyan, *Disability in the Hebrew Bible: Interpreting Mental and Physical Differences* (Cambridge: Cambridge University Press, 2008), 15–16; cf. 1 Sam 9:2.

15. Ibid., 17.

This, at least, is the rendering of the NRSV. The Darby translation, however, offers:

> In mine ears Jehovah of hosts [hath said],
> "Many houses shall assuredly become a desolation,
> great and excellent ones, without inhabitant."[16]

Both are possible, but since the term for "good" here (*ṭôbîm*) is the plural of *ṭôb*, I am inclined to prefer the Darby version. It is worth noting that the LXX renders *ṭôbîm* as *kalai*, which does not absolutely exclude the sense of beauty but may rather suggest that the houses were "well wrought" or "noble."

Now, just as the term *kallos* in Greek primarily indicates physical attractiveness, in Hebrew too there is a root that signifies beauty in this sense. The term is *yāpeh*, the forms of which occur much less frequently than *ṭôb*. In the adjectival form, *yāpeh* is sometimes rendered as *kalos* in the LXX, but it is worth noting that it is never translated as *agathos* or "good," whereas this is by far the most frequent Greek equivalent for *ṭôb* (e.g., Gen 50:20). On the other hand, *yāpeh* and its cognates are commonly rendered by the Greek *kallos*: examples include Ezek 16:14, in reference to Jerusalem (*en tō kallei sou*; see Ezek 16:15); Pss 45:3, to a man, and 45:12, to the king's lover; Prov 6:25, to an adulterous women (cf. Prov 11:22; 31:30); and Esth 1:11 to Vashti.

Sometimes *yāpeh* is ascribed to such items as especially handsome animals or trees (as an olive tree in Jer 11:6; a heifer in 46:20), but this is true also of the Greek *kallos*. But the contexts in which the word occurs give a sense of the primary meaning. We may note ascription of *yāpeh* to humans in Gen 12:11 of Sarah, 29:17 of Leah, 39:6 of Joseph (though also of the fatted cows); Deut 21:11, "Suppose you see among the captives a beautiful woman whom you desire and want to marry"; 1 Sam 17:42 of David, 25:3 of Abigail; 2 Sam 13:1 and 14:27 of Tamar, 14:25 of Absalom; 1 Kgs 1:3 of Abishag; Esth 2:7 of Esther; Job 42:15 of Job's daughters; and so forth. It will come as no surprise that the word is found eleven times in the Song of Songs. By tracking the uses of this root in the Hebrew Bible, we see that beauty is associated with women and with young men. If there is no recognized cultural practice of pederasty in the Hebrew text, there

---

16. John Nelson Darby et al., trans., *The Darby Translation Bible*, rev. ed. (Addison, Il.: Bible Truth, 1961).

is nevertheless an appreciation of male beauty that bears comparison with classical Greek perceptions.

5. Remorse and Repentance

Sexual behavior is one source of remorse and repentance. But is remorse an emotion? If so, is it recognized as such in ancient Greek texts? Here again, we come up against problems of translation from one idiom to another, which is to say, from one cultural construction of the emotions to another. Just as the Greek word *eleos* is rendered variously as "pity" and "mercy," importing a distinction into the original texts that may indeed be right but requires careful attention to context, so too the Greek words *metanoia* and *metameleia* have a still wider range of meanings, from a change of mind, which seems a strictly intellectual business, to the more emotive ideas of regret, remorse, repentance—and more.[17]

By way of illustrating the plain sense of changing one's mind, we may cite Menander's *Epitrepontes*, in which the shepherd Daos says to Syrus: "I gave you something of mine; if this is agreeable to you, keep it now, but if it is not, and you have changed your mind, then given it back" (*Epitr.* 287–98). Daos had found an exposed child and given it to Syrus, but not the tokens that had been set out with the infant; he now tells Syrus to be content with what he has received, or if he no longer wants it, then give it back. A fragment of Euripides runs: "Old age, what hope of pleasure you extend, and every person desires to arrive at you; but once they have you they also have *metameleia* and think there is nothing worse for mortal man" (*TrGF* 5:1080). *Metameleia* here has nothing to do with decisions, moral or otherwise, but simply indicates a change of view. Herodotus says several times that a benefactor will not have occasion in the future to rue his good deed (*Hist.* 3.140; 7.29; 9.89), and Xenophon speaks of restraining anger so as not to regret one's actions afterwards (*Mem.* 2.6.23; cf. *Anab.* 2.6.9); here the sense seems closer to a feeling of sorrow than a simple alteration of opinion. But if the previous passages suggest regret, they are still far from

---

17. For further discussion, see David Konstan, "From Regret to Remorse: The Origins of a Moral Emotion," in *Understanding Emotions in Early Europe*, ed. Michael Champion and Andrew Lynch, EER 8 (Turnhout: Brepols, 2015) 3–25; Konstan, "Regret, Repentance, and Change of Heart in Paul: *Metanoia* in Its Greek Context," in *Paul's Greco-Roman Context*, ed. Cilliers Breytenbach, BETL 277 (Leuven: Peeters, 2015), 119–33.

the more moral sense of remorse, which is defined in the *Oxford English Dictionary* as "a feeling of compunction, or of deep regret and repentance, for a sin or wrong committed."[18] We can see the difference clearly in a passage from Xenophon's novelized history *Cyropaedia*, in which a king declares: "I am not sorry that I killed your son, but that I did not kill you as well" (*Cyr.* 5.3.6). So too, Suetonius, in his life of Julius Caesar, reports that while Caesar was negotiating the surrender of Afranius and Petreius at Ilerda, the two legates "with a sudden change of mind" (*subita paenitentia*) killed all the partisans of Caesar in their camp (*Jul.* 75); they were hardly stung by a feeling of remorse for not having slain their enemies. In Menander's *Grouch* (*Dyskolos*), the misanthrope who gives the play its title is described by Pan, in the prologue, as being so unsociable that he refuses to greet anyone, except perhaps the god himself (that is, his statue)—and even then, he immediately regrets (*metamelei*) it (*Dysk.* 12).

In passing from a consideration of error to transgression, we move from the domain of regret to that of remorse proper, defined in one dictionary as "a gnawing distress arising from a sense of guilt for past wrongs";[19] "guilt" here is the morally operative term. We may note parenthetically that many scholars have denied that the classical Greeks and Romans recognized the concept of guilt, as opposed to shame. Yet there are passages in which the Greek and Latin terms in question do seem to take on a moral character. Lysias accuses his opponent of being "so far from feeling regret (*metamelēsai*) for the people he abused" that he compounded the wrong with further acts of *hubris* (3.7); Lysias is evidently suggesting that true regret would result in recognition of his fault and a change of behavior. Plutarch, in his essay *On Good Cheer* (*Peri euthumias/ De tranquillitate animi*), comments on a famous line in Euripides, *Orest.* 396, in which Orestes explains the madness with which he was afflicted after slaying his mother as his self-awareness (*sunesis*) of the terrible thing he has done. Plutarch affirms that the conscience (*to suneidos*) leaves regret (*metameleia*) in the soul like a bloody and ever-stinging (*nussō*) flesh wound, and the fact that no one but oneself is responsible (*epaitios*) for the wrongdoing makes the pain all the heavier (*Tranq. an.* 476f–477a). The historian Arrian, who was a disciple of the Stoic philosopher Epictetus and recorded his conversations, concludes his treatise on Alexander the

---

18. *Oxford English Dictionary*, vol. 13, 2nd ed. (Oxford: Clarendon, 1989), s.v. "regret."

19. "Remorse," *Online Merriam-Webster Dictionary*, https://tinyurl.com/SBL0396j.

Great (*Anabasis*) by affirming that it is no great surprise if he should have committed wrongs in a fit of anger, but adds that "Alexander is the only one I know of among old-time kings who repented (*metagnōnai*) of his errors by virtue of his nobility" (*Anab.* 7.21.1). Most, he says, have sought to disguise their wrongdoing; but this is a mistake, since "the only cure for error (*harmartia*), it seems to me, is to admit that one has erred and to make it clear that one regrets it (*ep' autō metagignōskonta*)," and this plants the expectation that one will not commit the same fault in the future (*Anab.* 7.29.2).

Beyond the recognition that one has done wrong, and more specifically, wronged another person, remorse usually entails the further consciousness of a defect of character as the root cause of the evil: not just the reflection that what I did was wrong but rather the acknowledgement that I was a bad person when I did it (hence the need to become a "new person"). Remorse is a result not just of an accident or a transient impulse but grounded in a deep defect of character. One has not merely done wrong, one is or was bad, and as a condition for overcoming the feeling of remorse one must change profoundly—a commitment not just to behaving differently in the future but to being different. It is here that remorse shades over into repentance, with the deep sense of guilt that this term implies. Amitai Etzioni writes in the introduction to *Repentance: A Comparative Perspective* that, in addition to remorse and punishment, "a third component, often overlooked, is actually of critical importance: To fully repent, 'sinners' must *restructure their lives* in line with the prevailing mores."[20] In the same volume, Harvey Cox explains that in the Liturgy for Holy Communion "the single and sole precondition for their participation in this feast of hope and anticipation is that they have repented and seek to lead a new life."[21] Again, in the same volume, Harold O. J. Brown writes, "Christian repentance involves not merely a turning away from what one has done in the past, but also a rejection of what one has been," and he notes that "at first, it seems to involve a kind of alienation from oneself."[22]

---

20. Amitai Etzioni, introduction to *Repentance: A Comparative Perspective*, ed. Amitai Etzioni and David E. Carney (Lanham, MD: Rowman & Littlefield, 1997), 12–13.

21. Harvey Cox, "Repentance and Forgiveness: A Christian Perspective," in Etzioni and Carney, *Repentance*, 30.

22. Harold O. J. Brown, "Godly Sorrow, Sorrow of the World: Some Christian Thoughts on Repentance," in Amitai and Carney, *Repentance*, 33.

Repentance, so conceived, is the necessary precondition to forgiveness, or the remission of sin.

This conception of repentance as a profound and deeply felt rejection of one's past seems to be grounded in the New Testament. According to Luke 3:3, John the Baptist "went into all the region around the Jordan, proclaiming a baptism of *repentance* for the forgiveness of sins" (cf. Mark 1:4). Or in the words of Jesus himself: "Thus it is written, that the Messiah is to suffer and to rise from the dead on the third day, and that *repentance* and forgiveness of sins is to be proclaimed in his name to all nations, beginning from Jerusalem" (Luke 24:46–47). Or again, in Acts 5:31: "God exalted him at his right hand as Leader and Savior that he might give *repentance* to Israel and forgiveness of sins" (Acts 5:31). In all these cases, the word translated as "repentance" is *metanoia*.

There are, however, passages that may raise doubts as to the precise sense of *metanoia* in these contexts. In Acts 19:4, we read: "Paul said, 'John baptized with the baptism of repentance [*metanoia*], telling the people to believe [*pisteusōsin*] in the one who was to come after him, that is, in Jesus.'" Here, in what is clearly an expansion of Luke 3:3, one might be inclined to understand the classical sense of *metanoia* as a change of mind, which results in abandoning old beliefs in favor of the belief in Jesus. When we read in Acts 10:43 that "all the prophets testify about him that everyone who believes in him receives forgiveness of sins through his name," we may note that belief here takes the place of *metanoia* as the condition of forgiveness or the remission (*aphesis*) of sins. The words *metanoia* and *pistis* (or faith) are placed in apposition in Acts 20:21, where Paul says: "as I testified to both Jews and Greeks about repentance [*metanoia*] toward God and faith toward our Lord Jesus"; the terms seem pretty much equivalent, suggesting that the change of mind is to be understood precisely as the adoption of the new belief. There is a similar conjunction of belief with the verb *metamelomai* at Matt 21:32: "For John came to you in the way of righteousness, and you did not believe him [*episteusate*], but the tax collectors and the harlots believed him; and even when you saw it, you did not afterward repent [*metemelēthēte*] and believe [*pisteusai*] him" (RSV). For "repent" here one could readily substitute "change of belief" (the NRSV in fact shifts to "change your minds").

This is not to say that a change of heart was never accompanied by pain or grief that we associate with repentance. As we read in Matt 11:21, "Woe to you, Chorazin! Woe to you, Bethsaida! For if the deeds of power done in you had been done in Tyre and Sidon, they would have repented long ago in sackcloth and ashes" (cf. Luke 10:13). The rough cloth garment and ashes have given repentance a reputation for harshness and grief and have contributed powerfully to the idea that *metanoia* in the New Testament, at least, implies deep sorrow and self-mortification for one's previous life. But this is not, I think, the predominant sense of the term in the New Testament any more than it is in classical Greek generally.

Indeed, in recent translations of the Bible, *metanoia* is sometimes rendered as "conversion" rather than as "repentance." In French, although the Louis Segond Bible (LSG) renders the verse "Et il alla dans tout le pays des environs de Jourdain, prêchant *le baptême de repentance*, pour la rémission des péchés," the Traduction Œcuménique de la Bible (TOB) has "Il vint dans toute la région du Jourdain, proclamant *un baptême de conversion* en vue du pardon des péchés"; still more radically, the Nouvelle Bible Second (NBS) offers "Il se rendit dans toute la région du Jourdain, proclamant *un baptême de changement* radical, pour le pardon des péchés." So too, La Bible Parole de Vie (PDV) renders the verse "*Faites-vous baptiser, pour montrer que vous voulez changer votre vie*, et Dieu pardonnera vos péchés."

Again, although the Spanish Nueva Versión Internacional (NVI) renders Luke 3:3 as "Juan recorría toda la región del Jordán predicando el *bautismo de arrepentimiento* para el perdón de pecados," and La Biblia de las Américas (LBLA), in turn, has "él fue por toda la región contigua al Jordán, predicando *un bautismo de arrepentimiento* para el perdón de los pecados," the La Palabra (BLPH) version has "Comenzó Juan a recorrer las tierras ribereñas del Jordán proclamando *un bautismo como signo de conversión* para recibir el perdón de los pecados." As "conversión" has replaced "arrepentimiento" here, the Traducción en Lenguaje Actual (TLA) offers the locution "turn to God": "Juan fue entonces a la región cercana al río Jordán. Allí le decía a la gente: '*¡Bautícense y vuélvanse a Dios!* Sólo así Dios los perdonará.'"

The Italian Nuova Riveduta (NR) has "repentance": "Ed egli andò per tutta la regione intorno al Giordano, predicando *un battesimo di ravvedimento* per il perdono dei peccati." But the Conferenza Episcopale Italiana (CEI) version gives: "Ed egli percorse tutta la regione del Giordano, predicando *un battesimo di conversione* per il perdono dei peccati."

Luther rendered the verses: "Und er kam in alle Gegend um den Jordan und predigte *die Taufe der Buße* zur Vergebung Sünden," that is, "penance." But the Gute Nachricht Bibel (GNB) has "Da machte er sich auf, durchzog die ganze Gegend am Jordan und verkündete: '*Kehrt um und lasst euch taufen*, denn Gott will euch eure Schuld vergeben!'" The latter opts for conversion as the basic idea.

These differing versions testify to a deep uncertainty about how to understand the Greek term *metanoia* and, most fundamentally, whether it is a sign of a new belief or an emotional response to a sense of past guilt.

When we turn to the church fathers, there is no such ambiguity. Basil writes in his letter to the Neocaesarians, "I pray that you all live amid tears and perpetual repentance" (*Ep.* 207.4). Ambrose, in his treatise *On Penitence: Against the Novatians*, insists that a person who has committed sins in secret, if he repents sincerely, will be reintegrated into the congregation of the church:

> I wish that the guilty person hope for pardon [*venia*], beg for it with tears, beg for it with groans, beg with the tears of all the people, entreat that he be pardoned [*ignoscatur*].... I have people who, during penitence, have made rivulets of tears in their faces, hollowed their cheeks with continual weeping, prostrated their bodies so that they might be trampled by all, and with their faces forever pale with fasting, presented the appearance of death in a breathing body. (*Paen.* 1.90–91)

John Chrysostom affirms: "For this life is in truth wholly devoted to repentance, grief (*penthos*) and wailing. This is why it is necessary to repent, not merely for one or two days, but throughout one's whole life" (*Compunct. Dem.* 1, 9 = PG 47:395, 408; cf. 47:394.1–9).

Christianity conferred a new meaning upon terms like *metanoia* and *paenitentia*, associating them not only with regret but with conversion and redemption through faith. But even those who had exhibited the profound change of heart implied in conversion might not adequately have abandoned their former state of sin, and repentance came to signify not just a deep moral regret for prior conduct but a lifelong sense of guilt and anguish for one's fallen state. This latter meaning became dominant, I believe, with the emergence of ascetic practices, with their emphasis on a lifelong discipline of self-punishment, motivated by a perpetual consciousness of guilt and sin, as the precondition for grace and forgiveness. It is at this juncture, I suggest, rather than in the Bible itself, that the terms *metanoia* and *paenitentia* assumed the intense emotional quality that we associate with them today.

I have briefly rehearsed a few of the issues that arise in examining the emotions represented in the Bible as a kind of envoi to the essays in the present volume. These essays offer richly detailed studies of various sentiments and represent a refreshing variety of approaches. Taken together, they skillfully show what can be done in the study of biblical emotions—and point to what still remains to be done.

Contributors

Samuel E. Balentine (sbalentine@upsem.edu) is Professor of Old Testament and Director of Graduate Studies at Union Presbyterian Seminary in Richmond, VA. He serves as general editor of the Smyth & Helwys Bible Commentary series, to which he contributed a volume on Job (2006); general editor of *Interpretation: Resources for the Use of Scripture in the Church*; and editor of *The Oxford Handbook of Ritual and Worship in the Hebrew Bible* (forthcoming). His most recent publications include: *Have You Considered My Servant Job? Understanding the Biblical Archetype of Patience* (University of South Carolina, 2015; Choice "Outstanding Academic Title"); *The Oxford Encyclopedia of Bible and Theology*, 2 vols. (Oxford, 2015), for which he served as editor-in-chief; and *Introduction to the Wisdom Literature* (Abingdon, forthcoming).

David A. Bosworth (Bosworth@cua.edu) is Associate Professor of Old Testament at The Catholic University of America in Washington, DC. His current research interests include grief and trauma, parent-child emotional bonds, and the motif of weeping in ancient Akkadian, Ugaritic, Hebrew, and Greek literatures. He is currently working on a book on the motif of weeping in Hebrew and Akkadian prayers. His work draws on modern sciences to help develop empirically-grounded lenses through which to analyze emotion. He is the author of *Infant Weeping in Akkadian, Hebrew, and Greek Literatures* (Eisenbrauns, 2016) and several related articles, including "Weeping in Recognition Scenes in Genesis and the Odyssey," *CBQ* 77 (2015): 613-33; "Ancient Prayers and the Psychology of Religion: Deities as Parental Figures," *JBL* 134 (2015): 681–700; "The Tears of God in the Book of Jeremiah," *Bib* 94 (2013): 24–46; "Weeping in the Psalms," *VT*, 62 (2013) 36–46; and "Daughter Zion and Weeping in Lamentations 1–2," *JSOT* 28 (2013): 217–37.

CONTRIBUTORS

L. Juliana Claassens (jclaassens@sun.ac.za) is Professor in Old Testament at the Faculty of Theology, Stellenbosch University, Stellenbosch, South Africa. Before moving back to teach at her alma mater, she spent thirteen years in the United States, studying at Princeton Theological Seminary and teaching in Green Bay, WI, Richmond, VA, and Washington, DC. She is the author of *Claiming Her Dignity: Female Resistance in the Old Testament* (Liturgical, 2016); *Mourner, Mother, Midwife: Reimagining God's Liberating Presence* (Westminster John Knox, 2012); and *The God who Provides: Biblical Images of Divine Nourishment* (Abingdon, 2004). She received an Alexander Von Humboldt Fellowship and spent twelve months in Münster, Germany, 2012–2015, working on a project on Gender and Human Dignity in the Biblical Traditions, published with Liturgical Press. She also serves as the Director of the Gender Unit at the Faculty of Theology, which seeks to offer a creative space for conducting research on an intersectional understanding of gender.

Michal Beth Dinkler (mb.dinkler@yale.edu) received her PhD in New Testament and Early Christianity from Harvard Divinity School and is currently Assistant Professor of New Testament at Yale Divinity School. Her BA and MA in English Literature are from Stanford University, and her MDiv is from Gordon-Conwell Theological Seminary. She is the author of *Silent Statements: Narrative Representations of Speech and Silence in the Gospel of Luke* (de Gruyter, 2013), as well as multiple contributions to edited volumes and articles in journals such as *JBL*, *NTS*, and *JSNT*. In addition to serving on the steering committees for the Society of Biblical Literature's Book of Acts and Gospel of Luke sections, she cochairs the Society of Biblical Literature's Speech and Talk: Discourses and Social Practices in the Ancient Mediterranean World section. Her current book project, *Literary Theory and the New Testament*, will be published by Yale.

David E. Fredrickson (dfredric@luthersem.edu) is Professor of New Testament at Luther Seminary in St. Paul, MN. He is the author of *Eros and the Christ: Longing and Envy in Paul's Christology* (Fortress, 2013). His research focuses on the tension between ancient poetry and philosophy over the topic of desire and the way this tension reappears in the writings of the New Testament. He is currently working on a book about reading the New Testament from post-structuralist perspectives.

CONTRIBUTORS

Deena Grant (dgrant@hartsem.edu) is Associate Professor of Jewish Studies at Hartford Seminary. She received her PhD from New York University, specializing in Hebrew and Judaic Studies, and her BA from Brandeis University specializing in Near Eastern and Jewish Studies. Prior to this she taught at Barry University (Miami, FL). She is the author of *Divine Anger in Biblical Literature* (Catholic Biblical Association, 2014), as well as a number of articles in the field of biblical theology and Israelite religion. She is currently working on anthropopathic depictions of God in the Hebrew Bible.

Katherine M. Hockey (katherine.hockey@abdn.ac.uk) is Kirby Laing Postdoctoral Fellow in New Testament at the University of Aberdeen, UK. Before taking up the post at Aberdeen, she was Postgraduate Research Associate at the University of Exeter, UK, where she worked alongside Professor David Horrell on the AHRC (UK) funded project "Ethnicity, Race, and Religion in Early Christian and Jewish Identities." She gained her AHRC (UK) funded PhD from Durham University in 2016 under the Supervision of Professor John Barclay with her thesis, "Seeing Emotionally: An Investigation of the Role of Emotion in the Rhetorical Discourse of 1 Peter." She was coinitiator and organizer of the Muted Voices Conference held in Durham, UK, in 2015, resulting in a coedited collection with Madison N. Pierce and Francis Watson, *Muted Voices of the New Testament: Readings in the Catholic Epistles and Hebrews* (T&T Clark, 2017).

Thomas Kazen (thomas.kazen@ths.se) is professor of Biblical Studies at Stockholm School of Theology, Sweden, where he has taught since 2002. He is author of *Jesus and Purity Halakhah: Was Jesus Indifferent to Impurity* (Almqvist & Wiksell International, 2002), with a corrected reprint edition (Eisenbrauns, 2010), *Issues of Impurity in Early Judaism* (Eisenbrauns, 2010); *Emotions in Biblical Law: A Cognitive Science Approach* (Sheffield Phoenix, 2011); and *Scripture, Interpretation, or Authority? Motives and Arguments in Jesus' Halakic Conflicts* (Mohr Siebeck, 2013); and a Swedish forthcoming book on same-sex relationships in the Bible and the ancient world. He is presently working on a book on apocalyptic language and imagery and beginning a long-term research project on ideas, practices, and rituals of moral repair in antiquity.

David Konstan (dk87@nyu.edu) is Professor of Classics at New York University. Among his publications are *Greek Comedy and Ideology* (Oxford,

1995); *Friendship in the Classical World* (Cambridge, 1997); *Pity Transformed* (Duckworth, 2001); *The Emotions of the Ancient Greeks: Studies in Aristotle and Classical Literature* (Toronto, 2006); "A Life Worthy of the Gods": *The Materialist Psychology of Epicurus* (Parmenides, 2008); *Before Forgiveness: The Origins of a Moral Idea* (Cambridge, 2010); and *Beauty: The Fortunes of an Ancient Greek Idea* (Oxford, 2014). He is a past president of the American Philological Association (now the Society for Classical Studies), and a vice president of the Bristol Institute of Greece, Rome and the Classical Tradition. He is a fellow of the American Academy of Arts and Sciences and an honorary fellow of the Australian Academy of the Humanities.

David A. Lambert (dalambe@email.unc.edu) is Associate Professor of Religious Studies at the University of North Carolina at Chapel Hill. He is the author of *How Repentance Became Biblical: Judaism, Christianity, and the Interpretation of Scripture* (Oxford University, 2016), which received the Award for Excellence in the Study of Religion in the category of Textual Studies from American Academy of Religion. Other recent publications include "Refreshing Philology: James Barr, Supersessionism, and the State of Biblical Words," *Bib Int* 24 (2016): 332–56; "How the 'Torah of Moses' Became Revelation: An Early, Apocalyptic Theory of Pentateuchal Origins," *JSJ* 47 (2016): 22–54; and "The Book of Job in Ritual Perspective," *JBL* 134 (2015): 557–75. His research focuses on the Hebrew Bible as a textual object whose interpretation tells us as much about its readers and their communities as it does about ancient Israelite origins. He is currently working on two book projects, one related to the dual concepts of Scripture and interpretation, and the other on biblical Hebrew terms associated with the self. He has received a EURIAS fellowship to work on the latter at the Institute for Advanced Studies in Jerusalem during 2017–2018.

Stephen D. Moore is Edmund S. Janes Professor of New Testament Studies at the Theological School, Drew University in Madison, New Jersey. He has authored or coauthored, edited or coedited around two dozen books, including *God's Beauty Parlor: And Other Queer Spaces in and around the Bible* (Stanford, 2001); *Empire and Apocalypse: Postcolonialism and the New Testament* (Sheffield Phoenix, 2006); *The Invention of the Biblical Scholar: A Critical Manifesto* (with Yvonne Sherwood; Fortress, 2011); *Untold Tales from the Book of Revelation: Sex and Empire, Gender and Ecology* (SBL Press, 2014); and *Gospel Jesuses and Other Nonhumans: Biblical Criticism*

Post-poststructuralism (SBL Press, forthcoming). He is also the author of *Revealing the New Testament* (Thinking Strings, 2017), a courseware introduction to the New Testament.

Dennis Olson (dennis.olson@ptsem.edu) is the Charles Haley Professor of Old Testament Theology at Princeton Theological Seminary. His academic focus is on Old Testament narrative, literary theory, and biblical theology with particular emphasis on the Pentateuch (Genesis–Deuteronomy). He is the author of several books, including the theological commentaries, *Numbers* (Westminster John Knox, 1996); *Deuteronomy and the Death of Moses: A Theological Reading* (Fortress, 1994; Wipf & Stock, 2005); and "Judges" in *The New Interpreter's Bible*, vol. 2 (Abingdon, 1998). He is currently writing a commentary and a theological study on the book of Exodus. He was General Acquisitions Editor (Old Testament) for the Society of Biblical Literature (1998–2004) and General Pentateuch editor for *The Encyclopedia of the Bible and Its Reception* (de Gruyter, 2008–2015), vols. 1–12.

Antony Dhas Prakasam (antonydhas1974@gmail.com) is a PhD candidate in Biblical Studies at The Catholic University of America, Washington, DC. He is a Catholic priest belonging to the Assumption of the Blessed Virgin Mary Province (Bangalore, India), of the Society of the Catholic Apostolate (Pallottine Fathers and Brothers). After obtaining his SSL from the Pontifical Biblical Institute (Rome, Italy), he worked as Dean of Studies and taught at the Pallottine Centre for Theological and Religious Formation (Mysore, India). His main research interests focus on self-conscious emotions such as pride, shame, guilt, and embarrassment, particularly how they influence characters in the Hebrew Bible and affect their relationship to themselves (self-image), to God (faith), and to other people (ethics). He is currently working on his dissertation, "Pride of Babylon and Zion in Isaiah in Light of the Theory of Self-Conscious Emotions." He intends to extend his research into other prophetic writings that explicitly condemn nations and individuals for their pride.

Matthew Richard Schlimm (mschlimm@dbq.edu) is Professor of Old Testament at the University of Dubuque Theological Seminary. He is the author of *From Fratricide to Forgiveness: The Language and Ethics of Anger in Genesis* (Eisenbrauns, 2011); and *This Strange and Sacred Scripture: Wrestling with the Old Testament and Its Oddities* (Baker Academic,

2015). He was also coeditor of *The CEB Study Bible* (Common English Bible, 2013). He is completing a book on what is lost in translating the Hebrew Bible into English (Abingdon). Schlimm holds a PhD from Duke University and is an ordained minister in the United Methodist Church.

F. Scott Spencer (sspencer@btsr.edu) is Professor of New Testament and Biblical Interpretation at Baptist Theological Seminary at Richmond, VA, where he has taught since 2002. He is the author of seven books, most recently: *The Song of Songs* (Liturgical, 2017); and *Salty Wives, Spirited Mothers, and Savvy Widows: Capable Women of Purpose and Persistence in Luke's Gospel* (Eerdmans, 2012). He is a past president of the Southeastern Commission for the Study of Religion (SECSOR) and current cochair of the Bible and Emotion section for the Society of Biblical Literature. He is working on a commentary on Mark (Smyth & Helwys) and a book on Jesus's emotions (passions) in the gospels.

Ivar Vegge (ivegge@fjellhaug.no) is Associate Professor of New Testament at Fjellhaug International University College, Oslo, Norway. Prior to this, he taught at Mekane Yesus Theological Seminary and Ethiopian Graduate School of Theology (both Addis Abeba, Ethiopia). He is the author of *2 Corinthians—A Letter about Reconciliation: A Psychagogical, Epistolographical and Rhetorical Analysis* (Mohr Siebeck, 2008). His current research interests include Mark; the rhetoric of characterization; awe and trauma studies; Christology; and 1–2 Corinthians. He was born in Ethiopia and lived twenty years in Ethiopia and Kenya.

Ancient Sources Index

Hebrew Bible/Old Testament

Genesis
3:16	5
4:7	5
4:10	119
6:6	50
12:11	363
12:18	119
13:16	192 n. 60
15:1	53
18:7	188 n. 50
18:12	187
18:21	157 n. 52
20:9	119
20:12	358
21:17	53, 128
24:67	359
26:10	119
26:24	53
26:27	64, 68–69
28:10–22	221
28:14	192 n. 60
29:17	188 n. 50, 363
29:20	169, 359
29:31	64, 68–69
29:33	64, 68–69
32:22–32	220
33:13	188 n. 50
34	359
37	35, 61, 69–73
37:3–4	70
37:4	64, 68–69, 71, 73
37:5	64, 68–69, 70 n. 35
37:8	64, 68–69, 70 n. 35
37:11	69, 71
37:18–22	72
37:19	72
37:20	72
37:23–28	72
37:26–27	73
37:29–30	72
37:32	72
37:33–35	128
37:35	122
38:12	122
39	359
39:6	363
42:28	259
44:27–31	128
44:30–31	127
45	36, 73–74, 253–55
45:3	254, 259
45:4–15	73–74
45:5	254
45:15	254
45:25–28	220, 254, 255
45:26	253, 254, 258
45:27	255
45:28	255
50:20	363

Exodus
2:6	128
3:14	261
8:12	192 n. 60
8:13	192 n. 60
12:16	255
15:11–16	36
15:16	258

ANCIENT SOURCES INDEX

Exodus (cont.)		35:9–34	107 n. 32
16:20	307		
20:5–6	45 n. 6	Deuteronomy	
22:21–22	147	2:25	259
33:19	261	4:31	45 n. 6
33:20	303	4:39	88 n. 53
33:22	261	5:9–10	45 n. 6
34:5–6	44 n. 4	5:15	54 n. 32
34:6	44–45 n. 4, 261	6:5	54 n. 32, 174
34:6–7	35, 44–49, 237	6:5–8	5
		7:1–5	35, 78
Leviticus		7:2	78, 89 n. 55
11	101, 109	7:5	78
12	1110 n. 36	7:7	174
12–15	101	7:9–10	45 n. 6
12:17	229	7:17	174
15	101 n. 15	7:17–18	54 n. 32
15:11–16	252–53	8:2	54 n. 32
16	158	8:17	174
16:1–28	157–58	8:18	54 n. 32
16:1–31	36, 157–58	9:4	174
16:29	158	9:7	54 n. 32
16:29–31	157–58	10:16	174
17–26	107 n. 32	14	101 n. 16
18	110 n. 36	14:3	101
18:8–18	357	15:7	258
18:22	358	15:15	54 n. 32
18:24–30	102	16:3	54 n. 32
18:25	81–82	16:12	54 n. 32
18:26	49 n. 18	19:1–13	107 n. 32
19:18	54 n. 32	20:8	188 n. 50
20	110 n. 36	20:16–18	81, 89 n. 55
20:11–12	357	21:1–9	107 n. 32
20:18	229 n. 40	22:11	363
20:21	102	21:15–16	64 n. 15
20:22–24	102	22:30	357
20:25–26	103	23:12–14	105 n. 29
23:26–32	36, 158	24:9	54 n. 32
23:29	158	24:18	54 n. 32
26	110 n. 36	24:22	54 n. 32
		28:24	192 n. 60
Numbers		28:54	188 n. 50
12:10–13	102	28:56	188 n. 50
14:18	44 n. 4, 45 n. 6	30:6	174
21:2–3	35, 85	32:4	218 n. 4

32:7	54 n. 32	1:18	150
32:39	261	2:8	149
		4:12–22	127
Joshua		9:2	362 n. 14
2	35, 87–93	10:27	237
2:1	87	13:11	119
2:11	88 n. 53	15:3	157 n. 51
2:13	89	17:42	
2:14	89	21:1–6	235
6	35, 87–93	25	36, 253
6:25	87	25:3	363
7:25	87	25:37	258
9:24	3	25:37–38	253
10:2	3	26:1	132
		26:23	218 n. 4
		26:25	132
Judges		28:4–11	128
3–5	26		
6:23	53		
10:10	165	2 Samuel	
10:10–16	36	1:24	187
10:13	165	3:29	102
10:16	165	3:39	188 n. 50
11:7	68–69	7:29	186–87
11:7–10	65	11–12	359
15:2	68–69	11:11	359
15:11	119	12:15–23	35
16:2	237	12:16–23	36, 150
16:4–21	359	12:16	150
		12:17	150–51
Ruth		12:18	151
2:2	132	12:22	150
2:8	132	12:23	128
2:22	132	12:24	119
3:1	132	13	359
3:10–11	132	13:1	363
3:16	132	13:12–19	36, 145
3:18	132	13:14–15	64
		13:15	68–69
1 Samuel		13:21–22	63 n. 13
1–2	36, 149–50	13:22	68
1:1–28	149	13:22–32	35, 63
1:5	359	14:25	363
1:6	149	14:27	363
1:8	151	18:19–32	127
1:11	149–50	19:1	127, 132

2 Samuel (cont.)

19:5	132
21:10–14	132
22:43	192 n. 60

1 Kings

1:3	363
8:23	88 n. 53
11:1–2	359
17	132 n. 46
19:11 (LXX 3 Kingdoms)	261
21:27	127
22:8	68–69
22:8–27	35, 63

2 Kings

4	132 n. 46
10:27	105 n. 29
12:16	218 n. 4
18:13–19:37	186 n. 39
19:6	53
22:7	218 n. 4

2 Chronicles

1:19	192 n. 60
11:1–2	359
18:7	68–69
29:5	102
30:9	45 n. 6

Ezra

8:21	147 n. 25, 157 n. 51
9	110 n.36
9–10	110
9:11	35, 102, 113–14

Nehemiah

1:5	45 n. 6
8:9	146 n. 21
9:17	44 n. 4, 45 n. 6
9:31	45 n. 6
10	110

Esther

1:11	363

2:7	363
2:17	359
4:4	151 n. 37

Job

1:9	192 n. 60
2:12	192
4:19	192
9:8	261
14:8	192 n. 60
14:19	192 n. 60
10:9	192
16:15	192
17:6–7	36, 252
17:7	256–57, 258
22:26	188 n. 50
27:10	188 n. 50
30:30	8 n. 19
39:14	192 n. 60
40:27	188 n. 50
42:15	363

Psalms

3:8	134
5:2–3	127, 134
6:2–3	134
6:3	259
6:4	259
7:6	192 n. 60
9:7	186
9:14	64 n. 18
13:2–5	127
18:7	127
18:17	64 n. 18
18:18	64
18:41	64 n. 18
21:8	64 n. 18
22:2–3	127
22:15	152
22:30	192 n. 60
25:19	64
32:4	218 n. 4
34:7	149
34:12	53
34:12–16	349

35:13	147 n. 25, 151 n. 38	11:22	363
35:19	64	12:17	218 n. 4
37:4	188 n. 50	12:22	218 n. 4
38:19	64	15:1	188 n. 50
39:13	127	22–23	52 n. 27
42:2–4	127	22:24	52 n. 27
43:1–2	134	25:15	188 n. 50
44:25	192	25:20	8
45:3	363	31:30	363
45:11	132		
45:12	363	Song of Songs	
51	108	7:10	5
69:2	134		
69:11–12	36, 152	Isaiah	
77:2	128	1:8	131
77:6	127	2:6–22	193
77:9–10	45 n. 6	2:17	193
77:19	261	3:26	192
78:38	45 n. 6	5:8	190
86:5	45 n. 6	5:8–24	190
86:15	44 n. 4, 45 n. 6	5:9	362–63
88:2–4	134	6:9–10	281 n. 66
103:8	45 n. 6	8:12	53
103:14	192	10–11	111 n. 39
103:17	45 n. 6	13–14	177
107:23–32	262	13:9	49–50
109:22	149	13:19	188
109:24–26	36, 151	14	194
110:10	53	14:1–4	177 n. 3
112:4	45 n. 6	14:4–5	194
116:5	45 n. 6	14:4–21	177 n. 3
117:1–4	237	14:6–8	194
117:29	237	14:9–11	194
120:1	127	14:13–14	194
135	237	14:16–17	194
145:8	45 n. 6	14:22–23	177 n. 3, 194
		25:12	192, 192 n. 60
Proverbs		26:5	192
1:7	53	29:4	192 n. 60, 193
1:8	132	30	110 n. 36
1:10	132	30:22	35, 102, 112–13
3:25	53	32:11–12	146 n. 21
6:25	363	34:7	192 n. 60
8:26	192 n. 60	37:6	53
9:10	53	40–55	135

Isaiah (cont.)

40:1	135
40:12	192 n. 60
41:4	261
43	135–36
43:10–11	261
43:16	261
45:5	187
45:6	187
45:18	187, 261
45:21	187
45:22	187
46:9	187
47	36, 136, 177–79, 183–94
47:1	184–85, 188, 192–93
47:1–4	184, 185, 191
47:1–5	191
47:3	184
47:5	184–85, 187, 193
47:5–6	188
47:5–7	184
47:6	188, 190
47:7	184–87, 190–91
47:8	184–87, 191
47:8–9	184
47:8–11	184–85
47:9	184, 191–92
47:9–11	189
47:10	184–87, 190–91, 193
47:10–11	184
47:11	184
47:12–13	184–85, 188–89
47:12–15	189
47:13	185
47:14	184–85
47:14–15	184–85, 191–93
47:15	184, 192
49:13	135
49:14–21	135
49:17–23	132
49:23	192 n. 60
51:3	135
51:9–10	261
51:12	135
51:19	135
53	282–83 n. 74
54:1–3	132
54:11	135
58	156
58:2–9	36, 155
58:3	147 n. 25
58:5	147 n. 25
58:13	188 n. 50
58:14	188 n. 50
63:3	55
63:7–64:11	111 n.39
63:10	50
64:6	35, 110
66:11	188 n. 50

Jeremiah

2:13–17	135
3:7	49
5:1	218 n. 4
5:3	218 n. 4
6:26	146 n. 21
11:6	363
20:7	49 n. 18
31:15	128, 132
32:4	188
32:18–19	45 n. 6
32:41	49
36:6–7	157 n. 53
36:24	146 n. 21
38:3	188
46:20	363
51	178 n. 4
51:34	187

Lamentations

1–2	35, 129–36
1:1	133
1:1–8	192 n. 59
1:2	130, 133
1:4	130
1:5	130, 134
1:6	130–31
1:7–9	134
1:7	130
1:8	134

1:9	130, 133–34, 193 n. 65	Hosea	
1:10	134	2:19–20	169–70
1:11	130, 133–34	2:22	218 n. 4
1:11–22	130	5:8	161
1:12	134	5:8–6:6	161, 167
1:14	134	5:13	161
1:15	130	5:13–6:4	166
1:16	130	5:14	161–62
1:17	133	6	161, 168, 173
1:18	130, 134	6:1	162, 166
1:19	130, 134	6:1–3	161–63, 165–70
1:20	130	6:1–6	36
1:21	134	6:2–3	166, 167
1:21–22	136	6:4	166, 170
1:22	130, 134	6:5	167
2:1	131, 192	6:5–6	167
2:9	193 n. 65	6:6	167
2:10	192	11:1–8	170
2:14	192 n. 59	11:5	169
2:21–22	135	11:8	51 n. 24
3:32	45 n. 6	14	168, 173
		14:1–3	168
Ezekiel		14:1–7	36, 168
4:12–15	105 n. 29	14:2	168
16:14	363	14:4	168
16:15	363	14:7	168
22	110 n. 36		
22:7–9	358	Joel	
22:10–11	102, 358	1:8–14	36, 153–54
23:18	49 n. 18	1:18	156 n. 51
24:7	192 n. 60	2:12–13	157 n. 53
27–28	178 n. 4	2:12–14	154 n. 46
36	35, 110 n. 36, 113	2:13	45 n. 6
36:17	102	2:15–17	154 n. 46
36:17–18	113		
36:25	113, 113	Amos	
36:26	113	2:7	192 n. 60
36:31	102, 113		
39:23	188	Jonah	
		1:1–16	262
Daniel		3:5	153
9:4	45 n. 6	3:5–10	36
10:12	147 n. 25	3:6–10	156–57
		3:8	154
		3:10	157

Jonah (cont.)		4 Maccabees	
4:2	45 n. 6	1:1	7
4:11	157	1:20	8
		1:22	8
Nahum		1:25–27	8
1:2–3	45 n. 6	4:25	9 n. 20
		7:1–5	8
Habakkuk		7:7	8
1:4	254 n. 35	9:8	9 n. 20
1:5	283	10:10	9 n. 20
2:4	218 n. 4	14:9	9 n. 20
3:15	261		
		1 Esdras	
Zechariah		4:18	362
3	105 n. 29		
7:5	154 n. 47	4 Ezra	
13:1	114 n. 44	7:132–140	45 n. 6

Ancient Near Eastern Literature

Ancient Jewish Writers

Instruction of Amenemope		Josephus, *Jewish Antiquities*	
2–4	52 n. 27	2.169	220
9–10	52 n. 27	2.169–171	221
12	52 n. 27	2.176	221
		5.1–7	90
Instruction of Ptahhotep			
2–4	52 n. 27	Philo, *De agricultura*	
25	52 n. 27	34	323

Apocryphal/Deuterocanonical Books

Philo, *De mutatione nominum*
167   276

Judith			
4:10	157 n. 51	Philo, *De specialibus legibus*	
		4.140	325 n. 35
Wisdom of Solomon			
14:2–4	262	Philo, *Legatio ad Gaium*	
		14	323
Sirach		189	254 n. 36
24:5–6	261		
		Philo, *Legum allegoriae*	
2 Maccabees		2.38	323
6:30	9 n. 20		
7:18	9 n. 20		
7:32	9 n. 20		
9:28	v		

New Testament

Matthew

1:5	90
2:3	259
5:11–12	347 n. 64
5:12	269
5:22	52
5:43–48	350 n. 79
6:25–34	53
10:25	347 n. 64
11:21	367–68
13:44	269
18:8	55
21:32	367
21:37–39	49
22:35–40	54 n. 32
25:21	269
25:23	269
25:41	55
26:26	306
27:18	18
28:5	53
28:10	53

Mark

1:1	235
1:16–20	239
1:22	244
1:27	244, 255
1:40–45	33 n. 95, 276 n.
2:12	244, 255–56
2:25–26	235 n. 55
3:5	36, 258
3:21	244
4:35–41	36, 249, 250, 256
4:35–6:56	246
4:40	245, 256
4:41	244–45, 250, 255
5:1–20	230
5:11–16	230
5:15	244, 255
5:20	244, 255
5:21–22	230
5:21–24	230
5:24–34	36, 228–34, 239–40
5:25	229
5:26	229
5:27	230
5:28	230, 239
5:29	229 n. 40, 234 n. 50
5:29–30	231
5:30	232
5:32	229
5:33	233–34, 244–45, 256
5:34	217, 234
5:42	244, 255
6:2	244
6:6	244–45
6:7–8	239
6:14–8:30	260 n. 47
6:20	244–45
6:23	269
6:30–44	260
6:45–52	36, 243–44, 259–63
6:47–48	261
6:48	261
6:49	259
6:49–50	259
6:49–52	259
6:50	238, 244, 259, 260 n. 52
6:50–51	259
6:51	244–45, 259–60
6:51–52	245, 252, 255
6:52	243–46, 258, 260–61
7:37	244, 245, 255
8:17	258, 261 n. 48
8:21–33	239
8:22–26	256
8:29	235
9:6	244–45, 255
9:15	244–45
9:32	244
9:41	235
10:20	269
10:24	244
10:26	244–45, 255
10:28–29	239
10:32	244
10:34	234 n. 50

Mark (cont.)		4:22	281		
10:36–37	238–39	4:28	281		
10:41–45	239	6:3	274		
10:46	234	6:27–36	350 n. 79		
10:46–52	36, 234–40	7:16	53		
10:47	235	8:1–3	277		
10:47–48	234–35, 239	8:1–15	37		
10:49	238	8:8	284		
10:50	238	8:13	281		
10:51	238	8:14–15	284		
10:52	217, 228, 236	8:18	282, 282 n. 72		
11:10	236	9:5	280 n. 65		
11:18	244–45	9:48	280 n. 65		
11:32	244	9:53	280 n. 65		
12:6–8	49	10:8–10	280 n. 65		
12:10–11	244	10:13	368		
12:11	244	12:1–34	53, 59		
12:12	244	15:5–7	49		
12:17	244–45	15:7	269		
12:35–37	236	15:9–10	49		
13:9–13	347 n. 64	15:10	269		
14:22	306	15:28	52		
14:33	244–45	15:32	49		
14:33–34	237	16:4	280 n. 65		
14:34	31	16:9	280 n. 65		
15:1–47	249	17:25	9		
15:5	244–45	20:13–15	49		
15:10	18	22:19	306		
15:34	237	24:26	9		
15:44	244–45	24:36–39	259		
16:1–8	37, 250, 275	24:46	9		
16:5	244	24:46–47	367		
16:6	244				
16:8	244, 250	*John*			
		1:1	48, 305		
Luke		1:13	305		
1:1	281	1:14	305		
1:1–4	281 n. 66	1:18	303		
1:3	282	1:29	302, 307 n. 77		
1:12	259	1:36	302, 307 n. 77		
1:14	269	1:46	235		
2:10	269	3:6	305		
2:28	280 n. 65	3:14	302		
3:3	367–68	3:16	303		
4:16–30	37, 280–81	3:29	269		

3:33	48	17:13	269
4:24	48	19:1	305
5:25	305	19:16	305
5:28–29	305	19:39–40	305
5:37	303	20:3–12	305
6:4	302	20:19	305
6:31	307	20:25	307
6:35	302	20:26	305
6:46	303	20:27	305, 307
6:48	302		
6:49–51	307	Acts	
6:50–58	306	1:1	281
6:51	302, 307	5:31	367
6:51–58	306, 306 n. 75	5:41	269–70
6:52	306	7:38	280 n. 65
6:54–55	306	8:14	280 n. 65
6:56	308	8:26–40	37, 279 n. 59, 280 n. 62, 283
6:58	307	8:28	280 n. 64
6:63	304, 308	8:30	280 n. 64
7:23	52	8:32	280 n. 64
8:12	302	8:39	281
9:2	237	9:31	53
9:3	237	10:43	367
9:5	302	11:1	280 n. 65
10:7	302	12:6–17	278 n. 53
10:9	302	13:9–11	237
11:3–4	302 n. 62	13:15	280 n. 64
11:11–15	302 n. 62	13:27	37, 280 n. 64, 283
11:25	307	13:40–41	37, 283
11:35	50, 298, 301, 303	13:52	269
11:35–38	37	14:17	269
11:38	303	15:21	280 n. 64
11:39	303	15:31	280 n. 64, 281
11:44	305	16:32	281
11:45–53	302	16:34	281
12:27	303	17	16
12:27–28	259	17:11	280 n. 64, 280 n. 65
12:40	258	18:9	53
14:1	259	19:4	367
14:2	306	20:21	367
14:27	259	22:5	280 n. 65
15:11	269	23:34	280 n. 64
15:18–20	347 n. 64	28:21	280 n. 65
16:24	269	28:26–27	281 n. 66
17:3	269		

Romans
  1:24–27   313 n. 5, 323 n. 31
  1:26   9
  1:27   323 n. 31
  1:29   18
  1:29–31   9
  2:6–8   50
  3:22   218
  3:26   218
  5:3–5   269
  11:7   258
  11:25   258
  12:17   349 n. 76
  12:19   351 n. 86
  13:1–7   349 n. 74
  14:17   269
  15:13   269

1 Corinthians
  4:8   270
  7:37   325 n. 35
  11:23–24   306
  13:12   37, 313, 321, 326–28, 326 n. 39

2 Corinthians
  3:14   258
  7:7–9   269
  12:2   231
  12:20   52

Galatians
  2:16   218
  3:1—4:11   14 n. 35, 218 n. 5
  3:22   218
  5:20   52
  5:21   18
  5:22   269

Ephesians
  4:13–14   324–25 n. 35
  4:14   325 n. 35
  4:18   258
  4:26   52
  4:30   50
  4:31   52–53
  5:21—6:9   325

Philippians
  1:8   18
  1:15   18
  2:2   269
  2:12   53
  2:16   18
  2:18   269
  2:29   269
  3:1   269
  3:9   218
  4:4   269

Colossians
  1:24   269
  3:5   9
  3:8   52
  3:18–4:1   325

1 Thessalonians
  4:5   9
  5:15   349 n. 76
  5:16   269

1 Timothy
  2:9–10   322
  3:9   218
  3:13   218
  4:1   218
  5:8   218
  6:4   18
  6:10   218
  6:21   218

2 Timothy
  1:4   269
  1:13   218
  2:18   218
  4:7   218

Titus
  1:13   218
  3:3   18
  3:3–7   324 n. 33

Hebrews		2:21–25	346
2:10	325 n. 35	2:22–23	341
4:1–11	324 n. 33	2:23	9, 339, 347, 350 n. 82
5:9	325 n. 35	2:24	346
5:14	325 n. 35	2:24–25	347
6:1	325 n. 35	3:1	339
7:28	325 n. 35	3:2–5	322
11:31	90	3:6	53, 336, 339
12:2	269	3:6–7	37, 313, 324–26
		3:7	324–25
James		3:8	335
1:2–4	269	3:9	337–38, 339, 341, 349–50
2:23–25	90	3:9–10	350
3:2	325 n. 35	3:10	339
		3:10–12	349
1 Peter		3:12	350
1:3	335	3:13	351
1:3–5	346	3:14	53, 339–40, 348, 351
1:6–7	346	3:15–16	339, 351–52
1:7	346	3:15–17	335
1:8	265, 285	3:16	338–41, 350 n. 82
1:8–9	335	3:16–17	339
1:9	346	3:17	340
1:11	346, 347	3:18	346
1:13	335, 350 n. 82	3:18–22	351 n. 85
1:14	348, 349	4:1	9, 339 n. 35, 347
1:17	335, 349, 350 n. 82	4:2–4	348, 349
1:17–21	350 n. 77	4:5	350 n. 82
1:18	348	4:7	335
1:19	346	4:12	340, 346, 347
1:21	346, 347	4:12–13	335
2:1	18, 349	4:13	269
2:1–10	340 n. 38	4:13–14	348
2:1–3:7	325	4:14	339, 340 n. 38
2:7–8	350 n. 82	4:14–16	338–39
2:12	338, 339, 341 n. 41	4:16	340
2:13–14	349	4:17–19	350 n. 82
2:14	348	4:19	339
2:15	339, 341 n. 41	5:10	340 n. 38
2:17–18	335		
2:18	339, 347	2 Peter	
2:18–19	339	1:3–11	324 n. 33
2:19	340		
2:20	339	1 John	
2:21	9, 346	1:5	48

1 John (cont.)
   4:7–12   48 n. 17
   4:8   35, 48
   4:16   35, 48

Jude
   3   218

Revelation
   1:17   53
   5:6   307 n. 77
   17–18   177, 178 n. 4

Rabbinic Works

Agadat Bereshith
   31   86 n. 42

b. Megillah
   10b   86
   15a   89

b. Sanhedrin
   39b   86

b. Ta'anit
   41   86 n. 42

b. Yebamot
   3a   358 n. 4

Genesis Rabbah
   55.5   86 n. 42

Midrash Tanhuma
   50   86

Early Christian Writings

Ambrose, *De paenitentia*
   1.90–91   369

Augustine, *De Trinitate*
   13.2.5   219

Basil of Caesarea, *Epistulae*
   207.4   369

Gregory of Nissa, *De vita Mosis*
   2.232   327

John Chrysostom, *Ad Demetrium de compunction*
   1   369
   9   369

Tertullian, *Contra Marcellum*
   1.26   56

Greco-Roman Literature

Achilles Tatius, *Leucippe and Clitophon*
   1.9.4–5   316 n. 11
   2.29   272
   2.36   315 n. 8
   4.8   316

Aelian, *Varia historia*
   9.13   257

Aeschylus, *Agamemnon*
   1331   312 n. 3

Aeschylus, *Persae*
   545   322

Anacharis, *Epistulae*
   4   324 n. 33

Andronicus, *De passionibus*
   4   337 n. 27

Anthologia Graeca
   5.78   316 n. 10
   5.255   312, 315, 318, 319
   5.275   312 n. 3
   5.279   319 n. 20
   5.281   319 n. 20
   5.288   319 n. 20
   5.290   319 n. 20

ANCIENT SOURCES INDEX

5.303	319 n. 20	Aristotle, *Rhetorica*	
12.21	321	1.11.9 (1370b)	356–57
12.22	319 n. 20	2.1.8 (1378a)	276
12.49	319 n. 20	2.1.8–9 (1378a)	6
12.65	316 n. 11	2.2.1 (1378a)	336, 355
12.81	319 n. 20	2.2.2 (1378b)	337
12.83	319 n. 20	2.2.3 (1378b)	338
12.92	319	2.2.5 (1378b)	338
12.99	319 n. 20	2.2.6 (1378b)	338
259	319 n. 20	2.2.11 (1379a)	339
		2.4.31 (1382a)	61, 65 n. 19
Apollonius of Rhodes, *Argonautica*		2.5.16 (1383a)	238
1.1232	321 n. 26	2.8.2 (1385b)	236–37
3.284	317		
3.960–972	320	Arius Didymus, *Liber de philosophorum*	
460–61	312 n. 3	*sectis*	
1009–1010	320 n. 22	78.1	325 n. 35
1065–1067	320 n. 22		
		Arrian, *Anabasis*	
Aristotle, *De anima*		7.21.1	365–66
1.1 (403a)	278	7.29.2	366
1.1.10–30 (403a)	6		
1.1.16–17 (403a)	357	Athenaeus, *Deipnosophistae*	
		12.549b	257
Aristotle, *Ethica nichomachea*			
1.7 (1097a–b)	207	Aulus Gellius, *Noctes Atticae*	
1.9 (1099b)	206	19.1	233
2.5.21 (1105b)	357		
3.5 (1113b–1115a)	206	Bion, *Epitaphius Adonis*	
3.7.4 (1115b)	6–7 n. 15	42–49	316
4.5.3 (1125b)	342		
4.5.5–6 (1126a)	342	Callimachus, *Hymnus in Dianam*	
4.5.6 (1126a)	342	191	321 n. 26
10.3.8–9 (1173b)	6		
7.7.12–17(1150b)	325	Calpurnius Siculus, *Bucolicae*	
10.4 (1174a–1175b)	7 n. 17	35	254 n. 36
10.7 (1177b)	206 n. 31		
10.7.27–28 (1177b)	209	Catullus	
10.7–8 (1177b-1178a)	206 n. 31	51	316 n. 13
Aristotle, *Metaphysics*		Chariton, *De Chaerea et Callirhoe*	
6 (1026a)	213–14 n. 52	1.1.6	320 n. 22
Aristotle, *Problemata*		Charondas, *Fragmenta*	
879b	323	60	325 n. 35

ANCIENT SOURCES INDEX

Dio Chrysostom, *De gloria i* (*Or.* 66)
1   321

Dio Chrysostom, *De regno iv* (*Or.* 4)
101   323–24

Dio Chrysostom, *De virtute* (*Or.* 8)
16   325 n. 35

Dio Chrysostom, *Venator* (*Or.* 7)
324 n. 33

Diogenes Laertius, *Vitae philosophorum*
7.86   276
7.111   267
7.113   337 n. 27

Epictetus, *Diatribai*
1.27.6   278
3.13.4–8   311

Epictetus
Frag. 9   233

Euripedes, *Orestes*
396   367

Epicurus, *Principal Doctrines*
7   343–44

Euripedes, *Iphigenia auldensis*
586   321 n. 26

Euripedes, *Iphigenia taurica*
414–415   312 n. 3

Euripedes, *Supplices*
79   322

Euripedes, *Tragicorum graecorum fragmenta*
5:1080   364

Galen, *De propriorum animi*
5.14   325 n. 35

5:34–36   325 n. 35
5.55   325 n. 35

Gorgias, *Helena*
8   271

Herodotus, *Historiae*
3.140   364
7.29   364
9.89   364

Hesiod, *Opera et dies*
66   318

Hippocrates, *De morbo sacro*
4   205 n. 24

Horace, *Epistulae*
1.6.9–16   254 n. 36

Julian, *Misopogon*
347   323

Lucian, *Dialogi mortuorum*
21.4   326 n. 38

Lysias
3.7   365

Menander, *Epitrepontes*
287–98   364

Menander, *Dyskolos*
12   365

Mimnermus, Fragment 1
1.1–5   360–61

Musaeus, *De Herone et Leandro*
100–107   320 n. 22
284   312 n. 3

Musonius Rufus, *Dissertationem a Lucio Digestarum Reliquiae*
12   323

ANCIENT SOURCES INDEX

Ovid, *Amores*
2.16.41–42   319 n. 21
16.103–104   320 n. 22

Perictione, *Fragmenta*
142   322

Philodemus, *De ira*
26.4–7   338
37.20–29   338 n. 29, 343
37.39–38.5   343
46.28–35   337 n. 25
47.18–41   337 n. 27

Pindar, *Fragmenta*
123   328 n. 42

Plato, *Cratylus*
420a   315

Plato, *Gorgias*
493d–494a   325–26

Plato, *Leges*
783d   321

Plato, *Phaedrus*
68c   322
108b   321
260e–272b   271

Plato, *Respublica*
329c   361
387b   15
387d–e   204
404a   321
439d   321
514a–517c   208–9 n. 38

Plato, *Symposium*
206d   321

Plutarch, *Amatorius*
759b   315

Plutarch, *Cato Minor*
44.1   221
44.7   221
44.7–8   222
44.8   238
56.2   222

Plutarch, *Consulatio ad uxorem*
609b   322

Plutarch, *De amicorum multitudine*
93c   322

Plutarch, *De garrulitate*
504d   322

Plutarch, *De proverbiis Alexandrinorum*
Frag. 7   326 n. 38

Plutarch, *De Stoicorum repugnantiis*
1047a   325 n. 35

Plutarch, *De tranquillitate animi*
4667f–477a   365

Plutarch, *Marcius Coriolanus*
31.3   254 n. 36

Plutarch, *Quomodo quis suos in virtute sentiat profectus*
84d–e   325 n. 35

Propertius
1.9.11   360

Pollux, *Onomasticon*
6.43   326 n. 38

Prudentius, *Psychomachia*
585   254 n. 36

Sappho, *Fragmenta*
23   320
31   317, 319–20, 321
34   313 n. 4

Seneca, *De ira*		26	199
1.9.4	342		
1.10.4	342 n. 44	Theocritus, *Idylls*	
1.11.1–3	342	23.32	361
1.12.1–2	342		
1.13.1–2	342 n. 44	Theodoros Kyzikos, *Epistulae*	
1.14	342	7	316 n. 13
1.17.1	342–43		
2.1.3	337	Timaeus, *Fragmenta*	
2.1.4	338	222	324 n. 33
2.4	233		
2.10.3–6	344 n. 56	Xenophon, *Anabasis*	
2.14.3	345	2.6.9	364
2.22.2	344		
2.27	345	Xenophon, *Cyropaedia*	
2.31.1–2	339	5.3.6	365
2.31.5	345		
3.5.8	345	Xenophon, *Memorabilia*	
		2.6.23	364
Seneca, *Epistulae morales*			
81.20	276	Xenophon, *Symposium*	
		4.25.4	315
Sophocles, *Philoctetes*	205		
Statius, *Thebaid*			
6.735–749	254 n. 36		
Stobaeus, *Eclogae*			
2.90–91	337 n. 27		
Stobaeus, *Florilegium*			
2.7.10	322		
4.28.19	322		
Suetonius, *Divus Julius*			
75	365		
Tablet of Cebes	36, 197–99, 213		
1–4	198		
5–7	198–99		
9–11	199		
12–13	199		
14–16	199		
17–21	199		
24–27	199		

www.ingramcontent.com/pod-product-compliance
Lightning Source LLC
Chambersburg PA
CBHW021929290426
44108CB00012B/771